To Lynda Haddon & Judy Wood

Preface

The Canadian courts have consistently upheld their fundamental confidence in the principle of "best interests of the child" as the primary consideration in deciding the fate of children of divorce. Although a constant tension exists in law and society between the needs of the child and the needs of the parents, especially the custodian, the courts have never been swayed to dilute their emphasis that decisions regarding children should be made on careful consideration of their needs. This notion that parents' and children's interests may not always coincide in the heartbreaking circumstances of divorce is rarely articulated but is often observed in the tussles and strains between angry and disappointed ex-spouses who may equate self-interest with what is best for their children.

Enter the family law lawyer upon whose shoulders falls the complex task of aiding the adult client in favourably settling matters for them and their children. To do this, not only must the lawyer support the parent's cause but, showing loyalty to a further ideal, peer over the shoulder of the parent to view what may be best for the children whose welfare rests on the legal system's ability to arrive at a sagacious conclusion.

No wonder then that the use of mental health assessments has become so widespread in cases of disputed custody. Such family assessments can provide a neutral and objective window that highlights the family as a human system that must be retooled to meet the changing circumstances of divorce. Such matters are often complex but are hopefully made clearer through the unique contribution of the assessment.

Of all the challenges in life, parenting must be the most difficult and the most rewarding. It is never quite what we imagine even at the best of times and it is certainly not what might be imagined during the discord of divorce. Sadly, during these very times that children need a special regard for their deeper needs and well being, their parents may be gripped by struggles with each other and the children's needs can go by the wayside. This underscores the value of assessments in bringing this implicit dimension to the forefront and to its accorded place in family law.

This underscores the reason for this book and how it evolved in the authors' minds. One of us (A.L.), a psychologist and psychoanalyst, became interested in family law through the attention given to joint custody during the middle 1970s. By and by, this led to assessments in custody disputes and an opportunity to know and appreciate the work of family law lawyers in the midst of their difficult job. Psychoanalysis has been called the "the impossible profession", perhaps, this is also true of family law. In any case, the idea for the book emerged following a family law conference which highlighted the benefit that a collaborative work between an assessor and lawyer might bring to this psychological dimension of family law. This led to the partnership of A.L. and R.M. and the volume now before you. A lawyer since 1972 and a specialist in family law since 1980, with extensive courtroom experience, R.M. seemed to ensure that this book would be aimed at the core of the practising lawyer's needs.

We hope that in reading this book, you will learn as much as we did writing it. Attempts to define guidelines for the resolution of custody and access issues will continue to change as the courts address the heartbreaking struggles of divorcing parents and behavioural science continues to investigate the psychological needs of families caught in the course of these struggles. What will remain a permanent feature, though, is the use of family assessments in the most complex and challenging of these cases. Hopefully, this volume will better prepare you to meet this daunting challenge.

Arthur Leonoff
Robert Montague

Table of Contents

CHAPTER 5

CHAPTER 6

CHAPTER 9

CHAPTER 10

CHAPTER 11

Table of Cases

1

Setting the Scene: Divorce and its Psychological Implications

1. DIVORCE

Perhaps it smacks of nostalgia, but it does seem that our views of marriage have changed. What was once a sanctified institution aimed at the bearing and raising of children has been transformed into a therapeutic one. Modern society, it seems, looks to marriage as a medium for the realization of one's potential. We look for the cardinal signs of a good marriage and a happy life — high self-esteem and self-fulfillment. In this regard, we expect a great deal of these unions and place them under great scrutiny. We seem less willing to compromise and we cherish our right to exit a bad situation. Additionally, we have also adopted a code of individual freedom and to the unhappily married we offer the cure of divorce.

The high frequency of marriages ending in divorce is no doubt attributable to many factors, many of which are positive despite the ill effects created by marital dissolution: feminism, increased awareness of individual rights, greater social mobility and economic opportunities for women, increases in disposable family income and greater parity of roles between the sexes. Other less positive factors may also be represented in the mix of reasons behind the higher divorce rate:

permissiveness in society, lack of commitment, impoverishment or instability in social values and increased sense of personal helplessness.

Despite these cultural changes, the majority of people still uphold that it is preferable for children to live with their parents as a united family. Faith in the superiority of the traditional family to sustain well-being remains a fundamental premise. As a corollary, although we are committed to our right to leave a frustrating marriage, we are equally committed to the needs of our children. This sets the stage for conflict.

Notwithstanding our awareness of mental health concerns and therapeutic strategies, we have not succeeded in removing the pain and trauma of divorce nor have we diminished its load of shame and recrimination for individuals. Children's concerns in divorce augment the complexity and human cost of marital dissolution and, despite a burgeoning knowledge of these issues, we cannot offset the emotional turmoil that these events produce. Hence, we can see the inherent paradox that increased personal liberty has led to more divorce with greater social and emotional costs to families and children. Although most jurisdictions have opted for no-fault divorce, the very strains between a permissive society and a therapeutic one have meant that divorcing spouses must dig deeper to justify their choice of divorce especially when children are involved. To say, for instance, that "we grew apart" sounds today vaguely hollow and unjustified. The modern discourse prefers themes of abuse, emotional instability and victimization and one sees a tendency in extreme cases for excesses of blame and self-rationalization.

In the midst of this social ferment is the family law lawyer whose role is to mitigate these concerns and to control the damage. Although critics abound who suggest that the courts fail miserably in resolving divorce conflicts, perhaps no other system has the stamina and time honoured methods of resolving the protracted battles of hurt and grieving spouses. Gradually over the past 20 years, the courts have modified their approach and rely increasingly on the input of mental health professionals as consultants, particularly in respect to the best interests of children. Mediation and arbitration have also taken their place in the family law arsenal although the ultimate reliance on the court and the judge's wisdom has remained as bedrock.

No one today would dispute that divorce is often a profoundly disruptive and disturbing life event. Moreover, divorce almost always follows a prolonged period of marital unrest and struggle. The separation is then but one moment in a series of events aimed at re-establishing personal and socioeconomic equilibrium. Although divorce may ensue from mutual consent, it often arises from the desire of one spouse more than the other. This adds greatly to the aura of conflict that often permeates the divorce process. It follows, therefore, that not only is divorce itself a serious stress but that unhappy marriages that end in divorce also undermine the spouses' capacity for coping and adjustment.

This domino effect of stresses impact on the integrity of the family system during the acute phases of divorce and often undermine the parents' capacity to protect and provide for children. These changes are multidimensional and include material changes, living arrangements and family relationships. Almost always, these changes occur without children exerting much or any control over the events that transpire between their parents.

Despite the enormity of these changes, and after an initial phase of disintegration, most children and adults can personally reintegrate and with time consolidate a new order. A sizable minority of parents, however, remain combative and unresolved with each other despite the passage of time. Conflict escalates and further weakens the family's capacity for adaptation. Family lawyers, the courts and their mental health consultants are often then called upon to render those choices and decisions that the parents themselves cannot make.

We should keep in mind that in these complicated cases often visited upon family law lawyers, separation itself may prove to be an inadequate solution for the problems faced. There is no guarantee that even divorce will prove sufficient to unravel the issues that bind ex-partners. Rather than entering into a period of restructuring, these more intractable couples will engage in an endless replay of their misalliance. Finally, as Wallerstein and Kelly[1] carefully documented in their longitudinal study, divorce does not automatically institute a period of renewal and reintegration and, even five years following separation, serious disruptions and adjustment problems may still be evident.

---

1 Wallerstein, J.S. and Kelly, J. (1980), *Surviving the Breakup: How Children and Parents Cope with Divorce*. New York: Basic Books.

We should keep in mind, therefore, that "divorce" is not really a specific moment but a chain of events that both usher in and follow separation and provide the backdrop or context in which the lawyer is asked to work. The divorce itself then is one component of an array of stresses that is likely to be part and parcel of the life of a divorcing family. The deleterious effects of these stresses can often be felt throughout an entire life span. Working regularly with such a client population, the family law lawyer learns to appreciate how extremely vulnerable and brittle clients may be at the very time they are seeking legal help.

Yet, impasse is probably least likely when guilt, loss and sadness can be openly expressed. In contrast, when defenses against guilt predominate and shame or humiliation are accentuated then the risk of regressive behaviour and protracted litigation increase. One can think, for example, of the client who is rife with indignation and bitterness and who, at every step, takes special aim at the esteem and well being of the offending ex-spouse. These are not people immersed in their grief but, rather, bereft litigants who cannot even begin to grieve. Psychologically speaking, one might say that they are just too angry to mourn.

Although we should not over dramatize the modern divorce, we should not, at the same time, simply view it as a transient upheaval simply because it occurs frequently. A newspaper report summarizing the life span findings from the Terman Study of Genius begun in 1921 by a Stanford University psychologist, Dr. Lewis Terman noted that those children whose parents divorced before they were 21 faced a 33 per cent greater chance of an earlier death than those whose parents remained married.[2] This effect does not seem to be explained by the general effect of loss as early parental death did not have the same impact on the subjects' longevity.

Although some may argue that divorce was less common and therefore more stressful in the years that these particular subjects experienced divorce, one reading of the literature would suggest that this may be wishful thinking. Divorce is a major ingredient in otherwise burdened families where high interparental conflict is often sustained. Such families are associated with poorer emotional adjust-

2 Coleman, D. (March 11, 1995), "Studied to Death", reported in The Globe and Mail, at D8.

ment in children as well as personality and academic problems.[3] One can observe the lingering effects of a parental divorce in adults who seek psychotherapy or psychoanalysis even though the actual event occurred so many years previously. In this regard, it is not simply the trauma of the divorce that is at issue but the subtle though pervasive changes in parental availability, empathy, tolerance, mental health and a plethora of other possible changes that impact on a child's state of mind.

The psychological literature is also replete with studies documenting the impact of divorce on children. The two most widely quoted studies are by Hetherington and colleagues in 1978[4] and Wallerstein and Kelly in 1980.[5] Together, these investigators dramatically outlined what had long been suspected: divorce is a major event in the life of a child and a family's capacity to alleviate its worst effects for children may be quite unsatisfactory.

The Hetherington group, from the University of Virginia, followed 48 preschool children for two years after their parents' divorce became final.[6] They were compared to a matched control group of 48 children from intact families. The study by Wallerstein and Kelly emerged from a five-year follow up investigation of 131 children from Northern California between the ages of 3 and 18 years.[7] This comprehensive longitudinal research design took as its starting point actual parental separation which occurred at least one year before the legal divorce. Both studies, however, focused on the children's response to divorce and examined the course and evolution of that response over time. Hence, despite their differences in research design and methodology, the findings of the two investigations revealed considerable concordance.

---

3 Veltcamp, L. and Miller, T.W. (1989), "Contested child custody as a stressful life event", in T.W. Miller (ed.), *Stressful Life Events*, Madison, Ct. International Universities Press, at 659-675.

4 Hetherington, E.M. Cox, M. and Cox R. (1978), "The aftermath of divorce", in J.H. Steves Jr. and M. Matthews (eds.), *Mother-child/Father-child Relationship*, Washington D.C.: National Association for the Education of Young Children.

5 *Supra*, note 1.

6 *Supra*, note 4.

7 Wallerstein, J.S. and Kelly, J. (1980), *supra*, note 1.

(a) Wallerstein and Kelly

For purposes of this discussion, we will focus in some detail on the more recent study of which in our view is still the most thorough and balanced assessment of the effects of divorce on children and their parents to date.[8] We consider the results of this ground-breaking study to be essential information for practising family law lawyers both as a guide for counseling parents during this critical period and for understanding the general impact of this rupturing life event on families.

This study, situated in Northern California, involved a comprehensive interview and examination of 131 children and adolescents along with their parents. This occurred at the time of marital separation. There was a re-examination of the families 18 months post separation and again at the five-year juncture. At five years, the original sample group was reduced to 103 children due to re-marriage and drop out.

The sample group tended to be middle class, 88 per cent white, and well-educated. The average age for the men was 36.9 years at separation while the average age of the women was 34.1 years. They had been married for an average of 11.1 years before separating. The children were all developing normally at the time of separation and none had been referred for mental health intervention. The sample group was, therefore, somewhat skewed in the direction of psychological and academic health. At least 35 per cent of the children were said to be functioning very well and 25 per cent were functioning within expected levels for their chronological age. Twenty per cent were either somewhat or moderately troubled.

Many of the children in the sample group had received consistent positive care from both parents. Forty per cent of the children, however, had significantly impoverished or pathological relationships with fathers while 25 per cent of the children had impoverished or pathological relationships with mothers.

Perhaps because of the high level of function and relative stability of this sample group, the results as reported were more shocking than had been expected. The children tended to experience the divorce as

8 Those interested in a more concise summary of the Wallerstein and Kelly findings, *ibid.*, can find it in: Wallerstein, J., "The impact of divorce on children", *Psychiatric Clinics of North America,* vol. 3, 1980, at 455-468.

a severe rupture with traumatic overtones. Intense anxiety, fixation on the family and overwhelming grieving seemed common place. These children were not mollified by the frequency of divorce in the community and they were often intensely worried about what might happen to them. They perceived divorce as the fragmentation of a needed structure and they tended to fear for themselves and for their parents. Many of the children had not been prepared for the departure of one parent from the family home and many had little or no prior warning that this would occur.

In many of the households studied, the ambiance of the family environment worsened in the few months prior to the separation, during the separation crisis, and for the year following. Parents were often unable to meet their parenting obligations and their capacity to protect their children diminished. Turmoil tended to erode the capacity to think and act and this led to lapses in parenting and adult psychological functioning. Bitterness, hostility and depressive symptoms increased following the separation.

The actual decision to divorce was rarely mutual, although both parents might agree that the marriage was in a sorry state. The tendency was for the women to insist upon the separation while the men were more inclined to resist its occurrence.

The children were often unprepared for the displays of violence, controversy and emotion that they witnessed in their parents. Normal discretion tended to break down between parents and children and the authors observed that the children were often bewildered, frightened or inappropriately stimulated by the mêlée between the adults.

Hence, at a time when children required more help from their parents, the adults were often less available and less effective than usual. Moreover, many children did not live near relatives and less than 10 per cent of the children were assisted by clergy, doctors and other adults who might have been available. The school often substituted for the dissolving home structure and provided a needed continuity. Yet, only half of the teachers were aware of the situation and some parents were reluctant to tell the school authorities for fear that their children would be labeled.

Of particular importance for lawyers in guiding client/parents as to expected childhood responses to separation, the study was able to distinguish four typical response patterns varying with age.

In the first, age 3 years to $5\frac{1}{2}$ years of age, the children were more likely to show signs of regression. Clinging, fears, aggression with peers, separation anxiety, thumb sucking or other self-soothing behaviours were all common findings in this age group.

Children in the 5 to 8-year-old range were more likely to express their feelings of sadness and mourning more openly. They tended to cry, to feel rejected and to long for a departed parent. They had intense fantasies of parental reconciliation and feared being replaced by a new family or child. They were often dubious that the separation would be sustained and they longed for the lost parent to return to them. About one-half of the children in this group experienced a significant decline in school functioning and reported problems in concentration.

In the 9 to 12 year old group, the children were more likely to blame one parent or the other for the decision to separate. These children also felt intensely helpless and powerless. They experienced deep anxiety and loneliness. They could be co-opted into the battle between parents and were willing to see one as a "good" parent and the other as "bad". School achievement and peer relations suffered in approximately one-half of these children.

The adolescent group suffered more than had been expected and the incidence of problems was high. In particular, adolescents feared for their own futures and tended to become preoccupied with these concerns. A year following the initial rupture about one-third of the teenagers appeared more troubled than they were at the time of separation.

The relationship between the non-custodial parent and the children was more likely to change. Close relationships unexpectedly deteriorated whereas previously poor or distant ones improved. Young children were more likely to be visited than older ones. Yet, some of the older children, adolescents included, tended to maintain close relationships with their father, especially when the mother was depressed.

The relationship of custodial parent to children also evolved. Many of the children developed close collaborative relationships with mothers and helped out considerably with daily tasks. Others experienced fears of being swallowed up by closeness and became more distant.

Even though the custodial responsibilities provided mainly by mothers led to much more contact and involvement with this parent, there was no evidence that the emotional significance of the non-custodial father lessened. Even when re-marriage occurred, children revealed little problem in making a place for the step parent without losing the place for their actual father. In fact, the emotional connection to the non-custodial parent, even when this relationship is limited or infrequent, maintained its importance to the children.

At the five-year follow up, the study was able to focus on what were the ingredients of a good post-divorce adjustment. In this group, families were able to maintain continuity of relationships and parental discord had not severed these possibilities. The parents had managed to restore their habitually good level of parenting following the initial decline. Where relationships with a parent had been destructive or incestuous, distance from that parent improved the climate for the child. This comprised approximately one-third of the over all group who were in good psychological health and had found solidity in the post-separation reality.

On the other hand, over half of the group looked back on the time that their parents were together and saw it as preferable to the present arrangement. They longed for a return to the time that their parents were unhappily together. Thirty seven per cent were emotionally troubled and in distress at the five-year mark. Feelings of rejection and neglect contributed to a high frequency of depression. Those who felt disappointed, rejected, or treated insensitively by the non-custodial parent were still feeling miserable and this did not seem to diminish with time. Very few of these children were able to get beyond the trauma of a parental relationship or to find substitute figures for identification.

As one might also expect, children left in the custodial care of a depressed, isolated or emotionally disturbed mother were likely to fare badly. The absence of the supportive benefits provided by the other parent were particularly evident in these situations.

The ongoing failure of divorce to ameliorate the situation between the parents proved to be a central cause of distress at the five-year juncture. Continued interparental strife weakened the family system and had a direct negative impact on children's well being. This was the major predictor of poor psychological outcome for children of divorce.

In contrast, and on the positive side of the ledger, children who benefited from contact with both parents seemed to be best off especially if this occurred in a low conflict atmosphere. Wallerstein and Kelly's results supported the conclusion that the easy availability of the non-custodial parent and the capacity of the children to link to that parent on a frequent basis was a major positive factor in post-divorce adjustment.

(b) Child Adjustment: Individual and Gender Differences

Although studies such as Wallerstein and Kelly's are best at elucidating trends and composites, it remains clinically true that children display a diversity of responses to their parents' marital breakdowns. One is often struck by the resiliency of even young children when seen in the midst of a stormy divorce. It is also common, though, for reactions to be delayed especially until the parents have resolved their own immediate crisis. In any case, anger, resentment, distress and self-blame are common initial reactions for children. The failure of parental "holding", hopefully transitory, will certainly affect children especially if they have known a prior period of stability where the parents functioned well within the home environment.

Fantasies of parental reunion are also ubiquitous in divorce and may endure for years. In one example, a young adult, whose parents had separated when he was 11 years old, sought help for extreme anxiety whenever he faced a serious disagreement with his spouse. Although he was always of the belief that the divorce was for the best, he often found himself fantasizing in the twilight before sleep that his parents were reuniting. This dreamy fantasy most often occurred when he felt under stress and it always had a quieting and soothing impact on him.

The longer term repercussions of divorce may not be related as much to the initial breakup than to other stresses that arise. This is especially significant in more vulnerable children who may not easily adjust to a parent's remarriage, changes in economic circumstances, emotional unavailability of a parent, blending and step-family complications, as well as the specific qualities of the parent-child relationships.[9]

---

9 Stolberg, A. L., Camplair, C., Currier, K. and Wells, M.J. (1987), "Individual, familial and environmental determinants of children's post-divorce adjustment and maladjustment", *Journal of Divorce,* 11:51-70; Hetherington, E. M.,

We should emphasize as well that each child brings their own resources as well as liabilities to a given situation and not all negative consequences can be directly traced to the conduct of any one parent. Children perceive and act in ways that are idiosyncratic and they are not simply reflections of their parents' influences. Commonly, though, stresses tend to be funneled through one child in particular who seems to suffer more than the others. If an older child, for example, is more vulnerable and more affected by the marriage breakup then the younger child will often seem to rise above the fray. This may be more appearances than substance, however, and subtle but undermining factors such as feelings of not mattering or lack of attention may contribute to later emotional problems.

What is often overlooked is that the stresses faced by children may be present years before the actual divorce occurs.[10] Unsupportive parenting and draining interpersonal tensions represent prolonged undermining factors often faced by children. Hence, these unremitting tensions are detrimental to the self esteem of children as they are to parents.

The psychological literature has consistently reported gender differences in adjustment to separation and divorce. Boys seem to be more affected by pre and post-divorce strain than are girls and are more prone to acting out, under-control of impulses and emotional volatility.[11] It may be helpful to discuss this gender issue further as it is often pertinent in assessments where custody is being disputed.

Following separation, 80 to 90 per cent of custodial (residential) care is provided by mothers with father's assuming varying degrees of secondary involvement. This exposes children to asymmetrical intimacy to a degree not often experienced in the intact family. Naturally, such a post-divorce arrangement enhances the closeness

---

Stanley-Hagan, M. and Anderson, E.R. (1989), "Marital Transitions: A child's perspective", *American Psychologist,* 44: 303-312.

10 Block, J., Block, J.H. and Gjerde, P.F. (1988), "Parental functioning and the home environment in families of divorce: Prospective and current analyses", *Journal of the American Academy of Child and Adolescent Psychiatry,* 27: 207-213; Hetherington, E.M., Cox, M. and Cox, R. (1982) "Effects of divorce on parents and children", in M. Lamb (ed.), *Nontraditional Families,* Hillsdale, N.J.: Erlbaum (at 233-288).

11 Hetherington, E.M., Cox, M. and Cox, R. (1985) "Long-term effects of divorce and remarriage on the adjustment of children", *Journal of the American Academy of Psychoatry,* 24: 518-530; Block, J., Block, J.H. and Gjerde, P.F., *supra,* note 9.

with the maternal figure while it lessens the link with the father. Developmentally, this may be seen as favouring emotional development of girls who generally benefit from close non-conflictive relationships with their mothers. Boys, on the other hand, must not only separate from their mothers psychologically but must further "disidentify" with her in order to secure their masculine development.[12] Without a consistent and meaningful paternal link, boys may experience greater conflict and gender role distress. Hence, boys unlike girls must locate their gender destiny outside of the primary maternal link that is nonetheless so essential in the early years. This likely explains why boys living with single mothers tend to show a higher incidence of behaviour problems in school and at home than do girls in the same situation.[13] Following divorce, and for two and even three years after, boys are prone to aggressive and non-cooperative behaviour.[14] There is also some evidence that girls in the custody of their fathers reveal higher levels of aggression and less adaptive social behaviour than girls raised with mothers.[15]

Hence, there is some support for the notion that children may benefit from being raised by the parent of the same gender. Of course, this will be mediated by other factors that naturally complicate any particular circumstance. In practice, therefore, the availability, adequacy and historical roles of the two adults along with the specific attributes and needs of the child will be more determining than the narrow dimension of gender. Yet, when severe conflict characterizes the parental relationship and spills into parent-child relationships, then the gender factor is germane if children are to be best protected from the worst aspects of their parents' interaction.

Besides the prevalence of mothers obtaining custody, there may also be some intrinsic biopsychological factors concerning boys that add to their vulnerability in divorce. Infant boys, for example, tend to be more irritable than girl babies and more difficult to soothe. They may also be more vulnerable to maternal depression and are more

12 Greenson, R. (1968), "Disidentifying from mother", *International Journal of Psychoanalysis,* 49: 370-74.

13 Hetherington, E.M., *supra*, note 8, at 305-306.

14 Hetherington, E.M., *supra*, note 11.

15 Camara, K. and Resnick, G. (1988), "Interparental conflict and cooperation: factors moderating children's post-divorce adjustment", in E.M. Hetherington and J.D. Arasteh (eds.), *Impact of Divorce, Single Parenting and Stepparenting on Children,* Hillsdale N.J.: Erlbaum (at 169-95).

emotionally reactive.[16] Studies have also indicated that boys are more vulnerable to disrupted relationships than girls and that they are more inclined in later years towards antisocial acting out.[17] In trying to understand how boys and girls react differently to stress, J. Block reasoned that boys tend to adapt by turning away from situations of stress whereas girls focus on maintaining continuity of relationships through assimilation to the stressful circumstance.[18] Such gender differences are not easy to interpret but we can likely accept that sex-linked differences in coping patterns exist.

Particularly important in evaluating the gender equation is the reality that mothers are not only likely to be custodians after divorce but also function as gate keepers of who else becomes involved with the child. In this role, they tend to colour the quality of those relationships including that with the father. Ideally, of course, both parents vitalize or validate each other as parents in the child's eyes. Where the mother is the dominant parent, she can validate the paternal parental identity and vitalize it.[19] Although this remains unexplored territory in family research, it may be true that many men take their cue from women and may be prone to assume the parenting role expected of them. In divorce, this can exert an added influence on identity development for children of both sexes as divorce can create varying degrees of father absence as well as empowering the woman in her maternal role. As gate keeper, therefore, the mother tends to interpret the father to the children and her attitude towards the father and men assume a greater impact than in the intact family structure.[20] Some researchers believe that the mother's attitudes as regards the father may be as influential to development as the actual presence of

---

16 Coates, S. and Wolfe, S., "Gender identity disorder in boys: The interface of constitution and early experience", *Psychoanalytic Inquiry:,* 15: 6-38.

17 Rutter, M. (1970), "Sex differences in children's response to family stress", in E. Anthony and C. Koupernik (eds.), *The Child in the Family,* New York: Wiley.

18 Block, J. (1982), "Assimilation, accommodation and the dynamics of personality development", *Child Develepent,* 53: 281-295.

19 Atkins, R. (1984), "Transitive vitalization and its impact on father representation", *Contemporary Psychoanalysis,* 20: 663-675.

20 Cath, S. (1982), "Divorce and the child: The father question hour", in S. Cath, A. Gurwitt and J. Munder Ross (eds.), *Father and Child,* Boston, MA: Little, Brown, at 467-479.

the father in the day-to-day affairs of the family.[21] Psychoanalysts, in fact, would take this issue further back in terms of the mother's experience of her own father and the degree to which her mother respected or endorsed her father's role. Such internalized representations influence expectations in the current context.

Although such findings and observations naturally take a back seat to the specific elements of cases met in family law, they form part of the background education to the field.

(c) Guilt, Blame and Divorce

Marital separation is most often stressful and for the emotionally unprepared it can be a chaotic time. It is a major source of psychic trauma and sufficiently endemic to be considered a public health concern. As family lawyers can verify, divorce often brings people in close touch with the destructive dimension of human emotion and experience. This is linked to the inner workings of fear, anger, frustration and sense of loss. People may experience this burst of negativity in different ways: acute anger or smoldering resentment, self defeating behaviour, chronic anxiety and fear, unremitting blame and aggression or severe defensiveness and undercutting of the ex-spouse especially in the eyes of children.

The most difficult task for anyone facing separation and divorce is to take responsibility for this personal negativity and to acknowledge it within themselves. This is most difficult when such emotions are directed at someone we love(d) and need(ed). It accounts for the turbulent push and pull that often describes the interaction of divorcing couples.

We can often perceive a close relationship between the capacity to accept responsibility for the full range of our feelings and mental health. Healthy people do not use a massive amount of projection of blame to deal with their anger and pain. Rather, they retain what might be called the healthy sense of guilt. Can the divorcing client face the inevitable and real guilt associated with marital failure? Toleration of uncomfortable and destructive (negative) feelings results in a capacity to be flexible and to problem solve. Of course, there is an opposite

21 Siegler, A. (1983), "Groupwork with single mothers", in E. Buchholz and J. Mishne (eds.), *Ego and Self Psychology*, New York: Aronson, at 95-111.

extreme in which a parent almost pathologically insists on bearing all the responsibility for the failure of the union. This slides into the dimension of masochistic solution and could only be properly addressed through individual psychotherapy.

In general, though, one can distinguish between the client who can acknowledge a deep sense of loss and failure and one who has to denigrate the other spouse in order to minimize any impression of loss or guilt. The former type of client can tolerate what is painful while the latter fights against it. What each type expects of the divorce process and of the legal system is therefore very different. In this regard, one sees people who maturely seek resolution in contrast to those who principally demand restitution and freedom from blame. The two are very different. Resolution is forward looking and is principally aimed at adaptation. Restitution is backward looking and seeks redress from the ex-spouse who is most likely the person least able at that moment to provide it.

Facing the precipice of marital failure, many people experience guilt so severely within themselves that they will distort perceptions to avoid feeling it. Such internal harshness may lead to a profound defensive stance in which blame and rationalization are prominent. Among the tell-tale signs, the rigid use of blame and moralistic thinking stands out as the most obvious symptom. This is especially true in those cases that require litigation to settle or regress due to it. What we often notice in such litigants is that they rarely can recognize the impact of their actions and they tend not to see their own aggression in what they do. These types of cases become major management problems for lawyers who may have a difficult time conveying to such clients a working attitude that is centred on resolution. This type of client may well join those clients, well known to family lawyers, who would rather fight than settle.

The tendency for parents to blame each other for their children's distress during custody litigation also stems from the psychic strain of the process. Although it is true that children can be coached and manipulated by their parents, it is also true that children may tell parents what they want to hear. The insecurity children feel in the hostile enclave between their parents is potentially considerable and they are likely to try and feather the new bed in order to minimize risks to their threatened security.

At the point that the lawyer is retained is often the stage just before or after separation when a high degree of discord is most apparent. Separation itself will probably intensify the hostility and mistrust as acrimony takes hold. The reasons for such antagonism are multiple and reflect individual differences as well as the enormity of our expectations regarding the institution of marriage. In the best of situations, though, a dynamic balance is maintained between dispute and a wish for resolution and parents are able to shield children from the depth of their anger and disappointment regarding each other.

More often than not, however, bonds are not as much broken as ruptured. Marriages take their cue from our earliest relationships with parents and when they rupture we are prone to feel that we have lost part of ourselves. Coupled with guilt and feelings of personal crisis, such disruption diminishes the adult's capacity to regulate their emotions and to think clearly. Unfortunately, at the very time that order collapses into the chaos of divorce it is also the time that people become involved in the legal process.

This underscores the vital stabilizing function that the lawyer can provide. The lawyer's psychological purpose, in this interpersonal context, is to act as a container for the anxieties and fears of the client while promoting a reasonable resolution of the outstanding legal issues so essential to eventual adaptation after divorce. Although the lawyer-client relationship may appear to be more one of alter ego than container, the failure on the part of some lawyers to recognize this essential holding and supportive function can lead to an exacerbation of conflicts with worsening consequences for the family.

2. BEST INTERESTS OF THE CHILD

The concept in family law of determining the best interests of the child may appear as a lofty ideal but it has had enormous impact on the process and outcome in specific cases. As parents are the payers and direct clients of lawyers, children can easily become an assumption in cases of custody dispute where everyone involved claims to speak for their needs. Although some of this is unavoidable especially when children are very young and have no actual voice in the process, this divided loyalty creates a tug of war as to who actually speaks for the child.

Despite this ambiguity, the ideal of determining the children's best interests acts as a stabilizing force that pulls the process away from being completely over run by the parents' needs and wishes. It is natural for most adults in conflict to equate their own desires with the needs of their children. The more psychologically minded and mature parent, however, will often be able to allow some small conceptual space between the two in which the children's ultimate need can be appreciated apart from their own. Assessing this capacity in the parent/client can be a useful exercise in predicting how the client will relate to the litigation process as well as how adjustment will fare when the initial furor abates.

It also appears that the best interests principle can still become a source of controversy in family law cases and there is always a readiness to displace the focus to the side of the parents. In *MacGyver v. Richards*, an Ontario Court of Appeal ruling, Abella J. described the best interests dictum as a lofty aspiration or ideal that can change regularly in the course of development.[22] Although the court might well have decided the case involving a custodial mother's wish to move from Ontario to Washington State on merit alone, the appeal judges chose to defer to the responsible custodian by linking the child's best interests with the best interests of the primary care giver. Although we could agree that this may often be the case, such a disassembling of this complex concept seems unwarranted and ultimately adverse to family law which loses important flexibility in responding to the unique aspects of each case. Moreover, such an equivalence effectively nullifies the specific child focus which has been instrumental to psychologically sensitive reforms in family law. Fortunately, a more recent Supreme Court decision restored legal confidence in the best interests principle and disagreed with an automatic legal presumption in favour of the custodian.[23] Writing for the majority, McLachlin J. modified the position by according the responsible custodian respect and serious consideration but stopped short of habitually assuming that the child's welfare will remain linked with the custodian even in the event of a significant material change.

Assessing the best interests requires a multi-dimensional analysis of the influences affecting a child in divorce. Moreover, this should not be interpreted necessarily as residing with only one parent and

22 *MacGyver v. Richards* (1995) 11 R.F.L. (4th) 432 (Ont. C.A.).
23 *Gordon v. Goertz*, SCC file 24622, May 2, 1996 (as yet unpublished).

should include a broad view of the total environmental field in which the child is raised. For example, a characteristic study by Hetherington, Cox and Cox[24] illustrated that the quality of the mother-child relationship was linked to the degree of social support available. The researchers observed that the parent-child relationship was least affected when the non-custodial father continued to be supportive to the family. The study focused on preschool children and the authors noted that mothers who lacked this support had greater problems in effectively controlling their children. The availability of other supports such as extended families correlated positively with the divorced mother's effectiveness as a parent. Although not surprising, these results underline that the best interests of the child must be understood within a relational context based on a parenting formula that best mixes and matches parental talents and availability with psychosocial needs of their offspring.

This determination of where the best interests lie is not something immutable and it could change. Hence, judges may request a reassessment if sufficient time has elapsed or material circumstances have changed significantly. Yet, the concept should not be seen as so fluid that it would ordinarily change from year to year or age to age. First, life is not so well organized and even in the intact family a parent may not be well suited to raise a child in one phase of development as compared to another. This is a fact of family life and not a sign that the child's best interests are being ignored. Hence, a custodial parent may have problems managing a pre-teen who is rebellious without acting contrary to the best interests of the child. It is also common for parents to have particular difficulties guiding children through life phases where they too experienced developmental problems. This is often the basis for the intergenerational transmission of emotional conflicts or deficits that plays such a prominent part in psychotherapeutic work and health promotion.

Consequently, in our opinion, the best interests formulation should be assessed at deeper level than simply how adept a parent is at one stage of development or another. On the other hand, a vulnerable child with a poor capacity to tolerate loyalty conflicts may react very poorly to the remarriage of the custodial parent. This may change the mix of parenting and psychological neutrality for the child to the

24 Hetherington, E.M., Cox, M. and Cox, R. (1976), "Divorced Fathers", *Family Coordinator*, 25, 417-28.

degree that the child's best interests are no longer being served. Although this is an extreme situation, it does occur and may require the parents to revisit the issue of residence and parenting relationships.

Continuing on this theme, it is not uncommon for lawyers and the courts to be faced with parents who seek to leave the region where the non-custodial parent resides. The question posed by the court in these matters is whether this is in the child's best interest to move, especially where the access to the non-custodian will be effectively reduced. Such a dilemma is often the type of circumstance where the best interests principle comes most clearly into focus. The appeal judges in *MacGyver v. Richards*[25] decided it on the basis of the formula — what is good for the custodian is good for the child. Because of its over reliance on this general principle, however, and its failure to give credence to case specific factors, such rulings seem unlikely to stand the test of time. The best interests guideline, though, should never be applied so rigidly that it would stifle adults from making appropriate and meaningful choices in their lives. Hence, we cannot see the purpose of binding parents with sole custody to a specific locale while their non-custodial counterparts have absolute freedom of mobility. In this regard, we have never heard of a custodian who attempted to have the non-custodial parent prevented from leaving a region on the basis of potential harm to the child's welfare. Rationally, it is clear that both parental relationships are psychologically important to children and best interests must be assessed within this bi-parental context. This issue becomes even more complex when parents' rights are measured against their responsibilities for the well being of their offspring which includes facilitating input and availability of the other parent.

Where the custodian's right to re-locate is questioned, the relationship of the non-custodian to the offspring will be highlighted and it will be argued by that parent that disturbing this non-custodial link will prove harmful to the child's long-term needs. Implicit in this argument is the assumption that although the non-custodial relationship may be viewed by the courts as secondary in legal terms, the child makes no such clear distinction. In some cases, loss of regular contact with the non-custodial parent could be detrimental as there is usually a major change in visitation pattern with less ongoing contact. This

25 *Supra*, note 22.

example does seem germane though to working through the problem of best interest. Again, the issue is complex. If the non-custodial parent's relationship to the child is strong, it will likely better absorb the stress of distance and dislocation. A parent, therefore, who argues that the relationship with a child is very close and harmonious may also be indirectly indicating that the relationship could withstand the change.

If, on the other hand, the relationship between non-custodian and child is essential to the well being of the child and is not simply a meaningful one, then it is reasonable to recommend that the custodian make an important sacrifice in their freedom of mobility for the sake of their child. This is never a unidimensional analysis, in any case, and will also have to account for the fallout for the custodian in the case of such a restriction and its secondary impact on the psyche of the child. Yet how might one know if the relationship was really essential to the child's coping system? In one case, for example, two boys were been raised by a mother who exhibited signs of an impulsive personality. The parents had been divorced for some time and the father had left the family home as he could no longer tolerate his wife's behaviour. Although he had left his two sons with the mother, he retained an active presence in their lives. When the youngest boy, by then a young adolescent, developed an acute, transient psychosis, the father remained with the boy and was instrumental to his recovery. Later, though, the mother became involved in a new relationship and arranged rather precipitously to move to another city. She very much wanted to have the boys residing with her. The intervention in this case was therapeutic and she accepted the advice that such a move would likely be harmful to their well being. The therapist stressed that the father's relationship was essential to their welfare and removing them from the jurisdiction would impose a heavy stress that might be too much for the younger boy to bear.

By focusing on this example, it hopefully becomes clear that the best interest rule can be applied without the appeal to legal presumption or any other generality. In different scenarios, the best interests of the child may hinge on distinct elements but these can be derived on issues of merit alone. On the other hand, as much as best interest should not be equated with either parent's wants, it should not be based on a simple measure of a parent's love or commitment. Such an oversimplification is likely to superficialize the question and reduce it solely to an issue of loss. This is not to undermine the importance of loving ties but it becomes unworkable in a psycholegal context. Best interests, in our opinion, should always have a deeper meaning tied to a careful scrutiny of the child's essential needs and relationships. It should represent something specific and identifiable in each case.

(a) Assessing the Best Interests

One possible view is that a child's best interest can be equated with what the psychoanalyst Donald Winnicott termed the "holding environment".[26] It depicts an environment which permits the child to develop personally and to realize their inherited potential. This concerns the adaptive care parents provide from infancy to adulthood. The result of this care is that the child develops a capacity for integration within the family, within school life and later within adult relationships. When a mental health assessor is consulting on a custody matter, it is generally this concept that guides their thinking and perspective.

Applying this concept to divorce, we could consider the following elements as being essential to the holding environment following marriage breakup:

- to be with the parent best able to represent the child's developmental needs;
- to have optimal access to the non-custodial parent which proves sufficient to permit a healthy resolution of that relationship in the life of the child;
- to be in a life situation where interparental strife and conflict is minimized;
- to live in a safe, secure physical and social environment which is conducive to the growth of the individual;
- to be subject to child rearing methods that are appropriate and reasonably attuned to the age and gender of the child;

26 Winnicott, D.W. (1960), "The theory of the parent-infant relationship", in *The Maturational Processes and the Facilitating Environment*, New York: International Universities Press, at 140-152.

- to have a custodial and access order in place that is feasible and explicitly defines post-separation parent-child relationships while not leaving too much to discretion or chance;
- to best protect a child from parental psychopathology by ensuring that the child is either not living full time with that parent or by arranging appropriate mental health intervention;[27]
- to be least vulnerable or exposed to the influences of bad parenting and such parental characteristics as excessive hostility, exploitation, blame and criticism, mixed messages, lack of appropriate boundaries, inconsistency, coercion or domination, unfair and inappropriate demands.

Listing these criteria does not make it any easier to assess what is in a child's best interests in specific cases but it does provide a general target. Mainly, it raises the level of analysis from a confrontation of parental demands to a focus based on the child's deeper and more long-term needs. It does seem that when both lawyers adopt a similar mind-set based on the best interests paradigm, then the adaptive capacities of the divorcing couple are often enhanced. This bears fruit in terms of quicker resolution with less conflict and rancour. In contrast, if the lawyers are focused solely on the parents' demands and the parents themselves insist that only they represent the child's best interests then the chances for real resolution are slim. It is often not obvious to litigating parents to view their children's needs separate from their own. In part this reflects the impact of divorce trauma on thought processes as well as the tremendous vulnerability experienced at this time. This is where the contribution of the family lawyer is essential. If we can accept that gauging the best interests of children is often done spontaneously and reflexively by most parents, then its impairment in divorce, although temporary, can be compensated by the perspective and guiding counsel of the family law lawyer.

It remains to discuss these essential ingredients that need be considered when the child's best interests are being determined. This involves a more detailed look at each of the above elements and how they translate into more concrete analysis of parental circumstances and behaviour:

27 For a discussion of personal correlates of parental psychopathology see, Rutter, M. and Quinton, D. (1984), "Parental psychiatric disorders: effects on children", *Psychological Medicine*, 14: 853-880.

(b) The Parent

This concerns parental aptitude and the capacity of the parent to appreciate the broader developmental needs of the child and to act wisely in their best interest. It is of course fundamental to all manner of good parenting. We could view it as a combination of skills: (a) attunement to the psychological needs of the child, (b) knowledge of child development and how children grow, (c) balance and perspective in dealing with children and (d) the ability to be accurate about one's children and to know them.

(c) Optimal Access

This emphasizes how essential is the contribution of the non-custodial parent to the well being and best interests of the child. It cannot be viewed, however, in isolation but should be conceptualized within a parenting formula that aims at optimal access. The formula represents a balance of forces that are designed to protect and provide for the child's well being during their remaining growing up years. There should be sufficient opportunity for a meaningful relationship between the non-custodial parent and the child. This should be optimized in reference to the capacity of that parent to contribute meaningfully and with consistency.

It is not uncommon, however, for the willingness of the custodian to accept the non-custodial parent's input to affect the frequency of access. Paradoxically, meeting a child's need for a link with the non-custodial parent may actually increase conflict with the custodian. This is always unfortunate and may require judicial intervention to curtail. As an example, a four-year-old boy was denied access to his 23-year-old father because the mother completely resisted his input. She alleged that he had raped her in an episode that occurred when they lived together. He denied any such happening and an analysis of his character traits revealed mostly passivity and personal inhibition. The tell-tale signs of aggressivity and poor impulse control associated with assault were not apparent and, upon observation, the boy seemed deeply gratified by contact with his father. Some limited access was recommended in the assessment but for this strong and assertive mother, optimal access meant no access at all. This was blatantly opposed to the boy's needs. The father's lawyer successfully moved in court that the recommendations be applied and the mother finally relented.

(d) Interparental Conflict

Research has shown that above all else it is the presence of unresolved conflict that is most damaging to children of divorce. Of course, this conflict does not begin after separation and often there is a long history of strife. The capacity of the parents to act as containers and provide a holding environment are seriously reduced by chronic strife. It undermines the security of children and keeps them interminably off balance. Conflicts may be based on sustained grief and sense of loss but may also centre on differing attitudes or expectations about divorce. Impasses in decision making as well as differences in parenting techniques may contribute to this negative factor.

Children deserve to live in an environment where such conflict is minimized. Some have argued that if this requires a reduced non-custodial access then so be it if it reduces interparental strife. In theory, we might agree although in practice it is difficult to apply when assessing families with custody in dispute. First, it is often prejudicial to "punish" one parent by drastically reducing access for a behaviour that clearly involves the other. Secondly, there is no guarantee that the child will live with any less tension if one parent completely triumphs over the other. The bereft or "losing" parent's grief may be no less appreciated by the child who may feel they bear some responsibility for the non-custodial parent's disenfranchisement.

(e) Safety and Security

This is a broad category and includes such major issues as residence, neighbourhood, and home life. One can think of a diverse list of safety and security concerns that may come into focus in determining a child's best interests. Assessors may be asked to consider such a wide array of matters as hygiene, baby sitting, seat belts, diet, health care, involvement of relative strangers in child care, leaving children alone and so on. Financial capability to provide may be considered in this category although it is more likely today to consider total family assets as well as work potential in evaluating this element.

In this category, as well, one may also describe a child's need to be free of parental violence either as a direct victim or indirectly in being exposed to it. The traumatic affect of such adult aggression on children is well documented and represents a serious risk to the later mental health of the child. In cases where one parent may be too emotive or under controlled in their grief or bitterness, then it is often wise to shorten access visits and/or reduce their frequency. We have observed that when children experience their parents as regressing into disruptive anger during the acute stages of a separation, they can lose a sense of innocence or trust in that parent that may never be repaired. It is possible that although love is not diminished, the child's sense of safety in regard to that parent will be.

(f) Appropriate Child Rearing

The best interests of the child are met when they are exposed to parental input that is appropriate for their age and gender. Perhaps describing a few examples might be helpful in briefly explaining this element:

- Adolescents need to be treated quite differently than younger children as they often react poorly to excessive control and punishment.
- Young children need a sense of holding and are not aided by excessive demands or role reversals. A child who must emotionally care for a beleaguered and distraught parent may not be in a position where their interests are being met.
- Fathers of pre-adolescent girls should not pat their daughter's behinds or thighs as they once were accustomed.
- Punishments should be appropriate, measured and educational without harming a child's self esteem or sense of security.

In one case where care was inappropriate, a father acted seductively in recruiting his 15-year-old daughter to his side in a custody dispute. He bought her whatever clothes she desired and courted her friends with tantalizing benefits such as tickets to rock concerts. The daughter grew quite bold and scornful of her mother who retained care and control of a younger son. The father was quite perturbed when it was suggested by the assessor that his behaviour was inappropriate and that the daughter's best interests lay in the girl living with her mother and receiving counseling to mend the link with her.

(g) Predictability

Children, whether living in intact families or in separated ones, require a sense of predictability in their lives. Any custody and access arrangement should respect this need and provide for needed continuity and stability. Clarity of routine and regularity in life style should be primary ingredients of good child care following divorce. Parents who cannot provide such stability or whose life circumstances introduce too much change or uncertainty cannot act in their child's best interests.

Further, best interests are supported when the custody and access arrangement allows for clear decision making in the life of the child. Although at times this may add an element of rigidity to the post-divorce family, it is often a necessary sacrifice. Joint custody with parents who cannot reasonably work with its demand on resolution and communication often represent families without a sense of control.

(h) Psychopathology

There is no clear division between health and illness in the mental sphere. In fact, mental health is to some extent the capacity to tolerate ill health and to work through its challenges. Hence, the presence of depressive symptoms is often a positive sign reflecting a mature capacity to take responsibility, to show concern and to reflect on one's conduct and situation.

A common pattern among parents who fight for custody is a conspicuous lack of depression. In its place one sees a combination of denial and projection of blame within a climate of hostility. Although most often unconscious, such people seek restitution as compared to mourning their losses and retrieving a sense of personal balance. Paradoxically, it is the absence of symptoms and the flight into apparent sanity that proves most troublesome. Such parents equate suitability for custody with being completely sane in contrast to being real or authentic. They are apt to attribute all ill health, responsibility or conflict to the other parent in an attempt to launder themselves of faults and failure. All of this suggests that some small measure of ill health is a welcome and reassuring sign when dealing with problems arising from divorce.

Obviously, though, serious psychopathology or personality disorder can be extremely disruptive to a family and sick parents are likely to produce sick children. Although this is undeniable, the legal system is not often at its best when coping with these problems. Judges, for one, are not mental health experts and, as experience teaches, everyone can muster a defence. What may be appraised as a serious mental problem in a litigant may be dismissed by that person's lawyer as a gross exaggeration, a misperception, a prejudicial judgment, or a traumatic result of victimization suffered at the hands of the other parent. In other cases, assessors may be too willing to excuse or underestimate the impact of a psychological problem and thus expose the children to the continued stress of the parent's problem.

In one case, introduced by the father's lawyer as "a case from hell", the conclusion was reached that the mother's allegations of bizarre sexual abuse of her daughters at the hands of the father and grandfather were false. Moreover, the unfortunate woman who had knitted anatomically correct dolls, videotaped the children's statement, and hammered 2x4's to their bedroom windows as protection, suffered paranoid delusions which linked to her problematic childhood. The welfare of these preschool girls was in jeopardy as they were under enormous pressure to reject their father and to accept their mother's version of reality. Each time unsupervised access was put in place for the father, new allegations of sexual abuse arose. The assessment recommended that the father be named as custodian and that he undertake the primary care. Although problems were noted concerning his character, his motivation and sincerity were judged as high.

Psychiatric care for the mother was proposed in the report with a gradual re-introduction of the children into her life. Despite a highly detailed report with many external sources consulted, the case dragged on well over a year without any resolution. The mere suggestion of abuse seemed to have sufficient power to stymie the courts until a complete re-assessment corroborated the original findings. We will not know for some years what impact living in such a psychotic milieu had on these girls. Needless to say, they have likely suffered serious abuse both from the fantasized father who was the perpetrator in the mind of their mother and from their mother who forced her psychic reality into her daughters' minds.

(i) Good Enough Parenting

Perhaps no element is as germane to the best interests of the child than adequate or good enough parenting. On the other hand, divorced parents are often so strained in their general life adaptation that their parenting skills are undermined. Hetherington studied the families of 48 preschool boys and girls from divorced families and compared them to an equivalent control group from intact homes.[28] Divorced parents were observed to have difficulties with parent-child communication, behaviour management and affection, and these were significantly compromised. Inconsistency in applying discipline, particularly problems for mothers controlling sons, and general lack of control over the children were prevalent in the divorced group. One can easily understand how a vicious circle evolves with ineffectual parenting leading to increased parental helplessness and depression which in turn leads to a worsening of the parent's response.

Despite this factor, parents in divorce are often held fully accountable for their conduct (especially by the ex-spouse) and they may be judged as to fitness at a time when they are least effective. This only adds pressure to an already strained situation. Yet, divorced or separated parents have no monopoly on bad parenting which is most often based on the personality of the parent more than what they do in any given situation. In this regard, parenting likely says as much about character as it does about technique.

Good parenting is often associated with self awareness, empathy and a deeper capacity to think in the parent. Bad parenting is often

28 Heatherington, C.M., Cox, M. and Cox, R., *supra*, note 4.

linked to personal maladjustment, lack of insight and projection of tensions so that the child must bear negativity on behalf of the parent. Bad parenting is by no means necessarily rejecting, but rejection is always bad parenting. Exploitation, control and its variants in over-protection, seduction and smothering, detail some of the many ways in which adults burden children in their own cause. In this regard, the best interests of the child are never served when there is too much bad parenting, especially when the parent has no insight into the harm they cause. On the other hand, good parenting supports the child's best interests and includes: capacity for insight, nurture, social skills, a non-defensive attitude, responsibility, consistency and firmness of boundaries.

Although parents must bear responsibility for their actions, the quality of the parent-child relationship is also a function of the specific nature of the child. There is no parent, in this regard, without a child and no parenting without a child's adaptive or non-adaptive response to that parent. It is not uncommon, for example, for a parent to be more effective with one child as compared to another. The disposition of the child and the degree to which this meshes with the parent will often predict the success of that relationship. As an example, one caring and motivated mother spent much of her own childhood contending with her ambitious, egocentric and preferred sister who dominated her own mother's field of interest. As a mother, she found herself too often locked in conflict with a daughter who uncannily resembled this sibling. In this relationship, she felt more vulnerable to confusion and emotional over response.

3. CONCLUSION

This chapter has hopefully introduced many of the concepts and notions that will be explored more deeply in the chapters to come. At best, it can set the scene and provide the background for the individual dramas that preoccupy the daily work of family law. We can conclude, though, that divorce has the capacity to be a distressing and disruptive time for families, more so for that subset who require assessment and litigation to resolve their disputes. Perhaps these parents never quite accept the reality of their divorce and they may compete and argue when they should mourn and resolve. Whatever the specific reasons for the conflict, post-separation antagonism can be intense and a direct challenge to the talents and wisdom of family law to intercede on behalf of the children.

2

Custodial Options: Which, When & Why?

Custody orders refer to the legal right and responsibility of a parent to make and carry out decisions that bear on the health, education and general welfare of the child. Custody and residence are usually intertwined so that the parent who has legal custody of the offspring also has physical custody or site of primary residence. In cases of joint legal custody, the physical arrangements vary more widely than in other custodial arrangements. A parent may have joint legal custody but the child will actually physically reside with the other parent the majority of the time. Joint custody can extend though to shared parenting where the child spends a fixed but substantial time with each parent up to and including 50 per cent time sharing. This is often referred to in the popular media as "co-parenting".

Although joint custody has been legally in place in Canada since 1985, in disputed cases decided in court women are favoured in the bulk of custody decisions. In 1991, women in Canada received custody in 73.6 per cent of disputed cases while father's were favoured 11.8 per cent of the time. Joint custody was awarded in 14.3 per cent of cases.[1] Most analysts would interpret these results as suggesting a traditional bias in the direction of maternal care in the mind of the judiciary. Although it is likely true that motherhood is more primal than fatherhood (though not less important), and judges are simply

1 Statistics Canada: quoted in the Globe and Mail, Saturday, August 12, 1995.

reflecting our societal preference for child care, these results may not fully reveal the extent to which our mental set is changing towards the notion of a generic parent, free of the idea of gender.

It is far more likely, for example, for fathers to seek greater involvement in their children's lives than the standard visitation model of every second weekend. Moreover, fathers are more likely to question and even legally dispute whether their children are best off being principally cared for by the maternal parent even where her essential adequacy is not in question. Finally, fathers are more likely to press for joint legal custody both to enshrine their expressed commitment in the lives of their children and to counter arbitrary maternal pre-eminence which they deem to be unequal and unfair. There may be the additional impetus gained from the perception that sole custody orders permit the custodian to act without regard to the needs and rights of the non-custodian in respect to children. Because parents focus on the rights of custody and not its responsibilities, including those to the non-custodian, being non-custodian is increasingly seen as a non-position. In a society where individual rights are being articulated and acknowledged, non-custodial parents may well feel left behind.

Hence, although judicial patterns may not be radically altering, there is more unrest in the custody arena and less acceptance of a subsidiary passive role for the non-custodial parent. This trend is likely to continue with further opportunities for conflict between parents arising as a result. The springing up of support groups for disenfranchised, mostly non-custodial fathers bears witness to this trend.

Family law practice, it seems, is challenged to walk a line between supporting custody arrangements that will lessen the chance of stalemate and arrangements that tip the scales alienating one parent from a meaningful parenting role. We would underline, in this regard, that both parents, custodian and non-custodian, bear a parenting responsibility that together predicts the children's adjustment during and following divorce. This element is often missed in the very cases where it should most apply. Observers of protracted litigation for custody often comment that although the process supposedly concerns the welfare of the children, it seems to be about everything but them!

Perhaps a manifesto listing parental responsibilities in divorce should be part and parcel of every divorce settlement. As we have enshrined the merits of prenatal education, so we might do the same for child care after divorce. My impression is that if the state is to interfere in the parents' rights to manage the care of their children by determining custody and access then it should go further and mandate a process to ensure that this is responsibly carried out. We cannot assume that parents in the throws of divorce fully appreciate the meaning of custody or how this might be blended with actual child care relationships. Custodial parents, for example, often misunderstand the responsibilities of their role and act as if custody is a licence to minimize the non-custodian's input. Too much stress on the primacy of the custodian further fuels parental conflicts and undermines family adjustment when it can least afford it.

1. SOLE CUSTODY

As matters now stand, sole custody remains the option of choice in most divorce situations which come before the courts. Joint custody, although a philosophical breakthrough in many respects, relies so heavily on collaborative strengths that it is usually not feasible in the majority of contested divorce cases, especially those that require the services of a judge to settle.

Sole custody offers the following advantages that have been well tested during the history of this option:

- it consolidates responsibility and provides a clear path for decision making in regard to children;
- it aids the process of separation by differentiating roles and affirming the reality of separateness between adults;
- it highlights parenting over spousal roles or relationships and brings child care into bold relief;
- it provides a clear base for children and promotes child development by reinforcing continuity and consistency of care.

Sole custody is not without its disadvantages and these can be formidable in the actual delivery of care and control:

- it places a special burden on the non-custodian to accept a lesser role in the children's lives even when they do not feel any less a parent;
- it requires children who put both parents on an equal emotional plane to accept the role dominance of one over the other;
- it can loosen ties between the non-custodial parent and a child and this may negatively bear on the willingness of that parent to visit or pay child support;
- at its extremes, such as a two-day visit with twelve days in between, it can be a source of psychological deprivation for children who may develop an emotional hunger for contact with that parent that cannot be abated.

2. SPLIT CUSTODY

Split custody should be considered a variation of sole custody in which each parent assumes care and control (physical custody) of one or more of the children of the marriage with access provided to the non-custodian. In our experience this has limited application and most often occurs in families where children are widely divergent in age or where other special circumstances apply. For example, the eldest child may be a 16-year-old girl while the younger two boys are respectively, nine and ten. The eldest may then choose to live with her father while the younger two share a residence with their mother. The location of a specific school, relocation of one parent, remarriages in which a child does not get along with a new spouse, as well as personality conflicts between siblings or with a specific parent may come into play in the choice of split custody.

To some extent, split custody resembles shared parenting at least in as much as it recognizes the parity of both parents as custodians. Two major drawbacks are notable. First, it can lead to a loosening of ties with the child's non-custodian as well as with the siblings who reside in the other residence. This is especially important in the case of adolescents whose social lives are already peer centred and further removed from home life. Secondly, it breaks up the family not just the parents and this introduces further emotional strain for everyone involved. Because of this latter factor, it is not an option worth considering in the majority of circumstances especially in families with younger children. On the other hand, it has its specific applications as described above and should be retained in the custody repertoire for these occasions.

3. DIVIDED CUSTODY

This describes the care and control arrangement whereby the child spends a year or part of a year residing with one parent and a year or part of a year with the other in alternation. Sole custody is deemed portable and is held by the parent providing the care at the time. This is sometimes applicable where the parents live in different cities or different countries usually at great distance and they decide to raise the children by taking turns. The advantages of such a method may be offset by the obvious lack of stability for the child but certain children and certain parents may come to such an unorthodox solution and presumably make it work. It is sufficiently idiosyncratic, however, to be left solely to the joint decision of both parents.

4. JOINT CUSTODY

Joint custody, which will be considered in detail in the next chapter, is an option worth considering in specific circumstances. When parents on their own agree to such an approach or when they can be swayed to its merits (as compared to being coerced), experience indicates that it stands a good chance of succeeding. Joint custody is understood to have two dimensions: (1) joint legal custody which outlines a shared division of rights without reference to the specifics of care, and (2) joint physical custody which defines a distribution of care in which each parent plays a significant role to a maximum of equal time with each parent.

The advantages of joint custody are not usually shared by families where the parents are locked in long disputes over custody and access. For one, joint custody is most often associated with frequent access and in high conflict families, access and conflict feed off each other. Johnston, Kline and Tschann reported that children who shared more days with each parent, in the presence of protracted conflict, were significantly more depressed, withdrawn and uncommunicative, had more psychosomatic complaints and were judged by their parents as more aggressive.[2] Hence, any custody order that stresses linkage and interaction between the parents is not well suited to such a post-divorce family. The danger in such a situation is that structure or control is lost all together.

In low conflict post-divorce families, especially where communication and collaboration in respect to children are well preserved, joint custody can succeed in enriching the lives of those involved. It may even succeed where such collaboration does not extend beyond minimal civility between the parents but even in these cases there will be an implicit respect for the joint arrangement and the role of the other parent.

The advantages of joint custody in this type of family situation are well known:

- it best mirrors the functioning of the intact family which is still considered the preferred social organization for the raising of offspring;
- it acknowledges that children have more than one primary or psychological parent and it highlights the unity of a parenting couple;
- it affirms the historical and psychological value of each parent and defends against emotional injuries to the pride and identity of either adult;
- it creates parity for children in relation to the two parents and minimizes an experience of guilt based on the children feeling that one parent is being unequally treated or deprived;
- it promotes bi-parental involvement in the lives of the children, including activities, interactions and monetary contributions;
- it provides a further viable option apart from sole custody for a select group of superior families, facilitating greater scope for cooperation among divorced parents who are equal to the task.

In relation to this final point, it may be helpful to simply outline the qualities that are often associated with success in joint parenting

2 Johnston, J., Kline, M. and Tschann, J. (1991), "Ongoing post-divorce conflict in families contesting custody: do joint custody and frequent access help?", in J. Folberg (ed.), *Joint Custody and Shared Parenting*, 2nd ed., New York: The Guilford Press.

and comprise what is meant by the qualifier "superior". These can be expressed in a series of questions that can be asked of parents when such an option is being considered:

- Do the adults respect each other as parents and do they place the bond with their children ahead of their own relationship and the fate of the marriage?
- Are the parents psychologically minded in their approach to child care?
- Is there a minimum of blame and a maximum of empathy with the needs and status of the children?
- Do the parents respect the limitations of joint parenting by acknowledging the autonomy of the other parent's role and relationship with the children?
- Are the parents flexible and reflective individuals who have good psychological health and an adequate personal adjustment?
- Have both parents been able to mourn the loss of their marriage and to clearly redefine their roles in terms of parenting?

Although, research in this field has not focused on child factors and suitability for shared parenting, this element should not be ignored. Most often children seek and are gratified by optimal contact with both parents as Wallerstein and Kelly discovered in their landmark 1980 study.[3] Certain children may prove particularly vulnerable, however, in an area that creates special needs. For example, a child with a learning disability, chronic medical condition or emotional disorder may do better under the care of one parent more than two for logistical or psychological reasons. Joint physical custody could introduce a strain and risk factor that may not be worth taking in these specific cases. On the other hand, this limitation should not apply to a situation where, for example, one parent expresses concern that the other parent is too "soft" or doting. Rather, this would be the occasion to address this issue with the other parent as compared to taking the position that joint parenting is contradicted.

Having articulated its merits and the type of people for whom it is best suited, it remains to mention some disadvantages of this option which should also be kept in mind:

---

3 Wallerstein, J. and Kelly, J. (1980), *Surviving the Breakup: How Parents and Children Cope with Divorce*, New York: Basic Books.

- it is administratively more complex as activities and possessions often have to be transported between homes on a regular basis;
- interactions between parents are enhanced by the sharing of care and control and this can fan existing conflicts or create new ones;
- it can be chosen for the wrong reasons which may have little to do with child care or the children's well being;
- it can be rescinded too easily and is especially vulnerable to the ambivalence of the parent who would most probably be named as custodian;
- it may set up expectations in the parents' minds that joint custody should solve all evils of separation and divorce and it is more likely than other models, therefore, to be blamed when this is not forthcoming.

As to the fourth point, this is often raised as a concern especially by fathers who seek joint custody apart from the wishes of their ex-spouse. The courts have been increasingly unwilling to impose joint custody when it is not the expressed desire of both parties. This has exposed the fragility of joint custody arrangements even when they are in place. They can be scuttled when one parent decides to reject its premise or exacerbates conflict and then claims that the joint custody is not working. Although some jurisdictions have stipulated what are justifiable reasons to retreat from a joint custody order, this vulnerability still exists.

The argument that might be made is that any parent who dismisses joint custody even on flimsy grounds of strategy, minor doubts or indecision may not be a suitable candidate in any case. On the other hand, might there be occasions where the court could uphold or support a joint custody agreement that has been in place when it is shown that extraneous factors are actually behind the change of heart? Although we would certainly agree that the courts should not be coercive in establishing joint custody, they should also not be open to changing these arrangements on arbitrary grounds. Such situations as a parent who is simply tired of the demand imposed by shared parenting, one who has remarried and it would no longer be convenient, or the gratuitous influence of a new lawyer who views all co-parenting as hogwash, are examples of spurious grounds on which to suspend a joint arrangement.

Joint custody has a definite place in the custody/access spectrum and in the right hands it can be a formidable bridge between an intact family and post-divorce adjustment. Although we do not see a place for mandating these arrangements against the will of parents, there is a definite place for the astute family lawyer to identify those parents who can work with joint custody in the bests of interests of their children.

5. RIGHTS AND RESPONSIBILITIES

In all forms of custody, a focus on responsibilities over rights seems closer to the real needs of children and parents. It is not that parental rights are secondary to a clear resolution of custody matters but they should not be viewed apart from the ethical texture of responsibilities that are essential to family adjustment following divorce. Figure 1 outlines a schema in which rights and responsibilities are labeled for each custody alternative and Table 1 summarizes the rights and responsibilities that correspond to the specific options for custodial, non-custodial and joint custodial parents.

Figure 1

	custodial	non-custodial	joint custodial
rights	A	B	C
responsibility	D	E	F

Table 1 Rights And Responsibilities For Various Custody Options

Rights/Custodial Parent

- the right to be the final authority and guardian as to decisions concerning the children's welfare;
- the right to plan and coordinate the activities of the children;
- the right to reside with the children for the majority of time as set out in the separation agreement.

Responsibilities/Custodial parent

- the responsibility of facilitating access and promoting the children's relationship to the non-custodial parent;
- the responsibility to provide the best possible environment for the children;
- the responsibility to consult and receive input on decisions of importance to the welfare of the children;
- the responsibility to coordinate and implement the health, educational and welfare needs of the children;
- the responsibility to appreciate the frustrations born by the non-custodial parent who must accept a lesser role than that played in a normal family setting.

Rights/Non-Custodial Parent

- the right to be consulted by the custodial parent regarding major decisions concerning the children's health, education and welfare;
- the right to be supplied all relevant information and feedback concerning the children which is of natural interest;
- the right to provide care and control of the children for the duration of the access visit.

Responsibilities/Non-Custodial Parent

- the responsibility of sustaining a meaningful and facilitating relationship with children during the limits of the access and telephone schedule specified in the separation agreement;
- the responsibility to contribute to the welfare of the children through support payments;
- the responsibility to contribute to the lives of the children by taking part in decision making and by demonstrating interest, commitment and concern;
- the responsibility to respect the custodial parent's ultimate answerability for decisions made on behalf of the children and to support this parent in that obligation.

Rights/Joint Custodial Parents

- the right to exercise care and control of the children during the time period in which the children reside with that parent;
- the right to contribute to the important decisions regarding health, education and welfare that are far reaching in their impact on the children;
- the right to be accorded equal respect and value as a parent and to have this sentiment communicated to the children.

Responsibilities/Joint Custodial Parent

- the responsibility to communicate and cooperate in the raising of the children in conjunction with the other parent;

- the responsibility to affirm and support the equal value and authority of the other parent in the eyes of the children;
- the responsibility to coordinate and cooperate in the formation of plans and schedules concerning the children;
- the responsibility to contribute financially to the welfare of the children on the basis of the formula established in the separation agreement.

All parents, we might conclude, exercise certain rights that are attributable to their adult status. As adults, they have the right to autonomously undertake the care and control of their children. When the parents on their own prove unable to make decisions after marriage breakdown and seek the intervention of the courts, then these rights are at least temporarily altered. As the goal is to move the family towards adjustment, the challenge for the legal system is to expedite the intervention and minimize the interval when the state must be involved. When lawyers, judges and mental health professionals become implicated, they add qualifiers to these rights by way of standards and legislative policies that govern post-divorce relationships between parents and between parents and children. The standard referred to as the "best interests of the child" is one such qualifier as it asserts that the child's needs should always take precedence over the parents' wishes. Children's needs are then paramount although the court most often favours frequent association and ongoing relationships with both parents as central to meeting childhood needs.

Another principle that seems to be of importance in family law is that of "the least detrimental alternative". Perhaps this is the corollary of "best interest" as it reflects the court's duty to ensure that children are as least harmed as possible by their parents' actions. By applying this standard, for instance, joint custody might be seen in certain cases as the least detrimental alternative for child care and, therefore, also the model of choice. In other circumstances, joint custody could well be judged as potentially highly detrimental and the option of least merit. We are often reminded of this principle of least detriment when faced with a custody dispute between two parents who are deficient in ways that impact on child care and the choice seems to be between negative options.

From an assessor's standpoint, the best interests of the children are always served when the detrimental factors are controlled to the extent possible through a parenting arrangement. For example, in one case, the mother of three children was completely unable to provide a minimal structure in the home environment. The house was a disaster area and extremely disturbing to the children. Moreover, the mother had serious problems controlling the children and seemed to become disorganized under pressure. Thankfully, there was no doubt that the father could provide this structure for he had done so prior to the separation. Yet, he was also a highly rigid closed personality who was intolerant of anyone with different views than himself. His psychological test scores were contaminated beyond interpretation whereas the mother, despite problems, showed more insight, more honest test responding and willingness to admit her failings. Yet, the children were adamant in their own way that some change was necessary and they could not tolerate the chaos of life with mother. The assessor had no choice but to recommend the father as custodian but suggested frequent, although briefer, access to the mother in order to make best use of her psychological strengths and to mitigate against the rigidity of the father.

One could also argue according to the same principle of least detriment that a conflict-ridden divorce would dictate reduced access to minimize the interaction. In support, we know that prolonged unremitting interparental conflict is very damaging to children and efforts to reduce it are essential to protecting children's welfare. This is not as clear cut in practice, though, and the matter is a complex one. If a mother, for example, is contemptuously treated by her overpowering ex-husband who also happens to be custodian, should she have to pay the price of reduced access in order to lessen the child's exposure to conflict? Moreover, clinically, one has to separate levels of needs and even levels of distress. Hence, even though it may be true that a child could become symptomatic or stressed if exposed to parents who are constantly in conflict, there may also be opportunities for quality time with that parent that might be emotionally protective. In such cases, it could be argued that the benefits outweigh the liabilities. This underscores how multidimensional the assessment must be in order to take account of the quality of parent-child relationships as well as the interaction between the parents when evaluating the component of detriment.

Another common presumption concerns the child's need to have relationships with both parents. This is sometimes expressed as the principle of "maximum contact" although a better term might be "optimal contact". Optimal, in this regard, refers to the balance between the relative potentials of the parents to provide for the child and the parenting arrangement established to meet the child's needs. As long as the parents fit that broad category of "good enough", then the child of the marriage should enjoy maximal contact with both parents to the degree consistent with the child's best interests.

It is not unusual, though, for one parent to seek to exclude the other, perhaps to replace them with a better candidate. In essence, such a parent unilaterally decides that optimal means no contact at all. As a typical example, one mother regretted her brief unhappy liaison which produced a child. She remarried with the clear purpose of having the new spouse fill the parental role. The child, in this case a young boy of four, longed for his father even though the step father was perfectly adequate and objectively more able than the father. A psychological assessment observed this need in the child and, and drawing on this principle, recommended some access. Although it was highlighted that access should be brief, the assessor recognized that some opportunity had to exist for the child to know his father and not to be left at the mercy of idealized fantasies about a magical father which would add a major risk element to his development. Hence, a corollary to the principle that a child benefits from having relationships with both parents is that some presence is always better than total absence unless the proximity of that parent would in fact be harmful to the well being of the child. In this case, the court has the duty to define optimal in highly restricted terms.

Lastly, there is the doctrine of "tender years" that has stood the test of time as a presumption in favour of the mother during infancy and the very young childhood years. Although we are not aware of any specific age requirement for a child to be deemed of tender years, it usually refers to the first three years of life and could extend to the first four but most certainly includes the pre-school years. Although there is a growing recognition that fathers are quite capable of being the primary parent to very young children, there remains a societal preference for mothers in the event of a choice.

This should not, however, be seen as a dismissal of the father's importance to the baby but rather a belief in the complementarity of roles. Yet, infant research would support that attachments for fathers are as significant as that for mothers and that each parent contributes to the social, emotional cognitive development as well as gender identity of their offspring.[4] The matter is a complex one and different theories prevail. Certainly, the nurturing role in our society is more often filled by women who, having given birth to life and being equipped to sustain it with their own bodies, are in a natural position to provide this elemental care. This does not preclude a father from offering the same care and nurture but it makes a preference for motherhood an understandable choice.

A major drawback in this maternal tradition concerning the tender years, however, is that it has underestimated the significance of the father link in a young male's life. In contrast, it has tended to serve the needs of female children who benefit from an uncluttered mother-daughter relationship. When the custody issue is decided within the tender years of the child and the mother is named as custodian, as is most common, access may be kept relatively brief to offset anxieties concerning separation from the mother. As the boy ages, though, access may not increase fast enough to meet the real needs for father contact that quickly develop. This element of deprivation can be harmful to the small boy's emotional and gender development. Often an assessor or judge can make an added contribution to the family in divorce when these developmental needs are addressed at the outset and circumvent the need to return to court at a later phase of the child's development.

In conclusion, what seems clear from this discussion of family law standards is that they modify rights and embed them in a matrix of parental responsibility. Although custody bestows a legal right to make decisions on behalf of the child, these are never fully independent of the ethical demand to enlist, include and value the importance to the child of the other parent. In the same way, non-custodianship has its own demands especially that of acknowledging that the bulk of child care falls upon the custodian whose position must be supported. Easier said than done perhaps in many of the disputes that lawyers and the courts handle. Yet, these ethical standards determine how we are likely to evaluate custody and access disputes and help frame the goal of intervention. Finally, these stand-

4 Gunsberg, L. (1982), "Selected critical review of psychological investigations of the early father-infant relationship", in S. Cath, A. Gurwitt and J. Munder Ross, *Father and Child: Developmental and Clinical Perspectives*, Boston: Little, Brown and Company.

ards place a demand as well on parents that steers them and the process towards a reasonable, sensible resolution.

6. PSYCHOLOGICAL PRINCIPLES AND THE MEANING OF CUSTODY

Besides rights, responsibilities and legal standards, psychological principles also have a bearing on how we understand custody and its relation to child welfare. In this regard, in order to be meaningful if not relevant, the notion of custody must have a direct connection to what is best for children. Adjudicating custody and access and determining what is best for children are considered one and the same. Psychologically, however, the issue of custody means much more than a legal distinction. It carries the notion of prediction. The parent who attains custody is predicted to be the parent best able to foster good development in the child. Hence, if an assessor recommends one parent over another as custodian, only time will tell whether this prediction is correct. Of course, the parents, custodian and non-custodian alike, have the real control over the fate of their children and we must not take more of the responsibility than they should. Yet, it still holds that custody, when determined by experts and the court, must rely on the future to justify itself.

Without an absolute presumption in favour of the mother, determining what is in the child's best interests has become much more difficult. When we consider the parents' personalities, mental and physical health, socioeconomic stability, parent-child relationships, children's and parents wishes and other relevant factors, the process can become quite complex. In litigated cases, the addition of testimony from neighbours, teachers and other interested parties can render the judge's task a veritable nightmare! In the end, judges may seize on only one or a few factors to make their decision as to custodian if only to control the complexity of the data. A good assessment, however, should facilitate that process and its merit will lie in the extent to which it informs the judicial process and supports it.

Ideally, the custodian is the parent best able to represent the child's needs as well as the one best equipped to manage the child's relationship with the non-custodian. This is very different though from the issue of least detrimental parent and has even less to do with who is the more righteous. In one case, for example, a 43-year-old mother had begun a new relationship with a family friend and, upon reflection, questioned the wisdom of her choice. Would it not have been sounder if she had left her marriage, established herself independently, and then pursued her new liaison? On the other hand, her two daughters very much wanted to accompany her and were of sufficient age to have meaningful input. The father argued that only he represented stability and that there was no telling what would happen in his wife's life. Although he had a point to his argument, he was not the children's choice, probably because he was somewhat obsessive and in his anxiety infringed on the children's right to think for themselves. The mother had a much better capacity to support their growing autonomy and the girls felt recognized by her. Although the father stood for stability and commitment, his moralizing may have missed the real emotional needs of his daughters. Although less faulty in one sense, he was also less attuned.

At least in theory, custody determination should reflect several aptitudes and strengths: (1) the aptitude to parent, (2) the aptitude to parent together despite divorce, (3) conflict resolution and communications skills, and (4) emotional maturity and psychological health. On the scale of custody alternatives, the cursor should be set at the point on the scale where the parents can best manage this complex task. The more negative the parental profile either in terms of aptitudes, willingness, circumstances or strengths, the more custody arrangements will have to reflect these limits. Conversely, greater aptitudes and strengths are associated with increased visitation, collaboration and prevalence of joint parenting. The art of custody and access determinations is to find that point on the scale that is most appropriate for the specific family circumstance. Too stringent and the tensions do not abate; too optimistic and care and control dissolve into mayhem.

It may be useful to consider some stages on the custody scale which ranges from sole custody with no access to shared or co-parenting parenting.

7. SOLE CUSTODY WITH NO ACCESS

Mrs. W felt that she had escaped her marriage when she forced her husband to leave but two years later she was still receiving furious and harassing telephone calls from him. Mr. W suffered from a manic depressive illness but his personality was also erratic, unstable and volatile. If perturbed, he would leave many angry messages and apologize after the fact. Yet, the children, both in the later primary grades, visited their father every second weekend, less it seemed out of desire and more because they feared saying no to him. He would blame their mother and inundate their lives with telephone calls and threats. Finally, an event occurred that gave them reason to act. Mr. W became embroiled in a fight with another man during one of the children's visits and the police were called. The younger of the two telephoned their mother who came to pick them up. They did not return and refused further contact. Finally, an assessment determined that Mr. W suffered from a mental disorder including bizarre thinking and that his judgment could be faulty. He had little capacity to respond to his children's needs and was extremely self absorbed with his problems. The assessor recommended that the children not be required to visit and that they would be better able to handle this relationship as adults.

8. SOLE CUSTODY WITH MINIMAL ACCESS

A woman lawyer specializing in cases of harassment and "stalking" successfully sought an assessment of an ex-husband who had been denied access to his two young sons. Although he denied malevolent intent, his conduct revealed serious lapses in behavioural control with a very low frustration tolerance. On psychological evaluation, this man was seen as hyperactive with immature and inadequate traits. Yet, he was also sincere and troubled and felt a longing for his sons as they did for him. It was less the case of a bad or unworthy person and more that of an undercontrolled man who had revealed his worst side during the separation. To his credit, he acknowledged his need for supervised access and accepted the validity of his ex-wife's anxieties. He accepted the conditions that he follow a program in anger management and parenting skills and that the visits would be professionally supervised. The assessment recommended supervised access of two hours per week to be held at a local community centre with an opportunity for adjustment if this proved stable and successful.

9. SOLE LEGAL CUSTODY WITH STANDARD ACCESS

Mr. P and Ms. B had a short one and a half year relationship that nevertheless produced two sons. Ms. B was pregnant with the second child when the liaison ended. Ms. B, a dynamic and successful executive was also somewhat rigid and unyielding although she was very thorough in advancing her case and putting Mr. P on the defensive. For one, she consulted a psychologist to advise her on child care, moved in the same vicinity as her parents who provided back up care, and engaged a live-in nanny. Mr. P was very sincere and genuine but also timid and restrained and slow to mobilize his own defense. He was plainly intimidated by his ex-girlfriend and consented initially to her demand that visits only take place at her residence and under her supervision. Gradually, however, his frustration grew and, as might be expected, he detested his secondary status which included being subordinated to the nanny.

Mr. P's lawyer sought a court order for an assessment. The evaluation revealed poor communication and deep mistrust between the parents as well as highlighting the intransigence of Ms. B. The assessment also revealed that Mr. P was deeply troubled by inadequacy feelings but could offer affection and good care to his sons. Yet, Ms. B's obvious poise and competence was undeniable and no one could fault the care she provided for the children. The need for unsupervised and natural access to take place at the father's home was also underscored and a recommendation for standard access was made despite the tender years of the children. The assessor took account of the youth of the children and suggested a staging of access that would increase with age. In its final form, though, it would comprise every second weekend with one short evening visit on a mid-week day. Holiday and special day visitation was specified but not equivalent to a complete sharing.

The depth of conflict between the parents, their personality limitations and propensity for strife, their lack of history together and the tender years of the boys, all contributed to the rationale for the parenting proposal. The assessor reasoned that it was best to recommend a visiting protocol that was within the mother's scope to accept rather than to suggest access that she would oppose and block likely at the expense of the two sons. The assessor emphasized that it was preferable at this stage for Mr. P to establish a precedent of solid relating and look possibly to revisit the matter when the boys were firmly of school age.

10. SOLE CUSTODY WITH AMPLE VISITATION

Mr. H had been married to Ms. B for nine years and they had two fine daughters. It was an unusual dispute in that Mr. H noted that he had been a stay-at-home dad and was at base the primary custodian. At the time of the separation, he had moved out and the mother, a successful investment broker, had moved to a more convenient location with the two girls. He saw them according to standard access provisions, mainly every second weekend plus holidays. There were no problems reported in the children's adjustment and the assessment confirmed their healthy academic, social and psychological strengths. Ms. B was a positive and skilled parent as well as successful in her career. She was an excellent role model for two young ladies growing up in this day and age. Mr. H was a resourceful person. He pursued his talents as an artisan and was very close to his daughters. Although he was ill at ease with some aspects of his masculinity, there was no doubting his capacity as a parent. The parents, although strained as regards the conflict, were still able to communicate and converse in respect to the children and did so often and freely.

The assessment acknowledged the mutual strengths and communication capacities and envisioned a more interactive model of parenting. The children seemed resilient and the mother was flexible in regards to the father's input as long as he did not claim to be primary custodian or caregiver. Yet, it was felt that joint custody still represented a risk of excessive conflict as there was an element of instability, especially in the father's personal and vocational life. The mother's strength as a role model for two preadolescent females was highlighted. The assessor recommended custody to the mother and an enriched visitation plan that included two weekends out of every three. Holidays were to be divided equally between the parents.

11. JOINT LEGAL CUSTODY WITHOUT SHARED PARENTING

Mr. and Mrs. L had been married for 19 years when their marriage ended with hurt and sorrow. Mr. L entered into a romance with a woman they both had known socially. It was a surprise to Mrs. L who was comfortable and content with her marriage and did not have any premonition that this might happen. The couple's three children were now teenagers and although they felt badly for their mother's hurt and devastation, they also noticed that their father became more outgoing and fulfilled. When one of the children suggested that he would prefer to live with his father and his new partner, Mrs. L insisted on an assessment to ascertain what was in the children's best interests. Underneath, she was alarmed that she might lose her family as well as her husband and this further distressed her.

The assessment established that the couple had shared the parenting over the years and that there was ample evidence for collaborative and communication strengths. Their children expressed a desire to maintain one home and to visit the other parent. The two eldest chose to live with their mother while the youngest decided to reside with her father. Visitation was arranged to establish specific opportunities for meals and times together with each parent. The rationale was that family integrity would be served if children and parents both knew that on one or two occasions each week there would be regular events with the children. On the other hand, joint legal custody was adopted without issue.

12. JOINT CUSTODY WITH SHARED PARENTING

Mr. and Mrs. K were both impressive, mature professionals in the same field of work. Moreover, they both had strong and caring relationships with their daughter and son, both in the later stage of primary school. Mrs. K was not without her concerns for her ex-husband's moods but she naturally accepted and promoted his welfare in her children's eyes. When their separation occurred, Mr. K obtained regular and liberal access but he strongly believed that the children wanted and needed equal time with each parent. Care and control was jointly maintained from the outset. The K's lawyers perceived that it was in the family's best interest to defuse this potential conflict and referred the parents for counseling and mediation. After seeing the parents, the mediator interviewed the children and ascertained after several meetings that they indeed wished to spend one week with each of their parents. They both felt that this would represent the best of both worlds and would be most protective of them. Mrs. K, although initially reluctant, consented to the plan with the provision that the mediator might oversee the change and ensure the children's healthy adjustment. Six-month and two-year follow ups revealed a successful adjustment for the children and less tension between the parents.

13. CONCLUSION

Although custody and access come in numerous combinations and formats, the one determining factor remains the best interests of the child. Divorce represents a fundamental change in circumstance for all members of the family and not all participants have the occasion to choose their own destiny. Although amicable divorces thankfully occur, surprising numbers of estranged parents prove totally unable to determine what is best for their offspring. More specifically, they may become hamstrung over the question of who is best able to assure the child's well being. Hence, assessors, lawyers and the courts may be asked to intervene to decide on what is best for the children of a dissolving marriage and hopefully soften the blow for all concerned. What this chapter has sketched are not only the variations on a theme of what works for children of divorce but also what principles and attributes may be applied to enhance the success of the outcome. Custody is certainly about rights and best circumstances but divorce itself highlights the continuing responsibility that parents bear their children over and above the fate of their union.

3

Joint Custody and its Challenge to Family Law[1]

1. INTRODUCTION

It was during the late 1970s that sole custody came under increasing scrutiny for its perceived failure to protect children of divorce from undue psychological trauma. With its legacy of infrequent visitation, sole custody was seen as a source of stressful deprivation for children from the non-custodial parent. This conclusion was soundly replicated by Wallerstein and Kelly in their 1980 ground breaking study described in the book "Surviving the Breakup".[2] The children who were best off were those who had frequent, uncomplicated contact with the non-custodial parent. Sole custody, as it was practised, appeared to inadequately serve the children whose welfare it was intended to protect.

Although the Wallerstein and Kelly study had not intended to look at custody issues, it indirectly supported the idea that co-parental access may well be a positive influence for children after separation or divorce. Sole custody, it seemed in this light, imposed alienating barriers between one parent and the children. It tended to disenfran-

1 A modified version of this chapter appeared in the Gazette, a publication of the Law Society of Upper Canada (1995), 20, at 29-50.

2 Wallerstein, J.S. and Kelly, J.B. (1980), *Surviving the Breakup: How Children and Parents Cope with Divorce*, New York: Basic Books.

chise fathers, in particular, whose involvement often diminished with time after the separation. Sole custody arrangements did not encourage a strong bond between the non-custodial parent and the child while saddling the custodial mother with a surfeit of duties and responsibilities.

In Canada, joint custody erupted into legal discourse on the impact of two cases heard by the Ontario Court of Appeal: *Baker v. Baker*[3] and *Kruger v. Kruger*.[4] Joint custody, it was believed, would reduce the trauma and estrangement of divorce, hopefully attenuating the severe adverse consequences that had been observed in children and adults who had undergone the divorce experience. Central but implicit in the movement that soon developed in support of joint custody was an implicit belief in the inherent worth of the nuclear family and the desirability of approximating this same structure in a post-separation framework.

Exponents of joint custody wrote elegantly of its many advantages.[5] It acknowledged the mutuality of parenting and it often led to a more balanced distribution of the work load. The children might be spared the loyalty struggles of the past as neither parent could automatically claim a distinct advantage in terms of influence. The sharing of custodial power should lead to a kinder, more humane divorce with quicker, healthier resolution for children as well as parents. The extended families on both sides would more likely find a place in such an arrangement and, coupled with the continuing proof of their parents' love and commitment, would feel less abandoned and rejected.

The rise of joint custody, then, was at the heart of public and private anguish concerning the pernicious impact of divorce on children and the subsequent societal pay out over many years. The tendency for the non-custodial parent, usually the father, to be marginalized while the custodial parent, mainly the mother, seemed fated to years of unremitting burden, led many advocates to argue that families should continue in their original form even if marriages fail. Dismal statistics outlining the failure of sole custody, as it was practised, further strengthened the joint custody argument. non-cus-

3 *Baker v. Baker* (1979), 8 R.F.L. (2d) 236, 23 O.R. (2d) 391 (C.A.).

4 *Kruger v. Kruger* (1979), 11 R.F.L. (2d) 52, 25 O.R. (2d) 673 (C.A.).

5 Elkin, Myer (1991), "Joint custody: in the best interest of the family", in Jay Folberg, *Joint Custody and Shared Parenting*, 2nd ed. New York, The Guilford Press, at 11-15.

todial parent's often withdrew following divorce or visited irregularly and this coupled with substantial incidence of non-payment of support added fuel to the momentum for change.[6]

Less rigid assumptions about role and gender, especially among the more educated classes, also inspired shifts in thinking about how the post-divorce family should be structured. Logically, it made sense to envision a shared distribution of labour with each parent shouldering a sizable part of the overall burden. This support held despite fears from some quarters that it could be used as a ploy by men to reduce child support and to exercise control over women. It was especially strong among social analysts who saw the traditional roles of woman as nurturer and man as provider breaking down in the post-modern society. There was an argument for a generic parent who can be either masculine or feminine in gender but whose parenting aptitudes can be assessed independent of stereotypes roles.

From a child rearing perspective, it was noted that children are naturally inclined to engage and love both their parents and to seek equal contact with them. Further, in sole custody, the non-custodian, usually the father, often played a far lesser role after separation than before independent of their degree of involvement or in spite of it.[7] Overall, then, spurred by public and professional interest, the time seemed ripe to re-think the whole issue of custody and access in the light of these findings and in view of changes in how society viewed the obligation to parent.

2. JOINT CUSTODY IN PERSPECTIVE

With its praises being sung from many quarters, some of us tended to view joint custody as the antidote to divorce and, perhaps, we asked too much of this or any custody option to offset the often severe familial consequences of separation and divorce. We hoped that warring parents, whose disputes expressed the enormity of the

---

6 Furstenberg, F.F., Jr., Nord, C.W., Peterson, J.L. and Zill, N. (1983), "The life course of children of divorce: marital disruption and parental contact", *American Sociological Review*, 48: 656-668.

7 Kelly, Joan B. (1993) "Current research on children's post-divorce adjustment: no simple answers", *Family and Conciliation Court Reviews*, 31: 29-49.

rupture triggered by divorce, would adapt more quickly if there was the mutual endorsement and empowerment intrinsic to joint custody.

There is a body of research that in varying degrees and circumstances has supported the virtues of joint custody when applied to families and individuals who can work within its borders.[8] Most often, this represents parents who have voluntarily chosen shared parenting rather than having it imposed on them by statute or judicial decree. When successful, mothers and fathers in joint custody relationships with their ex-spouse tend to be more satisfied than their peers in sole custody arrangements.[9]

Yet, Susan Steinman, in a respected study of cases in which joint custody was assigned by the court,[10] noted that even with children who have been living in joint custodial arrangements for a considerable part of their childhood, one-third were unhappy with the regimen and revealed signs of maladjustment. Issues of mastery over the environment and security issues can still be observed in joint custody families when even this method has failed to meet basic needs. Before blaming this one-third failure rate on this form of care and control, we should probably accept that the effects of divorce can often be far-reaching and might, in fact, resist the efforts of any post-divorce custody option to fully offset them. The shattering of family bonds even in so-called bad marriages can have enduring negative effects that last for years.[11] Wallerstein and Kelly[12] were plainly shocked in their longitudinal study of separated families to find that even five years after separation, many families floundered under the high stress effects of divorce. Interestingly, other studies have not replicated the negative findings of this study and the literature is inconsistent in this regard.

Ironically, what this likely depicts is the failure of divorce to provide a satisfactory remedy for all cases of marital conflict. Eventually, figure and ground meld and as life proceeds for children and parents, the residual effects are more difficult to discern as actually

8 Steinman, Susan (1984), "Joint custody, What we know, What we have yet to learn, and the judicial and legislative implications", in Jay Folberg (ed.), *Joint Custody and Shared Parenting*, Washington D.C., Bureau of the National Association of family and Conciliation Courts.

9 Wallerstein, J.S. and Kelly, J.B. *supra*, note 2.

10 *Supra*, note 8.

11 Galenson, E. (1986), "Divorce", in Arnold Aothstein (ed.), *The Reconstruction of Trauma: Its Significance in Clinical Work,* Madison: International Universities Press, at 121-134.

12 Wallerstein, J.S. and Kelly, J.B., *supra*, note 2.

stemming from the divorce. Yet, psychotherapists often see adults whose parents divorced when they were children and who still bear the impact of this early experience. Divorce causes a major lasting change in the life of a child which necessitates reorganization and adaptation. The wish to undo its effects can become an enduring fantasy, preoccupying the child long after it is actually relevant to their conscious lives. The undoing of schism, the fear of rupture, and conflicts around guilt and shame are often seen in people whose psyches were marked by divorce.[13]

Taking a realistic perspective, though, the outright condemnation of sole custody was perhaps premature as was the over zealous adoption of joint custody as a means of maintaining the effective relevance of two parents in the lives of their offspring. In the light of more recent research findings, however, the consensus is that for motivated parents who voluntarily choose joint legal custody with varying degrees of sharing and who meet certain fundamental personal criteria, joint custody can be a wise option. This is not to say that all studies confirm that joint custody in its various forms is well received by all children but, then, perhaps this has more to do with the children's sentiments concerning divorce itself rather than the lifestyle associated specifically with joint custody. Parents who gravitate to joint custody tend to be those people who, despite conflict, remain willing and able to communicate as regards the children even when this communication is strained by the severe disappointments they feel with each other.[14]

When custody can be considered as one variable along side other important predictors of post-divorce outcome, then it can be approached more rationally with better results for families who require assessment and court mediation. Other factors beside custody which are relevant to predicting outcome include: degree of conflict and interparental strife, the relationship of the children to each parent, the emotional adjustment and well being of the custodial parent(s), child rearing practices, gender of the children and, finally, remarriage.[15]

---

13 Kelly, J. (1988), "Longer term adjustment in children of divorce: converging findings and implications for practice", *Journal of Family Psychology,* 2: 119-140.

14 Lowery, C.R. and Settle, S.A. (1985), "Effects of divorce on children: differential impact of custody and visitation patterns", *Family Relations Journal of Applied Family and Child Studies,* 34: 455-463.

15 Ilfeld, F. Jr., Illfeld, H. and Alexander, J. (1982), "Does joint custody work:

The initial challenge is to predict when joint custody will work and when it will not. The second is to be realistic about what any custody option can offer and to not restrict measures only to soft signs such as happiness or voiced satisfaction as measures of success. Discontent may be endemic to all kinds of post-separation alternatives without being necessarily harmful or inadequate. It seems evident, though, that no single care and control option is appropriate for all families. Parenting formulas need to be tailor made to suit the individual characteristics of the family in question. At best, a well thought out custody and access formula will allow for a faster recovery from the turmoil of divorce, protect against re-litigation and incessant conflict and permit the relatively smooth regrouping of families.

If wrongly applied, joint custody can amount to no custody at all.[16] It can fuel interparental conflict and significantly prolong the adjustment process. At the same time, joint custody can be successfully practised by parents who dislike each other and who may not easily be on speaking terms. They will, however, relate when necessary concerning their children and inherently protect the other's parental space while valuing their own. It is not so simple, then, to say that joint custody is only for those parents whose communication and cooperation is optimal. Although the role of litigation on post-divorce relationships has not been specifically investigated, it is likely that prolonged litigation exacerbates conflict and hostility and adds to the hue of injury and mistrust.

One positive side effect of the joint custody movement in family law and the behavioural sciences has been the gradual clarification and amplification of the role and rights of the non-custodial parent. Our own opinion is that this is the major positive outcome of the joint custody impact on family law and societal reform. It is major impetus behind family law reform and we can now take for granted that the non-custodial parent will obtain relevant information and feedback from schools and doctors. Other innovations include: (1) more extensive visitation schedules such as two weekends out of three or extended weekend visits, (2) a growing tendency even in sole custody

---

a first look at outcome data from re-litigation", *American Journal of Psychiatry*, 139: 62-66.

16 Brotsky, M., Steinman, S. and Zemmelman, S. (1988), "Joint custody through mediation: a longitudinal assessment of the children", *Conciliation Courts Review*, 26: 53-58.

orders to share holiday periods and special days rather than restricting the non-custodial parent to two summer weeks in July or August, or (3) providing outlets to the non-custodial parent for arbitration in the case of a major disagreement. Hence, the role and contribution of the non-custodial parent has enlarged within a sole custody framework without there being necessarily a reciprocal increase in awards of joint custody. We suspect that joint custody will be an option to families who find their own way to it but that it will never be, nor should it be, a frequent option in parents who litigate to determine custody. When cases are litigated and assessments ordered, the chances that these same people are suitable for some type of shared custodial arrangement is, in our opinion, low.

With increases in the non-custodial side of the equation, though, have come more opportunities for conflict. This hearkens to an important book written in 1979 by psychologist/lawyer, Joseph Goldstein and psychoanalysts Albert Solnit and the late Anna Freud which concluded that attachment to one parent had to be decisive in order to meet the child's inherent need for security and continuity of care.[17] The three convincingly argued that frequent visitation when it created acrimony and opportunities for more conflict was of little use to a child who could only feel terribly exposed in the crossfire between the parents. Quite correctly, they underline that many custody decisions are in name only oriented to the child's best interests whereas in fact they are fashioned from the competing needs of their parents. Custody, they felt, should be based on the principle of least detriment and should reflect the child's need of continuity of being based on theirs and not an adult's sense of time. The authors did not oppose visitation in principle but suggested that the specific frequency be placed in the hands of the custodial parent. The danger, as they saw it, was that the child could otherwise be placed in the middle of a battle and fail to develop a sufficient tie to either parent!

We can identify, then, two trends that may conflict with each other. The first is the trend to support more access even in sole custody arrangements; the second is the propensity for greater access to be associated with greater conflict between the parents. This latter trend is especially important in litigated cases where non-custodial status is involuntarily imposed on a person described as "the loser". This is

17 Goldstein, J., Freud, A. and Solnit, A. (1979), *Beyond the Best Interests of the Child*, New York: The Free Press.

also where one's sense of fair play often takes a beating. If a custodial parent takes issue with the worth or contribution of the non-custodial parent, then it may be adding stress to the family to impose frequent access in a situation where it is unwelcome. One might also argue that the benefit to the child is in the quality of the relationship with the non-custodial parent out of ear shot and direct influence of the antagonistic custodial parent. No one, it seems, really knows the answer to these difficult dilemmas for they are multifactorial. Putting it another way, would a non-custodial parent or his lawyer readily accept a recommendation that he not see the child frequently because the custodian is too harshly opposed to their input? Lawyers, as well as clients, most often measure their success in litigation in terms of the extent to which they are accorded involvement. Ironically, this opposes what Goldstein and colleagues attest to be central to the principle of least detriment — an unequivocal decision that chooses only one psychological parent and formally cuts loose the other. Solutions to such paradoxes remain elusive.[18]

3. THE CHOICE OF JOINT CUSTODY

The collective experience in working with joint custody as an option in divorce is that it works well when one motive in particular dictates its choice — a deep underlying commitment to children and especially the nurturing of children. Those successful joint custody families have parents who uphold co-parenting as a key value. They will intrinsically and automatically show a respect for the worth and contribution of the other parent even if they disagree with certain aspects of their approach or personality. The right of each parent to parent in their allotted time will never be questioned no matter how hurt or upset they are with each other. Typically, examination of the family history will reveal close, genuine relationships to children before and after the separation.

We can conceive of a joint custody continuum beginning with joint legal custody with standard access provisions and ending with joint physical custody including 50 per cent sharing of the parenting. In the latter case, the utmost in co-parenting, parents should reveal the

18 *Ibid.*

above characteristics to a maximum degree. They should gravitate to shared parenting for the right reason and they should reveal a conspicuous recognition of the other's parental value no matter what the specific fate of their own personal relationship. Communication will be a usual occurrence as compared to being just possible and the parents will reveal some history of problem solving even after the separation occurred.

At the entry level of the joint parenting scale, parents should reveal some core aspects of the above but may have certain discordant factors such as life style differences, financial limitations, or parenting conflicts that would not permit a more elaborate shared arrangement. They should still be able to communicate and problem solve when necessary and it should be a choice of the parents or a recommendation that is acceptable to both parties.

Amongst these cases of joint legal custody without greatly enhanced access, we could specifically include those parents who assume a non-residential role but whose history of involvement has been substantial. Hence, when joint custody recognizes or acknowledges a non-residential parent's past and ongoing involvement with the children as a primary focus, it is an appropriate option. Some fathers, for example, may well have had major roles in their children's lives while in divorce financial limitations may limit the extent of care they can provide. Joint custody is a way of recognizing that parent's role while not insisting on equal sharing of time and resources. Again, though, this assumes that the other positive factors are also present as well.

As a rule of thumb, we would add that joint custody should always be a specific option in the parents' mind even if they are guided by others towards adopting it. It should not be a choice born of mediation to stave off the worst aspects of divorce or used as a bargaining chip to insure cooperation in settling other issues. We must also guard against promoting joint custody as a palliative against the pain of divorce or the injury of being the non-custodial parent. These are not rational reasons for selecting this option and they will likely put the family at greater risk of difficulties in the future.

Perhaps it may be helpful, at this juncture, to outline the major contraindications to any form of shared care and control. The presence of any one of these should eliminate the prospect of recommending such an option:

- When one of the parents, usually the one most easily designated as the primary caretaker, resists or rejects it out of hand. This should not be understood, though, in simple black and white terms. Such rejection of joint custody should be major and not founded on legal strategy or on a misinterpretation of what joint custody implies. In other words, rejecting joint custody because the parent wrongly believes that a child could only adjust with one substantial home should not be viewed as valid in itself. In this regard, what can be corrected through information and education should be differentiated from what is more entrenched resistance. Consequently, a parent who cannot tolerate the idea that they would have to include the input of the other parent and where the atmosphere is one of deep historical mistrust, would not be suitable for joint custody.
- When one or both of the ex-spouses employ to a major degree a psychology of blame. By blaming, this should not include finding fault with the other, for this is natural. Instead, blaming relates to those cases where the parent pervasively and rigidly disavows, denies and avoids any sense of personal responsibility and makes the incredible leap to viewing the other in almost intentionally evil terms. Constant blame seeking is a powerful defensive style and one will not observe any of the internal struggles and regrets of the free mind.
- When the child rearing premises of both parents are so discordant that the children are unlikely to be able to integrate them. This implicates attitude and character more than it does specific rules or methods. Children can synthesize differences such as in the case where one home is more rigidly structured by curfews and rules as compared to another that is not so rigorous in applying them. Children would find it harder, however, to negotiate a shared custody if one home valued education while the other did not.
- When one or both parents exhibit a sense of ownership over the children and negate the importance of the other parent. These are parents who have a tendency to defy the other and act with a haughty indifference to the other's legitimate claims. They are most likely parents who confuse their own needs with those of their children and they insist on an exclusive right to interpret the children's needs and best interests.
- When parents tend to argue through their children and use child rearing as a field of combat. For example, a parent clashes with the

other parent through the child by berating his school performance and blaming it on the mother's lackluster supervision during her week. Or, when the mother disciplines the son for rudeness while complaining that he is turning out like his father who thinks nothing of denigrating her. These parents seem to interpret their children's negative behaviours as a result of the negative influence of the other parent.

- When neither adult is adequate enough as a parent to assume the custodial role on their own. This may seem paradoxical for would not two halves make a whole. Unfortunately what in fact often happens is that both parents flounder while blaming the other. It is preferable to support one of the parents over the other and arrange supplementary and support services to ease the load.
- When there is evidence of mental illness, personality disorder or severe addiction in one or both parents.
- When there is hotly contested litigation over custody, shared parenting is most often not an option. Here, we are not referring to those contested cases where the parents, although reasonable people, cannot determine what is truly best for their children. These are people who are aware of the complex interactions of their family and are prepared to work matters out with the assistance of a family assessment. When disputes assume an irrational bent, however, and allegations and attacks on links predominate, joint custody, in any form, will not work.

4. DOES JOINT CUSTODY WORK?

Until recently, joint custody threatened to be more an ideology than simply an alternative custody arrangement for managing parent-child relationships following divorce. The initial research, spearheaded by the California experience, looked favourable, especially from the vantage point of relitigation statistics. If this index is accepted as a measure of reduced interparental hostility, then joint custody has been a major success.[19]

19 Johnston, J., Kline, M. and Tschann, J. (1989), "Ongoing post-divorce conflict in families contesting custody: do joint custody and frequent access help", *American Journal of Orthopsychiatry*, 59: 576-592.

More current studies, however, invite caution mainly because, as noted previously, conflict is not mitigated by joint custody awards. Rather, in low conflict families, joint custody is often a better option if other criteria are also met. For instance, low conflict based on one parent's essential disinterest would not qualify in favour of this type of arrangement. Where parents are both child focused and espouse nurturing as a major parenting goal and where there is a willingness to adapt, coordinate and communicate in the service of that goal, plus a core of healthy self esteem and flexibility in the parents, then joint custody may well be the preferred option. This is especially true when there is a mutual willingness to implement such a strategy or if they can be easily swayed to consider such an option. When criteria are applied accurately and rationally in generating the proposal for joint parenting, then it can and does work well. The problem seems to me that it is often assigned indiscriminately to parents who cannot make use of it, or worse, function more poorly as parents because of it.

Despite the ideal that joint custody parents must acknowledge the value to the child of the continuing presence of the other parent, this may receive lip service and may not be the primary reason joint custody is adopted. It seems to be a more likely occurrence, for example, in well-off families where financial support issues are weighed against the right of the wealthier parent to be fully recognized as a joint custodian. In other situations, an ex-spouse may prove so fanatic in their sense of ownership and narcissistic identification with their children that they may extract a joint custody arrangement from the other parent in order to be appeased.

Besides these more complicated reasons for joint custody agreements, others include: (1) a way of resolving work place and scheduling demands such as faced by people on shift work; (2) a way to deny the divorce and a defence against real separation with its threat of depression and loss and, (3) a way for one parent to soften the blow to the other when divorce is a unilateral choice unwelcomed by the other parent.

When successful, joint custody agreements tend to be applauded differently by men and women. Women, in general, celebrate the increased freedom the arrangement gives and feel liberated from the role of primary care giver. Men, on the other hand, will often speak of the close relationships with children that they would not have had otherwise. In this sense, joint custody reverses the usual gender distinction where men may be uncomfortable with intimacy while women clamor for more. Here, women can experience more freedom while men can enjoy the fruits of closer bonding with their children than they probably had before the marriage ended.

Having had enough years to receive feedback on the fate of shared parenting arrangements in specific cases, our experience has been that when established successfully it tends to age well. This is especially true:

- When the parents remain equally committed to the children's well being and manage to shift their own identities from co-spouses to co-parents. The ability make this transition is positively associated with increased satisfaction, ease of adaptation and security of identification as a parent.
- When the parents manage to separate from an embroiled intimacy and establish, instead, a cooperative sense of distance from each other. Although we often speak of the communicative links that must be apparent for joint custody, this may be less important than the capacity to separate psychologically and to consolidate separate lives. When joint custody fails, it is often because the two parents collapse into the hole of their failed marriage with the least provocation. This robs the children and parents of the neutrality and freedom from conflict that is most required if joint custody is going to work.
- When there are maternal misgivings that the father manages to heed and take seriously, then the mother is inspired to feel confidence and acceptance in the shared parenting arrangement. These fathers do not rebel and feel insulted by the other parent's anxieties or standards and accept that they must prove themselves as primary parents especially when this is a new role from that played in the marriage.
- When the parents feel that they have truly chosen joint custody rather than having it imposed during negotiations or legal proceedings. This is a major source of confusion in the literature regarding voluntary versus assigned joint custody which create entirely different mind-sets.

5. AGE AND GENDER IN DECIDING UPON JOINT CUSTODY

The success of a joint parenting arrangement is always multifactorial and no one age or gender is specifically indicated or not indicated when considering these cooperative formulas.

Although one might hope that shared parenting in itself would protect very young children (one to three years of age) from the strains of divorce, there is meager evidence to support this assumption. Yet, when it works, it is mainly because the parents can use the joint parenting formula to continue to meet the needs of nurture and continuity of care for the young child. It is always contraindicated when one or both parents are negligent or inadequate care takers or suffer from addictions.

Pre-schoolers from the age of three to five years are often malleable and will, on the surface, adapt readily. They are helpless, however, in protecting against parental negligence, disorganization or psychopathology and are greatly affected by any of these factors. Further, they are also sensitive to precipitous changes such as in the addition of a step parent. What may be underlined in these findings regarding young children is that the form of custody may have less impact on the outcome for children than factors inherent to the parents and their interactions.

There is agreement, though, that the most problematic group in establishing joint custody are teenagers who will likely have the most difficulty adapting.[20] Continuity seems essential at this age with peers, school life and patterns of living. If joint custody was established in earlier childhood, then the problems are minimized but if the break up occurs during adolescence, the effects will be maximal.

As to gender, it appears that boys may be more susceptible to adverse reactions when in sole custody arrangements, at least initially.[21] Boys in sole custody show more evidence of distress than

---

20 Saposnek, D. (1991), "A guide to decisions about joint custody: the needs of children of divorce", in J. Folberg (ed.), *Joint Custody and Shared Parenting*, 2nd ed., New York: The Guilford Press, at 29-40.

21 Guidubaldi, J. and Perry, J. (1985), "Divorce and mental health sequelae for children: a two year followup of a nation wide sample", *Journal of the American Academy of Child Psychiatry*, 24: 531-537.

girls in either sole or joint custody or boys in joint custody settings.[22] Such differences may meld with time as other factors such as the interparental climate exert their influences. It does, though, suggest that the operative factor for male children may be the active presence of a father.

The behavioural adjustment of girls may be negatively influenced by frequent access to both parents when the interparental atmosphere is angry and conflict ridden. It is not uncommon to see girls forming a close, emotionally dependent relationship with their fathers and an increase in the competitive and ambivalent relationship with their mothers. From a depth psychological perspective, the divorce enacts an oedipal victory where the girl wins her father's favour at the expense of her mother.

On the other hand, mid-childhood females may form close positive relationships with mothers in sole custody families even in the face of high conflict and dispute.[23] In this case, frequent visitation may not be the best answer in the long-term. In terms of boys, close relationships with non-custodial fathers may be important to their development even when conflict is high between the parents. The presence of a father link may offset other negative factors although they are still at risk to becoming embroiled in parental disputes. When interparental conflict is low, however, joint custody may be a useful option for both sexes and for most age groups except during the teen years.

In general, though, as children mature cognitively, they are more likely to be drawn into the parental morass as evidenced by loyalty conflicts and tendencies to ally with one parent over the other. The other prevailing finding is that research on contested and litigating families bears little resemblance to families of divorce who arrive at their arrangements either by themselves or with mediation. This is true whether sole or joint custody is being studied. There is no empirical support for imposing joint custody by statute or judicial ruling when it is not a goal of the parents themselves.

---

22 Heatherington, E.M. (1989), "Coping with family transition: winners, losers and surviviors", *Child Development*, 60:1-14.

23 Brotsky, M., Steinman, S. and Zemmelman, S., *supra*, note 16.

6. THE VISTA OF CUSTODY AND ACCESS

It may come as a surprise to lawyers who routinely litigate family matters and pursue access and custodial rights, that patterns of care and control may not be as important to the outcome for children of divorce as they may think. Instead, the emotional status of the parents, their capacity for empathy and support, and the quality of the parent-child relationships are the most vital factors in determining outcome independent of custodial pattern. Parents who can support and focus on their children's needs are better able to protect their children from the adverse consequences of divorce even in the context of parental hostility and dispute.

By viewing the extreme cases, the issue becomes more focused. Where there is severe narcissism in a parent, for example, especially in a primary or custodial one, limited empathy and capacity to separate one's needs from those of children will prove to be a serious handicap. This will be so no matter what custody and access option is extant. These parents possess their children, identify their needs with those of their children, blame the other parent for all problems, and usually expose their children to untold misery before the offspring can wrench themselves away on their own. In these cases, custodial status and access routines contribute less to the overall outcome for children than the qualities and limitations of the parents themselves.

Across cases, the literature is clear that parental personality, attitudes towards children and each other and the ability to redefine respective roles after separation, will determine more of what happens in the ensuing years than does the specifics of custody and access regimens. Johnston and co-workers estimate that approximately 20 per cent of the variance pertaining to children's maladjustment following marital break up is attributable to access patterns and interparental conflict.[24] Depression, personality disorder or psychopathology in the parent have a far greater impact. It remains a truism that ill parents create ill children.[25]

Conclusions such as these render making recommendations in custody and access matters a difficult task, indeed, in the more extreme cases, they often require assessment. Can a court readily

24 Johnston, J., Kline M. and Tschann, J., *supra*, note 19.
25 Giodubaldi, J. and Perry, J., *supra*, note 21.

distinguish a parent whose identification with a child is narcissistic from a parent who is devoted and genuinely concerned? In our experience, the answer is often blurred by the momentum of defense and rationalization which highlight contested cases. Even when such a parent acts out in blatantly destructive ways, their impropriety may be portrayed as ideal love gone awry due to the effects of divorce. Secondly, even if this determination is accurately made by the court, there is no guarantee that a judge will necessarily accept a psychological prognosis as sufficient evidence especially if this same parent has provided the major part of the care.

Here we confront the reality that the effectiveness of the family law system to protect children in divorce cannot exceed the aptitudes and personal resources of their parents. Although we can contest which parent should perform what role, we cannot fully shield children from the real impact of their parents. We can, it seems, add or reduce stress and tension, but we have much less control over outcome than do the parents themselves. As we see it, the challenge for family law and its consultants, is to accept this limitation and not act as if the parents' struggle is the same as our own. This may profitably shift the emphasis from one of parental rights to the higher plane of parental responsibility, even when this may mean stepping aside or accepting less access for the best interests of the child. Responsibility is a far more personally demanding dimension than rights and will often lead to very different conclusions. This ethical shift would place the legal process in the same plane as the psychological and would coincide more accurately with what is actually known about psychological outcome in divorce.

As an example, a lawyer who promotes the rights of a non-custodial parent may celebrate a victory in which the awarded access was plentiful. Yet, this may be a highly conflicted family where the parents use every opportunity to replay the marital struggle and the two always manage to find some detail on which to launch their next assault. In such a case, the responsible action would be to implement less access in order to spare the children the full and frequent impact of the parents' conflict. Although this may be said to be unfair to the non-custodial parent, who may even be the lesser contributant, it is more unfair to the children who are helpless to defend against their self-engrossed parents.

Occasionally, when doing family psychological assessments, assessors may be informed by a lawyer that it is their job to "win" and the assessor's job to be "moral". Such thinking evolves from the ambiguous relationship between the children and the lawyer hired and paid for by the parent. This can easily rise to the working assumption that the lawyer represents the best interests of the parents while the assessor represents the children's needs. Even if this latter perception is implicit, it still elicits a divided loyalty. The children's best interest may not coincide with a parent's wants which is why the emphasis must be on the responsibility of parenting and not just on parental defence. Our impression is that experienced family law lawyers often make this shift and the ethical texture of their practice reflects these principles. When it happens that both lawyers adhere to the same tenets, then the case is resolved along different dimensions than in the adversarial "father versus mother" mode.

7. BEYOND CUSTODY

Joint custody in Canada appears to be as frequently granted as sole custody is to fathers with both accounting for just over 10 per cent of divorce settlements.[26] Hence, it remains a minority choice although its impact has been more far ranging than its actual popularity in our society. Joint custody has received considerable scrutiny and parents as well as professionals are either enthusiastically for it or vehemently opposed. It is one of those issues that divides opinion as well as legal authority for children.

The origin of the debate around custody is firmly rooted in the role and societal changes that have taken place in the 1980s and 1990s. Divorce rates have risen enormously from their previous levels in the 1950s and 1960s. Money became more abundant, women redefined and expanded their roles and options, and men shed the model which equated fatherhood with provider. No one is sure whether any of this is a good or bad thing but it does seem to reflect permanent changes in society's fabric. In view of these changes and flux, it remains a major task to provide for the well being of children in divorce and to

26 Payne, Julien D. and Edwards, Brenda (1991), "Cooperative parenting after divorce: a Canad*ian* legal perspective", in Jay Folberg, *supra*, note 20, at 275-295.

promote their cause. This becomes more difficult as the expected roles of mothers and fathers dovetail and become less distinguishable from each other.

Some legal practitioners will maintain that custody itself is confounding and that parenting plans devised through mediated settlements will effect the same end.[27] Although we can agree in theory with such sentiments, it does not appear that custody determinations will disappear from the judicial landscape. In part, this is due to the nature of divorce itself which for the majority of people creates serious handicaps in trust and communication that can last for many years. Secondly, there is always a concern that failure to determine these matters in their entirety will lead more people to return to the courts for a second round.

8. CONCLUSION

Recently, in a family assessment over disputed custody, a woman, now in her late 40s and with several children, sobbed deeply over the separation. The separation she had in mind, however, was not her own but her parents' divorce which occurred when she was 11 years old. The traumatic impact of that experience continued to reverberate within her personality and was triggered by the current circumstance. Revealing the deeper perceptions of this prior experience, she mourned the fact that she was not good enough to prevent her father from leaving her.

Often, therapists treat adults who reveal massive repression of the significance of a parental divorce. On the other hand, psychotherapists often meet people who reveal an intense search for a missing anchor or some personal stability that eventually puts them face to face with the divorce experience they had endured as children. In such cases, the meaning of the loss becomes a focal theme as the person attempts to reconstruct the emotions and perceptions that burdened their psychic development. Unlike a death, which is permanent, divorce breeds intense wishes for the reconciliation of parents that may last a life time.[28]

---

27 *Ibid.*
28 Galenson, *supra*, note 11.

The descriptive research on divorce does stress how difficult an occurrence divorce is for children and their parents. Children can adapt and accommodate to its stresses, especially if they have understanding and supportive parents. Empathic parents can make a success of any custody model whereas rigid, projecting or blaming parents will invariably fail their children no matter what custody arrangement is in place. In those cases where negative factors predominate, the challenge becomes one of damage control as compared to the promotion of well being. A primary conclusion, then, is that custody is important but is less pervasive an influence on adjustment in divorce than the parents themselves in their close encounters with their children.

As to joint custody, we should remain faithful to its premises but realistic about its application. It has had a significant impact on custody decisions and no one, neither lawyer nor mental health professional, has not be influenced by its bold challenge to separate the roles of spouse and parent and to forge new alliances. Joint custody in the right parental hands can be a useful model for providing care to children after divorce. It is not the panacea for divorce, however, and should remain an option for parents who can meet certain stringent criteria. Clinical experience as well as the research literature does not support the blanket imposition of joint custody when it is not truly indicated. On the other hand, it should not be blamed for every mishap or moment of bewilderment that might befall a child in a joint parenting situation. Disruption and strain is endemic to divorce for children, especially in early stages, and to blame joint custody, *per se*, is to pursue a false ideal of a painless divorce. It also asks joint custody to be measured by a different standard than its counterpart in sole custody arrangements.

Perhaps the major benefit of the joint custody movement has been the impact on how sole custody is conceptualized and implemented. The willingness to award the child to the "winner" at the expense of the non-custodial parent has given way to a more sensitive and sophisticated assessment of the relative capacities both parents possess and what access schedule would best fit their potentials. The more attuned and enlightened family law lawyers routinely seek out these answers and, although, they stand by their clients' rights they maintain a keen eye on ways to protect and facilitate the children's adjustment. In this aspect, they remain responsible to the children of the family while they work to protect the rights of the parents.

4

Rationale and Purpose of Assessment

1. PURPOSE AND OBJECT OF THE ASSESSMENT

For the purpose of this chapter the authors are not dealing with child welfare which would usually require the involvement of appropriate social welfare agencies and, often times, local police authorities. It is felt that the issues in child welfare cases, including those cases involving assessments, are such that they require to be dealt with separately from a custody/access issue arising out of a family breakdown and thus are beyond the scope of this book.

The assessment process in a private custody/access case usually begins in the lawyer's office. A parent or other interested person, such as a grandparent or other relative, will seek legal advice from a lawyer regarding custody of children. At the time of the initial consultation a parent is probably either contemplating separation, or is in the early stages of a physical separation resulting from a breakdown in a marriage or relationship. On the other hand the client may be an interested person related to the child by blood (grandparent, sibling, aunt, uncle), by marriage (step-parent, aunt, uncle) or otherwise (family friend or otherwise concerned person), all of whom probably developed a close relationship with the child and/or are concerned for the child's welfare, and who, for their own reasons, do not feel that it is necessarily in the best interests of the child to remain with the person in whose care the child is currently entrusted.

The parties likely have been unable to come to any agreement with respect to the living arrangements regarding their children, with each parent feeling that the children should be in their custody, care and control. Usually each parent has no doubt in their mind that it would be in a child's best interests if that parent had custody. From an objective perspective, the reason for them so feeling may not be so much out of the consideration of what is in the best interests of the children as it may be out of consideration for a number of other factors that consciously or unconsciously cloud the vision of the parent when it comes to considering the welfare of the children.

Therefore, the lawyer has a client in the office who is seeking legal advice on how to solve a custody/access problem that, for the purpose of the discussion in this chapter, is not going to be settled by the parents and will not likely be mediated by the parties, although this could ultimately be the end result. A further assumption made in this chapter is that a lawyer has not been retained on behalf of the child or, that a lawyer has not been appointed for the child by the court for the purpose of assisting in the determination of the custody/access dispute.

Naturally, in the course of providing legal advice the lawyer will be obligated to canvass the options regarding custody.[1] In the course of doing so the issue of an assessment will ultimately have to be raised and explained to the parties as being an extremely important vehicle to be considered or resorted to, in appropriate circumstances, in custody/access disputes.

Whether the issue of custody and access is to be litigated or not, all relevant information pertaining to what is in the best interests of the child has to be investigated. In a situation where the parties are adverse in interest in this regard, they cannot necessarily be relied upon to achieve this objective as, naturally, they will be concentrating in putting forward all the information they deem relevant to advance their claim for custody, which information could be different than that information that is considered to be in the best interests of the child.

It will, in most cases, be explained to the parties that one of the fairest and most effective ways to supplement the gathering of information process, always keeping in mind what is in the best interests

1 Dealt with in Chapter 2, Custodial Options: Which, When and Why?

of the children, is to have an independent assessment carried out by an appropriately qualified expert, usually a mental health professional. It would be explained to the parties that the expert's findings could be adduced into evidence should the issue become litigious, and depending upon a number of factors that may have an effect upon the trial judge (or other trier of fact), a court may put a great deal of weight on the assessor's conclusions or recommendations.

It will be explained to the parent that the role of the assessor is not necessarily to make the final judgment in the case, although that may ultimately be the result for reasons later discussed in this chapter, but rather to provide expert assistance to the court and the parties by allowing them to make a determination of where the child's best interests lie.

Although the courts have no specific guidelines as to the purpose of an assessment, other than what guidelines or criteria may be set out in various provincial statutes,[2] some courts have attempted to describe and outline general guidelines of an assessor in the course of conducting an assessment which may be, in essence, summarized as follows:

1. The assessor must assist the child and the court by ensuring that in his report the important facts affecting the best interests of the child are set out.
2. The assessor must ensure that any recommendation that he or she sets forth in the report to the court has been presented to the parents, the child and their counsel and has some chance of acceptance especially if it involves more than usual activity or co-operation by them.
3. The report must give to the court an insight into the needs of the child and the ability of each parent to best satisfy those needs.[3]

---

2 In Ontario, see s. 30(1) of the *Children's Law Reform Act*, R.S.O. 1990, c. C.12, which provides that "The court before which an application is brought in respect of custody of or access to a child, by order, may appoint a person who has technical or professional skill to assess and report to the court on the needs of the child and the ability and willingness of the parties or any of them to satisfy the needs of the child."

3 *Boody v. Boody* (1983), 32 R.F.L. (2d) 396 (Ont. Dist. Ct.); *Busch v. Busch*, [1994] W.D.F.L. 1245 (Ont. Gen. Div.); *Sampson v. Sampson*, [1995] W.D.F.L. 652 (B.C. Master); *P. (M.J.) v. P. (P.A.)*, [1995] W.D.F.L. 404 (Sask. Q.B.); *Nichols v. Nichols*, [1995] W.D.F.L. 801 (B.C. Master).

The Ontario Psychological Foundation, the governing body for practising psychologists in Ontario, in its custody/access assessment guidelines, states that the purpose of a custody/access assessment is to arrive at those parenting arrangements which are in the best interests of the child within the capabilities of the family.[4]

The American Psychological Association has described, in its guidelines, the purpose of a child custody evaluation as being as follows:

1. The primary purpose of the evaluation is to assess the best psychological interests of the child. The primary consideration of a child custody evaluation is to assess the individual and family factors that affect the best psychological interests of the child. More specific questions may be raised by the court.
2. In a child custody evaluation the child's interests and well-being are paramount. Parents competing for custody, as well as others, may have genuine concerns, but the child's best interests must prevail.
3. The focus of the evaluation is on parenting capacity, the psychological and developmental needs of the child and the resulting fit. In considering psychological facts affecting the best interests of the child, the psychologist focuses on the parenting capacity of the prospective custodians in conjunction with the psychological and developmental needs of each involved child. This involves:
   (a) an assessment of the adult's capacity for parenting, including whatever knowledge, attributes, skills and abilities or lack thereof, are present;
   (b) an assessment of the psychological functioning and developmental needs of each child, and the wishes of each child, where appropriate;
   (c) the functional ability of each parent to meet these needs, which includes an evaluation of the interaction between each adult and child.[5]

---

4 "Custody/Assessment Guidelines", The Ontario Psychological Foundation, Toronto, Ontario, 1988, at 1. No part of the guidelines can be reproduced without written permission from the Foundation.

5 "Guidelines for Child Custody Evaluations in Divorce Proceedings", The American Psychological Association, Volume 29, Family Law Quarterly Spring 1995, at 51.

In summary, no matter what body promotes the concept of a family assessment, the objective or goal of an assessment is to attempt to provide as much information as possible with respect to the child and those persons who will impact on his or her life on a daily basis with a view to determining and identifying those factors that should be considered in ascertaining what is in the best interests of the child.

There are other valid and useful reasons for having an assessment conducted. An assessment may disclose to the parties, and to the court should the matter proceed to trial, certain areas of the parties' ability to parent or certain needs of the child that would not ordinarily form part of the evidence adduced by the parties and witnesses they call at trial.

A qualified mental health professional conducting an assessment may be able to identify special needs of the child, such as developmental, physical and mental lags, or any mental or physical handicaps or learning disabilities that would classify them as children having special needs. How the parents are able to deal with these problems and the parents' philosophy as to how the problems should be dealt with will be important to the trier of fact in determining the issue of custody/access. The assessment may also identify the parenting skills or lack of parenting skills of the parties. The interviews and testing of the parties, conducted by the assessor, may bring to light emotional, educational or behaviourial problems, all of which would impact on their ability to meet the needs of the child and to provide the highest and best level of parenting possible in the circumstances to the child in question. A well-qualified assessor should be able to flush out areas of concern of this nature and be able to provide a recommendation as to how the problems should be dealt with in the context of parenting skills and what is in the best interest of the child.

2. ROLE OF EXPERT — OPINION EVIDENCE

We have seen that the objective and purpose of an assessment is to provide an insight into the needs of the child and the ability of each parent to best satisfy those needs. One of the questions that has presented a historic difficulty to lawyers and the courts is the question as to whether, and to what extent a witness, generally speaking, is permitted to offer an opinion on any issue before the court. With respect to an assessment in a custody/access case, it is likely that the person conducting the assessment will be called as a witness at a hearing for the purpose of proffering an opinion on some aspect of the case. The question presents itself as to whether such a witness will be restricted in any significant manner as to the nature of the evidence he or she may be permitted to give. Will the assessor, as a potential expert, be permitted to testify and will the assessor be allowed to provide an opinion as to any of the issues in dispute?

There has been much debate in Canadian jurisprudence as to whether or not a witness can proffer an opinion in a case. This debate has not been solely restricted to opinions proffered by mental health professionals in custody/access cases. There has been a history of difficulty in Canadian jurisprudence which has plagued the admissibility of opinion evidence whether from the mouth of a layman or from the mouth of an expert.

Until recently-developed jurisprudence to the contrary, a lay witness' evidence was limited to describing precisely and exactly his or her observations and no more. Any inference to be taken from those observations was a matter for the court and the witness was not normally expected to provide an opinion. To otherwise allow the witness to give an opinion was to potentially usurp the function of the court or trier of fact. This opinion evidence rule was based upon the assumption that there is a clear demarcation between inferences and the facts which give rise to them. Under the rule witnesses could testify only to the latter.[6]

This rule particularly applied to the lay witness who was not considered to be a qualified expert in a particular field. For instance, let us assume that in a child custody case the child's teacher observed, during the course of two interviews with one of the parties at school, and during a visit to that party's home, that the party was under the influence of alcohol. The teacher observed the usual characteristics of alcohol abuse, such as alcohol odour, slurred speech and unco-ordinated movements. The question presents itself as to whether, in calling the teacher as a witness at trial, the teacher's evidence is to be restricted to his or her observations of the party without drawing any inferences or, whether the teacher's evidence will be such that he or she will be able to draw inferences based on his or her observations

---

6 John Sopinka, Sidney N. Lederman and Alan Bryant, *The Law of Evidence in Canada*, Butterworth's, 1992, at 524.

and thus provide an opinion that the party was under the influence of alcohol and, therefore, has an alcohol abuse problem.

The courts have gradually relaxed the layperson's opinion evidence rule to allow an opinion to be given provided such opinion will "help" the court.

In *R. v. Graat*,[7] Dickson J. concluded:

> Except for the sake of convenience, there is little, if any, virtue, in any distinction resting on the tenuous, and frequently false, antithesis between fact and opinion. The line between "fact" and "opinion" is not clear.

Dickson J. further stated: "The witnesses had an opportunity for personal observation. They were in a position to give the court real help."[8]

In applying this opinion evidence test for the lay witness to our above example of the teacher as a witness, an argument could probably be advanced that the teacher's evidence, being that the one party had an alcohol abuse problem, would probably be helpful to the court and would likely assist the court in determining what is in the best interests of the child as the court would not have had the opportunity to have observed the party as did the teacher in these circumstances. In such a case the teacher's evidence would clearly be considered opinion evidence as to whether that party had an alcohol abuse problem.

It would be another matter, and a subject-matter dealt with later in the chapter, as to the amount of weight that would be accorded to such opinion evidence after it is given.

3. EXPERT WITNESS OPINION EVIDENCE

If the assessor to be used in a custody/access case is a qualified expert, having the necessary technical and professional skills to conduct an assessment, it must be remembered that an expert is usually involved in a case for the purpose of providing an opinion and the question presents itself, as in the case of the lay witness, as to whether the expert assessor will be able to provide opinion evidence. As we

7 [1982] 2 S.C.R. 819 at 835.
8 *Ibid.*, at 836.

saw with respect to a lay witness' opinion, it is also the case with an expert witness, that receipt by the court of an opinion from an expert is an exception to the general rule that witnesses are not permitted to testify, or offer testimony, on matters not factually based and within their personal knowledge.

However, in Canadian jurisprudence the courts have recognized an exception to the opinion rule for expert witnesses, in order to provide the trier of fact with the necessary technical or scientific basis upon which to properly assess the evidence presented.[9] It is interesting to look at the recent jurisprudence with respect to what the test is regarding the role of an expert witness and the extent to which the expert may be restricted or permitted to provide an opinion.

In the decision of *R. v. Abbey*,[10] Dickson J. stated:

> With respect to matters calling for special knowledge, an expert in the field may draw inferences and state his opinion. An expert's function is precisely this: "Provide the judge and jury with a ready made inference which the judge and jury, due to the technical nature of the facts, are unable to formulate. An expert's opinion is admissible to furnish the court with scientific information which is likely to be outside the experience and knowledge of a judge or jury. If on the proven facts a judge or jury can form their own conclusions without help, then the opinion of the expert is unnecessary." *R. v. Turner* (1975), 60 Crim. App. R. 80 at page 83, per Walton, L.J.
>
> "An expert witness, like any other witness, may testify as to the veracity of facts of which he had firsthand experience, but this is not the main purpose of his or her testimony. An expert is there to give an opinion. And the opinion more often than not will be based on secondhand evidence . . ."

The above quote is used to deal with the threshold issue of the extent to which an expert witness may be allowed to give opinion evidence. Subsequent to the *Abbey* decision, it was said that the hallmark of admissibility simply should be whether the expert's testimony would be "helpful" to the trier of fact or the court.[11]

However in *R. v. Mohan*,[12] the Supreme Court of Canada decided that the word "helpful" sets too low a threshold and held that the word "necessary" should be used instead. The court explained that what is required is that the evidence "be necessary in the sense that it provide

9 Sopinka, Lederman, Bryant, *supra*, note 6, at 533.
10 [1982] 2 S.C.R. 24 at 42.
11 *Supra*, note 9, at 534.
12 [1994] 2 S.C.R. 9, 18 O.R. (3d) 160.

information 'which is likely to be outside the experience and knowledge of a judge and jury'."[13] The evidence must be necessary to enable the trier of fact to appreciate the matters in issue due to their technical nature. This element of "necessity" is only one of a number of elements listed by Sopinka J. in delivering the judgment of the court. In addition to the evidence being necessary it must be:

(a) relevant
(b) be given in the absence of any exclusionary rule
(c) be given by a properly qualified expert[14]

This chapter concentrates on the "necessity" element for the purpose of demonstrating that the role of the expert, particularly in offering the opinion of an assessor in a custody/access case, will most likely and, primarily, be based on whether or not the assessor's opinion is necessary to allow the court to draw inferences that it would otherwise not be able to do.

Let us assume that the assessor to be used in the custody/access case is a formally and properly qualified psychologist who has had vast experience in conducting assessments in custody/access cases and would therefore likely be qualified as an expert. Let us assume further that the psychologist assessor has properly conducted psychological testing of the parties and that one of the parties' psychological testing has revealed that he or she has a tendency towards aggressive anti-social behaviour and is very compulsive, exhibiting instant gratification tendencies. The question presents itself as to whether the assessor psychologist, as an expert witness, can provide an opinion that is restricted to the expert testifying that the testing revealed that one party does have anti-social behaviourial features and instant gratification tendencies, or whether, the assessor psychologist can further testify, that due to the findings and conclusions of the psychological testing it is his or her opinion the party should not have custody, care and control of the child which, in effect, is providing an opinion on the ultimate issue of custody/access.

In the above referred to example, the argument would be made that the assessor psychologist is an expert in a particular field and that due to the scientific nature of the psychological testing, the court

13 *Ibid.*, at 23, citing *R. v. Abbey*, *supra*, note 10.
14 *Ibid.*, at 20.

would be unable and unlikely to reach a conclusion as to the personality features and character of the party without the "helpful" or "necessary" assistance of the psychologist in the form of opinion evidence.

In applying the test as to the role of an expert as set out in the decisions of *R. v. Abbey* and *R. v. Mohan*, the assessor psychologist in our above example would likely be permitted to proffer an opinion as to the personality and character flaws of the party revealed by the psychological testing, as the court or trier of fact would not likely be able to formulate the said ready made inference or opinion without the assistance of the psychologist's opinion in this regard.

The measuring stick as to whether the opinion evidence of an expert witness can be given in a case seems to be whether or not the expert's testimony will be "helpful" or "necessary" to the court or trier of fact.[15]

4. EXPERT OPINION AS TO ULTIMATE ISSUE — GENERAL

In our lay witness example of the teacher proffering an opinion as to whether one party suffered from an alcohol abuse problem and in our expert witness example of an assessor psychologist proffering an opinion as to whether one party had anti-social behaviourial tendencies, those opinions were given on issues that surfaced within the ultimate issue of determining who should have custody of and access to the child. A further question presents itself as to whether in either scenario the teacher or the psychologist could offer further opinion evidence as to whether a party should or should not have custody of

15 In *R. v. Lavallee*, [1990] 1 S.C.R. 852, the Supreme Court of Canada held that expert evidence on the psychological effect of wife battering was both relevant and necessary. The expert evidence was required because the "battering relationship" was subject to a number of myths and thus was considered beyond the understanding of the average juror and therefore required an explanation through expert testimony. Such testimony could assist the jury in determining whether a woman who had killed her partner had a reasonable apprehension of death because of her heightened sensitivity to her partner's acts, and had thus killed in self-defence. In upholding the admissibility of the psychiatric opinion evidence, Madam Justice Wilson observed that the mental state of the woman could not be appreciated without the assistance of such evidence.

or access to the child, which of course, is the ultimate issue to be decided in the case.

We have seen that the courts now have greater freedom to receive opinion evidence from a non-expert witness or an expert witness, however, as such evidence approaches the central or ultimate issues that the courts must decide, one can still expect an insistence that the witness stick to the primary facts and refrain from giving their inferences regarding the ultimate issue. It is always a matter of degree. As the testimony shades towards a legal conclusion resistance to admissibility develops and the court is more inclined to reject the testimony. Obviously, the reluctance of the courts to accept this evidence is due to the fact that the court or trier of fact feels that such an opinion would usurp the function of the court.

There has been much ongoing judicial debate in Canada with respect to the "ultimate issue" rule. In the past the courts have been reluctant about admitting or allowing expert opinion evidence which was related to the ultimate issue in dispute.[16] However, the rule now seems to have been mostly ignored by the Canadian courts[17] given that the Supreme Court has made it clear[18] that the rule excluding expert evidence, simply because it suggests answers to issues which are at the core of the ultimate issue before the court is no longer of general application.[19] On the other hand there are numerous examples where courts appear to still apply the ultimate issue doctrine.[20]

In the final analysis the closer the expert's testimony, both in opinion and in words, comes to the very issue that the court has to decide, the more reluctant it becomes in receiving such evidence. This is so because the evidence then begins to overlap not only the fact-finding function of the court but the legal analysis that must be applied to the facts in rendering the ultimate decision. Even where the evidence may be helpful, courts are still nervous about the extent of the expert's influence over the trier of fact, in particular where the expert

16 *R. v. Neil*, [1957] S.C.R. 685.

17 *R. v. Fisher*, [1961] S.C.R. 535 in which the court canvassed a number of cases where the rule had been ignored.

18 *R. v. Mohan*, *supra*, note 14, at 24.

19 Pink, Joel E., Matthews, Kenneth, Tupper, Allison and Wells, Alvin, *The Expert: A Practitioner's Guide*, Carswell 1995, Chapter 1, para. 2.5.

20 *C. v. M.* (1990), 74 D.L.R. (4th) 129 (Ont. Gen. Div.); *Gorgichuk v. American Home Assur. Co.* (1985), 5 C.P.C. (2d) 166 (Ont. H.C.J.).

gives an opinion on the very fundamental issues that the trier of fact must decide.[21]

5. EXPERT OPINION EVIDENCE AS TO ULTIMATE ISSUE — CUSTODY/ACCESS CASES

In order for us to decide whether the psychologist in our expert witness opinion evidence example, would be able to give evidence on the ultimate issue of custody and access, it is necessary that one explore both the statutory jurisdiction and the jurisprudence as it has developed in family law with respect to this ultimate issue rule.

An example of statutory jurisdiction is section 30(1) of the *Children's Law Reform Act.*[22] The word "opinion" does not appear in the text of section 30(1). The section stipulates that the appointed person is "to assess and report" to the court. Do these words imply that an opinion may be given on the custody/access issue by the person who does the assessment and reports to the court? A strict interpretation of section 30(1) would suggest that the assessor is not to provide an opinion as to who should have custody of or access to the child, but rather should restrict itself to describing the needs of the child and the ability of the parents to deal with those needs.

Some judges have strongly expressed the view that it is not the role of the assessor to decide the issue of custody and access. In the trial decision of *Weaver v. Tate*[23] the trial judge, in referring to section 30 of the *Children's Law Reform Act,* stated:

> This section does not authorize the assessor to recommend which parent is to have custody. In my opinion, it is the duty of the trial judge to determine which parent is to be entrusted with custody and this decision cannot be delegated to a professional assessor regardless of his or her qualifications.

On appeal,[24] the Ontario Court of Appeal stated:

---

21 Sopinka, Lederman, Bryant, *supra*, note 6, at 546.

22 R.S.O. 1990, c. C.12 which provides: The court before which an application is brought in respect of custody of or access to a child, by order, may appoint a person who has technical or professional skill to assess and report to the court on the needs of the child and the ability and willingness of the parties or any of them to satisfy the needs of the child.

23 (1989), 24 R.F.L. (3d) 266 at 269 (Ont. H.C.).

24 (1990), 28 R.F.L. (3d) 188 at 189 (Ont. C.A.).

> We do not agree with the trial judge's criticism of the assessor appointed under s. 30 of the Children's Law Reform Act for including in his report a recommendation as to custody. Although s. 30 does not direct that such a recommendation be made, we are of the view that it should be open to an assessor to do so in cases where he or she considers it appropriate and where the court does not direct him or her to the contrary.

It is to be noted, however, that the judicial attitude reflected in the trial decision of *Weaver v. Tate* that it is the trier of fact who is to have the ultimate responsibility to decide a custody/access issue seems to be reinforced in the Ontario Court of Appeal decision of *Strohbridge v. Strohbridge*.[25] In that case a motions judge made an order granting interim access to the father of the child subject to the direction of an assessor at a Family Court Clinic. The order, in effect, left the issue of access to the assessor. The Ontario Court of Appeal in dealing with the issue stated:

> All parties agree that the motions judge erred in delegating the actual determination of access to the [Clinic]. In making the order he did, the motions judge brought a third party into the picture in the hope that an independent professional could "re-unite Mr. Strohbridge and his children". . . While I can understand why the motions judge proceeded as he did, I agree that he erred in assigning to the [Clinic] the decisions whether, and under what circumstances, access would be exercised. There is no statutory, or other, authority which would permit this delegation.[26]

The Ontario Court of Appeal seems to be saying that although only the trier of fact has jurisdiction and should be entrusted to make the ultimate decision as to who should have custody or access to children, in appropiate circumstances, an assessor will be permitted to offer an opinion on the ultimate issue of custody/access.

On the other hand, some judges clearly continue to adopt the same attitude and view as that of the trial judge in *Weaver v. Tate* and feel that the role of the assessor is not to provide a vehicle for resolving the custody and access dispute between the parties but, rather, their

25 (1994), 4 R.F.L. (4th) 169, 18 O.R. (3d) 753 (C.A.): See *Williams v. Ellul* (1995), 19 R.F.L. (4th) 40 (Ont. C.A.) where the Court of Appeal upheld a lower court's decision not to order an assessment. The Court of Appeal however overturned the lower court's ruling that a further motion for an assessment could not be brought without the recommendation of professionals currently working with children. The court stated that such allegation is inappropriate. See also *Kitzke v. Eisler*, [1994] W.D.F.L. 1508 (B.C.S.C.).

26 *Ibid.*, at 181.

role is to deal with clinical issues found to be existing in that particular family, that the assessment report is only one piece of evidence to be considered by a trial judge and the ultimate issue to be determined remains in the hands of the trial judge.[27]

It will be a matter of discretion to be exercised by the trier of fact in each case as to whether an assessor will be permitted to provide an opinion on the ultimate issue in a custody/access case. In applying the jurisprudence to our hypothetical examples of the teacher and the psychologist, it seems that it will depend on the individual trier of fact hearing the case as to whether or not they, as experts, will be permitted to provide opinion evidence as to the ultimate issue of custody and access.

In summary, although some courts, in appropriate circumstances, may permit the assessor in a custody/access dispute to provide an opinion as to the ultimate issue, the jurisprudence seems to make it unequivocally clear that the court, or trier of fact, shall almost always wish to retain the function and power of making the ultimate determination of custody/access, and not leave that responsibility to some expert such as an assessor, although the assessor's opinion or recommendations may be given varying degrees of weight depending on the circumstances peculiar to each case.

6. WEIGHT TO BE GIVEN TO THE ASSESSOR'S OPINION

Historically speaking, the courts commenced ordering assessments out of a need for assistance in determining what was in the best interests of the children in custody cases. Judges were reluctant to decide custody and access cases without the benefit of some input

27 See *Maganja v. Maganja*, [1995] W.D.F.L. 108 (Ont. Gen. Div.) where the court held that the assessment report is a useful tool but is only one factor to be considered. The court rejected a joint custody recommendation set out in the assessor's report and held that the ultimate issue lay with the court. See also *Fraser v. Fraser*, [1995] W.D.F.L. 440 (Man. Q.B.) and *Brown v. Brown* (1994), 3 R.F.L. (4th) 135 (Ont. Gen. Div.). The court held that the role of the family assessment was not to provide a vehicle for resolving the custody and access dispute between the parents but rather to deal with clinical issues found to be existing in the family. An assessor should not simply volunteer his or her opinion of who should have custody and access and on what terms.

from mental health professionals, whether it be a qualified social worker, psychologist, psychiatrist or medical practitioner.

Following the enactment of various provincial statutes, custody and access assessments were routinely requested, consented to and granted. In many cases where assessments were ordered, they were settled or decided on the basis of the recommendations in the report. The assessor was, in effect, the judge. What often resulted was an assessment that was basically the opinion of a mental health professional as to who should have custody of or access to the child. There emerged a growing judicial attitude, and an attitude among lawyers, that the mental health experts were probably more qualified than the courts to settle or determine the question of what was in the best interests of the child. The assessments were ordered not so much to have clinical issues decided, but to determine whether outside input could assist the court in resolving the custody/access issue.

As a result of the tendency of the courts to rely a great deal upon the input from mental health professionals, lawyers often found themselves advising clients that in most cases the recommendations in the assessment report would likely be adopted by the trial judge and, therefore, there was a tendency by lawyers to give an inordinate amount of weight to the recommendations in the assessment report. Cases would often settle on the basis of the recommendations in the assessment or upon some modified version of the principal recommendations without the assessment undergoing the scrutiny of cross-examination or an appropriate analysis of the contents of the report.

A review of recent jurisprudence would suggest that assessments continue to play an important role in custody and access cases.[28] However, a cautious attitude is emerging by the courts with respect

28 See *Smith v. Smith*, [1995] W.D.F.L. 608 (N.B.Q.B.) where the court held that an assessment is a significant factor in custody/access determination; *Swanson v. Armstrong*, [1995] W.D.F.L. 247 (Sask. Q.B.) where an assessment was a factor in the court reversing custody; *Kemp v. Kemp*, [1995] W.D.F.L. 259 (B.C.S.C.) where the fact that an assessor recommended arrangements similar to those in place militated against variation of a custody order. See also the following cases: *Swerda v. Swerda*, [1994] W.D.F.L. 1043 (Ont. Gen. Div.); *Binder v. Binder*, [1994] W.D.F.L. 1513 (Sask. Q.B.); *Rouillard v. Rouillard*, [1994] W.D.F.L. 1246 (Ont. Gen. Div.); *Smith v. Baldwin*, [1994] W.D.F.L. 1077 (Ont. Prov. Div.); *Voortman v. Voortman* (1994), 4 R.F.L. (4th) 250 (Ont. C.A.); *Neuman v. Bogan*, [1994] W.D.F.L. 1250 (N.W.T. S.C.); *T. (M.) v. T. (J.)* (1994) W.D.F.L. 1244, 1249 (Ont. Prov. Div.); *Lee v. Lee*, [1995] W.D.F.L. 899 (B.C.S.C.); *D'Andrea v. D'Andrea*, [1995] W.D.F.L. 450 (Ont. Gen. Div.) and *Jackson v. Hillen*, [1995] W.D.F.L. 470 (Ont. U.F.C.).

to the weight to be put on the recommendations and/or opinions set out in an assessment report or the opinion and recommendations provided by the assessor at trial.[29]

The fact that the assessment report is only one piece of evidence to be considered by a trial judge has always been highlighted in the jurisprudence. In the decision of *More v. Primeau*[30] the conclusions in the report of the psychiatrist who conducted the assessment were clearly inconsistent with other evidence adduced during the course of the trial. Mr. Justice Blair stated:

> Expert opinion is of great value in these cases, but the decision must be made by the Court. It is a responsibility that cannot be delegated. As Lacourciere, J. said in *Gauci v. Gauci*, [1973] 1 O.R. 393, 9 R.F.L. 189 at 193 . . . :
>
> > "The Court will, of course, treat the opinion of a highly respected child psychiatrist with great respect; however its delicate function in matters of this kind, as well as in other areas, cannot be surrendered or delegated to any expert however qualified. In the decision-making process, such opinion is considered as a helpful factor, to be weighed and assessed along with all other relevant evidence."[31]

Mr. Justice Blair in the *More v. Primeau* decision further made reference to the decision of *J. v. C.*[32] which was a decision of the House of Lords regarding a custody case. In referring to the report of a psychiatrist or other medical practitioner as to what was in the best interests of the child Lord Upjohn said:

> My Lords, such evidence may be viable if accepted but it can only be as an element to support the general knowledge and experience of a judge in infancy matters, and a judge, in exercising his discretion, should not hesitate to take risks, as I said when in the Court of Appeal, and go against such medical evidence if on the consideration of all the circumstances that Judge considers

29 See *Weaver v. Tate* (1989), 24 R.F.L. (3d) 266 (Ont. H.C.J.); affirmed 28 R.F.L. (3d) 188 (Ont. C.A.), where the trial judge held that if the finding of the trial judge differs in critical matters the opinion of the assessor may be flawed and of little assistance. See also *Maganja v. Maganja*, *supra*, note 29, where the court held that the assessment report is a useful tool but only one factor to be considered. The court rejected a joint custody recommendation as set out in the assessment.

30 (1978), 2 R.F.L. (2d) 254 (Ont. C.A.).

31 *Ibid.*, at 269.

32 [1970] A.C. 668.

> that the paramount welfare of the infant on the balance of probabilities (for that must be the true test) points to a particular test as being the proper one.[33]

Thus, the weight to be given to an assessor's opinion or recommendation in a custody/access assessment case is a matter of the excercise of discretion by the trier of fact. If the findings of the trial judge or trier of fact differ in critical matters from that of the assessor, the opinion of the assessor may be flawed and of little assistance with little weight being attached to it. On the other hand, if the court or trier of fact is of the view that the opinion of a properly qualified assessor is necessary and helpful, and that the opinion is consistent with the findings of the trier of fact on all the evidence presented at the trial or hearing, significant weight is likely to be given to the assessor's opinion.

7. OTHER USES OF THE ASSESSMENT

(a) Settlement

Whether an assessment has been conducted as the result of a court order or whether it was done on the consent of the parties we have concentrated, for the most part, on the uses of the assessment in the event the contested issue of custody/access proceeds to a hearing before a judge, or other trier of fact.

However, most responsible lawyers and most parties to a custody/access dispute will be hopeful that the assessment will lead to a settlement of the dispute without having to resort to the courts. In most cases where assessments are conducted the parties will settle the case, more often than not, by implementing and adopting the recommendations and conclusions set out in the report. In other cases the parties will be able to find a way to take the recommendations and findings of the assessor as a starting point for exploring ways of attempting to settle the custody/access dispute and entering into a satisfactory parenting agreement with the other parent.

The information set out in the report and the observations, conclusions and recommendations of the assessor may also impact on the

33 *Ibid.*, at 726.

parties in a way to cause them to attempt to settle the case. In other words, an attempt may be made to limit any damage that may be perceived by one party or the other to have been caused by the contents of the report. Once the recommendations are known, one party or the other may consider that they have "won" the assessment. On the other side of the coin the so-called "losing" party will be in a bargaining position that is less positive than it was prior to the recommendations in the assessment being known. Although one does not like to foster the winner/loser scenario, it can indeed impact on the parties' will to settle the custody/access dispute.

On the other hand, the parties may wish to settle the case not because one considers they have won and the other considers they have lost, but because they sincerely and genuinely are affected by the findings of the assessor in a context that causes them to wish to settle the case without further ado after considering what is in the best interests of the children. All family law lawyers can probably recall at least one file where the parents, upon requesting and insisting upon an assessment, were convinced that the children would unequivocally express to the assessor their wish or desire to be with that parent, only to later be taken somewhat aback, if not stunned, to learn that the child's preferences clearly are to be with the other parent. Most parents are capable, loving and good parents and thus are responsible when it comes to ultimately weighing all elements that should be factored into the consideration of what is in the best interests of the child. Most parents are mature and secure enough to consider the child's wishes in this regard knowing full well that the child's preferences do not necessarily mean that the child does not love that parent any less than the other parent.

The assessment may also cause the parties to reach a settlement as a result of the assessor having identified any special needs or handicaps of the children, identifying parental deficits that impact on the assumption of child care responsibilities; or as a result of the assessor flushing out incidents or circumstances regarding physical, psychological and sexual abuse, to give a few examples of identifiable family problems and conflicts that could affect the family. One parent or the other or both, may feel that in such circumstances it would be in the best interests of the children and the parties to avoid a public hearing on the issue of custody and access and that it would be in the best interests of the children to immediately attempt to find a solution to the problems identified in the assessment.

(b) Mediation

The differences and similarities between an assessment and mediation are canvassed in Chapter 6. However, an assessment can result in the parties either using the assessor or some other mental health professional to mediate their conflicts and differences with respect to a suitable parenting arrangement.

An assessment can be transformed into mediation either during the assessment process or after the assessment report is published with its conclusions and recommendations.

Upon digesting the contents of the report, whether the assessment was court ordered or done on the consent of the parties, the parties and their lawyers may feel that the continued adversarial approach to the issue will only inflict further psychological or emotional trauma on the children or cause the parents to become even more divisive and more incapable of arriving at a parenting regime that is in the best interests of the children. In situations such as these the parties will often turn to mediation feeling that it would be more conducive if they reach their own agreement with the assistance of a facilitator rather than having the matter litigated.

The assessment may expose for the parents problems or concerns regarding either the parties or the children, of which the parties had not been cognizant or aware prior to the assessment. The parties may feel that these concerns or problems should be dealt with outside the adversarial system and in a manner that is more consistent with mediation. The parties may decide to mediate because they have developed trust and confidence in the mental health professional conducting the assessment. If the parties are considering asking the assessor to mediate the custody/access issue, they should be made aware of the consequences of doing so.

The parties should be advised of the fact that nothing which is said to anybody in the course of the assessment is privileged and, therefore, whatever is said could become part of the evidence adduced at trial if the report is filed, or if the assessor is called as a witness. If the parties do embark on mediation after the completion of the assessment, but are still unable to settle the custody/access dispute, they must be made to understand that the assessor can still be called as a witness at trial and that whatever was said during the course of the assessment could be put into evidence, and that the assessor's recommendations and conclusions arising out of the assessment could also be put into evidence.

If the assessment process does lead to mediation, the mediation will likely be "closed" on the agreement of the parties and the mediator, the intent being that nothing said during the mediation can be subsequently used in court in the event the mediation fails. Statements made in the course of mediation have been considered by the courts to be privileged in the same context as statements made on a "without prejudice" basis in the course of settlement negotiations carried on during the conduct of an action.[34]

Given the above potential areas of concern, an assessor in a custody/access dispute should seriously consider whether he or she should also become the mediator between the parties if requested to do so. Although it is flattering that the parties may have developed enough trust in the assessor to request that he or she mediate the dispute, should the mediation fail the trusted mediator may, at trial, in the perception of one of the parties, be considered to be in a position of conflict of interest, the assessor having attempted to act upon a "with prejudice" basis in his capacity as an assessor and on a "without prejudice" basis in his capacity as a mediator.

The "trusted" mediator may also be seen by one of the parties as having betrayed the confidence of that party particularly if that party feels that something said during the mediation is now being used by the assessor in his or her report or in the evidence to be given at trial.

It is recommended that if the parties request the assessor to mediate the custody/access issue subsequent to the assessment report being completed, the assessor should decline the invitation.

If the assessor is requested to mediate the issue prior to the assessment being completed, it should be made clear to the parties, by the assessor, that if the mediation fails, a new assessment will have to be conducted by a different mental health professional.

34 *Porter v. Porter* (1983), 32 R.F.L. (2d) 413, 40 O.R. (2d) 417 (U.F.C.).

(c) Pretrial Conference

At a pretrial conference the assessment report can be introduced and reviewed by the presiding judge or pre-trier in the same way as any other experts' reports might be used for which privilege is not being claimed. However, a pretrial judge may or may not be impressed or moved by the observations and conclusions of the assessor. The pretrial judge's recommendation to counsel and the parties as to settlement of the case or as to how he or she thinks the case might be decided by the ultimate trier of fact could be based on the recommendations or conclusions set out in the assessment report.

(d) Use of Assessments on Interim Applications (Motions)

Prior to any assessment being completed, the parties will likely have been living with a verbal arrangement regarding interim custody of the children, will have entered into an executed interim agreement with respect to custody of the children, or there will have been issued an interim or interim-interim custody order regarding the children. If the recommendations or conclusions set out in the assessment are inconsistent with the status quo as reflected in the interim oral or written agreement between the parties, or as reflected in the interim custody order, the party who has received the favourable assessment may feel compelled to bring a motion to vary any interim custody agreement (oral or written) or to vary any interim custody order on the basis of the recommendations as set out in the assessment.

Although there is no reason why a court cannot vary an interim-interim or interim custody order when faced with the appropriate evidence to do so, the courts, generally, are reluctant to disturb the status quo in a custody case unless there is some compelling evidence that in their eyes will have a detrimental effect on the welfare of the child.[35]

---

35 *Larocque v. McComb* (1992), 43 R.F.L. (3d) 185 (Ont. Gen. Div.). The court held that although it should be cautious about varying an interim custody order, it may do so where there are exceptional circumstances. Further, the court may rely on an assessment report directed under s. 30 of the *Children's Law Reform Act* as the basis to vary the order.

In Ontario the test to disturb a *de facto* situation has not changed since the Ontario Court of Appeal decision of *Papp v. Papp*[36] where Mr. Justice Laskin stated:

> He contended [husband's counsel], however, that, on interim custody applications at least, credibility is irrelevant, and that the controlling question is what will best serve the interests of the children pending trial. This question could only be answered (so it was argued) in the light of a heavy onus on a parent who seeks to disturb *de facto* custody pending trial. In short, it was the submissions of the husband's counsel that the father's *de facto* custody could not properly be disturbed pending trial unless it would be clearly damaging to the children to leave them with him.
>
> It may be taken as a working rule that evidence to warrant an order for interim custody must more cogently support disturbance of the *de facto* situation than evidence to support an order for custody after trial on the merits.[37]

This test would suggest that it is more difficult to disturb the *de facto* situation on a motion for interim custody than it is to do so upon the hearing of the merits at trial. It is suggested that the same test will apply in an attempt to vary an interim custody agreement or interim custody order.

Unless the assessment reveals, in a compelling way, that the child is at risk or that it would be in the best interests of the child to be moved from the custody of one parent to the other, the assessment should not form the basis for varying interim custody. Assessment reports are often unclear and have not undergone the scrutiny of cross-examination prior to trial. Until the author of an assessment has borne the scrutiny of cross-examination, particularly with respect to the factual assumptions relied upon in arriving at the conclusions and recommendations set out in the report, it is almost always better to wait until the trial to determine the effect of the report.

An example of the trend of the court's reluctance to vary an interim custody order on the basis of an assessment may be seen in

---

36 (1969), 8 D.L.R. 389, [1970] 1 O.R. 331 (C.A.).

37 *Ibid.*, at 402-03. See *B.(S.I.) v. B. (F.H.)*, [1995] W.D.F.L. 024 (B.C. S.C.) where it was held that in the absence of urgency a recommendation in an assessment does not mandate a change in interim custody or access, between the date of the motion and the trial.

Crawford v. Crawford[38] where the parents signed a separation agreement by the terms of which custody was granted to the father. The mother then contested the permanency of the parties' agreement as a result of which the parties agreed to an assessment. The assessment recommended that the mother have custody of the child and she therefore moved for interim sole custody. In other words, she attempted to seek an order varying the provisions of the separation agreement. The Official Guardian argued that the trial judge should decide what weight be given to the report and that the status quo should not be changed. The court dismissed the mother's application and held that the report did not disclose convincing reason to disturb the status quo.

The use of the recommendations or conclusions in the assessment to change an interim custody agreement or interim custody order may or may not be successful prior to trial, and likely would not be, until the parties have had an opportunity to cross-examine the author of the assessment report, subject to the assessment containing compelling evidence that would justify a change in the status quo prior to the trial or hearing.

---

38 [1994] W.D.F.L. 010 (Ont. Gen. Div.). See also *Larocque v. McComb* (1992), 43 R.F.L. (3d) 185 (Ont. Gen. Div.) wherein the court held that although it should be cautious about varying an interim custody order, it may do so where there are exceptional circumstances and may rely upon an assessment as a basis for doing so.

5

The Assessment

1. CHOOSING A MENTAL HEALTH ASSESSOR

Depending on the community in which one resides, the availability of competent assessors is not uniform. Even in larger communities, many mental health professionals wish to avoid dealing with courts while some show insufficient caution and venture where wiser colleagues fear to tread. Not surprisingly, perhaps considering the nature of the work, professional colleges and regulatory boards receive more than their share of complaints concerning custody/access assessments. The positive side to such complaints is that these, in addition to the availability of more specific standards, have gradually sensitized health professionals to the complexity that custody assessments entail. Most would agree, though, that it is worthwhile work and a contribution to a legal system that has struggled to resolve custody conflicts in a sensitive and durable way.

Most often, unless the assessor is associated with a family court clinic, mental health professionals provide these assessments as one part of their clinical work. Many health professionals would see this as a preferable option to exclusive specialization in custody problems as it favours a broader clinical background with a wider scope for professional development. On top of this, a steady diet of such often stormy cases may be something to avoid.

Assessors come from various backgrounds and are well represented among psychiatry, social work and psychology. Each discipline may approach assessments somewhat differently but even within disciplines there is variation. This has never represented a serious problem although some practitioners in the field, especially psychologists, have called for uniform assessment techniques with standardized instruments. Although this would harmonize the data base for determining recommendations, it might also limit the individual assessor from employing their own specific method and techniques suited to their particular expertise and training. On the other hand, this would be most beneficial for the less experienced and less able assessors whose work would be strengthened by a more defined and guided process. We can probably expect developments in this area especially from American psychologists who are already busy developing instruments for this purpose.

As a general approach, assessors capitalize on their own clinical strengths and derive insight from the perspective of their training. A child psychologist may find much benefit in a careful scrutiny of parent-child interactions whereas an adult psychiatrist may derive most information from a careful clinical interview that accentuates history and current functioning. Besides careful interviewing, psychologists routinely administer a few major psychological tests and consider these indispensable whereas a social worker will likely gather and synthesize an abundance of observations from home, school and office visits that underwrite their conclusions.

Although diversity is quite acceptable, all assessors should bear a certain similar stamp and meet particular criteria in order to be qualified to do this exacting work. The family law lawyer should ensure that the assessor's qualifications and experience fit within the following framework.

- *They should be fully qualified, licensed or registered in a recognized health or social discipline.*

Although licensure reflects a bare minimum of qualification, it should be considered a necessary but not sufficient background to do the job. General clinical training such that psychiatrists and psychologists receive, or social work practicums, do not usually prepare practitioners to perform this type of assessment. The reasons for this are relatively clear:

(a) The litigants, although in dispute and less effective than usual as individuals or parents are unlikely to be psychiatrically ill or severely disordered which is the main subject of clinical internships and residency programs.
(b) Most mental health professionals are not well versed in the intricacies of litigation nor the ambiance and demands of the court room.
(c) The custody literature, with its focus on divorce and custody alternatives, represents a specific topic, a subspecialty, and is not the primary concentration of most mental health professionals.
(d) Determining custody and access recommendations is multidimensional and requires a working background in numerous areas including law, family systems theory, sociology, child and adult psychology, psychopathology, and specific clinical concerns such as disorders of aggression and sexual conduct. This is indeed a tall order.

The conclusion that can be drawn from the above is that the lawyer, in choosing an assessor, should be assured that the professional is well grounded clinically and has more than a primary licence to practice. Obviously, it is not up to the lawyer to determine the competence of the prospective assessor although reputation and track record are important guide marks. The lawyer might also request a sample of previous work that is already part of the public record or where names are deleted. Additionally, a meeting with the assessor may help establish confidence that the professional has the experience and depth of knowledge required.

- *If relatively new in their field, the assessor should be practising alongside a more experienced colleague who takes some active role in guiding their efforts.*

Inexperience is not a serious obstacle and this state of affairs is part of every professional's development. The inexperienced assessor, however, should have working access to a more senior colleague who can act as a supervisor. In any case, only straightforward custody and access disputes should be tackled by the less experienced assessor and high "risk" cases such as those involving abuse allegations or unusually litigious and protracted cases should be evaluated by the more seasoned assessor.

- *The assessor should be schooled in a standard accepted clinical method whether this be psychodynamic, social learning or a family systems approach.*

The assessor must be well versed in a clinical theory in order to understand or interpret the data collected. Clinical theory acts as a prism to separate and identify the important factors that will prove fundamental in deciding the direction that recommendations will take. Without this skill, clinical work can become an exercise in the superficial which accumulates observations that in the end amount to little. An absence of clinical theory, for example, might lead an assessor to lean heavily on behavioural signs without any knowledge of what weight to give them. Hence, an eight-year-old boy who tugs at his penis is said to be sexually abused, a little girl is considered to be ill treated during visitation because she is hard to handle after the visit, or a parent is seen as abusive and controlling simply because the other parent insists on this label. Such conclusions will not only impede resolution, they will exacerbate conflicts.

- *The assessor should work within a certain evaluation framework that provides several avenues of input among the following: diagnostic interviews, psychological testing, child evaluations, communications with extra-parental sources such as schools, counselors and physicians, parent-child interviews and home visits.*

As noted above, each of the major mental health disciplines has their own clinical vantage point and they may approach custody and access problems slightly differently. Differences are no obstacle or limitation in assessing these custody problems and there are numerous ways to achieve the same end. Assessors tend to rely on their specific strengths and orientations and they will choose or favour those clinical activities or procedures that reflect their own strengths and training.

Although this is a general point and not specific to the individual assessor, it may also be important to be aware that each mental health profession has its own limitations alongside considerable strengths. Human problems being as broad and multidimensional as they are, at least three main mental health disciplines have spawned to deal with the human condition: psychiatry, clinical psychology and social work. Yet, psychiatrists, for one, often have a limited foundation in normal psychology and the more mediocre practitioners among them may have little to say if the person is not mentally ill or disordered. Psychologists tend to give everyone the benefit of the doubt and may fail to recognize psychopathology unless it glaringly stands out in their psychological tests. Social workers may lack sufficient clinical training, especially diagnostic skills, and remain limited in doing this type of work by virtue of their social as compared to individual perspective.

On the other hand, each profession has made sizable independent contributions to the mental health movement and each is capable of training practitioners who can work effectively in this area. What should be stressed, though, is that the assessor should be from a regulated health or social profession which licenses or certifies its members and renders them accountable to the public. Psychiatrists, in this regard, are physicians who are licensed under provincial medical colleges while psychologists are certified or licensed under statute in all ten provinces. Social work may not always be regulated by statute, as for example in Ontario, although social workers may establish their own in-house certification.

One should be wary, in our opinion, of the assessor that is married to any one cause or special interest. As examples, assessors who are strictly feminist in orientation, religious, or experts on sexual abuse, transcultural issues, or power differentials between the sexes, do not in our experience make good assessors. Invariably they have an axe to grind and commonly appear in outraged rebuttal to a legitimate neutral assessment when recruited to do so.

- *The assessor should be prepared to document findings in a detailed, comprehensive report that arrives at specific and meaningful conclusions and recommendations that are clearly supported by the reported findings.*

The report is not a summary but a detailed record of the data that was gathered in support of the conclusions and recommendations made. The assessor must have reasonable writing skills and be prepared to spend the time and energy to convey the full breadth of their knowledge of the family in question. This is essential if the parents, lawyers and the courts are to adopt the assessor's proposals.

- *The assessor should be prepared in all cases to provide courtroom testimony when necessary and to have their findings examined in the context of the legal process.*

Testifying in court is like going through customs, it makes just about everyone nervous. Professional insecurities, persecutory fears, and fears of being on trial, are common sources of apprehension for assessors. Nevertheless, anyone performing these difficult evaluations should be able to present their clinical findings to the court in a cogent and professional manner. The assessor's responsibility to communicate this opinion and to outline how conclusions were determined also yields a valuable opportunity to directly inform the judicial process. Fundamentally, what the assessor conveys in both the written and oral reports is a clinical opinion. It is the court's responsibility to test the merits of this judgment in the light of the evidence raised by both sides. We believe that most lawyers and judges would agree, however, that a well documented and thoughtful report is normally very helpful in determining a rational outcome.

- *Assessors should be prepared to provide their services in a timely fashion that does not endanger the family's capacity to cope with the strains of the assessment nor the capacity of the lawyers and court to aid the family in question.*

Once the assessment begins, there is a reasonable time period in which the work can be completed most often with the full cooperation of the parents and children. Yet, undue delay and procrastination on the part of the assessor can induce heavy strain on a family's emotional resources at a time that they are most vulnerable. This can lead to regression in the family's coping resources leading to acting out on the part of the children and parents or other manifestations of chronic strain. In our experience, what is important is that the family is fully apprised of how the assessment will unfold and what time span is required.

Sometimes, however, waiting lists and long delays are unavoidable before an assessment can begin and this may represent a further problem in certain communities. It is always important, though, for the chosen assessor to provide some reliable estimate of a date for commencement in order to facilitate the parents' coping.

2. THE GOOD ASSESSMENT

Having looked at the common stamp that characterizes good assessors, it remains to briefly look at the attributes of the good assessment and worthy report.

Although it is axiomatic that good assessors will generally produce good evaluations, there is always good reason to appraise each family assessment on its own merits. In general, parents and lawyers tend to appreciate when the assessor has made a serious and comprehensive effort to grapple with the issues presented by the family in question. A superficial report or one that attests to the parents' charm and potential but sidesteps their serious conflicts will often not carry the day. In fact, it is our perception that such evasive reports feed the litigation as compared to helping resolve it. On the other hand, where there is a clear perception that the issues have been faced, discussed and weighed in the context of the children's best interests, then the majority of parents will work with the findings even if they are contrary to their wishes. Of course, there are parents who cannot accept less than their wishes but this is a question of character and exceeds any assessor's influence or control.

Although the good assessment is honest and direct in its method, the report should avoid being aggressive or combative. As a rule of thumb, the parents should have a place to stand and no one deserves to be humiliated or berated in an assessment. Hence, it is a question of balancing a regard for truth and insight with an equal regard for the feelings and self esteem of the family members. Having noted this, it may also be said that this can become problematic in those few situations where highly manipulative and controlling behaviour is highlighted in the report. In responding to such manipulative personalities, it may be difficult for the assessor to avoid being labeled as hostile or biased which is invariably the response to an unfavourable outcome. Unfortunately, the most manipulative, controlling and pathologically competitive parents, thankfully a small minority, are the most likely to claim that they are the victims of bias if the assessor fails to recommend what they desire. Although infrequent, such cases remind us that, despite efforts, the assessor is always open to the inference that the recommendation was based on pre-judgment, prejudice, or on non-psychological grounds.

One cardinal feature that helps to buttress the assessment against such criticisms is the inclusion of a breadth of information that documents the observed themes or tendencies. Consequently, the good report describes the full scope of the observations which ultimately mesh and lead to the conclusions and recommendations that follow. In this regard, the conclusions proceed from the data and do not appear arbitrarily tacked on or forced to fit. In one form of the poor report, the reader is aghast at the end for the conclusions seem to come out of the blue and may even clash with the prior findings. This is often discouraging to the court as well as being unconvincing for the parents. Generally, it limits the report's usefulness.

The above highlights that the assessment must not only be accurate, it must also be convincing especially to the parent who is asked to take a secondary role. This relates to the credibility of the exercise which, in turn, is linked to the capacity of the report to deepen understanding and shift the focus from the dimension of grievance to that of the well being of their children. The good assessment also expands the knowledge of the family and clearly tackles the issues that divide the parents. The reader should feel enlightened by the various views of the family members provided and it should move the case forward. The report should focus on the background of the parents, their personalities, the characters and needs of the children and the way that the parents interact with each other.

Additionally, the good assessment arrives at a feasible solution to the problems at hand and appears rational and considered to the reader. The recommendations are designed to be least detrimental and to protect the welfare of the children in the face of the divorce. In contrast, an assessment that recommends solutions that are logistically impossible or beyond the scope of the family to implement for emotional or other reasons will not be seen as effective. In this respect, the good report takes into account the reality of the situation and does not work solely with ideals that cannot be implemented.

Finally, the good assessment will sustain a balance between a clear division of authority and responsibility in child care with the child's right to meaningful post-divorce relationships with both parents. In this regard, reports that are draconian in their isolation of an adequate parent from the child's life, or conversely, a report that does not suggest a clear line of authority to safeguard the child from interminable strife, will both prove deficient.

In summary, therefore, the assessment that is good enough is one that strikes the reader as fair and comprehensive. The assessor is seen as having taken the matter seriously and with an open mind. The parents will feel that they had an opportunity to express their sentiments and the lawyers will feel that they can respect the process even if the outcome proves unfavourable to their client's wishes. The good assessment, in the proper legal hands, will help to move the case forward towards resolution and will not itself become a focus of further conflict. Although a tall order, a good assessment is no doubt a powerful tool for settling custody disputes in as much as it can be a potent focus for the energies of resolution. This is especially important in those cases where these positive energies seem too meager or too easily overwhelmed by the forces of discord.

3. ESSENTIAL COMPONENTS OF THE CUSTODY ASSESSMENT

(a) Prior Steps

In conducting a proper psychological evaluation, the assessor should have in his or her possession the affidavit and related material from both lawyers as well as a written agreement as to the payment and terms for the release of the report upon completion. The initial letter to the assessor should clarify whether the evaluation is court ordered or mutually agreed upon by the parents in question. In the case of mutual agreement, this should be verified by both legal counsels by letter to the assessor. As assessors are most often health professionals, they must be able to document that they have acted according to the consent of the parties or under the direct auspices of the court.

At this pre-stage, the assessor would not have had personal contact with the parents and, in general, it is not advisable for parents to make the initial contact with the assessor. As the entire exercise is grounded on the neutrality and independence of the assessor, any unilateral contacts could later be construed as having compromised objectivity or neutrality. In all cases, therefore, the impartiality of the assessor should be protected by the lawyers to ensure an untainted and more accepted result. On the other hand, if a parent feels a strong need to be assured of an assessor's stand on a specific issue, then it can be beneficial for that parent to discuss this point alone directly with the proposed assessor. For example, some parents may be comforted to know that an assessor will come to their home or that a new partner will also be interviewed. These are often facilitating contacts and serve to strengthen cooperation and trust in the evaluation process. Generally, the experienced assessor will guard the symmetry of the process by offering the same clarification to the other side.

What the assessor will want to avoid, though, are attempts to advocate for either side's interpretation or positions before the assessment has begun. In this regard, the first contact between lawyer and assessor is also important and represents the assessor's introduction to the case. From the assessor's standpoint, there is no advantage in receiving specific details or positions although some counsel find the opportunity too inviting to resist. It is more common for the lawyer who makes the initial contact to provide a brief synopsis without advocating any position. Most often this includes an outline of the task including the legal status of the assessment, how it is to be paid, the number of children, and any specific issues that will need to be addressed, such as allegations of spousal or sexual abuse or other complicating factors.

The initial telephone call to set appointments should be made personally by the assessor and this should not be arranged through the attorney's office. In our experience, this contact is very important as it sets the stage for what will follow and can be a reassuring contact for the anxious or guarded parent. A preparatory booklet, as provided in Appendix 1, can greatly alleviate these preliminary anxieties and it goes a long way to preventing misunderstandings that can distort the process. One can be sure that in the absence of facts and communication, litigants may fear the worst and this can interfere with the assessment by increasing resistance and fostering misperceptions. Although the assessor's self image is likely that of a helping professional, the parents' entry into the mental health system is, in this case, through the courts with its emphasis on conflict resolution. The mind-set, therefore, is entirely different and can be at odds with the assessor's standpoint. Although the assessment is by definition a psychological act with a strong potential to be therapeutic, the parents are not "patients" nor might they otherwise have contact with the mental health system.

At the same time, family assessments in custody/access matters differ markedly from the more adversarial format of other civil litigation disputes such as in personal injury cases. In the latter context, it is almost automatic that both sides will solicit favourable reports from experts, where as in family law the expert is chosen and agreed upon by the two sides and there is no presumption of multiple assessors. At the same time, both types of assessment can include a rigorous cross-examination of the report and an analysis of its methods and conclusions. Although there must be a paradigm shift for both lawyers and assessors working in the domain of family law, there is also much overlap with other areas of practice. Yet, in our experience, lawyers who treat custody and access conflicts with a no holds barred adversarial approach, complicate matters for the family and inhibit the power of the courts to help. They tend to traumatize family members and inflame conflicts more than resolve them. Likewise, assessors who deny the real context of litigation and erroneously view their function as a variant of family therapy, also miss the point and create added problems for divorcing families as well as for themselves. Such considerations speak to the reality context of the evaluation and pave the way for an optimal outcome.

It is best, in our opinion, then, to view the assessor as a consultant to the court capable of providing an expert clinical opinion based on a careful scrutiny of the family in question. If need be, the merits of that opinion can be tested through the normal channel of cross-examination within the context of a trial.

In choosing the assessor, many circumstantial factors may intervene including a limited availability of alternatives either because there are not many assessors in a community or because most have backlogs that would lead to a prohibitively long delay. Sometimes an assessor will be acceptable to one side but unacceptable to the other. This may arise because the lawyer had a negative experience with that assessor or is concerned that some bias such as a hospital affiliation or a particular point of view may interfere with the objectivity of the assessment.

The experienced lawyer may also be aware that some assessors may not have suitable or sufficient skills to adequately address the complexities of a specific case. Lawyers who have frequent contact with assessors quickly learn their relative strengths and weaknesses and can often advise the less experienced family law lawyer on these qualifying factors. Each assessor, however, deserves to have the final confidence of the lawyers and to be viewed as a neutral expert whose opinion will be respected even if not ultimately accepted by both sides. This assumes, of course, that the assessor satisfied their mandate and engaged the family in question in a reasonably thorough and acceptable assessment process.

Problems can arise when the assessor is clearly a second choice and is not mutually embraced by both counsel and parents as the most trusted professional to do the job. Lingering doubts as to the suitability of the assessor are bound to have a negative impact on the process or when the report is released, especially in a charged and highly conflictive situation. In this regard, the working alliance with the assessor is fundamental to a good result and it is essential that the lawyers and parents feel comfortable with their choice.

In this respect, parents should feel free to clarify matters with the assessor and should raise any concerns that may arise during the evaluation process. If, for instance, a parent feels criticized or dismissed by the assessor or if they lack sufficient opportunity to discuss their concerns, then the lawyer should advise the client to raise these directly with the assessor without fear of reprisal. As noted in the preparatory booklet reprinted in Appendix 1, assessors, especially those who also practice as psychotherapists, are accustomed to being questioned and they will appreciate any opportunity to improve both the rapport and the process. Consequently, they will welcome such communications and act to reduce confusion or concern. If the client reported, however, that these efforts have proved unsatisfactory, then the lawyer would be wise to communicate the client's concerns directly to the assessor. The underlying principle is that anything that promotes the alliance between the parents and the assessor is ultimately good for the assessment. On the other hand, and this distinction is crucial, this is very different indeed from, for example, telephoning an assessor to demand that pressure be exerted on the other parent to achieve some end. It is the difference between clarification and interference; the first is welcome while the latter is not.

Returning to the issue of choosing an assessor, it may arise that a professional suggested by a colleague is personally unknown to the lawyer. As a part of representing the client, the lawyer will want to ask certain questions of the proposed assessor to gain an impression and to glean the assessor's method. As to what questions are pertinent in this respect, we suggest the following:

- In what professional capacity does the assessor work, and for how long and what are the main clinical activities of the professional?
- How did the assessor learn to do this type of work?
- Has the assessor written or spoken to professional or community groups on this subject?
- What proportion of the assessor's work is represented by custody and access assessments?
- What is the usual method that the assessor follows and what time duration is devoted to each step?
- Is the assessor a regulated health or social service professional and has the assessor ever been found lacking by the relevant college or regulatory board in respect to their work?
- If the assessor is not experienced, is there a more senior assessor available for consultation and is it the habit of the assessor to seek guidance?
- If the assessor is a psychologist, what role do psychological tests play in arriving at a conclusion and what percentage of the assessment will they entail? If the assessor is a psychiatrist, what experience does the assessor have apart from treating patients with mental illness? if the assessor is a social worker, what experience and training does the assessor have of independently evaluating individuals in clinical terms?
- If there is a specific clinical problem involved such as addictions, abuse, joint custody, right to relocate, parental alienation etc., does the assessor feel confident to address this type of problem?
- Has the assessor appeared in court to defend their findings and recommendations and, if so, how often?

The intent of these ten questions is self evident. One seeks a professional with a multi-source approach who has some experience as well as a realistic sense of the limitations as well as the extent of their competence. They should convey an ethical, balanced orientation that reflects some efforts to develop and strengthen skills in this demanding area of work. The assessor should devote reasonable time to this professional activity and is best not a dabbler. At the same time, the assessor may well be steeped in therapeutics and need not offer these assessments as a full time endeavour. The assessor should address these questions without an air of defensiveness while the lawyer should simply pose the appropriate questions without interrogating. In the end, the lawyer should have a working knowledge of the assessor and the assessor's likely method and approach.

(b) The Essence of Clinical Assessment

An assessment as to custody and access is by necessity a psychological one. On the other hand, it may not always be done by a psychologist any more than all psychiatric diagnoses are rendered by psychiatrists. Yet, the evaluation must delve into psychological factors at sufficient depth and breadth to promote useful and sensitive recommendations concerning post-divorce parent-child relationships. Assessment, in this regard, implies a three-way professional relationship between the mental health expert, the family in question, and the court or its representatives. It is geared specifically to assess those pertinent factors inherent to the parents and children that will bear directly on questions of custody and access. It is not a therapeutic assessment but a psycholegal one. Only psychologists, for instance, are likely to administer psychological tests whereas all assessors will employ assessment techniques, be they interviews, observational procedures or home and school studies.

Competent practitioners in the mental health fields will employ a mixture of methods that make best use of their individual clinical strengths and are tailor made to answer the questions at hand. The lawyer will want to know, however, that the techniques chosen are valid procedures and capable of generating the necessary data and conclusions. Hence, for instance, a social worker who compiles a multi-page list of reasons to recommend one parent over another as custodian must be able to justify how these conclusions were derived and from what data. If these were generated by taking every version at face value without clinical scrutiny, then the procedures are inadequate. In the same way, if a psychologist sees a parent only briefly and administers an MMPI-2, a widely used personality test, which is then copiously interpreted without any supporting information, this too would be inadequate to support any conclusions on the matter. The lawyer in examining the report should perceive a concordance between the conclusions reached and the methodology used to generate them.

Family psychological assessments in cases of disputed custody should meet rigorous criteria for sophistication, comprehensiveness and validity that bear up well under cross-examination. They should be multifactorial and integrate findings from diverse standpoints in rendering an opinion. Assessment, therefore, is a complex clinical act and, in the case of custody and access disputes, involves a detailed appraisal of the parents, the parent-child relationships and the children themselves.

(c) Interviews with the Parents

Typically, a psychological assessment begins with the parents and not the children. The assessor seeks at this stage to construct a profile of the adults in terms of their character strengths and weaknesses and their mode of interaction with the assessor and the ex-spouse.

Some assessors automatically meet with the parents together for an initial interview. This is used as an opportunity to allay fears and misconceptions and to outline the procedures that will follow. Generally, the assessor will underline the purpose of the assessment and the task at hand. The parents may be invited to address specific concerns about their children and about their best interests. They may also agree upon what collateral sources can be contacted and appropriate consent forms will be signed. The assessor may also comment on how to introduce the assessment to the children and how to support them through this trying period. Mainly, the assessor will try and establish neutrality, objectivity and an ambiance of cooperation. The parents are likely to be told that resolution of whatever kind is far better for children than interminable conflict. Hence, this effort will hopefully help them to assist their children's adjustment.

Other assessors find that the atmosphere between the parents can be too strained for comfort and although some valuable data may be lost, they choose to do all interviews independent of the other parent. This is usually mandatory when there is a restraining order against one or both spouses prohibiting contact with the other. The guiding rationale should be to focus on those procedures that elicit the most data. If an assessor gains a special insight from these conjoint meetings then there is no inherent problem in holding them if the parents are willing. One risk of course is that the parents become more tense and antagonistic due to the meeting and the evaluation becomes too closely linked in the parents' minds to the battle as compared to its resolution. These matters are best left to the philosophy and approach of the assessor as well as the motivation and mind-set of the parents. It would be inadvisable, however, for an assessor to insist on a joint meeting in the face of one parent's fear or severe anxiety.

What follows in the assessment are a series of diagnostic interviews that cover a wide range of issues, including background, marital history, knowledge of the children, and family history. Generally, the assessor will begin by asking the parent to address the reason for the assessment as they see it and what has transpired to create a need for one. It is often interesting to view the differing perspectives of the parents and to identify their focal concerns.

In one example, for instance, the mother viewed the issue as one of choosing an appropriate parenting formula while the father sought to unmask the mother's inadequacy. His drive to discredit his wife was intense and obsessive although the two preschool children bore no apparent ill effects of her alleged incompetence and were relaxed and at ease with her. The assessment probed the reasons for his attack and sought to distinguish whether it represented a true response to his wife's conduct or a strategy either to enhance his own status or to win a court battle. In this case, the assessor learned that the father's underlying inadequacy feelings and regrets about his own choices and mistakes in life were being attributed to the mother's failings. Although his contribution to his children's lives was substantial and deserved recognition in the recommendations, the mother was viewed as more reasonable and forgiving and better able to respond to the children's needs in the long term.

It is not uncommon for assessors to spend four or more hours with each parent in obtaining information. This should all be detailed in the subsequent report that is issued. Although one or two hours with each parent is likely too limited an opportunity for even the most experienced assessor to fully appraise a complicated situation, it does not automatically follow that the more hours spent in the assessment, the better it will be. Inexperienced evaluators or those who use a more behavioural or observational method may require greater exposure to the parents to arrive at a confident understanding. The issue is one of balance and the capacity of the assessor to portray a cogent and meaningful portrait of the adults with the data collected. It should be realistic, balanced, fair minded and astute. In a good assessment, the reader has the impression that the assessor has made a sincere and thorough attempt to understand both parents and that the time spent was sufficient for the task.

When the meetings with the parents are concluded and the next phase of the assessment begins, the assessor should have a reasonable sense of the merits and problem areas associated with the adults as well as a measure of their interaction and what can be anticipated in the future. Although the assessor may feel pulled towards the perception and point of view of each parent at the outset, this will gradually shift to a more specific direction. As a rule of thumb, if at the outset the assessor feels partial to that parent's point of view then he or she has likely listened well. Gradually, though, perceptions form which help to build a model of the adults as parents and individuals in their own right.

In particular, the assessor should be able to answer some important questions concerning the parents:

- What is the dominant emotion and point of view of the parent?
- Can the parent relate, communicate or discuss with the other parent in regards to the children or other matters?
- Do they agree on major facts or is there a fundamental schism between them that seriously compromises any joint activity?
- Is there a sense that present functioning is characteristic of them or is psychological trauma severely compromising one or both parents and limiting their capacity to adapt at this critical phase?
- Is there evidence for psychopathology or character disturbance that will undermine one or both parent's capacity to adapt in the future?
- Are there strengths that are perhaps untapped that can be put to good use in planning for the post-divorce care of the children?

- Is there a capacity for empathy, concern or understanding regarding the ex-spouse or at least some identification with the children's need of this relationship with the other parent?
- Are there factors in the marital history that bear on the present dispute and can these assist in formulating a deeper understanding of the adults and their interaction?
- Are there factors in the personal history of each adult that can shed important light on the characters of each parent?
- How does each parent understand the children and do they agree or disagree on the basic personality, strengths and concerns regarding their offspring?
- Has there been a consistent involvement with the children over time and an ongoing relationship with them?
- Has there been any involvement with the police or courts, especially concerning such problems as driving while impaired, assault, or other criminal behaviour?
- Are there health concerns that might be of issue in providing the mainstay of the child care?
- Why does the parent want custody and are there actual plans in place to care for the children beyond just the sentiment to provide?

Although the above list is by no means exhaustive, it is meant to give a sketch or overview of the type of knowledge that should emanate from a complete evaluation of the parents.

(d) Psychological Testing

(i) Introduction

A psychological test is intended to be an objective yardstick of a trait or capacity on which people differ. Among the health professions, psychologists receive extensive training in their professional education on the use and misuse of such tests and how to assess their merits. The majority of psychologists who do custody assessments will employ psychometric techniques. In a survey study, W.G. Keilin and L.J. Bloom reported that almost three quarters of experienced assessors commonly use psychological tests in doing custody evaluations.[1] Mainly, these will be tests of personality although measures of intelligence and academic achievement may also be utilized when these issues are in question. As an example, an assessor may wish to measure a child's intellectual ability in order to comment on the likely validity of an account or the ability of the child to comprehend events they have described. Likewise, an assessor may administer an academic screening instrument to assess scholastic needs in relation to custody and/or access arrangements. Occasionally, a parent will be tested if there are specific questions as to their intellectual competence that would impact on the capacity to parent. Finally, structured questionnaires, checklists and attitude scales may also be employed to broaden the knowledge that the assessor has of the parents or children. They may be completed by the parents themselves or by teachers when designed for this function. There are some very useful questionnaires available, in this regard, that have been designed especially for this type of evaluation.

During the 1940s and 1950s psychologists developed several standard clinical instruments that are still used in a wide variety of settings. Initially, these had applications for hospital and clinic work and in the post-war era this expertise provided the entry point for psychology into the health provider system. Needless to say, the profession of psychology has gone well beyond these humble beginnings but the psychological test still remains the bedrock skill for many in the profession.

It should be pointed out, however, that these assessment tests were not specifically designed to address custody and access questions nor are they all tailor made to meet the rigorous criteria of the forensic context. This is not a criticism of the testing field but an acknowledgment that such clinical instruments were developed with a diagnostic intent to be used in a mental health setting where therapeutics was the ultimate goal. Measured against their original intent, the overall usefulness of these measures has stood the test of time.

On the other hand, there has been appropriate criticism that psychologists tend to use these tests indiscriminately as if they can be applied to any situation to generate the psychological data required to

1 Keilin, W.G. and Bloom, L.J. (1986), "Child custody evaluation practices: a survey of experienced professionals", *Professional Psychology*, 17: 338-346.

make sensitive predictions.[2] In other words, some assessors might intellectually evaluate every parent in a custody dispute instead of deciding which instruments are applicable in the specific situation. This "standard battery approach" is less likely to be geared to addressing the particular concerns that often arise in child custody determinations. For instance, they may generate psychological information as to the response patterns and intellectual levels of the parents but the actual relevance of this data to the substantive questions posed by a court is at best indirect. When it comes to which parent is best equipped to be primary custodian of a child, reliance on a standard clinical battery of tests as the mainstay of the assessment seems anachronistic and of questionable relevance. The mutidimensional factors that need to be addressed including parent-child relationships, parental availability, factors specific to the child's character, needs and development, and problems of life style, stability and reliability are not likely to be tapped by such global and non-specific procedures.

Consequently, by today's standards, a custody determination based solely on a clinical battery of tests without corroborating data from other sources, would not stand the test of peer scrutiny. For example, one psychologist recommended that a child be removed from his father's care due to responses on a projective psychological instrument that were interpreted as expressing the child's concerns for safety with that parent. The fact that the child was in the centre of a stormy fight between the parents and was far more under the mother's emotional control was not taken into account. The psychologist seemed unaware of a basic tenet of psychological assessment which is that validity can only be assessed in the real context of the subject's life. In another example, a psychologist was prepared to give evidence against a man who was charged with sexual molestation based solely on drawings done for a psychological associate being supervised by the psychologist. Fortunately, the lawyer for the father convinced the judge that this evidence was so weak and unreliable as to be inadmissible.

Although these are extreme examples, they convey the abuse of process that can occur if these instruments are idealized and given a role that they do not merit nor were ever intended. In particular,

2 Brodzinsky, David. M. (1993), "On the use and misue of psychological testing in child custody evaluations", *Professional Psychology: Research and Practice,* 24: 213-219.

psychological testing should only be employed as part of package of methods or procedures aimed at elucidating the psychological facets of the family in question. Even the most objective of psychological tests, therefore, must be understood in the specific context of the person being evaluated.

When used appropriately, though, psychological tests truly help to elucidate important information about the emotional health of the parents, personality features, adjustment and developmental issues. Their usefulness can be extraordinary and they provide a definite edge over interview data alone. For instance, two parents locked in a dispute about how to apportion child care became far more reasonable and communicative when they realized how psychologically vulnerable was the older of their two sons. Psychological assessment revealed a history of aggressive outbursts due to minor provocation, attention deficit, low frustration tolerance, and poor social skills and the psychologist/assessor questioned whether this may have a physical or neurological basis. This led to consultation with a neurologist, arrangements for social skills training and a recommendation to change schools. The parents were able to resolve matters when they could focus on the child's deficits and not blame each other for his dysfunction. They agreed to a shared arrangement where the children would live with the mother in her new neighbourhood during the school year while living with the father during the summers.

In a further example, a mother claimed that her daughter had raised concerns about boundary issues with the father after the onset of the separation. In this instance, the father had not sought custody and was supportive of the mother's role with their child. He saw his daughter on a frequent weekend basis and would not have challenged her role as custodian. There was little evidence to validate the allegation and although the mother insisted that this was her daughter's initiative, psychological testing revealed her intensely competitive nature as well as a deep underlying grudge against her ex-husband. Although not admitting it, it seemed clear that she was indirectly behind the charge. This was confirmed through other avenues of inquiry but the testing proved decisive in opening the door for other explanations that were more fitting than sexual abuse.

(ii) Application and Misapplication of Tests

Many mental health professionals are not clear on the difference between a clinical and forensic evaluation. In truth, most clinicians receive scant training in court-related work and bring a strictly therapeutic model to their scope of practice. Of course, the forensic and the therapeutic models share certain overlap but their coordinates and demands are quite different and it is a mistake to equate one with the other. In particular, what is acceptable practice in a clinical assessment may not easily fit within the more rigorous demands of forensic assessment.

As an example, projective techniques such as the Rorschach (unstructured ink blots) are not truly tests as they do not actually measure personality.[3] Rather, they generate hypotheses about emotional functioning that may help to paint a picture of how that person's mind works and how they process experience. The accuracy of the procedure is almost solely determined by the expertise of the clinician but the relevance to custody determinations remains to be specified. Of course, unconscious dynamics and intrapsychic processes should contribute to the total picture of that parent but the courts require a much broader insight and perspective of the person in the light of the real complexities of child custody determinations. Hence, the Rorschach is a fine instrument in capable hands for making accurate clinical diagnoses but most parents in custody disputes are not ill nor disordered and in need of a diagnosis. Even if the diagnosis can be made in a specific case, its relevance to parenting issues may not always be clear. This should not be interpreted as a repudiation of the Rorschach's value in custody assessments but the assessor would be on thin ice indeed if conclusions leaned too heavily on these findings unless there was a major diagnostic issue involved.

As much as psychologists or psychiatrists may overvalue psychological tests, lawyers may do so as well, viewing them as an "objective" window into the mind of the litigant. We might qualify this by saying that in capable hands, such measures enhance the image of the person and are more objective than simply building a portrait through several semi-structured interviews with someone intent on putting

3 Weiner, I.B. (1994), "The Rorschach ink blot method (RIM) is not a test: implications for theory and practice", *Journal of Personality Assessment*, 62: 498-504.

their best foot forward. Although weighty in their contribution, they are by no means infallible nor omniscient.

(iii) Personality Tests

Personality tests can be roughly divided into two major groups: (1) projective instruments and (2) structured personality inventories. In the latter group, the Rorschach or ink blot test is most well known and was developed by the Swiss psychologist Hermann Rorschach in the 1920s and represents the progenitor of this genre. We could also include in this group the TAT (Thematic Apperception Test) which presents a series of pictures depicting suggestive scenes and asks the subject to compose a story from the pictorial stimulus. Most clinicians score this procedure in an impressionistic way and look for repetitive themes that reflect underlying concerns and psychological processes. For example, the examiner may be able to note the most prevalent emotion and differentiate whether this is anger, anxiety or sadness for example. Additionally, attitudes regarding people and relationships may also be clarified based on responses to the cards. Although structured scoring systems do exist for the TAT, they are mainly used in research paradigms rather than clinical assessment. There are also refinements of the original TAT available as well as similar instruments that have been developed for children of various ages.

Finally, in this projective category, drawings may be used and interpreted in the light of specific formative features. The most common form of drawing test is referred to as the House-Tree-Person which asks the subject to pencil draw the three figures as best they can. Drawing the family is also a common procedure in the assessment of children and one can interpret the order of the family, who is standing next to whom, positioning of the figures, size dimensions as well as qualitative features such as expression and differentiation. There are clinical guides available that suggest specific hypotheses for particular features of the drawings. For example, does the house have windows, a door and appear welcoming? Does the tree have a knot hole, commonly thought to reflect psychic trauma? Is the person squeezed into a corner or is there a confident use of the available space? Again, these are simply hypotheses and whether these indications can be said to mean anything in respect to the particular subject's mental functioning depends on the entire context of the clinical appraisal. As with the TAT, there are refinements that expand on the drawing task. For instance, some assessors may ask the subject to draw a feeling, or action or use coloured pencils or crayons which can add a further dimension to the analysis.

Fortunately, there are structured and standardized instruments available and these can be defined as tests in the specific sense of the word. These are the second major group of personality tests. The most common such clinical measures is the MMPI (Minnesota Multiphasic Personality Inventory) which is the psychological test most commonly used in courts.[4] In the psychological world, it is in a league of its own in terms of established validity and relevance to many situations that arise in a forensic setting.

Although the MMPI was originally standardized on a mostly white middle class rural Minnesota sample in the 1940s, it was the first personality questionnaire developed by empirical methods that led to the development of scales focusing on abnormal behaviour. Having developed the scales, the authors, Hathaway and McKinley, were able to compare how various psychiatric groups such as depressives, schizophrenics, and manic depressives, among others, responded to the 566 true-false questions. This allowed the authors to analyze specific behavioural correlates that accompanied high scores on each scale. The combination of scale scores, expressed as a profile, could then be analyzed and compared to normative groups.

Adding to its validity, the MMPI contained several scales measuring response bias or test-taking attitude that could identify subjects who were either excessively defensive and "faking good" or excessively maladjusted and "faking bad". Thousands of well-designed studies and years of clinical usage have added to the wealth of data available on this test and have honed its clinical utility in forensic settings.

In 1989, a revised form of the MMPI, the MMPI-2, was made available and designed for use with adults 18 years and older. Although there is much continuity with the older test, the MMPI-2 has a modernized item pool and was standardized on a much larger contemporary sample that reflected American society as a whole. Psychometric weaknesses of the MMPI, especially the lack of percentile parity between scales, was eliminated in the modern version.

4 Lubin, B., Larsen, R.M. and Matarazzo, J. (1984), "Patterns of psychological test usage in the United States", *American Psychologist,* 39: 451-454.

Unless there is a special reason for using the old instrument, all forensic evaluations should now employ the MMPI-2.[5]

The MMPI-2 is easy to administer and is available in various booklet formats as well as special forms for the handicapped. It usually takes between one and one and a half hours to complete. The subject is asked to answer the questions as honestly as possible and to answer in terms of the current moment — that is how they feel and think today. The psychologist can easily score the test through a series of transparencies that contain the standard and supplementary scales that are commonly employed. The psychologist then interprets the profile by first judging its clinical validity and, secondly, given that it is not an invalid profile, incorporating a knowledge of each scale in relation to others to build a pertinent interpretation. Like any psychological measure, there is a rudimentary degree of interpretation and books to assist in this process. On the other hand, a true expert has many years' experience working with the instrument and can use the test in a specific context to understand many adjustment and personality factors that bear on the matter at hand.

There are scoring services available that will provide computer-generated MMPI-2 interpretations that may be sufficient for certain clinical settings including forensic ones. One positive feature of these services is that they make clerical errors unlikely and may provide scores on many more scales than can be reasonably derived by hand. The psychologist may have to explain, however, how they are certain that the profile and report are from the subject in question. If the assessor does choose to employ a computer-generated analysis, however, then it is essential that this be indicated in the psycho-legal report. The computer interpretation is often detailed but it must be kept in mind that these are simply hypotheses that need to be confirmed in terms of a complete analysis of all available material and extra sources of information.

In providing psychological assessments in custody cases, the MMPI-2 is extremely useful. It can provide valuable information about the openness and flexibility of a parent who is asking to be named primary custodian of a child. It can readily spot antisocial trends and emotional vulnerabilities that would likely impact on the capacity to parent. It can also help highlight strengths and allow the

5 As far as we know, there is no French translation yet available for the MMPI-2 and francophone subjects may still be required to use the MMPI.

assessor to measure capacity for insight and a willingness to maintain a balanced and mature approach to interpersonal relations. Hence, the test can help ascertain the credibility and maturity of the litigant and, in the context of other information sources, can be a valuable predictor of post-divorce conduct and parenting potential. In this regard, although the test is not specifically designed with custody disputants in mind, it can generate useful hypotheses that often bear on the legal matters at hand.

Adults caught in the tensions of a custody dispute sometimes go to great lengths to create a certain impression. Bluntly put, they are afraid to incriminate themselves by admitting to traits or problems that might blemish their image in the assessor's eyes. When these tendencies are at extreme, the profile validity may be so skewed as to render it invalid. Even when the clinician believes that the profile still has meaning, the need to exaggerate a favourable presentation over an accurate one is correlated with certain character traits. There are two particular scales that are most sensitive to these trends known as the L and K scales, respectively. The former is elevated in people who cannot admit to even minor flaws or failings and who claim near moral perfection. The K scale is less obvious and can be elevated in those individuals who possess an outstanding need to view themselves as well adjusted.

It is very rare, in a custody case where parents wish to put their best foot forward, that the issue of exaggerating problems or feigning mental illness will be met. If it did happen to occur, it would most likely be associated with a third validity scale designated as the F scale which would be greatly elevated and beyond a reasonable limit. Unless that person was confused or quite pathological in their make up, severe elevations on this scale could predict malingering or faked maladjustment. Most often, in the context of high L and K scales, the F value is very low, consistent with a response pattern that minimizes problems.

Having digested the response pattern of the subject taking the test, the clinician proceeds to an analysis of the clinical scales. There are ten standard clinical scales and numerous supplementary scales that are used at the discretion of the examiner. Once the scales are individually examined, the combination of scales and profile configurations are factored into the analysis.

The MMPI-2 profile contains a normal range which for all scales is between the 50th and 65th percentile. Scales are most clearly interpretable if they are above the normal limit or below it. If an interpretation is made, the lawyer should ask whether the scale elevation in fact exceeds the normal limit or is so low as to be also clinically significant. This is extremely important as interpretations will often be made even if a scale approximates clinical significance or if it is the highest scale overall in the overall profile. There is a major difference, though, between a profile elevation well into the pathological range and one that hugs the upper limit but still remains within normal values. This should be clearly communicated by the psychologist in the written report of results through use of qualifying terms such as "tendency towards" or "near significance".

It may be important at this juncture to mention several procedural issues that might be addressed by a lawyer in cross-examination:

- Who gave the instructions to the subject and what instructions were given? If this is not the psychologist but a third party, perhaps a clinical support staff person, then it may be useful to know their training and how the psychologist ensured that adequate instructions were given. The proper instructions to the MMPI-2 are for the subject to attempt to answer all questions and to provide a true response if it is mostly true and a false response if it is mostly false. The subject should consider their responses from the perspective of the present — that is how one feels today.
- If the psychologist does not specify, was the MMPI-2 administered or the MMPI? Although the new version is clinically comparable to the old, there are definite improvements in standardization as well as modernization of the item pool that make it a much preferable choice. Unless, there is a specific reason why the older test is administered, then the standard procedure in the field is to administer the MMPI-2.

In the MMPI-2 normative study, efforts were made to include diverse ethnic and regional backgrounds in the standardization sample. In fact, the MMPI has been translated into many languages and is used around the world. Consequently, the issue may be less one of culture than of language. If only an English version is available, for instance, and the subject is an allophone whose English is not especially fluent, then some caution should be in order to make certain that the subject understood all the questions.

- If the psychologist has used a computer-based interpretive report in litigation, then the lawyer may be wise to ask the expert whether all the descriptions given in the computer report actually describe the subject of the assessment. If not, then how has the psychologist made the decision as to what applied and what did not? Hopefully, the psychologist has not simply included every statement and observation, some of which will clearly not be pertinent to the subject in question. A personal analysis of a profile takes into account impressions gained from other sources that help to texturize the specific meaning of the profile with the nuances that arise from individual differences.

(iv) Alternative Testing Approaches

The future for psychological assessment in custody and access litigation will likely include standardized procedures that are developed specifically for the task of custody determination. Two quantitative approaches have been developed by B. Bricklin as well as by M.J. Ackerman and K. Schoendorf.[6] For example, one of the Bricklin tests requires the child to answer 64 questions concerning each parent's competence, support, reliability and the degree to which they possess positive traits. The parent who scores the highest on a numerical scale is considered to be the child's choice as preferred custodian.

Although such test instruments show promise in further objectifying custody evaluations, the validity of such data must await further experience and experimentation. One of the problems in developing such empirical methods is the question of what criteria to use in validating such scales. For instance, should the standard be judges' decisions, relitigation or other outcome measures taken at some point in the future. This addresses a fundamental weakness in the court system in that it presumes a good judicial decision without any clear way to measure the impact of that decision on future family adjust-

6 Bricklin, Barry (1984), *Bricklin Perceptual Scales*, Furlong, PA, Village Publishing; Ackerman, M.J. and Schoendorf, K. (1992), *The Ackerman-Schoendorf Parent Evaluation for Custody Tests (ASPECT)*, Los Angeles, Western Psychological Services.

ment. Test development is never an easy task and it is especially difficult in the custody/access field to measure the "success" of one decision or another. Sometimes, as we know, it is a matter of least detriment or a choice between options each with negative aspects.

(v) Summary

Among the mental health professions, psychologists are perhaps best identified with psychological tests and psychological assessments. In the 100 years or so of test history, these skills have proven very effective in many different domains from psychiatry to education to industry. In the realm of custody evaluations, both objective and projective personality measures have been successfully employed and evidence from these sources are readily accepted by the courts. The major advantage these tests can offer in the right hands is an independent and sensitive appraisal that focuses on a purely psychological dimension that stands apart from any particular child's or parent's subjective view. Used appropriately, these measures can highlight the important qualities of the person that are a reflection of character more than immediate events.

Of all these tests, perhaps one stands out as the single most widely used instrument in this class and this is the Minnesota Multiphasic Personality Inventory or MMPI. The capacity of this test to assess basic honesty and reliability of responding has given it an important advantage in the clinical psychology field. Being "objective" it can be readily interpreted by most trained psychologists, although true expertise is hard won and depends on an in-depth knowledge of the test profile.

Replying to the criticism that psychological tests are too general for the specific context of custody/access assessments, a number of other approaches have evolved to fill the gap. Custody questionnaires and more standardized procedures for assessing parental competency have been proposed as the route to follow. Additionally, and a new development in the test construction enterprise, certain batteries or combinations of procedures have also been created that are specifically aimed at custody and access issues. These should be considered preliminary at the moment but likely represent the future for psychological testing in this complicated area.

We have endeavoured in this section to emphasize that assessment is a more advanced notion than testing although tests can be an important part of psychological assessment. This component should not be idealized, however, either by the mental health professional or the lawyer and there should be ample room for appropriate scrutiny. Test usage should not be indiscriminate and the assessor should be able to support why a specific measure was used and to what extent its results can be trusted.

4. ASSESSMENT OF THE CHILDREN

(a) Preliminary Issues

Having provided a pertinent description of the parents in terms of their histories, personalities and views of the children, the assessor should then address the personalities and needs of the children and their respective relationships to the parents.

In general considerations of the task, there are two separate currents that must be balanced when assessing children of divorce. First, a child will likely gravitate to the parent who is perceived as most attuned to their needs. Secondly, and in contradiction, children can be highly influenced by a parent and will comply with a parent's wishes if they feel that their security is at risk otherwise. Fears of abandonment are ubiquitous in children of divorce despite the reassurances of their parents that it is only adults that do this to other adults! The most powerful examples of such a polarizing process occur, for instance, in cases of parental alienation where a child will refuse any contact with one parent due to intense psychological pressure from the other who, in turn, usually denies adamantly any such intention. It is best to view these currents as two opposing vectors that operate at different strengths in each situation. The assessor's task, at least in part, is to differentiate these proportions.

The situation is also complicated by the fact that cultural and biopsychological factors have favoured the primacy of motherhood, especially during the early childhood years. Fathers who oppose mothers for custody of young children not only must prove their own capability as a primary parent but must also overcome the natural preference for mothers in the early years. This is not a simple attitudinal bias but reflects a major cultural phenomenon. Most often, even in intact families, no matter what arrangement may exist in theory regarding child care, in practice it is mothers who become the primary caretakers. Research on two-parent families where the mother does not work outside the home suggests that fathers spend about 20 to 25 per cent as much time as mothers in one to one interaction with their children.[7] Moreover, mothers are more inclined to take the bottom line responsibility for child care as compared to just being involved. This translates into a culture of motherhood that influences the self perception of parents as well as of children. It might be acceptable to view motherhood as more primal than fatherhood which is not at all the same as saying that mothers are better parents than fathers. In any case, such role and identity distinctions in society are naturally mirrored by the courts.

Modern life has also added to the varieties of family structures and has additionally complicated matters for assessors and the courts. Women are as likely to be working at a job as compared to staying in the home. This has led to an enormous reliance on substitute care givers. The large numbers of single parents, mainly mothers but also including fathers, has also changed the expectations of both sexes. The joint custody and feminist movements have also had their impact on harmonizing the sexes which led to the blurring of gender role stereotypes that more than ever are viewed as outmoded. These societal trends, however, are not unopposed and they have become sources of debate and reflection. In varying proportions, depending on the mentality and ideals of the family in question, all of these factors may play some part in the real life issues of a custody dispute.

As to the relative competence of mothers and fathers in child care, the research seems helpful in dispelling the notion that there is some intrinsic evolutionary bias. Although mothers are more associated with child raising, fathers can be equally as good as parents. Interestingly, they are as proficient with new born children and can be as

7 Lamb, M.E., Pleck, J., Charnov, E.L. and Levine, J.A. (1987), "A biopsychological perspective on paternal behavior and involvement", in *Parenting Across the Life Span*, J.B. Lancaster, J. Altman, A. Rossi and L.R. Sherrod (eds.), Chicago: Aldine, at 111-142.

qualified dealing with infants as are mothers.[8] Nevertheless, if the mother provides the greater portion of the care, then she will likely become better at it and more sensitive to the children's needs. In this case, the gap in confidence levels between fathers and mothers continues to grow with time but is not irremediable. If circumstances arise that require fathers to become better parents or more involved, they can do so without any more difficulty than that experienced by mothers.[9] Hence, it is not an uncommon observation that father-child relationships evolve considerably after divorce and fathers faced with the loss of their families will redefine their roles as parents sometimes to the chagrin of the ex-spouse. In general, though, it remains more likely that even in these situations, the mother's and father's role may be distinguished, not by extent of involvement or accessibility but by the mother's more natural tendency to accept primary responsibility for child care, a role that is consistent with the legal definition of custody.

(b) Specific Assessment Procedures

Assessors differ in approach to this segment of the assessment depending on their own clinical training and perspective. For those professionals whose primary training has been child oriented, this component may be the most intricate and detailed. They may well show great interest in analyzing the parent-child interactions and the adequacy of the parent's responses to the child's needs as well as the quality of the relationship. For other assessors, a more general overview of the child's developmental and emotional status may suffice with the assessor's aim being to seek evidence of specific problems or needs that should be addressed through recommendations. In either case, however, assessors will seek intriguing ways to elicit psychological material even in preschool children.

---

8 Parke, R.D. and Tinsley, B.R. (1981), "The father's role in infancy: Determiniants of involvement in caretaking and play", in *The role of the Father in Child Development*, M.E. Lamb (ed.), New York: Wiley, at 429-458.

9 Lamb, M.E. and Oppenheim, D. (1989), "Fatherhood and father-child relationships: five years of research", in *Fathers and Their Families*, S. Cath, A. Gurwitt and L. Gunsberg (eds.), Hillsdale: The Analytic Press, at 11-26.

It is important to convey, though, that the assessor is interested in much more than the child's preference for one parent over the other. In pre-teen and older children, preference is a factor to consider strongly but families are a complicated array of forces and what a child expresses as preference may have deeper implications. Best interests of the child and the child's preference could well be different although they may also coincide. The assessor will tend to be on firmer ground in supporting a child's preference when a deeper understanding of the child's psyche and needs allow for a more sensitive analysis of what is best. Of course the situation can arise when an older child or teenager insists on a certain preference even though the assessor may view this as contrary to the child's best interest. As an example, this actually occurred in one family in which there were four children, three of whom were teens. The youngest child was a pre-teen boy and remained closest to his mother although very much in need of a strong father alliance. There were two teenage sons and one, in particular, insisted on living with the father who had left the marriage for a new relationship. There was only one spare bedroom at the father's new residence and this precluded the other two sons from staying over with any frequency. Although the son who took the initiative was vocal in his preference, he overshadowed his brothers who had no less need of their father. The assessor wrote that the best interests of the children were not met by having one son occupy a place the other's could not share. The more dominant son held to his position though, and the parents proved unable to make use of this part of the recommendations.

There is a definite difference between evaluating a very young pre-school child as compared to an older school age child. For example, the younger the child the more the assessor will rely on play techniques and the less on structured interviews or test data. Even with older children, the use of projective techniques often helps the assessor to derive a picture of the child's thoughts and perceptions. The child is able in such situations to project their psychic concerns into the play or test situation and not be influenced or intimidated by direct, anxiety provoking questions. In working with children who are sensitive to the politics of divorce, fears of alienating one parent or showing preference may be associated with excruciating anxiety. This need for absolute parity can even be seen in grown children of divorce who feel compelled to treat their parents symmetrically.

As best interests of the child are very much influenced by special factors that come into play, psychological, educational or medical factors might very well influence a custody/access recommendation. For example, an anxious or vulnerable child whose tendency is to regress in the face of the parents' conflict may profit from a more stable base with shorter, frequent visits with the non-custodial parent as compared to longer access periods that can be more disruptive. As a second example, a child with a learning disability may well benefit from an uninterrupted school week without access that could interfere with school progress. Finally, a child with epilepsy may require a schedule for visitation that is sensitive to the child's need for rest and appropriate "down times".

In all cases of child assessment, certain basic information is mandatory in building a comprehensive view of the child and their place in the family and at school. This would include: (1) developmental history, (2) an analysis of parent-child relationships, (3) child management and discipline issues, (4) description of the child's personality, (5) some understanding of the child's relationships outside the family, (6) parents' concerns about the child, (7) the child's adjustment to school and academics, (8) health issues, and (9) the history of custody/access since the separation in terms of how the child has fared overall. Most of this information is derived from interviews with the parents who are also given the opportunity to reveal how deep their understanding is of their child as compared to only sentiment and affection.

Most often, the assessor will endeavour to observe the parent and child in interaction either in a natural home environment during a home visit or in an office or observation room setting. The assessor will attempt to examine the style of parental engagement and the response of the child to that parent. At times it is possible to view how the parent responds to the child's concerns and needs and whether the child conveys a sense of confidence or ease with that parent. Needless to say, evaluations are stressful on parents and the assessor should take into account the artificiality of the situation as well as the anxiety that often permeates it. On the other hand, one can often perceive the model of parenting adopted by that parent and how the parent perceives their own involvement. For instance, one father made bacon and eggs during a home visit while another helped his child play games on the computer. One mother sat confidently in the living room and allowed the assessor to shape the visit while still being at the centre of the household; another seemed to orchestrate her children's activities and made certain that they were drawing pictures with equal numbers of crayons. This becomes very useful information when weighed in the context of other observations and data.

The assessor may consider several key factors in observing the style of relationship between parents and child as well as between siblings. Examples include:

- Does the parent encourage spontaneity or conformity?
- Is the parent responsive to the child or more interested in creating an impression?
- Does the child seem comfortable and confident with the parent?
- Does the parent feel comfortable and confident with the child?
- Does the parent attempt to shape or control the child's verbalizations?
- Does the parent provide firm boundaries that still encourage relaxation and openness for the child?

There are numerous assessment tools available and most assessors will employ some method to increase rapport and communication with the child. Drawings of the family as well as other projective drawing techniques are particularly useful in this regard. Creating family scenes in play or using structured story telling techniques also help to elucidate important information.[10] Another common device is sentence completion tasks which have the child complete a thought or phrase that begins a sentence. In addition, there are apperception tests which present drawings of scenes to children who are asked to use the stimulus to create a story. Assessors favour those questions or tools that provide a child with a non-threatening format in which to make their feelings and developmental issues known. This is no doubt in response to the frequent concern that young children especially are easily influenced and their "testimony" may be contaminated and unreliable. By using family drawings or imaginative story telling techniques, the assessor can plumb the child's attitudes and emotional structure without tipping the child off to the fact that this has a bearing

10 Miller, T.W. and Veltkamp, L.J. (1986), "Use of fables in clinical assessment of contested child custody", *Child Psychiatry and Human Development*, 16: 274-284.

on the dispute between their parents. The more conscious the child is of the relevance of a question to the parental conflict, the more the child may feel restrained and unable to respond freely. This is why projective and play-oriented methods have such a valuable place in the child custody assessment.

Naturally, older children may feel very strained if they are asked to differentiate or decide between their parents and loyalty issues may confound the process. Younger children may not easily understand complex questions and they can be easily coached or influenced. If a child is asked how they are disciplined at each home, they may find it threatening to admit that one parent makes them uncomfortable or scared. The assessor must be truthful with a child and not promise a confidentiality that is then not respected in the final report. On the other hand, it is perfectly legitimate to inform the child that a report will be written but that it can be kept very general and non-specific. In this respect, the assessor might say to a ten-year-old child: "Although I do have to write a report and I will have to say some things about you, I will not say anything to embarrass you or write anything that you would not want your parents to know that you said." This is often helpful in relaxing tense children who can feel caught between their parents or fear insulting a parent whose retaliation they may fear.

Through interviews, the parents' views of the child can be gathered and compared. It can be helpful to note the accuracy of the parent's knowledge of the child and of the child's needs. This includes evaluating the capacity of the parent to separate their own needs from that of the child, an aptitude that is not always prevalent in these matters. For instance, a mother may suggest that the father's influence is disruptive and stressful for the child whereas this may well describe her own reaction to the visits. On the other hand, another mother may grasp an essential part of the child's personality that is crucial to that child's adjustment whereas the father may be unaware and dismissing of his ex-wife's perceptions.

Through contact with teachers, especially after they have known the child through a good portion of the school year, one may garner a perspective of the child that is illuminating. Caregivers, especially those in day care centres and other professional settings, can also be excellent collateral resources for the assessor although the accuracy and neutrality of the opinion must never be taken for granted. It is important that the assessor communicate directly with the teacher or caregiver and not through one or the other parent. There is often a difference in openness, for example, between teachers who can privately convey impressions about a student without parental interference and the teacher who must communicate through a parent who insists on being the intermediary between the assessor and the school.

During the actual interview with the child, and depending on the child's age, the assessor may inquire about their feelings and points of view. In all cases, though, the rapport between assessor and child must be sufficient for the child to answer frankly. Examples of questions that may be posed to the school age child include the following:

- What is it like having your parents living apart?
- Do you remember what it was like before?
- What do you understand about why your parents are no longer together?
- Tell me about your mother? father?
- What do you enjoy most about your time with mother? father?
- What would you like to change about your mother? father?
- How does your mother/father show that he/she loves you?
- What happens when you get in trouble for doing something wrong at mother's? father's?
- Who is your best friend and what do the two of you do together?
- Do you have any difficulties with friends at school or at home?
- Whom do you talk to when you have a problem or are feeling unhappy?
- What do you do when you are with one parent and feel lonely for the other?
- How do you feel when your parents meet together?
- Do you find yourself thinking about your family's problems? When? What kinds of thoughts do you have?
- Are you having trouble with your sleep? Do you feel tense or have butterflies in your stomach?

Of course, certain children are more willing to communicate openly than others and the assessor must go with the flow. It is common, though, for a child to find some medium where he or she can communicate distress. This is not always verbally and sometimes drawings say much more than words. In one case, for example, a young boy of seven refused to include his mother in the family drawing but never offered a word of criticism regarding her. In this case, however, the mother was profoundly disorganized and the home was in serious disarray. In another, a small boy of four had not seen his corpulent father for several months due to much discord. The boy used doll figures to create a family with his mother present in the consulting room. At one point, he seemed to lose the father doll and asked his mother where "he" had gone. When the mother related that the daddy doll was behind the chair, the little boy exclaimed loudly and clearly, "No, the big fat one!"

(c) Home Visits

Home visits can be a very useful medium in which to observe children in their natural context. The assessor can act as a participant-observer for a brief time and by so doing glean a great deal of first hand impression about the family. The home reflects the ambiance of the parental environment and, in particular, whether the home is child oriented and responsive to the demands of child rearing. How a home is organized may provide valuable information about how that parent conceptualizes child development and how they aim to meet their children's needs though the physical environment. Moreover, the home visit can also elicit information about sibling relationships and parent-child modes of interaction. In this regard, the child in their home context is more likely to engage the parent in a natural way and to require some intervention from the parent. This is especially true with very young children who are best observed in their home where their personalities will be more naturally revealed. Finally, the home visit can also be helpful in preparing a child for an office visit and establishes an initial rapport between the child and the assessor.

By inspecting the child's bedroom, the assessor can perceive an aspect of the child's self expression as well as the parent's recognition and facilitation of the child's identity. It is not simply a question of material comforts but more specifically, the extent to which the child has elaborated their own private space in personal terms with possessions, drawings, creations, photographs or other collectibles of personal worth. Does the child have a hobby, a stamp collection for example, or some activity in their lives that reflects self investment and self discovery? Is the room functional as compared to self expressive? Is everything of interest crammed into a cupboard or is there an effort to display the identity and interests of the child? Are there books and what types? Is it a room designed by and suited for an adult or does it reflect a child's needs and perspective?

The assessor may utilize the home visit to explore the rapport and understanding between parent and child. Can the parent be natural during the visit and sufficiently confident to allow the visit to be spontaneous? Is it a child-oriented home where the child focus is spread about the dwelling? In contrast, is it an adult home with a child's bedroom added on and where the child space is obviously restricted? Such questions suggest that the home environment can join in the communication and reflect psychological features that are useful for the assessor to know.

Home visits are obligatory whenever there is any question about the physical environment in which a child lives or visits. They may be less important, at least in terms of comparison, if one parent has remained in the family home while the other is residing in temporary quarters or a newly rented apartment. Teenage children may not appreciate a home visit and may feel uneasy about allowing a stranger to view their bedroom. Often, however, a child feels most comfortable in their own bedroom and the rapport is deepened when an adult/assessor takes a sincere interest. As noted above, very young children in the pre-school years are best seen in the home environment even if office visits are subsequently arranged.

Occasionally, the home visit yields extraordinary information. During one occasion, a mother would not allow the assessor to enter the basement because this was the only room not cleaned for the assessment. The upper floor was rigidly ordered from the pillows on the sofa to the dining room chairs. Each of the two girls in the family had one toy available to play with during the visit and the mother choreographed the children's movements. Nevertheless, as the visit proceeded, the children's activity level increased rapidly and the mother's control unraveled before the assessor's eyes. One child hurt the family cat and the younger sibling jumped on the furniture. The mother threatened but was unable to assert meaningful control over these hyper-tense girls.

(d) Conclusion

In conclusion, it is apparent that through interviews with parents, observation techniques, child interviews, psychological testing, and discussion with teachers and other involved professionals, a picture of the child will emerge that is essential knowledge for the process at hand. The lawyer reading the report should observe that a combination of these procedures was employed and that the assessor has not relied on only one source of knowledge. Hence, a psychologist/assessor who administered, as a matter of course, a battery of psychological tests without really talking to the child or observing the parent-child interaction may not be in the best position to know that child or their needs. This is especially true if the testing procedures chosen are only indirectly relevant to the custody and access context. Likewise, an assessment that relied only on child-parent observation could also be seen as incomplete.

A further guiding principle, it seems, is that the assessment procedures must be suitable to the age and developmental stage of the child. Direct questioning of a three-year-old, for example, would likely be highly unreliable as would basing a child assessment of a 14-year-old solely on drawings or story telling techniques. The assessor should reveal an understanding of developmental theory and an appreciation of the impact of divorce on children of various ages.

Above all, an assessor should be able to differentiate between the psychic reality and material reality of the child. Psychic reality exists in the register of emotional life and is a product of real experience as well as internal factors, such as motivation, level of development, conflict and psychological defences. As an example, a three-year-old child observing a sexual scene between his or her parents may interpret what is occurring as violent even though the external reality is quite different. Yet, the child may well be affected by this perception even though it is psychic and not material truth. As another example, a five-year-old girl may compose stories that put her mother in a bad light not because her mother is evil but because of rivalry feelings incited by a recent marital separation. A hundred years of clinical work and research has taught us that memory and perception is malleable and affected by conflicts, pressures and fantasy. This is not license to disbelieve a child but it is certainly not license to conclude that children's reporting is always a direct imprint of objective experience.

Assessment of a child must always, therefore, be made in a developmental context so that issues related to development and psychic reality are carefully screened for what they actually indicate about external facts. Hence, a three-year-old who has problems in transition between mother's and father's home is probably reflecting an age appropriate response that is independent of the quality of relationship with any parent. Likewise, a little boy of four who has seen his father only on occasion in a 12-month period can be forgiven if he displays negative behaviour after a visit. At the same time, a child who expresses fear of a parent with documented emotional problems should not be dismissed as overreacting simply because that parent has done nothing specific to harm the child. Such nuances of meaning and interpretation make it clear that there is much more complexity involved in assessing these matters than simply determining truth or fiction. Even fiction betrays a deeper truth that may go a long way to understanding what is really important to a child.

Finally, the assessor should recognize that children inherently wish to love both their parents and they are unlikely to mirror their parents' splits. An experienced assessor would not directly ask a child with whom they prefer to live simply because this would violate the child's need and right of neutrality. Moreover, it could cause considerable guilt if the child felt ultimately responsible for a decision that denied one parent the much desired custodial role. Finally, it would lead the child and parents to equate best interest with preference which would be a gross over simplification of the complexity of the matter at hand.

Although courts, like assessors, are inclined to listen to an older child's point of view, it must be the role of the capable and responsible adults to ultimately recommend on the child's behalf. Hence, although assessors will not ask a child for a statement of preference, they are not opposed to listening to a child who speaks spontaneously and with authenticity. It is essential, however, to determine what the motivation of the child might be in taking such a stand. For instance, a child may express a preference to live with the mother simply because of a conflict with a sibling. Or, as another example, a daughter may indicate a preference to live with a father because the mother has a new boyfriend whereas the father is alone with no one to look after him. In both of these examples, expressed preference is based on spurious grounds and it would be erroneous to interpret these as *bona fide* choices.

On the other hand, a child may consistently feel more comfortable in the care of one parent over the other or feel extremely reluctant to change environments. In the latter case, preference may not be as much a matter of choice of parent as it is a choice of where to live. This is especially important in the case of older children and teenagers.

5. EXTERNAL (COLLATERAL) CONSULTATIONS

The role of collateral sources in a family assessment is to provide secondary information as to the functioning or needs of one of the family members. In contrast, the primary knowledge of the parents or children should be obtained exclusively through direct observation and evaluation by the assessor. In other words, collateral information should supplement a psychological assessment and not replace the clinical/analytic function of the assessor. The external consultation, in this regard, provides the assessor with an independent source of information and a further point of view.

There are good reasons why an assessment cannot be reduced to a collation of various opinions about a parent or child. First, one would not need an experienced assessor to do what amounts to a polling of opinions. Secondly, one would have no ability to assess the merits of these opinions or whether they were objective or accurate. This raises the important issue of who the assessor should speak to in preparing an assessment.

Mainly, the assessor is interested in consulting with those sources most likely to be neutral and objective and who are not allied with one side or the other in the custody dispute. Doctors, teachers, social workers, police and professional care givers are the sources most frequently consulted. The general principle is that these collateral sources should represent trusted individuals in the position to make an independent contribution towards the overall understanding of the family. Inappropriate collateral sources include all those who, either by kin or relationship, are likely to be polarized in the dispute or unlikely to make an uncontaminated contribution. Although in litigation neighbours and relatives may be called upon to testify, the means exist for the court to test the merits of this evidence. For an assessor to do so is rarely of value as objectivity is impossible to ascertain and the chances of contamination are high.

This restriction should also extend to psychotherapists or counsellors especially when clinical intervention depends on a strong therapeutic bond. A therapist with doubts or reservations about their patient as a parent may be unwilling to be frank with the assessor, especially if these comments are likely to be recorded in the assessor's final report. Besides, therapists and counsellors are not required to be objective evaluators in their clinical role. Therapists work through the medium of empathy and it would be at cross purposes to cast judgment on the patient's personality or potential. This may be less true if the therapist only saw the couple prior to the separation as the allegiance is less intense and the therapeutic role more suited to studying the interaction.

One possibility to avoid certain impediments is for the assessor to offer a general confidentiality regarding the therapist's input in order to allow more openness and frankness. This can also be helpful for other health professionals, such as physicians, who must face the patient beyond the assessment and continue in their healing role. The assessor can recount in the report that the consultation took place but can leave out any specific details that would interfere or compromise the therapeutic relationship in the future.

There does seem to be an unsettling tendency for health professionals, among others, to write supportive letters for divorcing patients in which they draw inferences about the other spouse. This cannot be a positive step as the therapist would likely not have met or evaluated that person and will only view them through the eyes of their patient. Not all psychotherapists seem to understand that what they are privy to is psychic reality that is no less important than historical truth but belongs to a different domain of experience. Hence, if a patient complains bitterly about their spouse to a therapist, it is not inconsequential but neither should these perceptions be presented as an objective estimate of the spouse's character.

Moreover, some litigants will engage a mental health professional with the strategic aim of furthering their own cause in a dispute. In this regard, they may ostensibly consult about the well being of children or about improving their parenting skills or degree of attunement. These parents will be intent on building an alliance and will be quick to solicit favourable letters and support from the therapist for their cause. Many well meaning but naïve professionals surprisingly are willing to be used for these purposes although therapeutic neutrality and caution would lead the experienced clinician to stay far removed.

As cases differ in their clinical demand, this component of the evaluation may assume various degrees of importance. Some consultation, however, is generally useful in almost all assessments. In a custody assessment where violence or sexual impropriety has been alleged, these consultations, especially with police or social agencies, often prove invaluable. The assessor has the opportunity to trace the history of a contact and to address the impression or experience that the agency has had with the parent or family in question.

Physicians, as well, can be an excellent resource to the assessor as they will have their own experience gained in a neutral context. Private care givers may or may not be independent sources of information and they are often partial to one side or the other. The larger professional day care centres staffed with early childhood educators, in contrast, will often prove very helpful in the evaluation of young children. Teachers, of course, are usually an important source of information and they are in a unique position to observe a child and sense their moods and temperament. Besides academic information, they are often able to gauge the involvement of both parents in the school life of the child as well as the child's relation to the family seen from the school's perspective. Hygiene and basic home organization may also be apparent to an observant teacher. Besides telephone and personal interviews, specialized questionnaires are available that can assist a teacher in communicating the nuances of behaviour and academics that are important for an assessor to know.

The failure to consult important external sources can represent a significant limitation in certain cases. It is conceivable that a reliable source may be able to offer pertinent feedback that could influence the conclusion reached in a major way. For instance, police and child protection services who have extensive experience in rooting out antisocial adult conduct can be an important independent source of information in matters of assault and abuse allegations. Likewise, a perceptive teacher may describe a certain parent-child interaction that is inappropriate and adds to the strain a child may be under. By excluding some collateral consultation, the assessor runs the risk, therefore, of omitting useful and even vital feedback considering the family in question. Even when it is not crucial, the assessor will still have forfeited an additional contribution that adds to the multi-source vista of the custody evaluation.

Perhaps the most serious failure, though, occurs when an assessor misconstrues the purpose of collateral consultation and speaks to those who are obviously polarized in their stance, including these comments as if it was reliable feedback. Interviewing a parent's best friend for a character reference, for example, would fall into this category of inappropriate consultation. In our experience, assessors who cannot distinguish neutral from biased sources are either biased themselves and lack the requisite neutrality to complete a proper assessment or are professionally ill equipped to pursue the task.

There are possible exceptions to this guideline and one might meet a circumstance where interviewing an obviously biased source could be perceived as useful. In the example that follows, the assessor saw merit in this approach but in hindsight recognized that it put the assessment seriously in question as it dipped too close to the warring parties. In this case, a man related that his whole street stood firmly against his wife in their custody dispute and he provided two damning affidavits that described his wife in a very negative light. As he appeared to be intensely competitive to a fault, the wife was provided an equal opportunity to locate neighbours who might speak on her behalf. The rationale, then, was to test his premise that the affidavits he had obtained represented a neighbourhood consensus rather than two polarized opinions in support of his cause. The risk for the assessor, however, born out in this example, is that it can increase the polarization of the conflict and entangle the assessor in the discord. Consequently, although we can note that exceptions may arise, it is best to restrict consultation to those whose neutrality is unquestioned and whose contribution is likely to be independent.

A final comment concerns the stage in the assessment at which external sources should be consulted. Most assessors would agree that these consultations are best done after the assessor has some personal knowledge of the family but not after conclusions and recommendations are firmly reached. The major principle, in this respect, is that the assessment should emanate from the assessor's primary knowledge and consultations should be supplemental and clarifying. To speak with external sources at a preliminary stage of the assessment might be more interfering than helpful. Equally important, the assessor can only maximize the precision of their questions in the latter stages of the evaluation. Moreover, the information from the collateral source is best interpreted or understood in a context derived from the assessor's own investigative process.

In summary, the multisource evaluation almost always involves some external consultation. This is part and parcel of the good assessment. Interviewing collateral sources provides an independent source of feedback that is often helpful to the assessor in their task. Moreover, it also provides a further reality check on the issues and concerns derived from the primary evaluation.

6. THE PSYCHOLEGAL REPORT

The psycholegal report that all assessors prepare fulfills the professional obligation to communicate the pertinent information and interpretations that led to the conclusions reached. Although some assessors have enlarged their scope of practice to include negotiated settlement even during a *de facto* assessment, the essential requirement and importance of the report should not be forgotten. Even when a mediated solution appears in reach, the assessor is obligated to provide a meaningful and detailed report of the findings. Then, if the momentum of conflict derails an apparent mediated solution in the last minute, as is often the case, the availability of the report will not negate the entire exercise.

The report, in this regard, represents the recording and distillation of all data and observations and should adequately reflect the breadth and depth of the assessment process. Hence, a five-page report summarizing fifteen hours of evaluation would be inadequate to express the full weight of the material gathered in the interests of the assessment. Lawyers and parents put a great deal of weight on these reports and each deserve a comprehensive description of all the relevant facts collected and interpretations made in support of the conclusions. Although there is no minimum length that can be stipulated, the reader, upon reading the report, will have a sense that the assessor listened and analyzed the material in accordance with an accepted clinical method. The depth of the evaluation and the depth of the report will be in balance and, although the conclusions or suggestions may be questioned, the report itself will offer a firm basis to do so. Finally, the report should be sufficiently spelled out that it provides ample opportunity for cross-examination in case of a trial.

The report should be written in a clear and organized manner and employ subheadings to aid the reader in understanding the components of the process. Although some overlap is inevitable, for the most part sections that relate history should be kept separate from sections that are interpretive in content. It can be most confusing, in this regard, when an assessor intersperses interpretations in material that is mostly historical or descriptive.

The first task is to specify what procedures were used in completing the assessment. The report should indicate the hours of individual meetings and with whom they occurred. If psychological tests were administered then these too should be listed and to whom they were given. Home visits, school visits and external consultations should be listed if these occurred. Finally, if written information was obtained or documents, affidavits and other reports were reviewed, then these should also be indicated at the outset.

The second task is to outline the reason for the assessment or, more exact, the statement of the problem as defined by each parent. This represents an initial sortie into the issues that divide the parents and have made the assessment inevitable. This is often an important section as it allows the reader to outline the different perspectives and concerns of each parent and provides the introduction to the material that follows.

The third component of the report is often quite detailed. This reviews the history of the relationship from the outset to its conclusion or breakdown. Assessors may dedicate one section to this topic or review it separately for each parent in order to stress their individual versions and the evolution of their concerns. The assessor is likely to describe in detail how the spouse perceived the relationship and how accurately they could interpret the behaviour of their partner. Indirectly, the assessor is also able to gauge the insight and perspective of the parent and their ultimate flexibility, tolerance and capacity to cooperate.

Having outlined the history of the marriage from both points of view, the assessor will then turn attention to the family and general background of each parent. The assessor will describe in detail the family, educational and vocational history of the parent and point out any major features or traumas that impacted on the parent as a child. The reader may well see a continuity between the family origins of the adult and their behaviour in the marriage. The marital and personal fate of siblings will be described as well as the personalities of parents and major themes of childhood. In this section, as well, the assessor should discuss other significant relationships that antedated the current situation.

If psychological testing was employed then this should be described in its own section. There should be a clear description of the test used, what version if this is applicable, and any details about its administration or interpretation. Each test result should be outlined separately. If the assessor relied upon computer-generated reports then this should be stated as well as how the report has been used in the final analysis. The analysis of the test data should be related to the person in question but it should also be clear to the reader how this has been applied.

Very importantly, if the assessor has relied upon clinical instruments with unknown or restricted empirical validity, then the limitations of the data should also be spelled out. For instance, if the assessor suggests a negative father-son relationship based on drawings of the family, then the tentativeness of this evidence should also be noted. The assessor may add that this was supported by other evidence but the reader should have a clear idea on what basis the conclusions were derived.

Following a comprehensive treatment of the parents, the assessor will then describe what they have learned about each child and the relationship of that child with his or her parents. The assessor will describe the methods used and how the child responded to each situation. Specific details and actual interchanges tend to be more convincing than generalities. The use of quotations is very useful in recounting the substance of an interview. Again, the detail provided must synchronize and support the conclusions and recommendations at the end of the report. Information from teachers and other external sources relevant to the children should be reviewed. Home visits should also be detailed in this section of the report.

The seventh major area concerns collateral consultations. These should be described with sufficient detail to give the thrust of their point of view. Sometimes, the assessor may not wish to undermine a relationship between a parent and the external consultant by detailing all their feedback and, as previously discussed, discretion on the part of the assessor is quite acceptable. In this case, however, the report should specify that only general themes will be described.

Next, if the assessor has reviewed and relied upon written documentation as other than general background, then this should be clarified within the body of the report. Reports from child protection services, health or mental health providers and other directly relevant material may assume importance in an assessment. The lawyer, judge or parent reading the custody report should be made aware of these sources and the meaning or importance ascribed to them.

Finally, following a careful exposition of all the relevant data, the assessor should then provide an overall conclusion that focuses on what has been understood. The assessor may have chosen to offer certain preliminary conclusions about each parent or the children in prior sections, but this final component should address the major questions posed by the assessment. It should not only specify which parent is the recommended custodian but why the assessor has reached this conclusion. In particular, the assessor should communicate those key factors upon which the recommendation for custody turned.

In contrast, a recommendation that seemed unlinked to the body of a report or remained unexplained would not meet the grade and will likely become controversial. In the same vein, a recommendation that seemed at cross purposes from the thrust of the data presented in the report and dangled without apparent rationale would also be questioned.

There is some ambiguity and difference of judicial opinion about what details should be provided in the access and supplemental recommendations. Some judges may view the specification of access and sharing of holidays as being in their purview and they do not welcome the entry of mental health experts in this component. Yet, as many of these disputes are resolved by negotiation or arbitration outside of a court room, it seems only reasonable that the assessor not limit the report's versatility and usefulness. Moreover, by detailing recommendations, the assessor can further clarify for the reader their vision of what would be best for the family in the future.

The recommendations should be very specific. They should remove ambiguity as well as the responsibility of interpretation from the shoulder's of the custodian. They should also provide the non-custodial or accessing parent with the clarity and predictability that they will also require in meeting the needs of their children. Many parents who reach a level of conflict at which an assessment is ordered will often verbalize this requirement as a safeguard against escalating tensions. In the majority of cases, the assessor should assume that flexibility and negotiation between the parents will remain at a minimum for a considerable length of time. Again, this also supports the legal process by providing sufficient detail for the lawyers to try and settle matters based on the thrust of the report.

The recommendations should stipulate the assessor's thoughts on how regular visits and occasions should be divided. These can include:

- Regular access (weekends, including day of commencement and return, times and where child should be returned, if weekend falls on statutory holiday)
- Summer holidays
- Christmas holidays (both the specific Christmas celebration and the school holiday)
- Spring holiday also known as March Break
- Easter Holiday (specifically Good Friday and Easter Monday)
- Children's Birthdays
- Mother's Day / Father's Day
- Hallowe'en
- School professional development days

Besides the division of times and occasions, certain ancillary recommendations are useful in facilitating the post-divorce adjustment of the parents in their new roles:

- Telephone access
- Access to health and education information
- Use of a diary to be passed between the parents at transitions
- Binding arbitration clause in case of future conflicts

Binding arbitration clauses can often function as a release valve in the case of parents for whom the awarding of custody may not be sufficient to resolve major parenting conflicts that can arise. The purpose is to define a process of dispute settlement, mainly for the non-custodian, in order to alleviate tensions and reduce the likelihood of re-litigation. The recommendation would stipulate three components: (1) the parents should agree on a mental health practitioner to act as arbitrator, possibly naming that person, (2) a method of presenting points of view to the arbitrator, and (3) a formula as to costs.

In summary, it may be said that the psycholegal report must be as convincing as possible as it has to constructively motivate parents at a time when reason and balance may be at a premium. The lawyer also requires a thorough accounting of the results and recommendations in order to best work with their client in pursuit of the children's best interests. Reports tend to be well received not only when they are favourable to one side but when the parents and lawyers perceive that the assessor has made a serious effort to understand and document the various issues and concerns raised by each side.

7. CONCLUSION

This chapter has sought to outline the linkage between assessor, assessment and report leading to a series of detailed suggestions intended to stem the tide of heartbreak and emotional damage in families of divorce. Although experienced lawyers recognize a good assessment when they see one, irrespective of what side it favours, it is not easy to measure degree of success in any long-term fashion. For one thing, what constitutes success may not be so evident and so many factors contribute to the outcome that are independent of control. If we were to evaluate success, should it perhaps be tied to the adaptation of children or their parents at some point in the future in those cases where the recommendations were followed? Or should it perhaps be tied to the short-term success of the report in helping to resolve the dispute at the time of its completion? This latter function correlates with what may be termed the political thrust of the report. Is it sagacious and tactful in promoting resolution and assisting the lawyers and the court in moving the family towards resolution? Until we have clinical research that can validly or scientifically answer these longer term questions, we should take solace from the frequent observation that a good assessment, in capable legal hands, is a powerful tool for resolving custody disputes in fragmenting families.

6

How an Assessment is Obtained

In canvassing how the issue of how an assessment is obtained a differentiation must be made between an assessment obtained on consent, obtained either by way of an oral or written agreement between the parties, an assessment obtained by way of a consent order and an assessment obtained without the consent of the parties by way of a court order or one obtained as a result of the court, of its own volition, ordering that an assessment be conducted.

1. ASSESSMENT ON CONSENT

In the normal course of events it will be explained to the parent/party seeking legal advice regarding a custody/access issue that the assessment process is a mechanism that can be used within the confines of litigation or as a mechanism to be implemented in a non-litigious or non-adversarial atmosphere.

The parents/parties and lawyers can co-operate with one another in this regard and consent to an assessment and consent as to who the assessor will be. In this scenario the parties, lawyers and assessor are part of a co-operative or team effort to help the parents solve their differences regarding child care arrangements. The goal in this scenario is for the parties to have an independent third party make recommendations regarding the children, which recommendations may ultimately be accepted by the parents. In the event the parents agree with the recommendations, the recommendations would likely be incorporated into a domestic contract to be executed by the parties in the settlement of their affairs.

Assuming that the assessment process is commenced in this non-litigious environment, and without a court action having to be commenced, the parents should, however, be made to understand that the assessment process and ultimate assessment report with its comments, observations and recommendations could ultimately be the subject-matter of litigation. If one of the parties does not accept the recommendations of the assessor as a consequence of which a court action is commenced and the matter proceeds to trial or arbitration, the assessment report will likely be adduced into evidence and the assessor will give *viva voce* evidence regarding his or her clinical observations, findings and recommendations.

It is imperative in such a circumstance that the parent/party understand that the assessment is not being conducted on a "without prejudice" basis and understand that the process is not a "closed" process in the same context that some forms of mediation are considered to be "closed".

It is our experience that most parents, and often times their lawyers, do not necessarily understand the difference between the assessment process and the mediation process, as those vehicles are used in settlement of custody/access issues.

Barbara Chisholm, in an article entitled "Preparing Your Client for Assessment or Mediation",[1] illustrates both the similarities and differences between an assessment and mediation as follows:

SIMILARITIES BETWEEN ASSESSMENT AND MEDIATION

Assessment	Mediation
1. The parents identify the problems.	7. The parents identify the problems.
2. The parents are the main source of information.	8. The parents are the main source of information.

1 (1987), C.F.L.Q. 385 at 387.

3. Children must always be seen, and interviewed if practical.	9. Children must always be seen, or included in the process, if pertinent.
4. The aim is not therapeutic, although that may be a by-product of the process.	10. The aim is not therapeutic, although that may be a by-product of the process.
5. The focus is Best Interests of the children.	11. Where children are the topic of the Mediation, the focus is their Best Interests.
6. Interviews are the main device.	12. Interviews are the main device.

DIFFERENCES BETWEEN ASSESSMENT AND MEDIATION

Assessment	Mediation
13. The process is for the Court's assistance.	25. The process is for the parents' assistance.
14. The Assessor uses his/her own judgment to arrive at opinion and to make recommendations.	26. The Mediator acts as a facilitator; does not express opinion or make recommendations.
15. The Assessor seeks as full as possible an understanding of the history of the marriage, early/later relationships, parenting skills, coping patterns.	27. The Mediator seeks only the information needed to orient self to the basis of the current need for conflict-resolution assistance.
16. The Assessor contacts (with consent) collaterals both within and outside the family to assist in full understanding.	28. The Mediator does not expand beyond the immediate family context (including new relationships). Some mediators do.
17. No option exists for anything but full disclosure through the vehicle of the Assessment Report.	29. The option exists for Open or Closed Mediation which affects the nature of the report to counsel.

18. The Assessor may be required as a witness in subsequent litigation, re the Report.	30. The Children's Law Reform Act, R.S.O. 1990, c. C.12, ss. 31(4) and 31(7) allows the Court to order mediation and filing of a report, either full or limited. Anything said to the Mediator will be privileged.
19. The Assessor determines the structure and the process.	31. The Mediator facilitates, but the clients determine, the structure.
20. The Assessment Report, with its Recommendations, is a final document.	32. A Temporary Working Agreement may be tried, subject to review in a specified period of time, and subject to alteration then.
21. The Assessor prepares the Report and its Recommendations entirely by himself/herself.	33. The Agreement reached by the mediating parties is prepared by them with the Mediator's assistance.
22. The Report is not vetted by anyone prior to completion.	34. The Agreement must be cleared through each party's counsel prior to completion and signing.
23. The Recommendations in the Assessment Report are just that, and may or may not be ordered by the Court.	35. So long as no one's rights are infringed and the Agreement is and feels fair, its terms will likely be confirmed.
24. Assessment is undertaken so the Court may be assisted to make its decision.	36. Mediation is undertaken so the parties may make decisions.

It is important that the parents and the lawyers understand the differences and similarities between the assessment process and the mediation process as, although the ultimate objective in each process is similar, the various elements involved in each process are different and can have a significant impact on the determination of a custody/access issue.

2. JURISDICTION

The issue of jurisdiction regarding the obtainment of an order for an assessment shall be restricted to the situation where the consent of one of the parties to having an assessment conducted is not forthcoming, but the other party feels that it is vital to have an assessment conducted so as to assist the parties or the court in determining what is in the best interests of the child or children involved in the dispute.

3. INHERENT JURISDICTION

It is only in recent years that the concept of assessments has become a commonly used vehicle in custody/access cases and, therefore, it is only within that period of time that the various legislatures in Canada have enacted appropriate legislation permitting courts to appoint qualified persons to assist the court in determining what is in the best interests of a child in a custody/access case.

Prior to appropriate permissive legislation being enacted in this regard the jurisdiction of the courts to order an assessment, or the equivalent thereof such as having the child interviewed by a psychologist or social worker, was not so clear.

The courts would, in cases where it felt justified to do so, resort to their inherent jurisdiction or to the *parens patriae* doctrine. In *Cillis v. Cillis*[2] the court was entertaining an application to vary custody awarded pursuant to a decree nisi that was granted pursuant to the provisions of the *Divorce Act, 1968*. The Official Guardian recommended that an assessment be conducted. The husband agreed but the wife refused. The court held that it did not have the power to order an assessment as the *Divorce Act, 1968* did not contain an express provision permitting same. However, the court invoked its inherent jurisdiction to stay proceedings, including the husband's child support payments, until an assessment was completed. The case was appealed to the Ontario Court of Appeal[3] which held that the court has inherent jurisdiction to make such orders as are necessary for the purpose of promoting a fair and satisfactory trial. The Court of Appeal further

2 (1980), 20 R.F.L. (2d) 208 (Ont. H.C.J.).
3 (1981) 23 R.F.L. (2d) 96 (Ont. C.A.).

stated that the court has jurisdiction to order a family clinic assessment where that assessment appears reasonably necessary to arrive at a just and proper decision in the best interests of the children. There are other reported decisions where the court relied on its inherent jurisdiction to order that an assessment be conducted in a custody/access case.[4]

4. STATUTORY AUTHORITY

Most provinces have now enacted legislation which permits a court to order an assessment.[5]

The *Divorce Act*,[6] does not specifically provide that a court may order an assessment. However, it is suggested that the wording of s. 16(6) of the *Divorce Act* is probably sufficient to permit a court to order an assessment in a custody/access dispute. That section provides as follows:

> 16(6) The court may make an order under this section [*custody*] for a definite or indefinite period or until the happening of a specified event and may impose such other terms, conditions, or restrictions in connection therewith as it thinks fit and just.

If a judge hearing a custody/access matter under the *Divorce Act* feels it necessary to order an assessment so as to assist the court in determining what is in the best interests of the child then it is arguable

---

4 *El-Sohemy v. El-Sohemy* (1980), 17 R.F.L. (2d) 1 (Ont. H.C.J.); *Roschuk v. Roschuk* (1980), 15 R.F.L. (2d) 196 (Man. C.A.); *Norton v. Korpesho* (1980), 7 Man. R. (2d) 39 (Q.B.). In *Soon v. Soon*, [1993] W.D.F.L. 1256: a master had ordered one of the parties and the children in her custody to attend upon a specific investigator for the purpose of investigation and preparation of a report under s. 15 of the *Family Relations Act* of British Columbia. On appeal it was noted that the *Family Relations Act* did not contain an express provision authorizing the court to order the attendance of a party or child for the benefit of the assessor as is the case in the Ontario *Children's Law Reform Act*. However, the court did hold that it had inherent jurisdiction, notwithstanding the absence of specific legislation, to order, in an appropriate case, the attendance of a party to a custody dispute and the children in that party's custody to attend for the purpose of investigation under s. 15 of the British Columbia *Family Relations Act*.

5 See Appendix III regarding legislation mandating assessments in custody/access cases.

6 R.S.C. 1985, c. 3 (2nd Supp.).

that such an order would be "fit and just" under section 16(6) of the *Divorce Act*.

The question has presented itself in Ontario as to whether section 27 of the *Children's Law Reform Act*[7] prevents the court from ordering an assessment under the provisions of the *Divorce Act*. Section 27 reads:

> 27. Where an action for divorce is commenced under the *Divorce Act* (Canada), any application under this Part in respect of custody of or access to a child that has not been determined is stayed except with leave of the court.

In the decision of *Booth v. Booth*[8] the court held that section 27 of the *Children's Law Reform Act* did not bar the appointment of an assessor as the words "except with leave of the court" contained in section 27 allowed the court to appoint an assessor pursuant to section 10(*b*) of the *Divorce Act, 1968*, which is the equivalent of section 16(6) of the current *Divorce Act*.

5. RULES OF PRACTICE

In all the provinces there are specific rules of court or rules of practice that will allow the appointment of an expert for the purpose of reporting to the court on any question of fact or opinion relevant to an issue before the court. In Ontario, the Ontario Rules of Civil Procedure[9] (rule 52.03(1)) provide that on a motion by a party or on his own initiative, a judge may, at any time, appoint one or more independent experts to inquire into and report on any question of fact or opinion relevant to an issue in the action. In the decision of *Jones v. Jones*[10] an expert was appointed under Rule 52.03 to prepare a report for the court in a custody case. In the decision of *Norton v. Korpesho*,[11] the court relied upon the Manitoba Queen's Bench Rules, Rule 351(2) in ordering an assessment.[12]

---

7 R.S.O. 1990, c. C.12.
8 (1983), 33 R.F.L. (2d) 330 (Ont. H.C.J.).
9 R.R.O. 1990, Reg. 194.
10 [1986] W.D.F.L. 389 (Ont. H.C.).
11 *Supra*, note 4.
12 *Courts of Justice Act*, R.S.O. 1990, c. C.43, s. 105.

The Ontario *Courts of Justice Act* provides that a " health practitioner" (the definition of which includes a psychologist registered under the *Psychologist Registration Act*) may conduct a physical or mental examination of a party to a proceeding where the physical or mental condition of the party to the proceeding is in question. Although the section is silent with respect to the examination of children the question presents itself as to whether an argument could be made to have a child custody assessment ordered under the section. It should also be noted that the enabling section makes ti clear that prior to such an order being made the question of the party's physical or mental condition must be relevant to a material issue in the proceeding and there is good reason to believe that there is substance to the allegations.

6. COURT ORDERED ASSESSMENTS (AT THE REQUEST OF THE PARTIES)

One of the most difficult tasks one could possibly impose upon a court is to ask a judge to determine which of two parents or other interested parties should have custody of a child.

Could any judicial function be more daunting or challenging than deciding who is to have custody of a child? This is an issue in regards to which almost all persons, particularly those who have children, feel they have some experience or opinion that would be worth considering. Because most parents can appreciate the complexities and frailties of human nature and how those complexities and frailties interplay with the development of a child, and because most parents can appreciate how their raising of a child is fraught with uncertainty and so many possible combinations of extraneous factors that affect the child's development such as good luck, bad luck, special needs, personalities, learning disabilities, lifestyle, family values, societal values, only to mention a few, most people would be hesitant or loath to attempt to decide such a serious issue as who should have custody of a child.

Deciding what is best for a child requires an examination of the purposes and values of life itself. Most persons would feel overwhelmed at having such a responsibility imposed upon them, particularly when one considers the profound affect the decision will have on the child and his or her future, let alone the effect such a decision would have on the parents. Some persons would be better qualified than others if asked to make such a decision. Some may have better life skills and life experience than others; some may be better trained or qualified in the area of social sciences or behaviourial sciences. Some may, therefore, be better prepared or qualified than others to make such a decision with all of its far reaching consequences.

Judges are no different than other people in society when it comes to evaluating the purposes and values of life. They are human beings. Some will be more competent than others in their ability to decide who should have custody of a child. Some will be less confident in their role as the final decision maker for such a difficult decision, and will look to assistance from sources other than that evidence that may come only out of the mouths of the parents or other interested parties or witnesses called on behalf of the parties, whose evidence may not be considered by a court as being independent or from a neutral source.

Some judges, then, are more likely to look for assistance from a mental health professional than are others. Some judges, as is the situation with some lawyers, are very uncomfortable dealing with custody/access cases and will look for all possible assistance in determining what is in the best interests of the children. Some judges do not at all feel qualified to make such a decision and, in ordering the assessment, are hopeful that the assessment process will settle the issue without the matter having to proceed to trial. The latter scenario is an example of the situation where some judges, in effect, foster off or pass off onto the mental health professional the ultimate decision-making task on the custody/access issue, notwithstanding the general reluctance of some judges to relinquish the final decision-making power in this regard.[13]

Unless there are justifiable grounds to have an assessment conducted some judges will not entertain an application for such an order. There is an increasing school of judicial opinion that feels that unless there is a strong case made to justify an assessment being ordered an application for same will be dismissed.[14]

---

13 *Weaver v. Tate* (1989), 24 R.F.L. (3d) 266 (Ont. H.C.J.); affirmed 28 R.F.L. (3d) 188 (Ont. C.A.).

14 In *Chapman v. Chapman* (1985), 49 R.F.L. (2d) 47 (Ont. Dist. Ct.) the court suggested that there was an onus on the person seeking the assessment to show

It is of interest to briefly review the court's attitude, perspective and approach to assessments in recent years.

Prior to 1990, the courts would almost always, upon an appropriate motion being made, order that an assessment be conducted in custody cases if material filed with the court in support of such a motion contained some evidence regarding the welfare of the child and, therefore, the assessment would be of great assistance to a judge in the determination of the custody issue. There were some exceptions.[15]

Professor Nicholas Balla in his excellent article "Assessing the Assessor: Legal Issues"[16] was, at the time of his article, justified in observing

> There are almost no reported cases which refuse an order for an assessment. This suggests that judges will order an assessment if either party request it, provided there is a genuine dispute over custody or access, and arrangements can be made to pay for an assessment.

Also, Professor Balla observed:

> While it is true that there is an onus on the moving party to justify the request, it is submitted that there will be few contested custody or access disputes in which an assessment by a competent independent assessor will not meet at least one of the criteria McLeod proposes (*reference to annotation by Professor McLeod as to criteria to be met on an assessment*) in *Chapman v. Chapman*, which would suggest it would not be a difficult onus to meet. Thus, if there is a genuine dispute, it may be appropriate for a resisting party to bear a tactical onus for demonstrating why an assessment should not be ordered.[17]

Since that article was written, there has been an increasing trend for judges to question the necessity of an assessment and the courts are now not so quick to order one. As discussed in Chapter 4, heading 5. "Expert Opinion Evidence as to Ultimate Issue — Custody Access Cases", some judges and lawyers feel that assessments may have too

why expert input was needed. See also *Saffin v. Saffin* (1992), 35 R.F.L. (3d) 250 (Alta. Q.B.); *Linton v. Clarke* (1994), 50 R.F.L. (3d) 8 (Ont. Gen. Div.); affirmed (1995), 10 R.F.L. (4th) 92 (Ont. Div. Ct.), and *Levine v. Levine* (1994), 50 R.F.L. (3d) 414 (Ont. Prov. Ct.).

15 See *Chapman v. Chapman*, *supra*, note 14. In this case the court suggested that there was an onus on the person seeking the assessment to show why expert input was needed.

16 (1990), C.F.L.Q. 179 at 190.

17 *Ibid.*, at 191.

much effect on the outcome of a custody case and, therefore, judges and lawyers are revisiting the issue as to the circumstances in which the ordering of an assessment will be appropriate. Some judges are now re-expressing the view that it is for them to decide the custody/access issue, not the mental health professional. They seem to be more mindful of their judicial decision-making function in this regard and are less reluctant to delegate that function to an assessor unless for very good reason.

Courts also had a tendency to rely too heavily on the recommendations in an assessment and would almost rubber stamp the conclusions set out in the report. Lawyers were no different, and there are many lawyers who in providing legal advice to their clients on the custody/access issue and in the course of reviewing the concept of an assessment with them, would advise their clients, particularly in the decades of the 1970s and 1980s, that a court would likely adopt the recommendations of the assessor, as set out in the report, unless there were obvious reasons for attacking and undermining the conclusions reached therein. Assessments in that period of time seemed to be ordered to resolve the issue of custody and access rather than for the purpose of determining whether any clinical issues existed in the family unit, on which issues a mental health professional could offer assistance to the court.

(a) Criteria to be Met

A review of recent jurisprudence would suggest that the courts are no longer prepared to rubber stamp the conclusions or recommendations of assessors, let alone even order an assessment unless satisfied that to do so is really necessary to assist the court in reaching its decision on the custody/access issue. The question presents itself as to what criteria must be met by the party requesting that an assessment be ordered to help determine what is in the best interests of the child. In the decision of *Saffin v. Saffin*[18] the court refused the request for an assessment and in doing so stated:

> In determining whether a psychological assessment of children should be ordered despite the objection of a custodial parent, a court should recognize,

18 *Supra*, note 14.

> on the one hand, that psychological assessments are intrusive, and, on the other, that psychological assessments may provide evidence useful in the resolution of custody disputes.
>
> . . .
>
> In determining which of these values weighs most heavily in this case, it is appropriate to examine the factors which must be assessed in custody cases, and the way in which a psychological assessment might provide evidence relevant to those factors in this case.[19]

In dismissing the application the court stated:

> In reviewing all the material on this application, I have concluded that since the custodial parent objected to a psychological assessment, and since no issue of fact has been raised suggesting that standard evidence would be inadequate to decide what is in the children's best interests with respect to custody, this is not a case in which a psychological assessment should be ordered.[20]

It is clear that the court wanted more than a bald allegation or assertion that an assessment, in general terms, would be required to determine what is in the best interests of the child. The court made it clear that there has to be some factual basis on which the argument is advanced that the assessment is necessary.

In *Linton v. Clarke*[21] the court dismissed an application for an order than an assessment be conducted. In considering the motion the judge remarked:

> It has become the practice to order assessments prior to trial in virtually every custody case. That is a practice that should be re-examined. The *Children's Law Reform Act* specifically provides that an assessment may be ordered by a trial judge at the time of the hearing, should that become necessary. An assessment that is ordered by a trial judge and is focused on a particular area of concern would, in my view, be of greater assistance to the court than a wide ranging report prepared without direction.[22]

In the decision of *Levine v. Levine*[23] the presiding judge, in refusing to order that an assessment be conducted at the request of one

19 *Ibid.*, at 254-55.
20 *Ibid.*, at 258.
21 *Supra*, note 14 (Ont. Gen. Div.).
22 *Ibid.*, at 12.
23 *Supra*, note 14.

of the parties, made reference to the decision of *Mantesso v. Mantesso*[24] where Justice Fleury stated:

> Notwithstanding that assessments have been granted by me and others as a matter of course, I am satisfied that where such assessment is not on consent, there is a duty on the party seeking the order to lay out the necessary ground work to justify the retaining of an assessor. Professor McLeod expressed it very well in an annotation to *Chapman v. Chapman* 49 R.F.L. (2d) 47. He stated:
>
>> "On the first point — the onus of proof — the approach of McDermid D.C.J. attempts to strike a reasonable balance. McDermid D.C.J. appears to have accepted the wife's submission that s. 30 of the *Children's Law Reform Act* is permissive, not mandatory. Such a conclusion accords with the language of s. 30 and seems beyond dispute. It would seem to follow on general principles that the person requesting the assessment must show a reason the special remedy of an assessment is required in the particular case . . . As a note of caution, the court ought not to assume that every assessment will raise new and pertinent evidence. The onus should be on the moving party to show at least some reason for the assessment. There should be some reason to expect that the assessment will add to the evidence if, as our law provides, the parties and child have a right to have the decision of custody or access made by a judge, not an assessor. To order an assessment merely because the parties dispute the issue would render the section in effect mandatory. There must be some evidence that the dispute is so intense as to prevent all the relevant factors coming out, or that there appears to be a parent-child problem that requires expert analysis and/or explanation, or finally that the assessment is necessary to allow the parties to understand the needs of the child and the need for cooperation."
>
> I agree.

---

24 (1991), O.J. 643 (Ont. Gen. Div.). In *Mantesso v. Mantesso* a 4-year-old child had been in the interim custody of the mother for 19 months. The father's access had been uneventful, he was employed full time and would rely on babysitter's if awarded custody. The court ruled that custody and access assessments should not be ordered unless the moving party established that the issue required expert analysis, or that it was necessary to allow the parties to understand the child's needs. In this case there was no question upon which an expert's opinion would be required. The court stated that the dangers of ordering an assessment as a matter of course included the cost, a disproportionate weight attached to the opinion of an unregulated body of experts in the determination of the custody issue and the introduction of a great deal of hearsay evidence.

The above referred-to decisions are just a sampling of the recent judicial trend by some judges in being reluctant to order that an assessment be conducted unless there is very good reason. That reason must be related to some problem identified in the evidence put before the court at the time the request is being made. The courts seem to be saying that if a particular judge feels that he or she can decide the custody/access issue in question based on evidence he or she feels will be offered at trial by the parties, without the assistance of a mental health professional's opinion or assistance, then they will not order that an assessment be conducted. Therefore, one has to conclude that the evidence before the court on an application seeking an order for an assessment must be such as to persuade the court that there are clinical problems[25] or areas of concern that do require the input of a mental health professional. As to what approach or perspective a particular judge or court will adopt upon hearing an application or motion requesting that an assessment be ordered will to a great extent, therefore, depend upon a combination of:

- the particular judge's juristic experience in custody cases and his or her confidence in their ability to decide the case on the basis of the evidence that the parties will be able to lead at trial; and/or
- the adequacy of the supporting material before the court upon which material the argument is being advanced that an assessment will produce evidence or information that pertains to the welfare or best interests of the child.

If upon an application for an order for an assessment the presiding judge is of the view that the material in support of such an application does not reveal a justifiable reason to order the assessment one will not be ordered.[26]

---

25 *Brown v. Brown* (1994), 3 R.F.L. (4th) 135 (Ont. Gen. Div.). The court held that the role of a family assessment was not to provide a vehicle for resolving the custody and access dispute, but rather to deal with clinical issues found to be existing in the family.

26 In the case of *Nawrocki v. Nawrocki*, [1990] W.D.F.L. 148 (Ont. H.C.) a 14-year-old child expressed the wish to live with his father, but have both parents share joint custody so that he could visit with his mother whenever he wished. The mother sought an assessment. The court refused stating that an assessment was unnecessary given the child's age and stated wishes. In *Winters v. Winters* (1992), 33 A.C.W.S. (3d) 454 (Ont. Gen. Div.) both the father and the mother requested that an assessment be conducted. The court

7. COURT ORDERED ASSESSMENTS (BY COURT OF ITS OWN VOLITION WITHOUT REQUEST BY PARTIES)

A court ordered assessment is not necessarily the by-product of one party or the other making the appropriate application to a court for an order that an assessment be conducted. A court may, with or without a request by a party to the action, appoint a person who has technical or professional skills to assess and report to the court on the needs of the child and the ability and willingness of the parties to satisfy those needs.[27]

The court's intervention in a case where it is likely to appoint a mental health professional without a request being made by either party is likely to occur in one of three settings, namely, at an interim hearing prior to trial, at a pre-trial conference or, at the commencement of or during the custody hearing.

8. INTERIM HEARING PRIOR TO TRIAL

In many custody/access cases an application is brought by one party or the other for an order for interim custody or interim access to the child pending trial or the hearing of the application in which custody/access is sought. It is usually at that stage of interlocutory proceedings that an assessment is requested by one party or the other. However, sometimes neither party nor their counsel feel that an assessment is warranted and, therefore, neither party ask that an assessment order be conducted.

However, the presiding judge at the hearing for interim-interim custody or interim custody will sometimes, upon review of the material filed in support of interim custody and access, or after having heard the submissions of counsel, feel that an assessment may be warranted. The presiding judge will feel that the ultimate trier of fact (which clearly may be a judge other than the motions judge) could

---

held that there was no concrete basis on which to find that an assessment was necessary for the benefit of the child and would not order one merely to make the matter easier for the parties to resolve.

27 *Children's Law Reform Act*, R.S.O. 1990, c. C.12, s. 30(1) and (2).

clearly benefit from input from a qualified mental health professional as to what is in the best interests of the child.

9. PRETRIAL HEARING

It is not uncommon at pretrial hearings for some judges to order an assessment of the parties and child or children. This usually occurs after the judge has read the pretrial conference memorandum of the parties' respective counsel in which relevant facts are contained and in which pretrial conference memoranda identify certain areas of concern regarding the welfare and best interests of the children. In some cases, the judge conducting the pretrial may be seized of hearing the custody trial or application particularly in a jurisdiction where case management is part of the litigation process. Even if the pretrial judge is precluded from conducting the custody/access hearing, as a pretrial judge normally would be in most circumstances, he or she may feel that the ultimate trier of fact should have the benefit of some input from a mental health professional or he or she may develop a feeling or sense that the welfare of the child requires that a clinical study of the family be conducted.[28]

It is not only the judge conducting the pretrial hearing who may consider that an assessment is warranted in the particular case. Counsel for either party may, by way of a motion returnable before the pretrial judge, make a request that an assessment be ordered.

10. ASSESSMENT ORDERED AT TRIAL OR HEARING

At the commencement of the custody/access hearing or during the hearing itself, an order may be made by the presiding judge that an assessment be conducted. Although it is not common for an assessment to be ordered at this late a stage of the proceedings, sometimes a judge, after reading the trial record or application record, or after having heard a portion of the evidence may adjourn the

28 In *More v. Primeau*, (1978), 2 R.F.L. (2d) 254 (Ont. C.A.) at the pretrial hearing, the pretrial judge made what was then commonly referred to as a "Haines Order" requesting a full psychiatric report on the child of the parties.

hearing until such time as a full or partial assessment of the needs of the family has been conducted. It is not too often that a judge would, at the trial application hearing stage, adjourn the hearing for the obvious reason that such a delay would be prejudicial to the non-custodial parent. Because of the importance attached to the non-disturbance of a child's environment and, therefore, the tendency of the courts to be reluctant to disturb the status quo, it would be unfair to adjourn the case not only for the party who does not have custody, but contrary to the child's best interests to prolong the uncertainty about his or her future.[29]

If the court does order that an assessment be conducted of its own volition and without the request having been made by either of the parties, it must also determine what procedures are to be followed in the assessment. Ordinarily these procedures would otherwise be determined by the parties and their lawyers if the assessment was done on consent. In the circumstance of a consent assessment the lawyers and parties will usually agree as to who is to conduct the assessment and will ordinarily have agreed on the terms of reference to be provided to the assessor, usually by way of a common letter of direction with the objective of the assessment being set out in the letter.

Where the lawyers and parties cannot agree on who should actually conduct the assessment or where they cannot agree on what the objective of the assessment is to be, most provinces, in their respective enabling pieces of legislation make appropriate provision for the procedure to be implemented.[30]

In Ontario, the *Children's Law Reform Act* provides that the court "Shall, if possible, appoint a person agreed upon by the parties, but if the parties do not agree the court shall choose and appoint the person."[31]

---

29 *Lotton v. Ralph* (1994), 43 A.C.W.S. (3d) 1122 (Ont. Gen. Div.) an application for an assessment was allowed although the report would result in a short delay in the proceeding as the interests of the children demanded an assessment in the circumstances.

30 See Appendix III regarding legislation mandating assessments in custody/access cases.

31 *Children's Law Reform Act*, s. 30(3), (4), (5): "30(5) . . . the court may require the parties, the child and any other person who has been given notice of the proposed order, or any of them, to attend for assessment by the person appointed by the order".

With this enabling section of the *Children's Law Reform Act* the court can appoint and name the assessor to prepare a report and report to the court within a specified period. It can further order the attendance of persons other than the parties or children at the assessment. Section 30(11) and (12) of the *Children's Law Reform Act* further gives the court power to provide directions in respect of the assessment as it considers appropriate. In some cases the court may order an assessment without specifically providing any direction as to which particular issue or area of concern is to be the subject matter of the assessment, leaving the assessor to decide which issues within the family unit are pertinent and have to be addressed in the report.

As earlier canvassed some courts will be more specific in giving directions to the assessor and probably more particularly so in the instance where the court is making the order of its own volition. In the circumstances of the court ordering an assessment on its own initiative such as at an interim hearing, a pretrial hearing or during the course of the trial or hearing, the court is more likely to have read evidence or heard evidence to cause it to identify a particular area of concern it feels should be addressed by a mental health professional.[32]

Another circumstance in which the court may order an assessment without being requested to do so by either of the parties, is in the situation where the children may be represented by counsel or by a lawyer appointed to represent the children on behalf of the province.[33] On the other hand, some courts are of the view that it is not necessary to have both independent counsel appointed to represent the children and an assessment conducted. In the case of *Lauro v. Lauro*[34] the

32 In *R. (G.E.) v. R. (A.K.)*, [1990] W.D.F.L. 62 (Man. Q.B.) the court held that access should not be specified until an investigation determined the effect of the visits upon the children. The husband had been convicted of indecent assault and of sexual assault on one of the children and, obviously, the court was concerned that the assessment be directed to this issue. In *G. v. G.* (1992), 30 A.C.W.S. (3d) 545 (Ont. Gen. Div.) a 4-year-old daughter alleged sexual misconduct by the father. The father was charged but the charge was dismissed when no evidence of any real misconduct was given by the daughter at trial. The father sought access. The court ordered that an assessment should be conducted. In *P. (S.) v. M. (D.J.)* (1994), 44 A.C.W.S. (3d) 1107 (Ont. Gen. Div.) the mother had not had any contact with the child for almost two years. The mother was a virtual stranger to the child. The court felt that it would not be in the best interests of the child to introduce the mother into the child's life without some expert evidence addressing the issue of advisability.

33 *Re O. (F.M.)* (1985), 45 R.F.L. (2d) 239 (Man. Q.B.).

34 (1988), 13 R.F.L. (3d) 189 (Ont. Dist. Ct.).

parties agreed that an assessment report relating to the custody of the children be prepared and filed with the court. The husband made a motion for an order appointing independent legal counsel to represent the children in order to ensure that their views were made known to the court. The application was dismissed and the court held that the assessment was designed to accomplish the same purpose.

11. SUMMARY RE EVIDENCE REQUIRED

The request for a court order that an assessment be conducted in a custody/access case is usually done at an early stage in the proceedings and most certainly well prior to the pretrial hearing or trial itself, although there are certain cases where an application is brought at the commencement of or during the trial.

The courts have in recent years made it clear that the practice of ordering assessments in virtually every custody case has to be re-examined. There now seems to be a duty on the party seeking an order for an assessment to lay out the necessary ground work to justify the retaining of an assessor.[35]

There must be some evidence that the dispute is so intense as to prevent all the relevant factors coming out, or that there appears to be a parent-child problem that requires expert analysis and/or explanation or, finally, that the assessment is necessary to allow the parties to understand the needs of the child and the need for the co-operation.[36]

35 *Linton v. Clarke* (1993), 50 R.F.L. (2d) 8 (Ont. Gen. Div.); affirmed (1994), 10 R.F.L. (4th) 92 (Ont. Div. Ct.); *Allwood v. Samuals*, [1995] W.D.F.L. 726 (Ont. Prov. Div.). In *M. (C.) v. M. (G.)* (1992), 40 R.F.L. (3d) 1 (Ont. U.F.C.) there was one assessment directed by the court which supported the mother and a second assessment, arranged by the father that did not involve an interview with the children but criticized the earlier assessment. The court held that although the first assessment was just one piece of evidence it should be given some weight because of its impartial and professional nature. The second assessment did not involve interviews and was more academic. It also included hearsay which went to its weight but not its validity or admissibility. However, the court was not prepared to give it the same weight as the first assessment report. See also *Mantesso v. Mantesso, supra*, note 24.

36 *Chapman v. Chapman* (1985), 49 R.F.L. (2d) 47 (Ont. Dist. Ct.) (annotation of professor McLeod).

In summary, the factual basis relied upon by the party which ordinarily would be set out in pleadings or in a notice of motion and accompanying affidavit or affidavits, must be particularized and specific enough so as to clearly demonstrate that an assessment could produce evidence or information that would otherwise not be available solely through the evidence presented by the parties at trial and that in determining what is in the best interests of the child, the additional input of a mental health professional could possibly assist the court in determining the ultimate issue.

It is unlikely that an appeal court will reverse a judge's order to grant or refuse an assessment[37] and, therefore, it is important that the supporting material for an application for an order that an assessment be conducted be as complete as possible.

12. REFUSAL TO UNDERGO COURT ORDERED ASSESSMENT

There are instances where one party may advise his or her counsel that they do not intend to undergo an assessment as they do not wish to incur the expense or because they feel that it is unnecessary notwithstanding that an assessment has been ordered by the court. It must be explained to that party that a judge or court may draw an adverse inference if a party refuses to participate in an assessment without good reason.[38]

It is really a question of facts peculiar to each case as to whether there is good reason not to attend a court ordered assessment. In the case of *Knockwood v. Knockwood*[39] it was held that although it was not assuming that the first assessment report was invalid, nevertheless the assessor was not native and therefore unable to have a proper perspective about the contribution the father could make *vis-à-vis* the

37 *Linton v. Clarke*, *supra*, note 35; *Carignan v. Black* (1994), 138 N.S.R. (2d) 61 (S.C.).

38 *Haggerty v. Haggerty*, [1994] W.D.F.L. 1579 (Ont. Prov. Div.). Section 30(6) of the *Children's Law Reform Act* of Ontario reads: "Where a person ordered under this section to attend for assessment refuses to attend or to undergo the assessment, the court may draw such inferences in respect of the ability and willingness of any person to satisfy the needs of the child as the court considers appropriate."

39 [1991] W.D.F.L. 818 (N.S. Fam. Ct.).

children's relationship with the native side of their heritage. This decision raises the question as to whether the father could have refused to attend the assessment without an adverse inference having been drawn. On the other hand, in cases where there are cultural issues at play, and where the parties are of different cultures, it may not be possible to always retain a mental health professional who is familiar with both cultures. More likely than not, in a situation of this nature the court is likely to order that both parties attend the assessment, however, any deficiency in the report based on the fact that the assessor is unable to culturally relate to one party or the other, would become a question of weight by the court that is to be given to the report.[40]

13. SECOND ASSESSMENTS

A court does have jurisdiction to order a second assessment report where the first assessment is deficient and incomplete.[41]

One of the problems in our court system is the undue length of time it sometimes takes to have a case reach trial. Often an assessment will have been completed in a case but because of either the long wait for trial or a change in family circumstances since the report was completed, the value of the assessment deteriorates with time and, thus, the less value the assessment has in assisting the court in deciding what is in the child's best interests.[42] In these circumstances a court has jurisdiction to order another assessment, however, the party seeking a second court-ordered assessment must clearly do more than demonstrate that they are simply dissatisfied with the original results.[43]

Where there is no evidence to indicate that the situation between the parties has changed since an assessment was done, there is no justification for ordering a new custody/access investigation.[44]

40 *More v. Primeau* (1978), 2 R.F.L. (2d) 254 (Ont. C.A.) at 268.

41 *M. (S.P.) v. M. (W.B.)* (1988), 15 R.F.L. (3d) 301 (Ont. H.C.).

42 *Longaphy v. Tupper* (1995), 139 N.S.R. (2d) 287 (Fam. Ct.).

43 *Naumetz v. Naumetz*, [1988] W.D.F.L. 1633 (Ont. H.C.). In *McClinchy v. McClinchy* (1988), 12 A.C.W.S. (3d) 427 (Ont. Dist. Ct.). In this case the husband sought an order appointing a second assessor to assess the first assessor's assessment report. The court held that a new assessment was not necessary as the previous assessment could be brought up to date.

44 *L. (J.) v. R. (H.)*, [1994] W.D.F.L. 1011 (B.C. S.C.).

For the purpose of having a second assessment conducted the courts will most likely want to use the original assessor so as to control the cost factor that would be involved. The original assessor can do an up-dated report for a lot less than having a different assessor do a completely new report unless circumstances such as distance costs warrant that a different assessor be used. In *Tremblay v. Tremblay*[45] an assessment report had been completed in Calgary in 1992. The court ordered an up-date of the assessment prior to setting a new trial date. The mother wanted the original assessor to complete the report, however, the court held it would be far more efficient and less costly for an up-dated assessment to be made by a resident of Winnipeg where the mother resided. The decision obviously was made on the basis of the cost involved. It would seem that unless it can be shown that there were errors in the methodology used by the original assessor, or that an element of bias or preference was exhibited by the original assessor, or that the original assessment is otherwise deficient, the court will likely use the same assessor.

Often times circumstances have significantly changed since the making of the report and a decision must be made whether a new assessment should be conducted or at least up-dated to reflect the change in circumstances. In *K. (M.M.) v. K. (U.)*[46] a report prepared in 1988 was unfavourable to the mother based on her emotional and psychological statement of mind. At the time of trial in 1989 the doctor who prepared the report had a much more positive opinion of the mother and testified that the mother had recovered since the report was initially prepared at which time the family was in distress. The experts were unanimous that custody should remain with the mother. The trial judge awarded custody to the father relying on the 1988 assessment. The mother appealed and the court held that the trial judge erred in disregarding the testimony of the doctor one year after the report was made.

In the decision of *Britton v. Britton*[47] an assessment prepared three years prior to trial recommended custody to the father, however, at trial the said assessment was rejected by the court as not accurately

45 [1994] W.D.F.L. 092 (Sask. Q.B.).
46 (1990), 28 R.F.L. (3d) 189 (Alta. C.A.); leave to appeal to S.C.C. refused (1991), 31 R.F.L. (3d) 366.
47 (1991), 37 R.F.L. (3d) 253 (Ont. Gen. Div.).

representing the current state of affairs and was therefore of little assistance. A second and more recent assessment, which recommended custody to the mother, addressed the current situation.

In situations where there has been a significant change in circumstances from the time the report was completed and the evidence adduced at trial is inconsistent or materially different than what the facts or evidence were at the time the assessment report was completed, the court is unlikely to follow the recommendations in the assessment. The court will likely refer to the original assessment report as being but one piece of evidence to be weighed in determining what is in the best interests of the children.[48]

There are occasions, during the course of the assessment, where one of the parties may express reservations about the assessor which reservation is usually brought about when that party feels that the assessor is not relating to him or her and, therefore, is of the perception that the assessor is exhibiting a bias in favour of the other party. If the party is of that view part way through the assessment process it is open to that person to bring a motion to a court at that time for the purpose of seeking an order for a new assessment. Not to do so at the time of the expressed concern may ultimately be prejudicial in the sense that the court, at such a late moment in the proceedings (the assessment having been completed and substantial cost having been incurred), may be reluctant to order that a new assessment be conducted.[49]

14. UNILATERAL ASSESSMENTS

A not uncommon situation to occur in custody/access disputes is for one party to obtain an assessment which is conducted by a mental health professional at the request of that party, but to the exclusion of the other party. Sometimes this is done with or without the knowledge of the other party and, ultimately, the party obtaining the unilateral assessment wishes to use it as evidence at the custody/access hearing. This is sometimes done without any other assessment having been

48 *Kosokowsky v. Kosokowsky* (1992), 95 D.L.R. (4th) 309 (Ont. Gen. Div.); *McMahon v. McMahon*, [1993] W.D.F.L. 1310 (Ont. Gen. Div.).
49 *M. (C.) v M.(G.), supra*, note 35.

conducted earlier and sometimes it is done where an independent assessment has been done (that is agreed to by the parties or having been ordered by the court) but one of the parties is not happy with the recommendations and conclusions or opinions set out in the independent assessment. These unilateral assessments are usually conducted without the assessor having interviewed the other party or child, or persons the other party might normally suggest that the assessor interview in the course of an independent assessment involving both the parties.

The question that one has to ask oneself in considering whether to obtain a unilateral assessment is whether or not a mental health professional would conduct such a unilateral assessment and the extent to which a court would put weight on such an assessment if that party attempted to introduce the assessment into evidence and have its opinions and recommendations relied upon by the trier of fact.

Most mental health professionals would not likely conduct such an independent assessment as to do so would likely cause them to be in breach of their profession's rules of conduct or guidelines by which they are governed. For example, in Ontario the Ontario Psychological Foundation has published custody/access guidelines which provides as one of its underlying assumptions "that a complete and impartial custody/access assessment cannot be conducted on a one-sided basis (i.e., not on behalf of one parent alone, but only on behalf of the family as a whole)".[50]

Generally speaking an independent assessment carries more weight than an assessment arranged by one of the parties in a unilateral fashion, the corollary to which is that an assessment which includes all of the interested parties carries more weight than an assessment that does not.[51]

The unilateral assessment will likely only provide one perspective of events as seen through the eyes of the party arranging for the assessment. For obvious reason the situation could create an incomplete marshalling of the facts and could cause the assessor to make a

50 "Custody/Assessment Guidelines", The Ontario Psychological Foundation, Toronto, Ontario, 1988, at 1. No part of the guidelines can be reproduced without the written permission of the Foundation.

51 *Allwood v. Samuals*, *supra*, note 35.

recommendation based on that one party's perspective of events, which could be extremely prejudicial to the other party.[52]

52 *Whey v. Brenon* (1984), 41 R.F.L. (2d) 30 (Nfld. C.A.). In *M. (C.) v. M. (G.)*, *supra*, note 88 at 9 where the father, questioning the abilities of the assessor in the midst of the assessment, retained a psychiatrist for a second opinion. The psychiatrist did not meet with the children or the parties and assumed that the complaints of the father were true. The court gave little weight to the psychiatrist's report.

7

Assessing the Assessment

1. IN ANTICIPATION OF THE ASSESSMENT REPORT

A considerable period of time would have been spent in advising clients on the rationale and purpose of the assessment, in selecting an assessor and in preparing them for the assessment process. The clients, their children and any other persons affecting their lives, will have gone through the assessment process in some manner whether it be direct or indirect.

The clients and children will likely have undergone psychological testing and interviews. A relationship will probably have been forged between the parties and the assessors. The relationship between the parties and the assessor will vary depending upon the many different factors and personalities at play throughout the process.

Of even more importance is the fact that the children will have spent a great deal of time with the assessors and, possibly, where a team assessment is involved, their support staff regarding interviews and testing. Throughout the assessment process the players and characters in the assessment drama have been measuring one another in a number of different ways. Parents and parties (non-parents seeking custody or access) and their significant others, if any, will in particular be pondering what impression they may have made on the assessor and those involved in the process who may have some bearing on the outcome of the assessment. They will have many questions in their minds:

1. Did they suitably or appropriately impress the assessor?
2. Does the assessor understand their position as to why they feel they are best suited to have custody of or access to their children?
3. Does the assessor understand that they are loving and caring parents?
4. Will the assessor misunderstand or understand them regarding things told by them to the assessor? Will the assessor accept what they say?
5. Does the assessor like them? Were they too open or honest with the assessor?
6. Does the assessor seem to have a similar philosophy to them on how to raise, nurture and discipline children?
7. Does the assessor have the same cultural values and background?
8. Does the assessor understand that the other parent will be attempting to use his/her charisma and charm to influence the assessor in leaning towards a recommendation in favour of that parent?
9. Did one parent attempt to paint the other as a bitter, vindictive, self-centred, uncaring parent who will do and say almost anything to obtain a favourable recommendation? What if the assessor believes that parent?
10. What if the parent was not provided an opportunity to defend oneself against the vitriolic attack of the other?
11. Will the assessor truly understand the personalities, character and special needs of the children as only that one parent is capable of understanding given their closeness to the child and special bonding to that child acquired with years of unmitigated devotion and nurturing of the child's welfare?
12. Will their past conduct be morally judged by the assessor?
13. The children will ponder and wonder how they may have presented themselves to the assessor.
14. The children will be concerned as to whether throughout the process they have exhibited disloyalty to either parent and whether that fact will be revealed in the assessment process, which may then affect their relationship with that parent.

The parents and the children will most certainly have the above questions and many others in their minds at the completion of the interviews and tests. They will be anxious to see what recommendations the assessor will make. They know and fully appreciate, particularly the children, that the process will have a profound effect on their lives. It is with a great deal of trepidation and anticipation that they will await the formal recommendations of the assessor.

The children will probably wish that the assessor did not have to make a recommendation as they, by this stage of the process, will understand that the final outcome may very well, in a most profound way, affect their relationship with their parents and with their siblings. Most children would prefer that the parenting arrangement be settled by the parents without the involvement of third party professionals. Awaiting the recommendations of the assessor is similar to awaiting judgment day. In a sense, to the parents and children, the assessor's recommendations are indeed a judgment of the parties. The assessor will be reaching conclusions regarding the parents and children that will have a direct bearing on the final recommendations made and, therefore, possibly on the outcome of the custody/access dispute. The parents and children will be judged in such areas as intelligence, personality traits (good or bad), character, general preferences and dislikes, inter-personal skills, coping skills, ability to relate to children and, most importantly, a judgment will be made by the assessor as to how much time the parents will spend with the children, without whom both parents feel they could not possibly survive and carry on a full and balanced life.

When a client is advised by the assessor or lawyer that the final report has been completed it is almost universal that mountains can be moved and schedules changed forthwith so that a copy of the report can be picked up for perusal by the parents.

2. SOLE ASSESSMENT/TEAM ASSESSMENT

The mental health professionals available to do an assessment may vastly vary in terms of formal qualifications, such as in the examples of a social worker, psychiatrist and psychologist. Each of these professionals may have a wide range of experiences and courses in their formal education. As far as clinical experience is concerned each of these professionals may have branched out into various disciplines and sub-specialties within those disciplines, thus allowing them to develop a particular area of expertise. For instance, the psychologist and psychiatrist may be psychoanalysts or may not be. The psychologist may have developed an expertise in sexual abuse cases or may have developed an expertise in dealing with adolescents only. The experience and expertise of the assessor selected for the assessment process will vary and that expertise and experience will impact on the number of professional persons involved in the assessment process. Some assessors feel they are qualified to conduct the entire assessment process without the need of resource staff, such as technicians for conducting various psychologist tests or for social workers for the purpose of carrying out home studies or conducting interviews with teachers or other persons relevant in the child's life. On the other hand, there are many clinics established in major urban areas that are staffed by psychologists, technicians and social workers for the purpose of conducting assessments. These clinics in the various urban centres are generically referred to as "Family Court Clinics" and concentrate on a group or team approach in the assessment process.

It does not really matter whether a "sole" assessor approach is used in the assessment process or whether a "team" assessment approach is used. What is important is to ultimately determine whether the assessment process has considered all the appropriate activities and proceedings required to collect all necessary information and data allowing the assessor(s) to identify the clinical issues that have to be solved and to allow the assessor(s), where given the appropriate mandate, to make recommendations as to what is in the best interests of the child.

In the team assessment process, the likely leader of the team will be a psychiatrist or psychologist who inevitably will sign the report and will be the person in whose name the recommendations are made.

In situations where the assessor relies upon input from support staff, such as technicians or social workers, the lawyer should request the production of any reports, memos, written documents, tapes or other original instruments of source of information upon which the assessor(s) has relied in gathering facts and making reference to those facts in the assessment report. The assessor(s) on the other hand should maintain these original instruments of information at source in anticipation that they may be requested by a party's lawyer.

It is essential in the situation where the lawyer or his or her client has any concerns about the information collected in the assessment process, that the lawyer review the original sources of information relied upon in the assessment process. Such a review may disclose, by way of example, that the assessor in having reviewed the original source of information, has misinterpreted it, taken it out of context or simply misunderstood it. The client may suggest that he or she was not properly quoted. The client may even deny that what was purportedly said by the client was not what was said at all.

Therefore, in the situation where there is a concern about the data collected, one should request to see the notes prepared, for example, by the social worker from his or her home study visit or interviews with relevant persons; or the test results conducted by any technicians involved in administering personality testing, intelligence tests or other psychological tests of any of the parties or children; and doctors' reports or notes upon which the assessor may have relied or made reference to in the body of the assessment report.

3. PREPARING THE CLIENT

It is with great expectations that the parents and other interested parties await the assessor's final report. Will they be pleased with the outcome or will they be upset and disappointed?

The lawyer, on the other hand, will know that most clients, even those who perceive that the custody/access recommendations are favourable to them, will likely be unhappy with some aspect or feature of the report and its recommendations. It is a counsel's duty and obligation to not only prepare the client for the various steps in the assessment process, but also to prepare them for the day when the final report and its recommendations are available to be read and analyzed.

Counsel should attempt to emphasize in the client a frame of mind and perspective that the purpose of the assessment not be forgotten or go unheeded, that is, that the assessor wishes to assist the court and the parents in determining what is in the best interests of the children. An attempt should be made to prepare the parents for the positive and negative features of the report. An example, and a most common one, is that usually a parent will express shock, disbelief and utter hurt over the unequivocal preferences expressed by a child that the child wishes to reside with the other parent or be in the care and control of the other parent.

It is of extreme importance that the parents understand, as most likely will, that the child, out of loyalty to that parent and for fear of negative consequences, could tell that parent one thing regarding with whom they wish to spend time, but could tell the assessor quite another thing, either directly or indirectly.

The expectations of the client/parent have to be tempered with a dose of anticipated reality. The client must also understand that the assessment report and its recommendations can be used in a number of ways in order to achieve the ultimate goal of determining what is in the best interests of the children.

It is assumed for the purpose of this chapter that the assessment whether ordered by the court or consented to by the parties has been done with the intention that the issue of custody/access of the children will be proceeding to trial.

Once the client understands that the report will only be one piece of evidence at the trial, it will be necessary to review the report to determine if the assessor has met the main objective of its having been ordered by a court or the main objective of the assessment having been consented to by the parties and whether the information in the report is correct.

Was the assessment done as the result of a court order or did counsel and the parties merely consent that an assessment be conducted for the purpose of litigation?

If the assessment was the result of a court order did the court order set out a mandate or provide specific directions as to what the purpose or goal of the assessment was. Sometimes a court order is very general and simply orders that an assessment of the family be conducted. Some court orders are more particular and, for example, may provide that the assessment be restricted to certain areas such as determining the wishes of the children where they can be reasonably ascertained, or may be broad such as determining the ability of the parents to have custody or access to the child.

The earlier trend in the courts would reflect that the courts were prone to make an order for a general comprehensive assessment of the parties without any direction. Recent jurisprudence would suggest that judges, in ordering assessments, should focus on a particular area of concern and be specific in the directions regarding the area of concern to be explored in the assessment as this would be of greater assistance to the court than a wide ranging report prepared without direction.[1]

Where counsel or their clients have agreed that an assessment be conducted without having been ordered to do so, they often times send a common letter to the assessor setting out the mandate or the question or issue to be reviewed by the assessor. In such instance a careful review of the report should be done to see that the mandate, as set out in counsel's letter, has been met by the assessment.

There are many different components to an assessment although there do not appear to be any standardized guidelines as to the format or content of a report. Some reports are more detailed than others and focus on all the major areas of the information collected whereas in other reports the assessor simply gives general, overall impressions of the parties and the dynamics of the families in question. Thus, when counsel and clients sit down to assess the assessment they should keep in mind a number of factors when analyzing the report.

Given the enormity of weight that could be accorded by a court to an assessment report, it is a lawyer's job to assess the report in a most thorough fashion. Some assessors are more qualified than others. Some assessors will provide a good report that is complete in all respects. Some assessors are less qualified or skilled than others. Some assessors, for example, lose sight of the main objective of the report and become meshed in a personality clash with the parties. It is for the lawyer to analyze the report for the purpose of identifying its deficiencies or strengths. The client has retained the lawyer for this purpose.

The lawyer must put aside his or her personal beliefs and not judge the parties in a contested custody or access dispute. The lawyer may personally not have any objection to the recommendations or conclusions set out in an assessment report and actually feel that it would, from an objective point of view, be in the best interests of the children that the recommendations be adopted. A lawyer must sometimes step back from this objective perspective if the custody/access

---

1 *Linton v. Clarke* (1993), 50 R.F.L. (3d) 8 (Ont. Gen. Div.); affirmed (1994), 10 R.F.L. (4th) 92, 21 O.R. (3d) 568 (Div. Ct.); *Tyabji v. Sandana* (1994), 2 R.F.L. (4th) 265 (B.C. S.C.).

issue is proceeding to trial, and review the assessment from an adversarial perspective. The question the lawyer must ask himself is whether the conclusions of the assessment can be challenged effectively in court or whether the conclusions can be supported in court based on evidence that will ultimately be adduced.

The above comments should not be construed to mean that the adversarial approach must be adopted at all times. The adversarial approach will probably only be adopted once the lawyer and client have decided after an exhaustive analysis of the report that the recommendations and conclusions therein cannot be adopted as being in the best interests of the child. Obviously, if the client after an exhaustive analysis of the report can find his or her way to accepting the recommendations as being in the best interests of the child then hopefully, at that stage, serious consideration would be given to settlement of the custody/access issue based on the recommendations.

A lawyer will usually approach the task of assessing the assessment from one of two perspectives. If the report is favourable to his client the lawyer will wish to analyze it for the purpose of ascertaining whether the conclusions or recommendations can be supported at trial by the assessor. If the report is unfavourable to his client, the lawyer's analysis will attempt to find the areas that can be successfully attacked such as factual assumptions relied upon by the assessor. If the assumptions are incorrect or if the findings of the trial judge and the assessor differ on critical matters, the assessment may be flawed and of little assistance. It is obvious that where the assessor's recommendations are consistent with the facts established at trial and the law pertaining to those facts it will be given a considerable amount of weight. On the other hand, where the assessment is in any way flawed or based upon an incomplete investigation or has disregard for any significant evidence, the court will not put any weight on the recommendations set out in the assessment report.[2]

2 *Carlson v. Carlson* (1991), 32 R.F.L. (3d) 383, 81 D.L.R. (4th) 185 (B.C. C.A.); *Fasan v. Fasan* (1991), 32 R.F.L. (3d) 121 (Ont. Gen. Div.).

4. REVIEW OF ASSESSOR'S RECOMMENDATIONS OR CONCLUSIONS PRIOR TO PREPARATION OF FINAL REPORT

The question presents itself after the assessment process has been completed but prior to the final written report being prepared as to whether the parents and/or their lawyers should be advised by the assessor as to the recommendations and conclusions the assessor is inclined to make in the final report.

Assessors differ in their approach in this regard, with some having a meeting with the parents alone to discuss the recommendations the assessor has in mind and which are about to be inserted into the written report. Some assessors will include lawyers in this meeting.

Some assessors in accordance with the guidelines of The Ontario Psychological Foundation will make a verbal presentation to the lawyers and parents prior to writing the report. The purpose of such a presentation to counsel would be:

(a) to inform the lawyers as to the outcome of the assessment;
(b) to explain the process of the assessment and the rationale for the findings;
(c) to allow counsel to ask questions, offer comments, or make factual corrections;
(d) to give counsel an opportunity to achieve a settlement regarding a parenting plan;
(e) then to co-operate with counsel in facilitating the acceptance and implementation of the plan; and
(f) to advise counsel, should the matter be proceeding to trial, of the assessor's availability to meet with them, preferably together, to prepare for trial, and of the assessor's willingness to be cross-examined by counsel for any of the parties.[3]

Some assessors, on the other hand, prepare a draft written report which is prepared on a "without prejudice" basis or on a "for discussion purposes only" basis. The purpose of the above referred to

3 See "Custody/Assessment Guidelines, Report of the Interdisciplinary Committee for Custody/Access Assessments", The Ontario Psychological Foundation, 1988, Toronto, at 9.

approaches is to provide the parents and their counsel with an opportunity to voice their objections or concerns prior to the final version of the assessment being completed. This is a highly recommended procedure. Such an opportunity not only allows the clients to satisfy themselves that any concerns they may have had about the assessment process are answered, it also provides them with an opportunity to clarify any statements or information given to the assessor that they feel required some type of qualification. On the other hand, such an opportunity may bring to the assessor's attention facts or background of which the assessor was previously unaware. The process may shed light on an incorrect statement of fact or assumption reflected by the assessor in the report and on which the assessor's recommendations or conclusions are based.

It would probably be diligent of the lawyer prior to any assessment being conducted, whether by way of court order or at the request of counsel without the benefit of court order, to ascertain from the assessor in question as to what the process will be. Will the assessor be advising the parents of the recommendations or conclusions that are being considered prior to the report being prepared in its final form?

If a letter setting out the client's complaints regarding the contents of the draft assessment is sent to the assessor, the assessor, in some cases will respond in writing in which case the written response could effectively be considered part of the assessment report and therefore admissible in evidence.[4]

5. REVIEW OF THE FINAL WRITTEN ASSESSMENT

There are many factors to be considered in the review of the assessment report for the purpose of determining whether the mandate imposed on the assessor by the court, in the event of a court ordered assessment, or whether the mandate given to the assessor by counsel in the form of mutually agreed upon written instructions, without the necessity of a court ordered assessment, has been met.

4 *Darling v. Chung* (1988), O.J. 1334.

Where there is no specific mandate other than counsel and the parties having agreed that an assessment be conducted in the general sense, there are no universally accepted standards as to the features that should be contained in an assessment.

In the decision of *Boody v. Boody*[5] Justice Perras stated that the assessment should contain the following information:

- An outline of the assessor's professional qualifications.
- A list of the issues presented for assessment.
- A description of the assessment process including the number of interviews and other participants.
- A detailed summary of the facts developed in the course of the assessment.
- An insight into the needs of the children and the ability of each parent to best satisfy those needs.[6]
- An assurance that the recommendations in the report have been presented to the parents, child and counsel and that ways in which these can be implemented have been determined and discussed with all of the parties.

5 (1983), 32 R.F.L. (2d) 396 (Ont. Dist. Ct.) at 399-400. For other interesting reading with respect to standards see, by way of example:
Mayers, Nadine, "Effective Processes in Custody/Access Assessments" 11 C.F.Q., p. 147 at 155; Gindes, Marion, "Guidelines for Child Custody Evaluations for Psychologists: An Overview and Commentary" (1995), 29 Family Law Quarterly at 39; American Psychological Association: "Guidelines for Child Custody Evaluations in Divorce Proceedings" (1995), 29 Family Law Quarterly at 51.

6 See the following decisions where in essence it was held that a properly conducted custody/access assessment should identify the needs of the child following the family break up and the respective abilities of the parents to meet a child's needs: *Bush v. Bush*, [1994] W.D.F.L. 1245 (Ont. Gen. Div.) where the assessor concluded there was no abuse. *Sampson v. Sampson*, [1995] W.D.F.L. 652 (B.C. Master) where it was held that children were under emotional and physical stress; *P. (M.J.) v. P. (P.A.)*, [1995] W.D.F.L. 404 (Sask. Q.B.) where it was held that the assessment addressed the parenting strengths and weaknesses and children's needs; *Nichols v. Nichols*, [1995] W.D.F.L. 801 (B.C. Master) which case underlines the principle that an assessment should also provide a judge with insight into the relationship between the parents. It was held in that case that an assessment should deal with the conflicting stories of needs of the child and the ability of the parents to meet those needs.

- An outline of possible alternative solutions, with advantages and disadvantages, which have been presented to parents, child and counsel.
- The recommendation or favoured solution of the assessor, together with reasons.

The client must also understand that the report with its recommendations set out therein is not necessarily the determinative factor in the custody assessment issue and that the amount of weight to be given to the recommendations, and their author, have yet to be subjected to the scrutiny of cross-examination. The client should also understand that just as courts can give a great deal of weight to a sound report that offers recommendations based on correct assumptions, the court can also disregard those recommendations in a report if there are flaws or other reasons to lead the court to disregard those recommendations. Depending on the circumstances peculiar to the family in question, and other evidence called at trial, the recommendations set out in the report may, in the discretion of the court, be given a great deal of weight in determining the ultimate outcome, or be given little or no weight. In determining what weight to be put on an assessment a judge can take into account the skill of the assessor, any bias or preference of the assessor, the methodology employed by the assessor and the reasonableness of the conclusions reached by the assessor.[7]

The point cannot be made strongly enough that the assessment is only one piece of evidence available to the court in a custody/access trial. The court's function is to hear all of the evidence adduced at trial and to weigh and assess it in a judicious manner. The court, in doing so, will decide what amount of weight shall be put on each piece of evidence in arriving at its decision as to which of the parties shall have custody of or access to the children in question. In addition to the assessment report being adduced into evidence, there will usually be an abundance of other evidence, not the least of which is the evidence of the parties themselves. It is not unusual that relatives, close friends, teachers, family physicians (children's doctors) and other persons will also testify at the trial so as to give the arbiter of fact as much evidence as possible to be considered in deciding such a difficult issue as to

7 *C. (R.M.) v. C. (J.R.)* (1995), 12 R.F.L. (4th) 440 (B.C.S.C.). In this case the court determined that the psychologist was impartial, experienced, knowledgeable and wise and, therefore, his report was given a great deal of weight.

what is in the best interests of the child. Although some of these witnesses may have been interviewed by the assessor or the assessor's support staff in the course of the assessment process, some will not have been interviewed. Those who were interviewed and whose comments or observations have been relied upon and referred to by the assessor in the report, will be subject to undergoing cross-examination at which time their comments would be more closely scrutinized.

Upon the client receiving the assessment and having digested its contents, whether favourable or not to their case, he or she will want to know from the lawyer whether the conclusions or recommendations in the report will be accepted by a judge and what bearing the recommendations or conclusions will have on the ultimate outcome of the case.

(a) Client's and Lawyer's Concerns

It is essential that the lawyer and the client read over the contents of the assessment prior to meeting with one another, in particular to allow the client time to digest the contents of the assessment report. It can be extremely difficult for a client to read a report that may be unfavourable to the client or critical of the client in a most personal manner. Most clients should allow themselves a few days reaction time to digest the contents of the report. If they insist on meeting with the lawyer immediately, and it is clear that they will be in an emotional state, it is probably wise to postpone the meeting with the client until the emotions have abated somewhat.

Have the client identify for you, in writing if possible, all concerns he or she may have about the report prior to your meeting. In obtaining this information go through your personal check list of elements that you would wish to review in the report and compare them with the list provided by the client.

In meeting with the client it will become clear that certain complaints can be dealt with quickly in the cases where he or she can be assured that the element or component of the report of which they complain is either irrelevant to the advancement of their position or can be explained to the client in a satisfactory manner.

The client will have to be placated regarding those elements of the report about which they are upset but which elements in the view of the lawyer are irrelevant to the issue of custody and access. A simple example of this might be in the observation of the assessor as to how the client dresses, or an observation may be made that the client appeared to be "suffering from a mild to moderate degree of anxiety". Such observations by an assessor are simply part of the process of accumulating overall factual background and information regarding the client. These specific observations by themselves will not likely have any bearing on the recommendations about to be made by the assessor or on the outcome of the custody and access issue at trial.

It is the concerns of the client that, in the view of the lawyer, may indeed be relevant to the client's case that have to be dealt with. The lawyer, as well, may have his or her own concerns about certain elements and matters raised in the report. A decision will have to be made as to what approach, strategy or tactic should be employed in dealing with the concerns of both the client and the lawyer. Generally, these concerns will be dealt with through the process of the lawyer writing a letter to the assessor pointing out the concerns and in some cases requesting that the assessor respond in writing to the concerns raised by the lawyer. In some cases the lawyer, either with or without the client, will meet with the assessor and discuss the concerns. Whether it is done by way of the lawyer writing a letter dealing with the concerns or done through a meeting with the assessor, the idea and intent is to have the assessor reconsider those areas of the assessment to which the client and lawyer object and that the report be amended in this regard. This, of course, can cause problems because it is somewhat akin to a referee or umpire in an athletic event changing their mind after having made a judgment call. An amended report would usually cause the opposing counsel or other parent to then become upset with the amendment made by the assessor. The assessor will have to decide how he or she would deal with the situation where he or she has decided to amend the assessment as a result of concerns raised by one parent or that parent's counsel.

A close review of the report by the lawyer and client will also, of course, reveal all of the positive aspects emanating from the assessment's conclusions or recommendations. The revelation of positive factors will, of course, allow one to measure the element or components of the report that will serve as corroborating evidence in the advancement of your position at trial on behalf of the client.

It is of vital importance in circumstances where an assessment is favourable to your client that you have a "fireside chat" so that it be impressed upon the client that he or she not be seen or perceived by the other parent as "gloating" or being "smug" over the conclusions and recommendations in the report. The positive or favourable aspects of the report should not be used to provoke the other parent or in any way exacerbate the wounded ego or offended mind set of that parent who would have read the report which, in their view, is deemed to be unfavourable. The client who is the beneficiary of what might be considered a favourable report should be encouraged, through counsel, or in direct communication with the other parent where feasible or possible, to persuade the other parent that the recommendations are in the best interests of the child or children. This should not be done with an attitude that might be perceived by the opposing counsel or the other parent as being one of "I won - you lost".

One approach to be considered in persuading the other parent to accept the recommendations is for the parents to have a meeting with the assessor to discuss those recommendations. This meeting would have to be on a "without prejudice" basis with or without counsel in attendance, so that the parents are free to express themselves without worrying whether their remarks may come back to haunt them.

A review of the assessment may also reveal to the lawyer a great deal about both parents that previously was unknown, such as personality traits, character strengths and flaws, likes and dislikes, background information regarding criminal activities, background information regarding medical histories, history of alcohol or substance abuse, or any other background or facts that will be of significant interest to the lawyer. Such information disclosed about the other parent may provide the lawyer with ammunition with which to effectively cross-examine that parent. The awareness of pertinent information may cause the lawyer to commence investigation of areas not previously thought to be relevant to that parent's ability to care for the children. Is there a history of prior criminal offences? Is there a history of previous psychiatric problems and care regarding which there may be medical records and reports to be subpoenaed and reviewed for the purpose of cross-examination?

Of course the report could also reveal information about your client about which you were previously unaware. The client may have intentionally or unintentionally overlooked disclosing to you what might be a most important fact or important information relating to his or her ability to care for his or her children. In these circumstances the opportunity should be seized upon to extract from the client an explanation for the oversight and/or to have the client make full and complete disclosure of all background, particularly those facts or incidents that may later surface to be used at trial during cross-examination of the client.

An in depth review of the report will have to be made in order to identify what concerns the client or lawyer may have and whether these concerns should be addressed with the assessor.

It is extremely important that the client and lawyer be satisfied that the collection of data and information by the assessor and the compilation of same be complete, particularly as that collection of data relates to the interview of the parties, the children where feasible, or other persons whose input may be considered instrumental or relevant to the assessment process.

(b) Interview of Parties

In the review of the assessment the first area to examine would be to determine whether the client feels he or she had the opportunity to fully express themselves to the assessor regarding all relevant aspects of the assessment, including their concerns regarding the child and/or their concerns of the ability of the other parent to have custody of or access to the child.

Generally speaking, clients will feel they had an opportunity to freely express themselves to the assessor or the assessor's support staff. However, upon review of the report they may feel that the assessor has failed to put any emphasis or enough emphasis on some of the information they provided to the assessor and which they feel would have an important impact on the assessor's view of things. The lawyer should determine what the client feels is missing from the report in this regard and then decide what tactic is to be employed in addressing the problem.

(c) Interview of Child

The child, of course, will be interviewed by the assessor. One should probably examine the content of what the child told the assessor and determine whether, in the view of the parent, the content or comment is consistent with what would ordinarily be expected of that child. Sometimes the child's comments will, to the parent, seem uncharacteristic. Therefore, one has to review the circumstances in which the child was interviewed. Some children, for example, will simply not be comfortable and relaxed during an interview conducted in the assessor's office or some other environment that may not be user friendly or that may not be familiar to the child. In these circumstances the child may well be inhibited in how they answer questions during the course of the interview. Therefore, the report should be reviewed to determine whether or not the child was interviewed at home in addition to being interviewed at the assessor's office. It is important that home interviews be conducted as the child may feel more comfortable and relaxed in a home environment and thus less inhibited. In a friendly home environment the child will likely speak more freely and openly.

It is essential, if home interviews are conducted, that they be conducted in each of the parents' homes. This will dictate against one parent suggesting that there may be a bias on the part of the assessor with respect to having selected the home of the other parent as the more appropriate place for the interview. Perhaps even more important, however, it is sometimes interesting to observe how the child or children react or respond to the interview in the home environments of the parents. The nature and manner of the child's response could be revealing. If the child is more subdued in one home than the other, the question may be asked, for example, as to whether this is due to the fear of one parent or whether it relates in some other way to that parent's inability to provide a relaxing atmosphere and thus provide appropriate care for the child. From counsel's perspective these elements of the child's interview could be extremely important in preparation for the cross-examination of the assessor. The admission by the assessor of his or her observation that the child's inhibition in that particular parent's home is of concern could be used in argument when asking the court to draw an inference that it would not be in the best interests of the child to be with that parent given the child's inhibitions and perhaps fear or reluctance to be with that parent in that parent's home.

The contents of the report should be closely read with respect to where the interviews of the child took place to determine whether the child's or children's responses were appropriate or inappropriate having regard to some of the factors above described. As to whether the child's comments are admissible in evidence or as to whether the child's comments are hearsay is a matter discussed in that part of the chapter dealing with cross-examination of the assessor.

(d) Children's Wishes

In most jurisdictions the relevant legislation governing custody/access matters sets out the criteria and factors it will consider in determining what is in the "best interests" of the child. In almost all jurisdictions one of the criterion that courts consider of paramount importance in a custody/access case is that of determining the views and preferences of the child where such views and preferences can reasonably be ascertained.[8]

In dealing with this issue it is assumed that it has been predetermined that any effort to ascertain the wishes and preferences of the child will be exercised through the process of a formal assessment, and that the children will not be testifying at the hearing.

In the vast majority of cases of separation, the views of the parents as to what is in the best interests of the child will suffice as in fact the parents usually do know what is in the best interests of the child. They will therefore reach an agreement without involvement of the courts, an assessor, or any other person or institution in helping to decide what is in the best interests of the child. However, where no agreement can be reached between the parents in this regard, the issue of the child's wishes and preferences will present itself whether the assessment is being done within the litigation process or whether the assessment is being done outside the litigation process. In the former situation the parties are already within the adversarial process, whereas in the latter case, although they are not within the adversarial process in the context of litigation, they are in fact being adversarial

8 Children's Law Reform Act of Ontario, R.S.O. 1990, c. C.12, s. 24(2)(*b*).

to a certain extent, otherwise it would not be necessary for an assessment to be conducted in order to assist the parties or the court in determining what is in the best interests of the child. Either way, the parents are engaged in some sort of adversarial circumstance regarding the issue of who should have custody of or access to their child.

The underlying element of the adversarial process is that each parent is ultimately responsible for adducing or leading evidence that is consistent with the advancement of their case or position, that position being that the child should be in their respective care and custody. Thus, a parent may lead evidence that concentrates on supporting their position or claim and not necessarily lead evidence that is in the best interests of the child. The interest of the parents may differ from the interests of the child. This can cause problems, particularly in that not all of the evidence that is relevant to the issue of what is in the best interests of the child may be put before the court as part of the parent's case, including the views of the child where such views can be reasonably ascertained. Hopefully an assessment by a qualified mental health professional will assist the court in attempting to determine the views of the child.

The child should not be a passive and dependant non-participant in the consideration of what is in his or her best interests. The "best interests of the child" test demands that children's wishes not be excluded from consideration by the court. To the contrary, the child's wishes, views or preferences should be made known to the court.

Children are persons in their own right and have a right to be heard. We are not aware of any published guidelines or policy in Canada that specifically sets out the rights of children in separation or divorce actions. However, we are reminded of the "Bill of Rights of Children in Divorce Actions" as published by and relied upon by the Family Court in Milwaukee County, Milwaukee, Wisconsin. The rights according to this Bill of Rights are set out below.

I The right to be treated as an interested and affected person and not as a pawn, possession or chattel of either or both parents.

II The right to grow to maturity in that home environment which will best guarantee an opportunity for the child to grow to mature and responsible citizenship.

III The right to the day by day love, care, discipline and protection of the parent having custody of the child.

IV The right to know the non-custodial parents and to have the benefit of such parent's love and guidance through adequate visitations.

V The right to a positive and constructive relationship with both parents, with neither parent to be permitted to degrade or down-grade the other in the mind of the child.

VI The right to have moral and ethical values developed by precept and practices and have limits set for behaviour so that the child early in life may develop self-discipline and self-control.

VII The right to the most adequate level of economic support that can be provided by the best efforts of both parents.

VIII The right to the same opportunities for education that the child would have had if the family unit had not been broke.

IX The right to periodic review of custodial arrangements and child support orders as the circumstances of the parents and the benefit of the child may require.

X The right to recognition that children involved in a divorce are always disadvantaged parties and that the law must take affirmative steps to protect their welfare, including, where indicated, a social investigation to determine, and the appointment of a guardian ad litem to protect their interests.

In the tenth provision referred to, reference is made to steps being taken to protect the child's welfare, including, where indicated a social investigation to determine, and the appointment of a guardian *ad litem* to protect their interests. It is suggested that a guardian *ad litem* may be substituted with the appointment of an assessor who could be involved in determining or ascertaining the views of the child.

The child's wishes, views and concerns must ultimately get presented to the court and in doing so it is important that the evidence led, whether through the assessor or otherwise, be accurate, complete and consistent. It is important for the lawyer and the client to be satisfied that in so far as possible, given the age and circumstances of the child, that the preferences and views of the child be expressed freely and without duress from any other party or person.

In a disputed custody case it is essential to determine the child's views as to how they feel about either parent, their daily lives and activities, their concerns and needs, their relationship with friends and teachers, and any other of the multidimensional facets of their well being.

In reviewing the circumstances under which an assessment makes references to a child's views, concerns or preferences, there are some fundamental questions that will have to be asked. For instance, is the child capable of expressing his or her views. Are they the child's views, or are they the views of someone else such as a parent or other adult figure in their lives.

What explanation did the child provide for offering a view or preference? Was it based on the more attractive living arrangements in one household as opposed to the other? Was it based on the discipline and structure or rules of one parent which in the eyes of the child may be more lenient or more strict than the other parent? Does the preferred parent allow more sleep overs than the other? Are curfews more relaxed in one household than the other? It would be impossible to make reference to the multiple and complex factors that may be relevant or important in the mind of a child when offering his or her view as to with which parent the child prefers to be with.

If the assessment makes reference to the child having expressed a preference or views regarding any matter concerning their welfare, the report should provide as much detail as possible and be explicit as to how the child's views or preferences were elicited by the assessor. Was it done by direct questioning or indirect questioning? Did the child simply volunteer his or her preference or wish? Was the child prodded? Were leading questions asked of the child suggesting an answer? All of these factors are extremely important and counsel should insist of the assessor, in appropriate circumstances, that full details be given with respect to these areas of interest or concern.

Counsel will wish to examine the circumstances under which the child's express preferences have been exacted so that in the case of a favourable response, it can be reasonably ascertained that the circumstances under which the wishes, views, preferences or concerns of the child were obtained cannot be challenged in court. In the case of an unfavourable response, counsel should do an exhaustive review of the report and the circumstances under which the child's interviews were conducted to see if such circumstances can be challenged as not having been the proper or appropriate circumstances under which to exact a response from the child. Thus, the report should provide full details *vis-à-vis* the child talking about his or her life and the role of the parents and the role of other significant persons in that child's life. This detail will better enable the lawyer and parent in the review of the report to grasp the child's needs or preferences if so expressed. If either counsel or parent has concerns regarding the circumstances under which the child's views were elicited, counsel should ask the assessor for all notes or records kept in this regard. Without disclosure and full detail of the said circumstances counsel cannot be as effective as they might otherwise be in cross-examination in revealing the weaknesses of the assessment. The assessor should, on the other hand, maintain a complete record of all interviews with the child and the circumstances under which the interviews were conducted and should be prepared to release that information, if not to counsel, then to produce it at the time of trial if subpoenaed to do so.

(e) Weight to be Put on Wishes of Child

Clearly, a review of the circumstances in which the child's views and preferences are elicited leads to the ultimate goal of measuring what weight counsel feels a court will put on the express views of a child at trial.

One of the most common questions a parent will put to counsel with respect to the assessment making reference to a child's views or wishes is the extent to which such views or wishes of the child will be given weight or consideration by a court in the determination of what is in the best interests of the child with respect to the ultimate custody/access issue.

A review of the jurisprudence reveals that there is no practice, policy or guideline carved in stone in this regard as developed by the courts, other than suggesting that the courts listen to and often give effect to the wishes of the children who are in older age brackets. There is legislation dealing with preferences of the child as evidenced by the *Children's Law Reform Act* of Ontario,[9] section 24(2)(*b*) where it is provided that in considering the best interests of the child, the views and preferences of the child, where such views and preferences can reasonably be ascertained, are to be a factor to be considered by the courts. It should be noted however that the *Divorce Act* (Canada) is silent with respect to the wishes of the child.

9 R.S.O. 1990, c. C.12.

There are many examples of cases where a child's views or preferences have been relied upon by an assessor in making a recommendation that the child reside with one parent or the other but which recommendation has not been accepted by the court for various reasons. For example in the decision of *Tapley v. Tapley*[10] the court found that the assessor's opinion was not sensitive enough to the wishes of the child which were lost in the process.

The Ontario Court of Appeal decision of *Docherty v. Beckett*[11] is an example of a case where the assessor relied too much on the child's preference. The court stated:

> It is clear from Dr. Chiarot's opinion, as stated above, and his viva voce evidence that he has concluded on the basis of what he has been told by the child that the child has a strong desire to live with the father and in Dr. Chiarot's opinion if this wish was not accommodated, the child would develop an increasing resentment towards the mother. The difficulty with the opinion of Dr. Chiarot is that it appears to be based entirely on statements made to him by the child that the child wished to be with his father. When the child was interviewed by Dr. Murray G. McGovern on October 22, 1987 the child told him precisely the opposite. . . .
>
> . . .
>
> It is obvious to us that the preference of this child as to his custodial parent was not consistent and certainly little weight should be attached to his wishes in the circumstances.[12]

---

10 [1983] W.D.F.L. 763 (Ont. U.F.C.).

11 (1989), 21 R.F.L. (3d) 92 (Ont. C.A.); leave to appeal to S.C.C. refused (1990), 23 R.F.L. (3d) xli. See also *Hudson v. Hudson*, [1989] W.D.F.L. 637 (Man. Q.B.). The court ruled that the assessment report was not helpful as it was rushed and too much emphasis had been given to the children's wishes (the assessor had based her recommendation primarily on the wishes of the children, aged 12 and 9). The court further held that the husband had an undue influence upon the children. The mother was a manic depressive but her condition was under control and it did not necessarily affect her parenting ability. Nonetheless the father advised the children that the mother was mentally ill and unfit to care for them. He also told them of the assessment report, which recommended that he be awarded sole custody. The court further held that the assessor, by accepting the children's statements and wishes as true and reliable, was in effect asking the court to let the children write their custody order on the prompting and direction of one of the parents.
See also *Tarling v. Tarling,* [1995] W.D.F.L. 063 (B.C. S.C.) where the court held that the assessment was significant in the court refusing to accede to a child's request for a change in the custodial arrangement.

12 *Ibid.*, at 95 and 96.

(f) Age at Which Child's Wishes Are Given Weight

At what age does the court consider it appropriate to consider the views and preferences and wishes of the child in determining what is in the best interests of the child? A review of some of the various approaches taken by the courts over the years yields some interesting perspectives.

For instance, in 1971 a well-known study in Ontario was conducted into "The Attitude of Judges at the Supreme Court of Ontario (as it then was) with Respect to Child Custody Cases.[13]

In that study, the judges were canvassed in the context of interviewing children in chambers in custody cases in order to determine their views and preferences. This led to determining the views of the judges as to at what age they considered appropriate in consulting children with respect to their views. Some of the judges believed that every child over the age of nurture should be consulted. They believed that they could detect when the child was saying what he or she has been told to say as opposed to when he or she was speaking his or her own mind. Some of the other judges took an intermediate stand, stating that the older the child the more likely they are to consult with them, but they did not make a habit of this practice in every case. The majority took the line that the opinion of the child over the age of 10 years carried great weight in every case, but that under the age of 10 years, the weight attached to the opinion depends on the circumstances; in the latter cases the child's opinion usually only settled the case in borderline situations, whilst in the former cases, the opinion overrides all but exceptional evidence suggesting a contrary judgment.[14]

On the other hand, D.M. Siegel and S. Hurley, suggest that the assessment of the child's capacity to state his or her views be made according to the circumstances of each particular case rather than by the arbitrary application of age guidelines.[15]

---

13 Bradbrook, A., "An Empirical Study of the Attitudes of the Judges of the Supreme Court of Ontario Regarding the Workings of the Present Child Custody Adjudication Laws" (1971), 49 Can. Bar Rev. 557 at 559–560.

14 *Ibid.*, at 559–560.

15 Siegel D.M. and Hurley S., "The Role of the Child's Preference in Custody Proceedings" (1977), 11 Family Law Quarterly at 2.

The suggestion that the circumstances of each particular case be reviewed in this regard is, from a common sense perspective, difficult to challenge as most mental health professionals would probably suggest that all children develop differently and that one child's degree of emotional maturity at a particular age may be quite different than the emotional maturity of another child the same age.

In a booklet published for children by the Ontario Ministry of the Attorney General entitled "Where Do I Stand? A child's legal guide to separation and divorce", it is suggested that if the child is at least 14 and getting old enough to make some of his or her own decisions, he or she may be able to do that.

Clearly, although the wishes of a child are not necessarily the ultimate deciding factor or controlling factor in assessing the best interests of the child they become increasingly more important as the child grows older and could therefore be given considerably more weight the older the child.

(g) Wishes of an Older Child (Age 10 - 14)

Where children have reached their teenage years, and the children have made it clear in some manner what their wishes are, then likely a fair amount of weight will be given to their wishes unless there are compelling reasons not to do so.[16]

The question presents itself as to whether or not a court is likely to ignore the wishes of an older child such as one in their mid to late teens when they are determined to live with one parent as opposed to the other. The courts generally concede it would be fruitless to ignore the wishes of such a child.[17]

The courts have also ignored the wishes of an older child where they consider that the child's preference is not in the child's best interest.[18] This decision underlines the point that one should not confuse the issue of ascertaining the preferences of a child with the

---

16 *Hagan v. Hagan*, [1983] W.D.F.L. 1034 (Ont. H.C.); *Tapley v. Tapley*, *supra*, note 10; *Corrado v. Corrado*, [1989] W.D.F.L. 1387 (B.C. S.C.).

17 *Sweeney v. Sweeney* (1993), 139 N.B.R. (2d) 60 (Q.B.); *Sharpe v. Sharpe* (1974), 14 R.F.L. 151 (Ont. H.C.); *El-Sohemy v. El-Sohemy* (1980), 17 R.F.L. (2d) 1 (Ont. H.C.).

18 *Stanley v. Stanley* (1988), 84 N.S.R. (2d) 411 (Fam. Ct.); *Martel v. Vatcher*, [1989] W.D.F.L. 1335 (Nfld. T.D.).

paramount issue of what is in the best interests of the child. They may be two different things.

Obviously the younger the child the less likely is the court to put a great deal of weight on the wishes expressed by that child. Depending on the circumstances of the case, a review of the case law would show that children between the ages of 10 and 14 can affect the outcome of a custody decision by having their wishes adopted by the court[19] and other cases would show that the wishes of children between the ages of 10 and 14 will not be given any weight.[20] In these cases it really becomes a question of weight to be given to the wishes of the child by the trial judge in the exercise of his or her discretion.

(h) Wishes of a Child Under the Age of 10

As a general rule, the courts have placed little or no reliance on the wishes of a younger child. Children under the age of 10 years are more impressionable than older children and as has been pointed out earlier are more likely to be subject to subtle and not so subtle influences by adults. Thus the courts generally are of the belief that young children are not old enough to make a mature and reasoned decision when it comes to what is in their best interests. In most

---

19 In *Hiscocks v. Marshman*, [1991] W.D.F.L. 1136 (Ont. Gen. Div.), a 13-year-old did not wish to be returned to his mother's custody in California and the psychologist, therapist and Official Guardian assured the court that the child's wish was sincere. The father in Ontario was awarded interim custody. In *Togyi v. Togyi*, [1985] W.D.F.L. 554 (B.C. S.C.), the court awarded custody of twin boys, aged 13, to the mother based on the boys' preference to remain with her. The court made the decision despite the adverse views expressed by social workers in two separate custody reports prepared for the court.

20 In *Alexander v. Alexander* (1986), 3 R.F.L. (3d) 408 (B.C. C.A.), custody of an 11-year-old child was awarded to the father despite the child's express wish to remain with his mother, who had been the custodial parent for 11 years. The court felt that the mother had allowed the child to become too much the focus of her life, resulting in a loss of perspective such that she could not respond objectively to the child's needs. In *Rudaniecki v. Rudaniecki*, [1987] W.D.F.L. 2273 (Ont. U.F.C.), the court held that the whim of the eldest child, a rambunctious and impulsive 11-year-old, to be with his father was not a deciding factor in determining his custody as the mother's overall home surroundings were otherwise satisfactory, healthy, stimulating and settled.

instances it is probably safe to say that the courts will put little weight on the expressed wishes of a child under the age of 9.[21]

Given the weight that could be accorded a child's wishes it is imperative that all the circumstances surrounding any statement made by the child in this regard and the circumstances and data relied upon by the assessor in determining what he or she believes the child wishes or preferences are, be completely disclosed and examined by counsel.

(i) Biases

Some assessors will have biases or distinct prejudices that can affect the outcome of an assessment. In appropriate cases the qualifications of assessors should be questioned and any elements of bias against either a father or mother should be thoroughly canvassed. A litigant may have a justifiable fear of bias if an assessor has preconceived notions on the occurrence of certain events or conduct. Judges should be conscious of preventing even the appearance of bias to maintain the integrity of the litigation process. For instance, in the decision of *Children's Aid Society of Perth v. Tumber*[22] it was held that the fact an expert was called in to consult in a child protection case was not indicative that the expert witness came to the task with preconceived notions in favour of one party. In any event, the potential for so-called bias in the context of the assessor having preconceived notions did not mean an approach which was contrary to the children's best interests. By way of example, some assessors may have a strong belief in the doctrine of tender years which is a rule of common sense (but not a rule of law) that many courts apply in custody cases and which rule provides that a child of tender years should be in the care

21 In *Simms v. Simms* (1976), 15 Nfld. & P.E.I. R. 238, the court refused to hear evidence of a 6-year-old child as she could offer no mature observation. In *Re Brown*, [1986] W.D.F.L. 1816 (Nfld. T.D.), it is unwise to attach significant weight to the wishes of a child who is only 6 years old. In *Gilson v. Gilson*, [1987] W.D.F.L. 1560 (Ont. Dist. Ct.), given an 8-year-old child's age and her conflicting expressions of opinion the child's views and preferences could not be reasonably ascertained. In *Schultz v. Schultz*, [1984] W.D.F.L. 233, the court in awarding custody of two children to the mother disregarded the express wishes of the older child, aged 9, to remain with her father because the paternal grandmother would be the primary care taker of the children if they were placed with the father.

22 [1994] W.D.F.L. 1576 (Ont. Prov. Div.).

and custody of its mother unless there is compelling evidence by the father to show that it would be detrimental to the well being of the child not to be.[23] If the assessor believes in the doctrine of tender years, then, in the perception of some lawyers and parents, the assessor is clearly showing a bias and a father of young children could certainly have his case prejudiced by having an assessor who believes in the doctrine of tender years principle, conduct an assessment involving children of tender years.

There may be a strong personality conflict between the assessor and one of the parents that interferes with the assessor's ability to provide an impartial assessment, thus resulting in a bias.[24]

Bias may lie in the fact that the assessor has failed to interview a number of interested persons who support one party, or worse, the assessor only interviews persons whose names are provided by one party but chooses to not interview persons suggested by the other party.

Religious beliefs and spiritual beliefs can contribute to bias or prejudice on the part of the assessor. Any allegation or claim of bias on the part of a judge or the assessor based on religion may simply be in the perception of one of the parents. It may be the tact of one parent, who is not happy with the recommendations in the assessment, to raise the issue of religious bias on the part of the assessor.[25]

The religious background of the parties and the religious training of the child are important criteria to be considered in an assessment. Not only would one look for bias on the part of the assessor, but one would look to ascertain if the parties' views on religion and their views on the religious training of the child in any way might impede or affect their ability to care for the child.

---

23 *S. v. S.* (1992), 35 R.F.L. (3d) 400 (Ont. C.A.); *Talsky v. Talsky*, [1976] 2 S.C.R. 292, 21 R.F.L. 27.

24 *Avitan v. Avitan* (1992), 38 R.F.L. (3d) 382 (Ont. Gen. Div.). In this case a strong personality conflict existed between the father and the assessor to the degree that it interfered with the assessor's ability to provide an impartial assessment and the court could not rely on the proposed recommendations.

25 *Voortman v. Voortman* (1994), 4 R.F.L. (4th) 250 (Ont. C.A.). In this case the assessment discussed religious differences of the parties and recommended custody to the father. The mother appealed on the grounds that the trial judge made the decision based on religious prejudice. However, the Court of Appeal held that the judge's conclusions were reasonable and properly supported by the evidence.

In the not too distant past certain provincial statutes provided that the child's religious education was to be a decision for which the father's authority was paramount.[26] Current legislation has no similar provision, however, the courts consider that the religious background or religious training of the child can be of significant interest in deciding what is in the best interests of the child.[27]

Cultural and native heritage is certainly an important factor to be considered in the assessment process. One of the unique and special features of Canada is that it is a multi-cultural society. As Canada grows there is a growth of the many cultures that exist in the country, each of which has its distinct customs and traditions. A multi-cultural society spawns cross-culture relationships, partnerships and marriages. In the event of a separation involving cross-cultural partners in which an assessment is to be conducted many problems can surface.

There can be serious disruptions or even termination of a child's culture and heritage or of any of the many characteristics or features of a child's particular culture or heritage as a result of the separation. The parents may feel that the child's development and education of a particular culture and heritage is threatened by the separation and they will wish to be assured that the mental health professional or professionals conducting the assessment are qualified in the context of understanding any cultural nuances or traits that will be significant in the development of the child.

---

26 *Infant's Act*, R.S.O. 1970, c. 222, s. 2.

27 In *Hockey v. Hockey* (1989), 21 R.F.L. (3d) 105, 69 O.R. (2d) 338 (Div. Ct.), custody of twin sons had been awarded to the mother. The children had been christened in the United Church. Later both parents took up different faiths. The mother had applied to vary the father's access rights so as to effectively preclude him from being able to take the child to services of his faith. On appeal this restriction on access was reversed. The court made it clear that such religious discrimination would not be tolerated by the courts. In *James v. Page*, [1991] W.D.F.L. 157 (B.C. S.C.), the courts declined the invitation to choose between Jehovah's Witness and Anglican religions by granting the care and control parent sole decision-making power in this regard. In *Solomon v. Solomon*, [1991] W.D.F.L. 230 (N.S.T.D.), two male children were born to a Jewish father and a formerly Catholic mother who had converted to Judaism upon marriage. After separation the wife returned to the Catholic faith. The court had to decide whether or not the boys would have Bar Mitzvah's at age 13. The court decided the boys would have their Bar Mitzvah's because it was in the children's best interests to have the opportunity to know two different faiths and to be able to choose later in life.

More often than not the assessor may not realize that a comment in the report smacks of prejudice or bias, or that a comment may be perceived by a party as having an element of bias as the assessor may not realize that he or she is exhibiting a bias. The effect of cultural differences between an assessor and a party may fall short of resulting in bias but could well make it difficult for the assessor and the party to relate to one another. The courts, in appropriate circumstances, will give consideration to and put weight on the principle that cultural heritage and cultural identity be maintained in a child's life.[28]

The suggestion of bias or prejudice existing in an assessment can be an extremely difficult and sometimes delicate area of concern to be dealt with by the lawyer and client. Some times the element of bias is quite apparent and some times it is more subtle and thus not so apparent.

An example of this may be seen in the decision of *More v. Primeau.*[29] In that case there was a custody action between a parent (mother) and non-parent (stepmother) with respect to a nine-year-old boy. The mother was French Canadian, the assessor was Anglo-Indian. The step-mother was white Anglo-Saxon Protestant. The assessment recommended that the stepmother have custody of the child. The trial judge stated:

> Third, having seen both [the assessor and the mother] in the witness-box, I am in a position to draw conclusions which I do without any reflection on

28 In *M. (C.) v. H. (H.)*, [1990] W.D.F.L. 1141 (Alta. Q.B.), the father was Jamaican, the mother was Caucasian. The mother gave up the child for adoption shortly after its birth and the child was in the care of prospective adoptive parents for over a month. The father sought custody. The father was awarded sole custody. The court found it was in the child's best interests for racial and cultural reasons to be in the care of her father. In *Lin v. Lin*, [1991] W.D.F.L. 364 (B.C.S.C.), the father's wish was that the children become educated and retain their Chinese culture. The court held this was in the best interests of the children and the father was awarded custody. In *Camba v. Sparks* (1993), 124 N.S.R. (2d) 321 (Fam. Ct.), the father was a white French-Canadian; the mother was an anglophone African-Canadian. The mother was granted sole custody as she was more likely to support and encourage the mixed racial and multicultural background of the child. In *Maier v. Chiao-Maier*, [1990] W.D.F.L. 1288 (Sask. Q.B.), the mother was Chinese, the father was white Roman Catholic. The mother was teaching the 3 1/2-year-old child Cantonese and had arranged for him to learn Mandarin. The father did not have a similar interest in the child's Chinese background, therefore, the mother was awarded custody.

29 *More v. Primeau* (1978), 2 R.F.L. (2d) 254 (Ont. C.A.).

> either the assessor or on the mother. I conclude that there is little in common between these two ladies, and that in a realistic sense, one could not easily communicate with the other. [The assessor] is precise and orderly, reflecting her distinctive Anglo-Indian background. It seems clear to me that she would have the greatest difficulty in achieving a rapport with a vivacious French Canadian lady like the [mother]. On the other hand, it would be easy to see that she would relate easily, as she obviously did, to the [stepmother]. In no sense do I wish to be construed as suggesting that the conclusions of [the assessor] are biased or injudicious, but I have been forced to conclude that she was simply unable to comprehend fully the position of the [mother].[30] (The mother was awarded custody of the child).

In Canada cultural problems also surface on a regular basis in assessments that involve families where one parent is a Canadian Indian (native heritage) and one parent is non-Canadian Indian.[31] It is extremely important for the lawyer or client, preferably before the assessment process is even commenced, to voice any concerns they may have with respect to whether the assessor may have any biases or prejudices that might affect their case.

The problems of bias do not necessarily fall within the domain of the assessor. The parent may very well create the problem and prejudice his or her own case due to a cultural belief that may be misinterpreted in the Canadian courts. If one parent unwittingly, in the course of the assessment, makes a comment concerning his or her views on custody and access, which views accord with his or her cultural traditions, and which views would be considered in the best interests of the child within his or her culture but which views in the mind of a Canadian court or assessor may not be considered to be in the best interests of the child, such comments could have a direct bearing on the recommendations in the assessment report and could influence the trier of fact.[32]

30 *Ibid.*, at 268.

31 In *Gordon v. Little Mustache*, [1991] W.D.F.L. 094 (B.C. S.C.), the court took into account that the child's native heritage was more likely to be preserved if she remained with her mother. In *L. (J.P.) v. M. (J.W.)*, [1990] W.D.F.L. 666 (N.S. Fam. Ct.), the mother was awarded custody where the father and his parents, who had been caring for the child, down played the child's dual heritage. The mother wished the child to be exposed to and learn Micmac culture.

32 *Darling v. Chung* (1988), O.J. 1334. In this case the father was Chinese, born and raised in Hong Kong. The wife was Canadian. In the assessment the assessor stated he had concerns in how the husband's cultural background flavoured the husband's perspective on what would be in the child's best

(j) School Visits and Home Visits

(i) School Visits

It may not be necessary that the assessor visit a child's school in the case of every assessment, however, whether such a visit is deemed appropriate by the assessor will depend upon the circumstances of the child in question.

There will be cases where the assessor, after having interviewed the child, will want to learn more about the child's schooling and the extent to which the child is prospering or not prospering in the school environment. Some assessors, as a matter of course in the assessment process, will conduct a school visit whereas others will only do so where they feel that the circumstances peculiar to the case in question call for it. In some cases one of the parents will consider it important that the assessor visit the child's school so as to gather as much information as possible regarding the educational environment of the child. Counsel for the parent will want to know to whom the assessor spoke and what information was obtained from the school whether as a result of discussions with the teachers or as a result of being provided documentation concerning the child, such as report cards or means of evaluation used by the school. Copies of any documents relied upon by the assessor should be requested and reviewed by counsel.

If a school visit is conducted it will be important to the assessment process to gather information regarding the child's overall performance and, more particularly, the child's academic, behaviourial and social performance.

(ii) Home Visits

The parents will likely want a home study to be conducted by the assessor as part of the assessment process for obvious reasons. Most assessors will agree to do this. Most parents feel that the home

---

interests. The husband told the assessor that in Hong Kong there was major shame involved in the breakdown of a marriage. In such a situation it was his belief that one parent should leave the scene entirely and the child be told that that parent had died. Fortunately the trial judge did not take the husband as literally as did the assessor and awarded joint custody of the child to the parties.

environment they have established for the child is conducive to their developmental growth and nurturing. The parents feel more relaxed in their home than in an outside environment. They will therefore think it important that the assessor come to their home to interview them and the child. Such a visit will also afford the assessor an opportunity to observe the parent and child interact and perhaps divulge information that is not easily obtained in the assessor's office.

A house visit will also allow the assessor to observe first hand the physical layout of the home, the specific accommodation for the children, and the feel of the home in the context of whether it provides an aura of healthy and advantageous environment for the child.

In the review of the assessment one should look for a detailed summary of the assessor's home study and be satisfied that appropriate consideration of the home has been given.

The school visit and the home visit are just one of many elements in the assessment process, however, it is important that if the school or home visit is relied upon by the assessor in the report, the assessor should have prepared written school visit reports and written home study reports. These reports should be available to counsel or the court if necessary. Unless the reports are uniform, objective, professional and provide an independent judgment they will sustain criticism by a court and not likely be accorded much weight.[33]

6. HOW TO DEAL WITH CONCERNS

Where, upon review of the assessment counsel or the parties have any concerns about the contents of the report, communication should be made with the assessor about the concern or concerns. The most obvious first step would be to consult with opposing counsel to see if an agreement can be reached that the assessor amend the assessment so as to provide the appropriate opinion requested pursuant to a court order or as requested by counsel. This step should be taken even though the inappropriate opinion is favourable to your client although, the initial reaction of counsel, for obvious reasons, may be one of reluctance to do so.

---

33 *Hudson v. Hudson* (1986), 39 Man. R. (2d) 42 (Q.B.).

The next step would be to communicate with the assessor for the purpose of expressing counsel's view or preference that the perceived offending or inappropriate opinion be deleted from the report given that it falls outside the mandate initially imposed by court order or requested by counsel.

When the lawyer or client approaches the assessor it should be done in a very diplomatic, courteous and tactful manner. The idea is to raise the concerns as a matter of constructive criticism and not necessarily as an attack of the assessor.

Obviously, there are many ways in which communication with the author of the assessment report can be done. Suffice it to say that if initial contact by counsel is made by way of telephone or letter, a conference call should be held including counsel for the other parent, or at least the opposing counsel should receive a copy of any letter sent to the assessor thus affording the other counsel an opportunity for input as to how the concerns raised might be dealt with.

Some assessors will have no objection to meeting with the parents to consider their concerns or any questions they may have with respect to the recommendations in the final report. Some assessors will invite counsel to be present at the meetings.

Some assessors do not like to have follow up meetings either with parents or with counsel as they feel that they have done a thorough report and have considered all the facts and relevant matters affecting the best interests of the child issue.

If a meeting is agreed to by the assessor it is an opportunity for counsel to evaluate the assessor's manner and demeanour and perhaps his or her philosophy on various concepts or doctrines applied to the issue of what is in the best interests of the child. Such a meeting could afford counsel an opportunity to have the assessor answer questions in anticipation of cross-examination and to get a sense of how the assessor might handle questioning.

On the other hand, the meeting may result in the assessor agreeing to amend the report for the purpose of correcting any of the contents where it would be appropriate to do so.

If the assessor, for whatever reason, does not deem it appropriate to address the concerns raised by counsel or the parties and, therefore, does not revisit the report or take corrective steps in this regard, then the concerns raised can be dealt with ultimately through the process of cross-examination at trial.

In most cases, assessors will have developed their own strategies, methods or policies for dealing with concerns raised by lawyers and/or the parties after the written report has been completed.

8

Introducing the Assessment into Court

1. FILING AND SERVICE OF ASSESSOR'S REPORT

The rules of procedure and process regarding the serving and filing of the assessor's report varies from jurisdiction to jurisdiction according to the regulatory process in place pursuant to which an assessor has been appointed. As seen in Chapter 4, there are a number of legislative enactments and rules of court procedure in the various provinces which permit the appointment of an assessor but which also make provision as to how an assessment is properly put before the court and into evidence.[1]

For example, the Ontario *Children's Law Reform Act*, in providing for the court appointment of an assessor, stipulates that the person appointed as an assessor shall file the report with the clerk or registrar of the court, who shall in turn give a copy of the report to each of the parties. The said report is admissible in evidence in the application being heard on the merits. Any of the parties may require the person appointed to attend as a witness at the hearing.[2] Whether the assessor is appointed by order of the court or on the consent of the parties, there

1 See Appendix III setting out provincial legislation in this regard.
2 See s. 30(7) to (10).

are usually rules of court procedures in place in the various jurisdictions which govern the serving and filing of an expert's report. In some provinces the rules of civil procedure require the party calling the expert witness to serve a copy of the report, signed by the expert, setting out his or her name, address and qualifications and the substance of his or her proposed testimony not less than 10 days before the commencement of the trial. Other provinces require that such a report be served at least 30 days prior to the commencement of the trial.[3]

Failure to comply with these requirements means that the expert is prohibited from testifying except with the leave of the trial judge. Clearly these rules dealing with expert witnesses would be applicable to assessors in custody/ access cases where a report has been prepared setting out the findings and conclusions of the expert.

At trial, or at the appropriate hearing dealing with the custody issue, the assessor's report should be marked as an exhibit, thus ensuring that the assessor will be able to refer to his or her report during the evidence. Marking the report as an exhibit allows the trier of fact to have a copy to refer to throughout the proceeding which in the case of a persuasively written report will be beneficial to the party calling the assessor as an expert witness.

2. WHOSE WITNESS IS THE ASSESSOR?

The determination of which party calls the assessor as an expert witness will be very much influenced by the circumstances under which the assessor has been appointed and the conclusions and/or recommendations set out in the assessment report.

Often the parties will have consented to the appointment of an assessor and to the naming of an assessor without the necessity of a court order. Sometimes a consent order is issued whereas in other circumstances the consent of the parties is housed in either an interim or final domestic contract.

When an assessor is appointed in the above referred to circumstances, it is usually intended by the parties that they obtain both a neutral assessment and a neutral assessor. It is probably also accurate

3 Pink, J., Matthews, K., Tupper, A. and Wells, A., *The Expert: A Practitioner's Guide* (Carswell, 1995), Chapter 1, para. 3.5.

to suggest that in most cases where the parties have consented to an assessment being conducted each party reasonably contemplates that the recommendations of the assessor will be favourable to their position, that is, that there will be a finding by the assessor that it is in the best interest of the child that he or she be in the care and control of that particular parent. Both parties also reasonably expect that they will be seen in reasonable light by the assessor. Assuming that the assessment will invariably contain recommendations that one party or the other will consider to be more favourable to the other party a quandary could very well present itself as to how the report and its recommendations will get before the court, and as to which of the parties will call the assessor as an expert witness for the purpose of providing opinion evidence. It is not unreasonable to expect that the party who considers the report to be favourable to his or her case will likely wish to call the assessor as an expert witness. However, in some cases of a custody/access assessment, the situation can present itself where both parties have concerns about the findings in the assessment and, therefore, both wish the right to cross-examine the assessor, or for whatever other reason, the parties cannot decide who will be obligated to call the assessor as a witness, both wishing to preserve the right to cross-examine the assessor. Whose witness is the assessor in these circumstances? In these circumstances do the normal rules of evidence apply even though the parties had consented to the appointment of a neutral assessor? Is the party who calls the assessor as a witness restricted as the party calling the witness would normally be, to direct examination with the opposing party only having the right to cross-examination?

Generally speaking it is the role of the parties, not the court, to call and examine witnesses. Counsel have the right to determine what witnesses to call, in what order, and what evidence to adduce from them. Parties in the same interest have the right to examine the witness, but not to cross-examine. Parties adverse in interest have the right to cross-examine, a right of fundamental importance.[4] Therefore, the party who calls the assessor as an expert witness may be limited to examination-in-chief only.[5] However, due to the so-called neutral-

---

4 Sopinka, John, Lederman Sidney N., Bryant Alan, *The Law of Evidence in Canada* (Butterworths, 1992), Chapter 16, at 821.

5 See *Sawyer v. Sawyer* (1984), 42 R.F.L. (2d) 374 (B.C. S.C.). In this case an assessor was appointed by the court to conduct an assessment of the family.

ity aspect of the assessment process some courts feel that all of the parties to a custody action should have the right to cross-examine the assessor who prepared the report.[6]

At the time that the parties to a custody case consent to the appointment of an assessor, consideration should be given to putting a formal agreement or arrangement in place that either party may call the assessor as a witness and that either party may cross-examine the assessor. If necessary, the agreement should be reduced into writing by way of an exchange of letters, a consent order, or a domestic contract. If such an agreement cannot be worked out and the parties cannot agree as to whose witness the assessor is or as to who will have the right to cross-examine the assessor then an application to the court or trier of fact should be made for directions in this regard. In a situation where the assessor is appointed by court order directions regarding who shall have the right to call or cross-examine the assessor should be sought at the time of the making of the order.

Notwithstanding who calls the assessor as a witness, the assessment report will likely have to be served on the opposing party and made admissible into evidence pursuant to the appropriate rules of court procedure and statutory guidelines that might apply from jurisdiction to jurisdiction as canvassed earlier.[7]

In certain jurisdictions counsel should be aware of the provisions of any statute that deals with the introduction of expert reports into evidence, such as the Ontario *Evidence Act*,[8] which for example, contains provisions dealing with the admissibility of medical reports, which provisions could be applicable to an assessor if the person appointed to conduct the assessment is either a registered psychologist

---

One of the parties elected to call the assessor as a witness. The court held that the party who called the assessor as a witness was not entitled to cross-examine the witness.

6 See *Mernick v. Mernick*, [1992] W.D.F.L. 1164 (Ont. Master). The parties hired a doctor to determine what custody arrangement would be in the best interests of their five-year-old. The mother sought to call the doctor as a witness in order to cross-examine him. The father objected. The court held that counsel for both parties may examine each professional called in a custody case. The doctor was pivotal to the resolution of the custody case. See also certain rules of different courts such as the Unified Family Court of Ontario and the Provincial Court (Family Division) of Ontario which provide that when an assessment is ordered in "child in need of protection" cases any party may summon the assessor and cross-examine that person.

7 *Supra*, note 3.

8 R.S.O. 1990, c. E.23, s. 52.

or a psychiatrist. The Ontario *Evidence Act* in dealing with medical reports, provides for the admissibility of any report prepared by a "practitioner" which definition includes a registered psychologist under the *Psychologist Registration Act.*[9]

A report obtained by or prepared for a party to an action and signed by a practitioner, and any other report of the practitioner that relates to the action, are, with leave of the court, and after at least 10 days' notice has been given to all other parties, admissible in evidence in the action.[10] All parties are entitled to a copy of the report failing which the author of the report shall not be permitted to give evidence. Therefore a psychologist who is appointed or retained for the purpose of conducting an assessment would appear to be governed by these provisions. The Act further provides for allowing the expert's report to be filed and to be admissible evidence without the expert giving *viva voce* evidence. Generally speaking, a party cannot proceed both to file the doctor's report and call the doctor and must elect what course he or she will pursue.[11] If he or she elects to file the report and leave is given to do so, then in most cases the doctor cannot be called by that party to give *viva voce* evidence. A doctor whose medical report has been tendered under the *Evidence Act* is the witness of the tendering party notwithstanding that he or she is subpoenaed to testify at trial by the opposite party.[12] In other words, at least in Ontario, if one party gives notice to the opposing party that he or she elects to file a doctor's report, or, in the case of a custody action, an assessor's report which has been prepared by a psychologist, the opposing party may insist that the electing party call the doctor to testify so that the opposing party may cross-examine him or her.[13] If an assessment report is obtained, whether on consent or by court order, the parties may decide to file the report, but not call the assessor. The trier of fact may insist that the assessor be called in any event in which case both parties would be entitled to cross-examine the assessor.[14]

9 R.S.O. 1990, c. P.36.
10 Ontario *Evidence Act, supra*, note 8, s. 52(2).
11 *Ferraro v. Lee* (1974), 2 O.R. (2d) 417 (C.A.).
12 *Kapulica v. Domancic,* [1968] 2 O.R. 438 (C.A.).
13 *Briand v. Sutton* (1986), 57 O.R. (2d) 629 (H.C.J.).
14 *More v. Primeau* (1978), 2 R.F.L. (2d) 254 (Ont. C.A.).

3. DISCLOSURE AND PRIVILEGE OF ASSESSMENT REPORTS

The Ontario *Evidence Act*[15] makes reference to the filing and admissibility of not only reports signed and prepared by a practitioner, but also to "any other report" of the practitioner that relates to the action. This raises the issue in custody/access cases of the extent to which any report prepared by an assessor has to be disclosed, and once disclosed, whether it has to be produced or whether privilege can be claimed for the document. By way of example, a party in a custody case may obtain a private or unilateral assessment through a qualified clinical psychologist notwithstanding the fact that a neutral assessment has been conducted as the result of a court order or the consent of the parties. The party who obtained the unilateral assessment may not be enamoured with the conclusions in the said report and, therefore, is not too willing to either disclose the fact that the report exists or produce the report for inspection by the opposing party. In such an example the question arises as to whether the report would have to be disclosed and produced.

Again one would have to look to the various rules of court procedure and relevant statutes in the various jurisdictions dealing with the admissibility of expert's reports. The Ontario *Evidence Act* seems to make it clear that all reports of a practitioner, the definition of which includes a registered psychologist, must be filed and produced if the party intends to rely on any one of the reports prepared by that doctor. Thus, in the above example, assuming the party who obtained the report does not intend to rely upon it, the psychologist would not have to produce the report, assuming there were no other reports prepared by him or her. However, assume that, for whatever reason, the psychologist had prepared two reports, and the party only wished to produce and rely upon one of them. The *Evidence Act* suggests that both reports would have to be produced, and unless otherwise ordered by the trier of fact the psychologist would not be able to claim privilege for the second report. It would appear, under the Ontario *Evidence Act*, that even in the situation where the reports are prepared two or three years apart, which can often be the case in custody assessments due to the delays in getting the case heard, both

15 *Supra*, note 10.

reports would have to be introduced into evidence if an attempt is made to rely on only one of them.

In continuing to use the above example, if the party who obtained the private unilateral assessment elects not to rely upon it, and thus does not disclose its existence how does the opposing party learn of the assessment's existence, the contents of which may be extremely relevant for the trier of fact in determining what is in the best interest of the child? Does the opposing party have an obligation to ultimately produce the report? One would look to the appropriate rules of court procedure to obtain the answer to these questions.

In most jurisdictions the existence of expert reports prepared by an expert engaged by or on behalf of a party to the action has to be disclosed at the examination for discovery stage of the action, including the opinions, findings and conclusions of the expert unless they were made or formed in preparation for contemplated or pending litigation and for no other purpose *and* the party being examined undertakes not to call the expert as a witness at the trial or hearing.[16] A word of caution is necessary here. The question presents itself as to whether an assessor, appointed to perform an independent or neutral assessment, is considered to be "an expert engaged by or on behalf of" one of the parties. It is probably debatable as to whether a neutral assessment falls within this definition. However, a unilateral or private assessment would likely be considered as containing the opinions, findings and conclusions of an expert engaged by one of the parties. Should the unilateral assessment, using the above example, have been obtained subsequent to examinations for discovery, and the party obtaining it wishes to rely upon it, then appropriate notice would have to be given to the other party.[17] In using the above examples of a unilateral or private assessment it has been assumed that only one of the parties and the children have been interviewed by the assessor. If an expert retained by one party interviews the other party, there may be a strong inference that any privilege was waived.[18]

Some assessors prepare draft or preliminary assessments prior to doing a final report. They then seek input from counsel and/or the

16 Ontario Rules of Civil Procedure, R.R.O. 1990, Reg. 194, Rule 31.06(3).

17 *The Expert: A Practitioner's Guide, supra*, note 3, Chapter 1, para. 3.5. Ontario *Evidence Act, supra*, note 10, s. 52; Ontario Rules of Civil Procedure, *ibid.*, rule 53.03(1).

18 *K. (C.R.) v. K. (G.F.)* (1987), 5 R.F.L. (3d) 433 (Sask. C.A.).

parties regarding the contents of the draft report and subsequently make amendments resulting in a final report that contains findings and conclusions that are different from those set out in the draft report. Would the draft or preliminary report have to be produced for examination in circumstances where one of the parties intends to rely upon the contents of the final report only and intends to introduce the said report into evidence? In Ontario, at least, there appears to be a difference of judicial opinion in this regard.[19] Some judges consider the preliminary and draft reports of an expert witness to be privileged and others do not. In a custody case it is difficult to imagine a situation where the trier of fact would not insist on the production of all relevant evidence including preliminary or draft reports. On the other hand there are triers of fact who would respect the fact that one is entitled to claim privilege and would not, therefore, draw an adverse inference from the fact that one has claimed a privilege to which he or she is entitled.[20] If one of the parties becomes aware of the existence of an assessment obtained by the other party for which privilege is claimed (even properly) one might raise the matter in argument at the conclusion of the hearing in the hope that the trier of fact will consider, in reflection on the merits of the case, why it is that the said party would claim privilege for a report, the contents of which probably are directly related to the issue of what is in the best interests of the children.

---

19 See *Cheaney v. Peel Memorial Hospital* (1990), 73 O.R. (2d) 794 (Masters). This case dealt with the request on examination for the production and disclosure of an expert's findings and conclusions. The court held that the applicable rule (rule 31.06) is not restricted to final opinions, findings or conclusions of experts nor to written reports; it requires disclosure of any finding, opinion or conclusion of an expert that is expressed in a sufficiently coherent manner that it can be used by counsel. See also *Kelley v. Kelley* (1990), 42 C.P.C. (2d) 181 (Ont. U.F.C.). In dealing with a request for production of a draft report pursuant to rule 31.06 the court held that preliminary drafts of a report prepared by an expert witness for the purpose of litigation are not "findings, opinions or conclusions of the expert" within the meaning of rule 31.06 and are privileged.

20 *Wentworth v. Lloyd* (1864), 10 H.L. Cas. 589 at 590-92, 11 E.R. 1154.

4. EXAMINATION OF ASSESSOR PRIOR TO HEARING

In most custody cases involving an assessor it is not necessary to consider the question of examination prior to trial or the hearing as upon request the assessor will likely co-operate in answering any questions regarding the contents of the report. Not to do so may suggest an element of bias which could taint the credibility of the assessor and, thus, the conclusions in the report. Can a party insist on the right to examine an assessor in a case where the party, for instance, feels that there is not sufficient information in the report in support of the conclusions set out therein and the assessor is not prepared to release any information to the party prior to his or her testimony? There does exist, in the various jurisdictions, the right to examine non-parties to an action with leave of the court but the exception to this right usually relates to an expert engaged by or on behalf of a party in preparation for contemplated or pending litigation.[21] Thus, once again, the question presents itself as to whether the assessor is the witness of one of the parties only or whether the assessor is considered to be the witness of both parties as is usually the case when a neutral assessor is appointed. Even if the assessor falls within those rules of procedure that allow for the examination of a non-party prior to trial, the test to be met in obtaining leave for such an examination is rigid and difficult to meet. One must exhibit that a request for information from the assessor has been refused and could not be obtained through the examination of one of the parties.[22]

5. ADMISSIBILITY OF EXPERT OPINION EVIDENCE

(a) Test for Admissibility

If a custody/access case involving an assessment proceeds to a hearing whether it be by way of a trial, an arbitration, or some form

21 Ontario Rules of Civil Procedure, rule 31.10(1).

22 *Famous Players Development Corp. v. Central Capital* (1991), 6 O.R. (3d) 765 (Div. Ct.); affirming (1990), 1 O.R. (3d) 672 (Gen. Div.).

of alternate dispute resolution, it would usually be the case that the assessor will be called to give evidence. If the assessor is called as a witness the purpose of his/her testimony would likely be to provide:

- Evidence based on his/her first-hand experience such as their personal observation of the parties and their children, or based on facts proven at trial. Any personal observations will allow the assessor to testify as to the veracity of the facts of which he/she has first hand knowledge like any other witness, and would also allow the assessor to give opinion evidence based on these facts.
- An opinion on certain issues in the case which opinion may be based on information, facts or knowledge of which the assessor does not have first hand knowledge, such as, for example, empirical data obtained from authoritative works authored by others, or information obtained as a result of discussions with other persons who will not be witnesses at the hearing.

In these circumstances a very fundamental question presents itself, that being, whether or not the opinion evidence of the assessor is admissible into evidence, by the trier of fact.

A good amount of the jurisprudence dealing with the admissibility of opinion evidence emanates from criminal law cases involving a judge and jury, where the question of admissibility is quite literal in the sense that the judge will have to determine whether the evidence should be admitted for consideration by the jury. As family law cases do not involve juries in this country the issue of admissibility of opinion evidence in a custody/access case is not so literal. In any civil matter involving a judge alone the question becomes not so much one of admissibility as it becomes a question of the amount of weight to be given to the evidence by the trier of fact. In most civil cases, including custody/access cases, the opinion evidence will likely be admitted, even if, at the outset, objection is made by counsel, unless it is obvious at that stage, that the said evidence is inadmissible. In most custody/access cases the trier of fact will likely have to hear all of the opinion evidence in order to determine if it meets the basic criteria for the admission of evidence and whether any significant weight will be given to that evidence.

The test for the admission of expert opinion evidence is as set out in the Supreme Court of Canada decision of *R. v. Mohan*,[23] where Sopinka J. stated:

> Admission of expert evidence depends on the application of the following criteria:
> (a) relevance;
> (b) necessity in assisting the trier of fact;
> (c) the absence of any exclusionary rule;
> (d) a properly qualified expert.

This test would have to be met in any custody/access case where an assessor, in the capacity of an expert witness intending to offer an opinion on any aspect of the case, will be called as a witness. A review of the criteria regarding the admissibility of evidence and their applicability to assessments is therefore warranted.

(b) Relevance

Relevance is the threshold requirement for the admission of expert evidence as with all other evidence. Relevance is a matter to be decided by a judge as a question of law. There is a distinction to be made between logical relevance and legal relevance. Logical relevance is so related to a fact in issue that it tends to establish the fact.[24]

Evidence that is otherwise logical may be excluded if its probative value is overborne by its prejudicial effect, if it involves an inordinate amount of time which is not commensurate with its value, or if it is misleading in the sense that its effect on the trier of fact is out of proportion to its reliability.[25]

An example of logical relevance in a custody/access case might occur in the following scenario. The assessor in the course of the assessment has interviewed a 13-year-old child who has unequivocally expressed to the assessor that she wishes to reside with her mother. At trial the assessor wishes to offer the opinion that it would be in the best interest of the child that she be in the care and custody

23 [1994] 2 S.C.R. 9, 18 O.R. (3d) 160.
24 *R. v. Mohan, ibid.*, at 20 and 21 S.C.R.
25 *Ibid.*, at 21.

of the mother. Such opinion evidence, in part, will be based on the statement the child made to the assessor. The child will not be a witness at the trial. The evidence of the assessor in these circumstances is seemingly logically relevant in that the wishes of the child, as expressed to the assessor, has such a direct and immense impact on what is in the best interest of the child, that it should be made admissible.

On the other hand, an example of evidence that may, in its own right, have logical relevance, but not be legally relevant to the issue before the court, is described as follows. In the course of a custody/access assessment, the assessor in taking the history of the parties makes copious notes of the respective parties various allegations that the other was responsible for the breakdown of the marriage. Assume that the parties have been married for 15 years and that they, as is not untypical in a family breakdown, both strongly feel that the cause of the separation is terribly important to the issue of who should have custody of their children. The assessor has formulated an opinion as to who is responsible for the breakdown but has also concluded in his own mind that the conduct of the parties throughout the marriage, as related to him by them, does not in any way affect their ability to parent the children. At trial counsel for one of the parties asks the assessor to give his opinion as to who was responsible for the breakdown of the marriage. In using this example, bear in mind that most legislation in Canada, dealing with custody/access matters provides that past conduct of a person is not relevant to a custody/access determination unless the conduct is relevant to the ability of the person to act as a parent to the child.[26]

In the above scenario, the evidence probably would not be considered as legally relevant due to the fact that the inordinate amount of time it would likely absorb in the trial process would not likely be commensurate with its probative value. Most judges, in the above scenario, would not permit such opinion evidence to be introduced, or, if they did, would attach little weight to it.

26 *Divorce Act*, R.S.C. 1985, c. 3 (2nd Supp.), s.16(6); *Children's Law Reform Act*, R.S.O. 1990, c. C.12, s. 24(3).

(c) Necessity

Opinion evidence of an expert witness must be "necessary" to enable the trier of fact to appreciate the matters in issue, due to their technical nature, prior to the evidence being made admissible.[27] In the *Mohan* decision, Sopinka J, in delivering the judgment of the court, referred to the comments of Dickson J. in *R v. Abbey*: "If on the proven facts a judge or jury can form their own conclusions without help, then the opinion of the expert is unnecessary."[28]

By way of example, assume that a formally and properly qualified psychologist has conducted psychological testing of the parties in a custody/access dispute. The testing reveals that one of the parties has a personality trait that features anti- social behaviourial tendencies which lend themselves to episodes of anger and abusive treatment of the children. Assuming that these personality traits would not be evident to a trier of fact, by observation of the party at trial, and, therefore, that the trier of fact could not draw such an inference or conclusion without the assessor providing an opinion regarding same, then it would seem that the opinion evidence of the assessor would be "necessary" to the court, so as to allow it to form its own conclusions. The amount of weight to be given to the evidence would be a matter of discretion to be applied by the trial judge.

The closer the expert's opinion gets to the ultimate issue in the case, the more rigid the court could be in exercising its discretion in admitting the expert opinion evidence. Although it is clear that the ultimate issue rule is no longer of general application, judges are still wary of admitting expert opinion evidence that touches too closely upon the ultimate issue to be decided.[29]

---

27 *R. v. Mohan*, *supra*, note 23, at 23.

28 [1982] 2 S.C.R. 24 at 42.

29 Pink, J., Mathews, K., Tupper, A. and Wells, A., *The Expert: A Practitioner's Guide* (Carswell, 1995), Chapter 1, para. 2.5. Also see *Weaver v. Tate* (1989), 24 R.F.L. (3d) 266 (Ont. H.C.J.); affirmed (1990), 28 R.F.L. (4th) 188 (Ont. C.A.).

(d) The Absence of An Exclusionary Rule

(i) Hearsay as a Component of Expert's Knowledge

Expert evidence is subject to the rules which govern the admissibility of all witness' evidence.

Although it has been asserted that the expert's opinion must be based upon either personal knowledge or facts presented at trial, it cannot be completely devoid of a hearsay element. Since the expert by definition possesses a special skill or knowledge in a material area superior to that of the court, the expertise is founded, to a large extent, upon hearsay data. An expert's opinion will be based on experience and education received. The expert's education is naturally comprised of the study and readings of works of authorities in the field and information and data culled from numerous sources. Therefore, an expert's knowledge is made up of the distilled assertions of others not before the court. Recognition of this hearsay basis of expertise has been acknowledged by Canadian courts for some time.[30] This type of hearsay evidence is a component of the expert's knowledge that he/she may draw upon in providing an opinion and such type of opinion evidence is admissible and generally has appropriate weight attached to it by a trier of fact.

In a custody/access case involving an assessment, the assessor's conclusions or opinions will often be based on a combination of his/her clinical experiences and upon the assertions of others as set out in authoritative literature which is recognized as such by those in a similar field of expertise to that of the assessor. A common example of this is often seen in assessor's reports such as where reference is made to the assessor's observations of children made during the course of the assessment. The assessor may offer the opinion, for instance, that the symptoms exhibited by the child are normal or abnormal for a child going through a separation process. The report is silent with respect to the basis upon which such an opinion is offered. The opinion is likely based on knowledge obtained by the expert through his or her readings of relevant literature generally relied upon by other experts in his or her field of expertise as being

30 Sopinka, Lederman and Bryant, *The Law of Evidence in Canada* (Butterworth's, 1992), at 546-547; *R. v. Anderson* (1914), 22 C.C.C. 455.

authoritative. For example, the assessor may opine in the report that a five-year-old child exhibited a feeling of mourning and sadness which is characteristic of a child that age going through a divorce.

If the assessor were asked how one can conclude, necessarily, that these symptoms are in fact typical for a child in those circumstances the assessor could likely make reference, for example, to studies done by noted child psychologists Wallerstein and Kelly[31] who in their studies concluded that a typical response in a separation for children aged five to eight was that they were likely to express feelings of sadness and mourning openly and that they tended to cry, feel rejected and long for a departed parent.

A further example of this can be seen in the decision of *Young v. Young*[32] where a doctor of psychology and an expert in the field of clinical psychology testified that it was her opinion based on clinical literature, that if a person is an abuser and does not take therapy that person is likely to be an abuser in another relationship. The psychologist's evidence was not only admitted by the trial judge but was relied upon by the court in arriving at its decision to grant custody to the mother.

This type of opinion evidence, although consisting of hearsay, is generally admissible, and would have significant weight attached to it by a trier of fact. Although the said evidence has a hearsay element to it, it consists of a component of the expert's knowledge.

(ii) Hearsay as a Component of the Expert's Opinion

The issue of admissibility of an expert witness' opinion becomes a little more complicated where the expert's opinion, rather than being based on first-hand knowledge facts or information, is based on second-hand knowledge and information, other than that acquired as a result of assimilation of the assertion of others as set out in authoritative literature, as canvassed above. This may occur in the case of a custody/access assessment where the basis for the assessor expert's opinion are facts, knowledge or information obtained, for example, from conversations with doctors, school teachers, nannies, or even neighbours or friends of the parties; or where the basis of the opinion

31 See Chapter 1.
32 (1989), 19 R.F.L. (3d) 227 (Ont. H.C.J.).

is based upon empirical data obtained from studies done by persons other than the assessor, such as studies regarding novel theory or scientific technique.

On a practical level, the reason for calling the assessor as a witness in a custody/access case will likely be for the purpose of having the assessor provide an opinion of some sort, which opinion is probably going to be based on, at least in part, second-hand information or data, without which the trial judge will not likely have before him or her all relevant evidence necessary for a final determination of the custody/access issue. As Dickson J. stated in *R. v. Abbey*:

> An expert witness, like any other witness, may testify as to the veracity of facts [of] which he had first hand experience, but this is not the main purpose of his or her testimony. An expert is there to give an opinion. And the opinion, more often than not,will be based on second hand evidence.[33]

It is worthwhile to review the issue of second-hand evidence that may present itself in the course of calling an assessor as an expert witness in a custody/access case and, to consider the extent to which such evidence may or may not be admissible.

If an expert witness testifies as to the statements made by a person who does not appear at trial to give evidence, and such evidence is proffered for the purpose of proving the truth of the statement, such evidence is hearsay, and unless there is an applicable exception to the rule against hearsay, such evidence is inadmissible.[34]

However, such evidence may be introduced for the purpose of demonstrating the basis for the expert's opinion, but the facts upon which the expert relies must be established prior to the court attaching any weight to the evidence.[35]

In the Supreme Court of Canada decision of *R v. Lavallee*,[36] the court, in following its decision in *R. v. Abbey*, held that an expert opinion is admissible if relevant, even if based on second-hand evidence, i.e., hearsay. However, hearsay is admissible to show the information on which the expert opinion is based, not as evidence going to the existence (or truth) of the facts on which the opinion is based. If the expert's opinion is based in part on statements made to

33 *Supra*, note 28, at 42.
34 *The Expert: A Practitioner's Guide*, *supra*, note 29, para. 2.6.
35 *R. v. Abbey, supra*, note 28, at 46.
36 [1990] 1 S.C.R. 852.

him or her, the statements are admissible as part of the material upon which his or her evidence is based, but failure to prove these facts independently will depreciate the weight given to the opinion.

R. v. Abbey had raised the interesting question of whether each of the second-hand facts upon which the expert's opinion is based, and comprising a component of the opinion, must be proven in evidence before any weight can be attached to it.[37]

In *R. v. Lavallee*, Wilson J. attempted to clarify any such confusion that may have been caused by the *Abbey* decision, by holding that as long as there was some admissible evidence to establish the foundation for an expert's opinion, the evidence is admissible, but the more the expert relied on facts not proven in evidence, the less weight a court (jury) could attribute to the opinion.

In *R. v. Lavallee*, Sopinka J. in a concurring opinion with Wilson J. suggested that a trier of fact could distinguish between evidence that an expert obtains and acts upon within the scope of his or her expertise and evidence that an expert obtains from a party to the litigation touching a matter directly in issue.[38] As seen earlier this is due to the fact that evidence which an expert obtains and relies upon within the field or area of his or her expertise is often times based on forms of enquiry (literature, seminars and lectures) and clinical experience that are deemed to be accepted means of decision within the expert's field. It is often within the scope of an expert's skill and training to evaluate the reliability and accuracy of information derived from various sources.[39] There are strong circumstantial guarantees of trustworthiness surrounding opinions arrived at under these circumstances and they deserve to be given weight.[40] Sopinka J. went on to say that any second-hand evidence obtained from one of the litigants, or from any other source that is inherently suspect, touching one of the issues in the litigation, ought to be independently proven.

The seeming result of the Supreme Court of Canada decisions in *R. v. Abbey* and in *R. v. Lavallee* is that the expert can rely on hearsay evidence in the formulating of his or her opinion, but if the hearsay comes from one of the parties to the action or some other interested

37 *The Law of Evidence in Canada, supra*, note 121, at 552-553.

38 *Ibid.*, at 554-555. See also *The Expert: A Practitioner's Guide, supra*, note 29, para. 4, at 1-17.

39 *R. v. Wilband*, [1967] S.C.R. 14.

40 *R. v. Jordan* (1984), 11 C.C.C. (3d) 565 (B.C. C.A.); *R. v. Zundel* (1987), 56 C.R. (3d) 1 (Ont. C.A.).

source, and the hearsay touches on one of the issues in the litigation, the hearsay should be independently proven. The less the facts upon which the second-hand evidence is based, is proven, the less the amount of weight that will be accorded to the opinion evidence by the trier of fact. The law of admissibility of expert evidence as canvassed above, applies, of course, equally well to the admissibility of an assessor's opinion evidence in a custody access case, where invariably, the assessor's opinion evidence will likely, in part, be based on second-hand information and thus have an element of hearsay to it.

By way of example, assume that in the course of conducting an assessment the assessor speaks to the neighbour of the father of the children in question. The assessor is told by the neighbour that he has seen the father, on a few occasions, selling drugs to unsavoury looking characters in the backyard of the father's residence. At trial the neighbour is not going to be called as a witness. However, the assessor will be attempting to provide an opinion that the father should not have custody of the children which opinion, in part, will be based on the conversation that the assessor had with the neighbour. In this example there are no facts before the court to support the opinion of the assessor, at least to the extent that the opinion relates to the father's alleged drug trafficking. If the drug trafficking allegation could be established as a fact by proof thereof, then obviously a court would be inclined to give more weight to the evidence than they otherwise would. Absent any other corroborating evidence of the father's drug trafficking some judges or other triers of fact may be reluctant to give any weight to the assessor's opinion evidence in this regard.

In some custody/access cases, involving the expert opinion evidence of an assessor, hearsay evidence will be tendered at trial, either *viva voce*, or by being set out in the assessor 's report, which hearsay evidence will be intended to form the basis of the assessor's opinion. As in the case of any expert opinion evidence, the weight to be given to such hearsay evidence will be in the discretion of the trial judge and, to a great extent, will depend on whether or not the secondary facts or information relied upon in providing the opinion are proven or are considered reliable by the trier of fact. In some cases the hearsay evidence will not be admitted,[41] and in some cases it will

41 In *Bruno v. Bruno*, [1984] W.D.F.L. 119 (B.C.S.C.), the court did not follow the custody consultant's report since it was based on hearsay evidence which could not be tested before the court by cross-examination. There was also little

be,[42] depending on the weight attached to the evidence by the trier of fact.

A particular problem regarding hearsay evidence and second-hand evidence in a custody/access assessment can arise particularly in those situations where the team assessment approach is used. Often times assessments are referred to family court clinics, organizations or even individual assessors where a number of persons are involved in the assessment and, thus, a team approach is used regarding same. There may be a number of differently qualified people involved in various aspects of the assessment. A social worker may deal with school visitations and home studies. A psychologist may interview the children and the parties. A psychometrist may conduct the psy-

---

factual material in the report against which the court could gauge the consultant's conclusions. In *Cardinal v. Cardinal* (1988), 17 R.F.L. (3d) 23 (Alta. Q.B.), the court ordered that a home study be done in a custody case. The report consisted entirely of interviews conducted by the author of the report and a statement of her opinion. The report consisted entirely of hearsay evidence and included a discussion of the mother's alleged drug dependence. The mother was not awarded custody of the child. On appeal a new trial was ordered based on the fact that the trial judge had relied too heavily on evidence which should have been ruled inadmissible as hearsay. In *Sherry v. Sherry* (1993), 1 R.F.L. (4th) 146 (P.E.I. T.D.), a home study was carried out by two social workers who made a recommendation as to access of the children based on information provided them by many individuals to whom they spoke during the course of the assessment. At trial, one of the social workers admitted that if any of the information provided her was not correct she would not have the grounds to make the recommendations. The court held that a trier of fact should be reluctant to accept opinions arrived at in this manner. The opinions only bear merit if based upon a direct professional observation of the facts. In *R. v. Olscamp* (1994), 95 C.C.C. (3d) 466 (Ont. Gen. Div.), a psychologist testified regarding the alleged sexual abuse of a 7-year-old girl. She did not personally interview the child or her parents. The psychologist based her opinion, that there was sexual abuse, on the observations of a psychometrist who had conducted play therapy sessions with the child, and on her own general clinical experience. However, she could not offer any evidence supporting the reliability of her clinical judgment. The trial judge refused to admit the opinion evidence.

42 In *Re Ammon* (1984), 47 Nfld & P.E.I.R. 176 (Nfld. U.F.C.), the court stated that given the nature of court ordered assessments and reports in a custody dispute, some hearsay evidence will be tendered or used to form opinions. The weight to be given to such reports is to be determined by the judge having regard to the source of such information and the nature of the allegation. In *M. (C.) v. M. (G.)* (1992), 40 R.F.L. (3d) 1 (Ont. U.F.C.), the court, in reviewing the contents of an assessment report in a custody matter, held that the fact that a report included hearsay went to its weight and not its validity or admissibility.

chological testing. Yet another psychologist may sign the report itself. Should a trial or other form of hearing be conducted, the person who signed the report will likely be called as a witness to provide an opinion regarding certain conclusions reached by the assessment team. His or her opinion will be based on the findings and conclusions, in part, of the other team members. To the extent that the evidence is based on the others' findings presents a potential hearsay problem. Will the assessor's opinion evidence be considered reliable and have appropriate weight attached to it, or, will all members of the assessment team have to be called to give evidence? In a situation of this nature, counsel responsible for calling the assessor should make certain that the other team members are available for the hearing if necessity so dictates. The best possible approach, of course, would be to assume that all team members be prepared and ready for trial.

(iii) Reliability of Expert Opinion Evidence (Novel Theory or Scientific Technique)

In *R. v. Mohan*, the Supreme Court of Canada explained that evidence that is otherwise logically relevant may be excluded if its probative value is overborne by its prejudicial effect, if it involves an inordinate amount of time which is not commensurate with its value, or if it is misleading in the sense that its effect on the trier of fact is out of proportion to its reliability.[43]

The reliability test is particularly relevant when dealing with novel theory or scientific technique as it may relate for example to the science of human behaviour such as in a custody/access case relying on the opinion of a psychiatrist or, when dealing with the issue of alleged sexual abuse where the expert evidence is often based on either behaviourial science testimony describing behaviours commonly observed in sexually abused children. Expert opinion evidence dealing with novel scientific theory or technique is likely to be excluded, or given little weight, on policy grounds because there is a danger of such evidence having an effect on the trier of fact which is out of proportion to its reliability.[44] To guard against this danger one

43 *R. v. Mohan*, [1994] 2 S.C.R. 9, at 21, 18 O.R. (3d) 160.
44 *The Expert: A Practitioner's Guide*, *supra* note 29, at 1-4.

of the factors considered in determining its admissibility is, therefore, whether it meets a threshold test of reliability, as set out in *Mohan*.[45]

In recent years, in custody cases, we have seen an explosion of new and unique syndromes, usually relied upon by one party in attempting to have the other denied custody or access to children. In the course of custody assessments we see allegations, for example, of brainwashing, parental alienation and sexual abuse of children. In order to establish or prove that such syndromes or theories are reliable and therefore admissible into evidence, one would ordinarily expect that expert evidence would be led to establish that the theories in question are accepted by the scientific community regarding the field of expertise in question, and the theories in question are accepted by the clinical community of the field of expertise in question.

In custody/access cases, one, on a more regular basis, sees the use of evidence involving psychiatry, psychology and other behavioural sciences in order to establish the existence of syndromes and to prove the novel theory or scientific technique related to the said syndromes. In the case of an assessment where an allegation is made of any one of the above syndromes the assessor will be required to launch a full scale investigation into not only the facts, but into the studies and literature and empirical data regarding any syndrome involving a novel theory or scientific technique. In ultimately formulating an opinion the assessor will most likely base it on a combination of clinical observations, clinical experience and an element of hearsay evidence in the context of relying on empirical data gathered by others or relying on expert assertions of others such as the opinion of a child psychologist specializing in child abuse cases, who might, for example, opine as to the significance of drawings done by a child or the behavioural patterns of a child who allegedly has been sexually abused by one of the parents. In circumstances such as these the basis of an assessor's opinion in a custody/access case will bear special scrutiny, which topic will be more specifically dealt with in Chapter 9.

Prior to any such expert evidence being admitted and being given an appropriate amount of weight the trier of fact will wish to be satisfied that the assessor possesses special knowledge with respect to the subject-matter in question. The more an assessor expresses an opinion based on a novel theory or scientific technique, which likely

---

45 *Supra*, note 43.

involves relying on the expressed assertions of others or relying on empirical data and the conclusions of others, the more the assessor, or any expert for that matter, is exposed to expressing an opinion beyond his or her area of expertise, in which case the degree of reliability becomes potentially less, with less weight therefore being placed on the evidence by the trier of fact.[46]

If an assessor, as an expert witness, attempts to provide an opinion that appears to be beyond his or her field of expertise, the assessor should be challenged on his or her qualifications.

In *R v. Marquard*,[47] McLachlin J. stated:

> The proper practice is for counsel presenting an expert witness to qualify the expert in all the areas in which the expert is to give opinion evidence. . . . As a practical matter, it is for opposing counsel to object if the witness goes beyond the proper limits of his or her expertise. The objection to the witness' expertise may be made at the stage of the initial qualification, or during the witness's evidence if it becomes apparent the witness is going beyond the area in which he or she was qualified to give expert opinion. In the absence of objection, a technical failure to qualify a witness who clearly has expertise in the area will not mean that the witness's evidence should be struck. However, if the witness is not shown to have possessed expertise in the area, his or her evidence must be disregarded and the jury so instructed.

In a custody/access matter being heard before a trier of fact alone, the expert evidence will likely be admitted and the question becomes one of the amount of weight to be attached to the evidence after having reviewed the assessor's qualifications and the reliability of the basis upon which the evidence is presented. This is particularly so in a case

46 See *M. (C.) v. M. (G.)* (1992), 40 R.F.L. (3d) 1. In this case a doctor, a recognized expert in the field of assessing children's credibility gave testimony in a custody case involving an allegation of child sexual abuse. One of the issues was whether the application had so alienated the children from their father that one of the children felt compelled to fabricate the sexual complaint in order to please her mother. The doctor testified at length in this regard about the role of the "parental alienation syndrome". However following a most effective cross-examination by the applicant's counsel it became clear that the concept of the parent alienation syndrome was a theory which the doctor had personally identified and labelled which he believed to be present in all custody/access disputes. The judge stated that "Without commenting on the theory's validity suffice it to say that he (the doctor) acknowledged that in this case it (parental alienation syndrome) exists at less than 10 per cent of its potential, and not, certainly, to the extent of being a protection concern or a significant factor in formulating a parenting regime."

47 [1993] 4 S.C.R. 223 at 243, 85 C.C.C. (3d) 193 at 224-225.

dealing with syndrome evidence which may deal with novel theories or scientific technique.

(e) Properly Qualified Witness

(i) Qualification of Assessor

The last of the criteria with respect to the admissibility of expert opinion evidence, as set out in *R. v. Mohan*[48] dictates that the evidence must be given by a witness who is shown to have acquired special or peculiar knowledge through study or experience in respect of the matters on which he or she undertakes to testify.

When selecting the person or organization that is going to do the assessment in a custody/access case a great deal of consideration should, at that time, be given to the qualifications that the assessor may possess. A full and complete investigation should be made of the assessor's background and experience prior to the actual selection being made so that one is fairly well assured that the selected person is potentially capable of giving reliable evidence to which an appropriate amount of weight will be accorded should the matter proceed to a hearing. It will be too late to wait until the eve of trial to discover that the assessor may not have the proper qualifications to be proffering expert opinion evidence. Some of the factors to be considered in assessing the qualifications of a possible assessor are worth reviewing.

The selection process of an assessor in a custody/access dispute is different in one major area from the selection process of an expert witness in other civil cases. In most civil cases requiring the utilization of an expert witness the parties to the dispute will usually be selecting their own expert for the purpose of obtaining expert opinion evidence regarding a particular issue.

In a case involving the selection of an assessor for a custody/access assessment, the parties and their counsel are usually concentrating on the selection of just one expert who is to conduct a neutral assessment on behalf of the parties and all other interested persons as a result of having either mutually agreed to have an assessment carried

48 *Supra*, note 43, at 25.

out, or, as a result of a court having ordered that the assessment be conducted. In either case, the parties are not competing with one another for the purpose of retaining an expert so as to assist them in the advancement of a better prepared case than the other with a view to winning at all costs. Rather, they are, in effect, forced to collaborate on the choice of the assessor. This process causes the parties and their counsel to more readily concentrate on the primary issue before the court, that being, a determination of what is in the best interest of the child. In these circumstances the parties will be concerned that the most qualified person and the most impartial person or institution be selected for the task in question. All concerned parties will require that the assessor be independent in all respects and, therefore, it is in everyone's best interest that the best qualified person be considered for the assessment. As opposed to other civil cases involving the use of expert witnesses, in the case of a custody/access assessment the parties and the lawyers are truly seeking a neutral expert witness who will be qualified to proffer an opinion in a particular field of expertise and whose evidence will, in the eyes of a trier of fact, be reliable in the context of being relevant, and of assistance to the trier of fact in drawing inferences or reaching conclusions that it would otherwise not be able to do without the said expert evidence. By having a neutral expert involved the risk of having expert evidence adduced which might be less than independent is greatly reduced, unless, of course, it is subsequently discovered during the course of the assessment by way of example, that there is an element of bias apparent in the assessment or in the approach or philosophy of the individual assessor.

In the selection of a neutral expert to act as an assessor in a custody dispute all interested parties will likely have in mind basic criteria to be met so that as competent as possible a person is in fact selected. What criteria does one consider? Judge Stephen Borins, in an article entitled: "Family Assessments In Custody And Access Disputes Under The Children's Law Reform Act, 1977"[49] made reference to a paper by Dr. Sal V. Levine, "The Role of the Mental Health Expert Witness in Family Law Disputes" who had posed the following insightful questions:

---

49 (1982), 24 R.F.L. (2d) 90 at 97.

> Is he an expert in name only? Is he truly familiar with the voluminous and often conflicting literature? Is he "up" on the latest research findings . . . which might force him to reassess his thinking? Is he open to change his mind, not to impose *a priori* his theory and dogma? Is he aware that what is factual in our field today is often heresy tomorrow? Is he dedicated to the preservation of the traditional family above all else? Does he know about the growing data on the success of all kinds of alternative families?
>
> Why is he pursuing this line of work? Does he enjoy the fray, the combativeness of litigation? Is he a lawyer in drag, or a mercenary? Does this line of work enable him to exercise his exhibitionistic needs (in court), or afford him an affluent life style, because of its lucrativeness? Is he a social reformer, a do-gooder, a crusader?
>
> What all of these questions are pointing to are the potential limitations of the role of the expert witness in family court proceedings. The court should have confidence, based on satisfactory answers to these questions, that the expert is knowledgeable and skilled, well-read and open, interested and committed both to the welfare of his patients or clients and the cause of justice. The issues are so complex and vital that the . . . court cannot accept anything less than excellence in this type of work. And even with the *best* of expert witnesses the judge should have at her (his) disposal, corroboratory or supportive . . . reports — from schools, daycare centres doctors, etc. — in order to render a decision.

This concern regarding an expert's qualifications was reflected in *R. v. Mohan* where Sopinka J. stated:

> Finally the evidence must be given by a witness who is shown to have acquired special or peculiar knowledge through study or experience in respect of the matters on which he or she undertakes to testify.[50]

If the assessor selected by the parties or appointed by the court to conduct the assessment is ultimately considered by the trier of fact not to be properly qualified to give an appropriate opinion on a matter in issue, the evidence will either be ruled inadmissible or will be accorded little weight, in which case an enormous waste of time and money will have been incurred by the parties not to mention the emotional cost that likely will have been borne by the parties and the children to that point in the proceedings.

Obviously, the search for the right expert in a custody/access case will not produce the ideal or perfect expert witness. It has been said that the ideal expert or assessor would have the following characteristics:

50 *Supra*, note 43, at 25.

> The ideal expert is someone who can present dynamic riveting testimony to dazzle the trier of fact. The person should be pleasant and charming, intuitively know when to be quiet, and have every possible degree and credential, an impressive array of awards and honours, and a long list of authoritative publications that address the main issues in your case, as well as considerable hands on knowledge of the people places, or things at issue. If you find such an expert please let me know, but in the meantime, you must determine which characteristics are most important in your case.[51]

Appreciating the fact that the ideal expert assessor will not likely be found, nonetheless, in venturing out to seek the most qualified person to conduct a custody/access assessment, one should keep in mind some of the more relevant factors to which one would look as reviewed below. In most custody/access cases involving an assessment the assessor will likely be selected from one of the three mental health professional disciplines of psychiatry, psychology, or social work. The normal formal qualifications of these professionals and the strengths and weakness they bring to the arena of custody/access assessments are set out in Chapter 5, heading 1. "Choosing a Mental Health Assessor".

(A) Expertise. In the course of conducting a search for the appropriate person or persons to be retained as the assessor one has to assume that it has been determined by either the parties to the action or by a judge, that a particular problem, concern or issue has been identified, thus warranting that an assessment be conducted. Therefore, a properly qualified person, having the expertise to deal with the specific problem in question, must be sought out. One will wish to be insured that the potential assessor or persons forming part of a team assessment will possess the requisite formal training and clinical or work-related experience in the necessary field of expertise. In a custody/access assessment where one might be dealing with, for example, new theories, scientific technique or the science of human behaviour, such as in situations of alleged sexual abuse, close scrutiny should be given to the assessor's qualifications to ensure that he or she is capable of providing relevant, necessary and reliable evidence which includes the assessor being in a position to prove the basis upon which his or her opinion is based.

---

51 Wilder, J. Ross, "Choosing The Right Expert Witness", Spring 1990 Family Advocate 44.

(B) Reputation. The more prominent the expert witness the more likely that witness will have an impact on the trier of fact. In a custody/access assessment case one will usually be selecting a local expert, but even then, it is important to have the parties select (and they in all likelihood will be relying on the recommendations of counsel) the most reputable of the local assessors. One of the best and most reliable ways to identify the best qualified person is to consult with other counsel who have had the experience of using an assessor in other custody/access cases. Another means of determining an appropriate person is from the reading of the law reports that have dealt with assessments. The reading of the cases will, in addition to identifying the experts, also probably disclose the manner in which the expert's evidence was received by the trier of fact in the context of whether it was rejected or accepted and given any appreciable degree of weight.

Another means of locating the appropriate person for the purpose of the assessment would be to speak to other mental health professionals who for one reason or another may have had reason to deal with qualified persons who possess the nature of expertise required for a particular assessment.

Intertwined with the reputation of the assessor expert is the important element of his or her personality and general demeanour. Even though an assessment will not involve competing experts, as in other civil cases, it does involve consideration of what is in the best interest of the child and, therefore, it is important that the assessor expert be presented as a credible witness. The person selected for the task must exhibit the qualities of being open-minded, unbiased, and independent. It is important that the assessor be viewed as open-minded and not as being intractable or intransigent in his or her views. When dealing with syndrome evidence or the science of human behaviour it is vital that the expert not adopt a position of advocacy on behalf of one of the parties or, more importantly, not be seen as proffering expert evidence beyond his or her area of expertise. To do so will obviously have a direct bearing on the credibility of the assessor and, consequently, have a negative impact on the threshold issue of determining what is in the best interest of the child.[52]

---

52 In *Olver v. Olver* (1987), 6 R.F.L. (3d) 334 (Ont. C.A.), a psychologist retained by the mother did not consult the father or consider the relationship of the father and children and, therefore, was seen as advocating the position of the

*(C) **Publications.*** Although it is not considered as vital as in the situation of a case involving competing experts, it is a relevant and important factor to consider, the extent to which a potential assessor has published in the field of assessments or even generally in a family law related field. Are his or her views with respect to the subject-matter of assessments generally accepted by peers within the clinical community of which the assessor is part? One should read the published material of the potential expert to ascertain whether, for instance, he or she is married to any one cause or whether he or she advocates a point of view or philosophy that is contrary or at odds with the views or philosophy of one of the parties. Ascertaining the philosophy of a potential assessor is of particular importance in a custody case where, clearly, the assessor's point of view could have a significant impact on the trier of fact. Does the expert in question ascribe to the rule of common sense that children of tender years are better off with the mother? Does he or she believe in the concept of joint custody or, rather, is he or she of the belief that it is more beneficial for the children that they be in the care and control of one parent? Does he or she have a particular point of view on such other relevant areas as separation, divorce, the roles of men and women as fathers and mothers, the type of lifestyle one is expected to lead, or on any other matter that may be significant when it comes to making recommendations in an assessment which recommendations may be given considerable weight by the trier of fact?

The assessor must have a full understanding of typical patterns of divorce, including the effects of divorce on children of different ages both in the short and in the long term. The assessor should understand research on the success of various types of custody and visitation arrangements. The occurrence of sexual abuse allegations requires knowledge regarding the appropriate assessment of this most difficult issue. An understanding of acceptable sexual abuse interview and assessment procedures as well as a thorough grounding in the

---

mother. In these circumstances the Court of Appeal expressed considerable reservations about the evidence of the psychologist and gave little weight to it. See *R. v. Olscamp, supra*, note 132 where the psychologist testified regarding the alleged sexual abuse of a child. The psychologist was perceived as attempting to testify beyond her field of expertise regarding an area of human behaviour not yet accepted by the scientific community within her field of expertise.

research and clinical applications of the findings of children's symptoms, memory and suggestibility is required.

Although the assessor should have some experience in the treatment of children and adolescents, child custody assessments are essentially an assessment task not a treatment task. Advanced skills in the assessment of child and adult personality and psychopathy, family dynamics, intellectual functioning and parenting skills are required. An assessor should also be up to date. Many years of experience may be of importance but a lack of familiarity with the current literature in the field may leave the clinician out of touch with important trends and findings. The assessor should have a working knowledge of the use of tests and test data and the proper dissemination of psychological information.

The decisions required in child custody assessments can reflect some of the most controversial social issues such as daycare, father's rights, homosexual parents, traditional and non-traditional families, religious and cultural differences and the rights of biological versus custodial parents.[53] It is, therefore, important to know the assessor's personal belief's and philosophy in this regard. It is best, of course, to have predetermined this prior to the cross-examination, if possible. The best way to do this is to read publications of the witness to ascertain whether there is an element of bias or a degree of partiality exhibited in the assessor's views relating to any of the social issues above referred to.

(D) Methodology. The major point to be made about methodology of a potential assessor is how it will impact on the assessor's credibility before the court. The methodology used by the expert must be both clinically and scientifically valid in the eyes of others who offer expertise in the same field. The issue of methodology is more exhaustively dealt with in Chapter 5, heading 2. "The Good Assessment".

53 Clark, Beth, Phd., "Acting in the Best Interest of the Child: Essential Components of a Child Custody Evaluation", 29 Family Law Quarterly, Spring 1995 at 19.

(ii) *Qualifying The Expert Witness*

Qualifying an assessor in a custody/access assessment is to be distinguished from the situation, as is usually the case in a civil action, where competing experts are called to give competing expert opinion evidence. In the latter case each expert will call his or her own expert for the purpose of providing opinion evidence and, ordinarily, the witness will be qualified at the commencement of his or her evidence as the result of a combination of examination-in-chief and cross-examination conducted at that time and being restricted to the narrow issue of whether the expert witness is qualified to provide an opinion on the issue in question. If the qualification of the expert is not dealt with at the commencement of the expert's testimony, it will almost certainly be challenged during cross-examination conducted during the course of the trial.

In a custody case, there are unlikely to be competing expert assessors being called to provide competing opinions on any matter in issue. In most custody cases the assessor is being called as a neutral expert witness and, thus, there will be absent the circumstance of competing opinions. There can be exceptions in a custody case such as where, in addition to a neutral assessment having been done, one of the parties, not being happy with the conclusions set out therein, has obtained a private unilateral assessment, that is, one that is obtained without the consent or involvement of the other party or even the involvement of all of the children. Another example would be where a second and complete full assessment has been conducted by an assessor other than the assessor who conducted the original assessment, with the two assessments containing diametrically opposed conclusions, observations or opinions. In these circumstances it is certainly a possibility that one of the parties will call one of the assessors resulting in competing opinions being put before the court. Assuming that in most custody/access cases a neutral assessor only will be called to give opinion evidence it will have to be determined as to what procedure will be followed in the context of whose witness the assessor will be and, therefore, who will be calling the assessor as a witness. The factors to be considered in this regard have been canvassed in this chapter, heading 2. "Whose Witness is the Assessor?" Will the assessor be deemed to be the expert witness of one party only or deemed to be the witness of both. Will both parties have the right to cross-examination?

In any case, in the very initial stages of the assessor being called as a witness, he or she will have to be qualified as an expert. Prior to any evidence of substance being heard from the mouth of the assessor, it must be demonstrated to the trier of fact that the assessor possesses significant background in whatever area, subject, topic or matter he or she will touch upon, so as to be able to assist the trier of fact in any appreciable manner.

The test of expertness is whether the witness has skill in the field in which the assessor intends to testify and in the field in which his or her opinion is sought. The admissibility of such evidence does not, as we canvassed earlier, depend on the means by which that skill was acquired. As long as the court is satisfied that the witness (assessor) is sufficiently experienced in dealing with the subject-matter at issue,[54] the court will not be concerned with whether his or her skill was derived from specific studies or by practical training, although that might affect the weight to be given to the evidence. The Supreme Court of Canada has acknowledged that an expert's opinion evidence, more often than not, is likely to be based on second-hand evidence or information.[55] The expertness as far as qualification is concerned was dealt with in *Rice v. Sockett*,[56] where Falconbridge C.J. stated:

> The derivation of the term "expert" implies that he is one who by experience has acquired special or peculiar knowledge of the subject of which he undertakes to testify, and it does not matter whether such knowledge has been acquired by study of scientific works or by practical observation. Hence, one who is an old hunter, and thus has had much experience in the use of firearms, may be as well qualified to testify as to the appearance which a gun recently fired would present as a highly-educated and skilled gunsmith . . .

The point to be made here is that prior to the assessor expert being permitted to give opinion evidence, the admissibility and weight of which will be later determined by the trier of fact, the assessor must first be qualified as an expert. In other words, the issue of the expert's qualifications to give an opinion becomes a preliminary question to that of whether the expert's opinion is admissible or deserving of

54 *R. v. Mohan*, [1994] 2 S.C.R. 9 at 25, 18 O.R. (3d) 160.
55 *R. v. Abbey*, [1982] 2 S.C.R. 24 at 42.
56 (1912), 27 O.L.R. 410 (Div. Ct.) at 413.

having any significant weight attached to it. The idea is to qualify the assessor to testify in a particular field so as to allow him or her to give expert opinion evidence in that field, i.e., a practising psychologist who has had years of experience conducting custody/access assessments and testifying regarding same in court. Therefore, it is for the trier of fact to make a factual determination of a witness' qualifications to give opinion evidence regarding any particular field of expertise.

(iii) Procedure to Qualify Expert Witness

In dealing with the issue of qualification the obvious should not be left unsaid. The situation will develop in some cases wherein counsel for the parties will not consider it necessary to have to formally qualify the assessor, both accepting the assessor's credentials. This usually happens in circumstances where the assessor's qualifications are either well known to the counsel involved in the case or, perhaps, even more importantly, in the case where the trier of fact is familiar with the assessor based on prior court appearances having been made before him or her. One may not wish to try the patience of the trier of fact if it is clear that he or she considers the assessor to be a qualified expert witness without having to go through the formality of proving the qualifications.

Generally speaking, the court will hear the qualifications of the assessor with questions being put to him or her by the lawyer who calls the assessor as a witness. The opposing counsel will in the normal course of events, have the right to cross-examine the assessor prior to the trier of fact making a ruling as to whether the assessor is qualified to proffer an opinion in his or her field of expertise.

When considering, as a preliminary step in the proceedings, whether to formally qualify the witness, it is essential that counsel keep in mind the distinction between the issue of an expert witness being qualified as an expert in a particular area or field of expertise, and the issue of the formally qualified witness, subsequently in the course of the proceedings, providing an expert opinion that may or may not be admissible or that may or may not be worthy of having any weight attached to it. This distinction is of particular importance for counsel to appreciate when considering whether to seek the indulgence of the trier of fact in leading evidence as to the assessor's credential's or in deciding whether or not to cross-examine the assessor on his or her qualifications.

It is not uncommon for the situation to present itself in a case, for instance, where counsel wishes to challenge the expert opinion of the assessor, who, otherwise is generally considered to be a well-qualified expert by both counsel and the local judiciary. Should one, during the preliminary process of qualifying the assessor, challenge his or her credentials, or should one wait until the assessor provides an opinion on the merits of the case and then cross-examine him or her at that time? Knowing that the assessor has an established reputation, in the eyes of the trier of fact, and knowing that it is difficult to prevent an expert from being qualified, and so as not to risk incurring the ire of the trier of fact, it is suggested that counsel wait until cross-examination on the merits of the case before embarking on the challenge. However, it is probably tactically prudent, at the time of qualification of the assessor, to go on the record, advising the trier of fact that you intend to later challenge the opinion of the assessor and the assumptions and facts on which the opinion may be based. It should, at that time be made clear that in admitting or consenting that the assessor is qualified, to testify in his or her field of expertise, you are not to be seen as agreeing with or as accepting any opinion evidence subsequently given by the assessor in the course of his or her testimony.

More often than not, at the conclusion of hearing evidence regarding an expert's qualifications the trier of fact will rule that the assessor is qualified to give opinion evidence in the appropriate field of expertise. The obvious exception would be in the situation where the evidence reveals serious weaknesses or shortcomings with the person's credentials, such as where, for example, it is clear that the expert will be testifying in an area of expertise outside his or her field of expertise.[57]

On the other hand, counsel calling the assessor as an expert witness may wish to lead the assessor through evidence relating to credentials and ultimate qualification, notwithstanding the fact that opposing counsel is prepared to admit that the witness is a qualified witness. Sometimes the fact that a trier of fact actually hears the witness describe his or her formal training and experience (as opposed to reading about them in a *curriculum vitae*) impacts more and makes more of an impression in the mind of the court. This may be of

57 *R. v. Olscamp, supra*, note 41.

particular importance in the case where counsel anticipates that the opinion of the witness on the merits of the case will bear special scrutiny from opposing counsel, or where, for example, the opposing party will be calling an expert witness of their own. The better qualified the assessor the more likely he or she will be considered or accepted by the trier of fact as being credible.

(iv) Examination-in-chief on Qualifications

Having decided to establish the qualifications of the assessor, counsel would advise the court that he or she intends to lead evidence in that regard for the purpose of obtaining a ruling that the witness is qualified. The proper practice in this regard is for the counsel presenting an expert to qualify the expert in all the areas in which the expert is to give opinion evidence.[58] Upon being called to the witness-box the assessor should be asked to produce a current *curriculum vitae* which would set out the assessor's training and experience, including, by way of example, the following:

- Educational history including a description of degrees, diplomas, certificates and special courses related to the field of expertise.
- A reference to any awards or honours granted in the assessor's area of expertise.
- A list of memberships in associations or societies in the relevant field.
- List of continuing education conferences attended by the assessor at which he or she delivered papers, gave speeches, or sat as a member of a panel in matters relating to his or her field of expertise.
- A list of any published works of the witness, including articles, books or papers.
- A description of any teaching experience in the related field of expertise.
- A description of previous court experience including the number of occasions, if possible, when the assessor's opinion evidence was accepted by the court

58 *R. v. Marquard*, *supra*, note 47.

Counsel should lead the witness through the evidence in such a manner so as to emphasis the qualifications. Leading questions in this regard are considered acceptable and will be permitted unless their is a valid objection by opposing counsel or by the trier of fact, which will be rare. Do not simply ask the assessor to state his or her qualifications as some witnesses are more modest than others and may be prone to understate their qualifications, or, for example, they may leave out an important factor or criteria not believing it to be relevant. As counsel leads the witness through the evidence the witness should be given the opportunity to expand on his or her qualifications where appropriate.

(v) Cross-examination Regarding Qualifications

At this stage of the preliminary question of determining a so-called expert's qualifications, counsel will focus on the assessor's background skills and base of expertise in order to ensure that the expert is qualified to give reliable expert opinion evidence in his or her field of expertise and so as to ensure that the expert is not about to attempt to give expert opinion evidence in an area of expertise outside that field of expertise for which the expert has been qualified. An expert witness or an assessor may be qualified to give an opinion in one field of expertise but not in an associated field and, therefore, it is essential at an early stage of the proceedings to attempt to discern whether, firstly, the witness is qualified to provide an opinion in his or her so-called field of expertise and, secondly, whether the witness will be attempting in subsequent testimony to proffer opinion evidence outside his or her field of expertise. As a practical matter, it is for opposing counsel to object if the witness goes beyond the proper limits of his or her expertise. The objection to the witness' expertise may be made at the stage of the initial qualification, or during the witness evidence if it becomes apparent the witness is going beyond the area in which he or she was qualified to give expert opinion.[59]

An example of this problem may be seen in the decision of *Young v. Young*.[60] At the beginning of the trial the trial judge, with certain misgivings, qualified an *amicus* investigator as an expert witness. In

59 *R. v. Marquard, ibid.*
60 (1986), 48 R.F.L. (2d) 390 (Ont. H.C.J.).

that capacity the trial judge allowed the investigator to express an opinion with respect to the welfare of the children. In the course of delivering judgment the trial judge had reservations about having qualified the investigator as an expert and noted that although the witness may be an expert investigator, questioned whether the expert investigator was qualified to express an opinion with respect to what was in the best interest of the children. The judge stated:

> For reasons indicated at the trial, with certain misgivings, I did qualify the amicus investigator as an expert witness, and in that capacity allowed the investigator to express an opinion with respect to the welfare of the children. There are two issues here. As is obvious from the title used by the amicus witness, that person might be considered an expert investigator. In this capacity, and with reservations as expressed above relating to hearsay on litigious issues, this person might provide convenient, compendious,evidence on the general circumstances of the parties and the children.
>
> However this particular investigator had no professional education, training or background in family assessment or therapy. What qualifies her to express an opinion as to what is in the best interest of the children, as opposed to, for example, a women who was a mother and who had a university degree in engineering and who had seen the film relating to joint custody upon which the investigator appears to have relied? The investigator herself at one point stated that her recommendation seemed to her to be a matter of common sense. It will be clear from the jurisprudence, of course, that in matters of common sense no expert can be called; common sense is the domain of the trier of fact and not an expert.[61]

It is essential that this problem be dealt with at this preliminary stage of qualification so as to reduce the risk of any potential prejudice to one of the parties, or more importantly, to the children as a result of having allowed the admission of expert opinion evidence which the assessor is not qualified to give. More often than not, however, it will not be readily apparent at the qualifying stage of proceedings as to whether the assessor will be attempting to proffer an opinion in areas in which he or she is not qualified. In such an event the issue will have to be dealt with on general cross-examination of the assessor on the merits of the case.

If at the preliminary qualification stage of the case counsel is concerned about the general qualifications of the assessor, or is concerned about the nature of the evidence to be given and its

61 *Ibid.*, at 394.

reliability, a vigorous cross-examination should be conducted. In a custody/access case counsel will have, prior to trial, likely read the assessor's report which will have been served on counsel pursuant to the appropriate rules of procedure that govern in the particular jurisdiction. For example, the case may involve an allegation of sexual abuse of a child. The assessor, in his or her report, may conclude that based on certain behavioural patterns of the child as observed by him or her, there was sexual abuse. Although the assessor may be qualified as a clinical psychologist and has clinical experience in conducting custody assessments, the question may present itself as to whether the assessor is qualified to give opinion evidence in this field of behavioural science. Upon what basis is the opinion based? Has it been scientifically proven that a child's behavioural patterns are necessarily consistent with those of one who has been sexually abused? Can the factual foundation upon which the opinion is purportedly based be proven? If these questions cannot be answered then the assessor may not be qualified to give that opinion evidence as referred to in his or her report and should not be permitted to testify in that particular area of expertise.[62]

It is extremely difficult to prevent an expert witness from being qualified. It is not uncommon in custody/access assessment cases for the trier of fact to qualify the assessor to give opinion evidence, only to subsequently rule that, in fact, the assessor is not qualified to have given such evidence or decide that little or no weight be attached to the said evidence.[63]

We have seen that it is for opposing counsel to object if a witness goes beyond his or her field of expertise.[64] If objection is not taken as to the assessor's qualifications it seems that the failure to do so could

---

62 *R. v. Olscamp* (1994), 95 C.C.C. (3d) 466 (Ont. Gen. Div.), *supra*, note 41 for facts. See also *Catholic Children's Aid Society of Hamilton-Wentworth v. S. (J.C.* (1986), 9 C.P.C. (2d) 265 (Ont. U.F.C.). In this case the applicant attempted to qualify one of its social workers as an expert witness in order to render opinions on what the best interests of the child were. The social worker had a two-year diploma in social services from a college and one-year of schooling at a university in a general program. The trial judge held that the witness could not be called to give her opinion on the issues proposed as she had not demonstrated the requisite skills in assessments. The witness had not "by a dint of training and practice acquired a good knowledge of the science or art of the assessment of needs of children and their parents".

63 *Young v. Young, supra*, note 60.

64 *R. v. Marquard, supra*, note 58.

have a prejudicial effect on one of the parties.[65] However, if it becomes clear that the witness does not possess the requisite expertise in the field the evidence should be disregarded. On the other hand in the absence of objection a technical failure to qualify a witness who clearly has expertise in the area will not mean that the witness' evidence should be struck (or disregarded).[66]

Once examination-in-chief and cross-examination on the preliminary issue of the person's qualifications has been completed the counsel who called the assessor as a potential expert witness would ask the trier of fact to make a ruling that the assessor is "qualified" to give opinion evidence and thus be permitted to give expert opinion evidence on those issue or areas of expertise in which he or she has been qualified.

Once the ruling has been made qualifying the witness as an expert counsel would then tender the assessor as a qualified expert witness for the purpose of providing opinion evidence in an appropriately related field.

65 In *Tobias v. Meadley* (1991), 33 R.F.L. (3d) 349 (B.C. C.A.); leave to appeal to S.C.C. refused (1992), 38 R.F.L. (3d) 255, an assessment report regarding custody was prepared and supported the position of the mother that she have custody. At trial the father's counsel did not cross-examine the author of the report. The Court of Appeal held that by not cross-examining on the report, the husband was deemed to have accepted the report as *prima facie* proof of the statements that it contained. In *Kahn v. Kahn* (1973), 13 R.F.L. 269 (Ont. S.C.), which case involved a custody dispute, the views of a qualified doctor set out in a report filed in evidence were not challenged. The court held that because the report was not challenged the court felt bound to give effect to the said expert testimony.

66 *R. v. Marquard, supra*, note 58.

9

Examination of the Assessor

1. EXAMINATION-IN-CHIEF

A party who calls a witness examines that witness in-chief. Evidence adduced on examination-in-chief is generally designed to serve the following purposes:

- build or support the calling party's case;
- weaken the opponent's case;
- strengthen the credibility of the witness;
- strengthen or weaken the credibility of other witnesses.[1]

The approach and the amount of time it takes in order to prepare a qualified assessor to testify at a custody/access trial very much depends upon the experience of the assessor and the nature of the issues that might be involved in the course of the assessment, particularly if the issues include syndrome issues such as child sexual abuse, parent alienation syndrome or any other exceptional issue that might have presented itself in the course of the assessor having carried out an investigation.

---

1 Sopinka, John, Lederman, Sidney N. and Bryant, Alan, *The Law of Evidence in Canada* (Butterworths, 1992), at 832.

It is of fundamental importance, of course, that the lawyer who decides to call the assessor spend a considerable period of time with the assessor in preparing him or her for trial. The most important feature of an expert witness' evidence, including the expert evidence of an assessor, is that of credibility and reliability. If the assessor has no credibility or if the assessor's evidence is not deemed reliable by the trier of fact, then no weight will be put upon it. Therefore, time has to be spent by counsel with the assessor in the preparation process, dealing with how the assessor's evidence should be presented in such a way as to come across in a credible fashion. The most important aspect is to prepare the assessor so he or she would be able to explain things clearly. If a witness, whether it be the assessor or some other person, cannot explain things clearly to the lawyer that is going to call the assessor as a witness, then the assessor will not likely be able to explain it to a court or to a trier of fact. It is therefore important that the assessor be able to give evidence, to the extent the area of expertise involving a particular issue in question will allow him or her to do so, using simplified layman's terms. On the other hand, one cannot ask the assessor to over-simplify the evidence to the point of perhaps jeopardizing its credibility. The more the evidence coming out of the assessor's mouth is seen by the trier of fact as being esoteric the more likely the trier of fact will have difficulty understanding the evidence. Therefore, the assessor has to be prepared to give evidence in such a way that he or she can explain in a comprehensible manner what the opinion is and why the opinion was given. If the assessor cannot explain the opinion or explain the theory on which the opinion is based to the counsel calling him or her as a witness, then the assessor will not likely be able to explain it to the trier of fact.

The other major aspect of maintaining the assessor's credibility is to remember that the fundamental criteria to the acceptance of the assessor's opinion, or recommendations or conclusions will be whether or not the trier of fact considers them to be correct. In other words are the facts, information and data gathered by the assessor, and as referred to in the assessor's report, or throughout the assessor's evidence, correct and provable? If the assumptions upon which the conclusions and recommendations in the assessor's report or in the assessor's *viva voce* evidence are correct then the greater the possibility of the opinion evidence of the assessor being accepted. Most assessors, on cross-examination, will be attacked or challenged on their assumptions relied upon in arriving at their recommendations or conclusions in their report.

In preparing the assessor for trial time should be spent on how to present the assessor's evidence in such a credible manner that the trier of fact will be attracted to the assessor's evidence and develop a confidence in the assessor. Counsel who intends to call the assessor as a witness in the custody/access case should approach the task of preparing the assessor from both the perspective of how the assessor will give his or her examination-in-chief and how to prepare the assessor for cross-examination.

2. REVIEW OF THE REPORT

In preparing an assessor for examination-in-chief the assessment report should be reviewed at length with a view to determining whether the assessor is able to corroborate, either first hand or through collateral sources, all of the facts, data or information referred to in the body of the report so as to make certain that the recommendations or conclusions are based on correct assumptions or information. By way of example, if the assessor is a clinical psychologist and his or her conclusions or recommendations are a matter of clinical judgment the assessor should be able to explain, if necessary, how that clinical judgment was determined or arrived at. If the psychologist makes reference to the fact that it is normal for a 10-year-old child to exhibit certain behaviourial symptoms during divorce or separation then the assessor should be able to refer to studies, empirical data, or the authoritative works relied upon in forming the clinical judgment. More often than not, because the corroborative sources form part of the assessor's knowledge within his or her field of expertise reference will not be made to the said corroborative sources in the assessor's report.

If the assessor, in the assessment report is relying upon a theory or technique the assessor should be prepared to prove that the theory or technique relied upon is generally accepted within his or her community of expertise and, in the case of a novel theory or novel technique, be able to prove that same is accepted not only within the clinical community of expertise of which he or she is a part, but also that it is accepted within the scientific community within his or her field of expertise. In the latter case counsel should probably ask the assessor for authoritative literature to which counsel can make reference and which supports the assessor's theories or techniques and which authoritative literature can be put to the assessor in the course of examination-in-chief. In the support of any theory, an expert is permitted to refer to authoritative treatise and the like, and any portion of such text upon which the witness relies is admissible into evidence. If the written work forms the basis of the expert's opinion, then counsel is allowed to read extracts to the expert and obtain his or her judgment on them. The written view of the author thereby becomes the opinion of the witness.[2]

While reading the authoritative literature that supports the assessor's theory or technique in question, counsel should also be directed to any authoritative literature that may be contrary to what the assessor's opinion may be. In this regard the assessor should be prepared for cross-examination as it should be assumed that well-prepared counsel will, on cross-examination, put contrary authoritative literature to the assessor, and ask him or her whether they acknowledge the specified works of others as being authoritative. If they are authoritative then the assessor will be asked as to whether he or she accepts the expert views of others in this regard and, if not, how they can reconcile the different views relating to the issue in question.

In dealing with theory and technique counsel should also attempt to determine whether the assessor seems to be attempting to provide an opinion in a field of expertise that is really beyond his or her field. This has been seen to occur by way of example, in cases dealing with alleged child sexual abuse. Counsel and the assessor should put their heads together to determine whether or not it is necessary to call some other expert who may be more comfortable or more recognized as an expert within the field in question (child sexual abuse) and whose evidence may therefore be considered or perceived by a trier of fact as being more credible because that person is deemed to be better qualified than the assessor.

A further area to explore with the assessor in the preparation for giving *viva voce* evidence is to review the assessment report to determine the extent to which the recommendations, conclusions or opinions of the assessor are based on second-hand information or

---

2 *Ibid.*, at 560. (For a further discussion of the use of authoritative works see heading 12. "Use of Authoritative Works".

hearsay. To the extent that they are, the sources of the said second-hand information should be reviewed with the assessor in order to determine the reliability and credibility of same, and to determine whether the said information or data has been corroborated by other sources. It is extremely important to do this, for as seen in the jurisprudence[3] earlier referred to, if the assessor, as an expert witness providing expert opinion evidence, relies upon second-hand information of others, such as oral statements or written documents, little weight may be given to the said opinion unless the said second-hand information, upon which it is based, can be proven at trial.

If counsel and the assessor in the course of preparation for trial are of the view that said second-hand information is not reliable, then the primary source of the said information, that is those who made the oral statement to the assessor, or those who made a written statement in this regard, should probably be called as witnesses for the purpose of giving evidence.

To summarize the above, a complete review of the assessor's report should be done so as to be assured that the conclusions or recommendations set out therein fit the findings made in the body of the report and to be assured that the conclusions and recommendations are based on facts that can be proven as reliable and credible.

3. MANNER OF TESTIMONY

The importance of the assessor's personal appearance, demeanour and the manner in which he or she projects while giving evidence cannot be underestimated. Judges and other triers of fact will engage in very close scrutiny of the assessor as he or she gives evidence. The assessor will be observed with respect to his or her dress, which should be comfortable but professional, body language, demeanour and the manner in which the evidence is given. The assessor should give evidence in a forthright, candid, precise and concise manner where possible. If the assessor is seen as being defensive or evasive the credibility of the evidence will be affected.

3 *R. v. Abbey*, [1982] 2 S.C.R. 24; *R. v. Lavallee*, [1990] 1 S.C.R. 852.

The assessor should be told that questions will be put to him or her in such a way as to entice the assessor to highlight particular areas of the evidence and so as to keep a logical narrative flowing. It is important that it be explained to the assessor that when dealing with any matters in dispute, no leading questions should be asked by counsel. This is probably the most often breached rule of evidence that one will observe in a trial. The assessor should understand that the evidence is more credible if it comes out of his or her mouth without a suggestive answer or other type of leading question being put to him or her. It is the evidence of the assessor and not the lawyer that is important. Some judges and opposing lawyers do not vocally object to leading questions, however, this does not mean that what the assessor says will be accepted by the trier of fact. Some triers of fact will put little weight on evidence extracted by way of leading questions even though there is no objection to same. The role of counsel during the examination-in-chief process is to keep the narrative moving and to be certain that all requisite areas of the evidence are covered in the course of the assessor's testimony.

In an ideal situation the assessor should probably be encouraged to attend court some day prior to the hearing in order to monitor some other cases at which an expert witness, preferably an assessor in a custody/access case, is testifying. The assessor should be shown around the court room so that he or she is familiar with the physical lay out and so that there is some feeling of familiarity when he or she ultimately testifies.

Lawyers often times will forget that a court room can be very intimidating for witnesses, particularly those who have never previously testified as an expert witness in a custody/access case. An effort should be made to demystify, to the extent possible, the judicial system and the court room environment. The assessor should not be distracted by all that is going on around him or her in a court room and an attempt should be made to have the assessor focus on what is going to be said during the testimony. The most important person with whom the assessor has to communicate is the judge or trier of fact. Thus, the assessor should be counselled on how to address and communicate with the judge. The assessor should be familiar with such expressions as "Your Honour" or "Your Lord" or whatever other appropriate expression should be used (in the case of an arbitration, Mr. Arbiter). The assessor should always make eye contact with the trier of fact and when answering the lawyer's questions, whether during direct examination or cross-examination, and should look at the trier of fact as opposed to counsel, in order to maintain communicative contact. The tone to be used by the assessor should professional and conversational. The best possible dialogue that the assessor and the trier of fact can have is one where the two are seen to be engaging in a conversation. The assessor should be confident and not afraid to highlight what his or her qualifications are. This likely would have been done during the "qualification" process earlier dealt with when dealing with admissibility of evidence. Although counsel may have many ideas for an assessor as to how he or she may deliver his or her evidence, the bottom line is that the assessor give evidence in the style and form in which he or she is most comfortable. It is probably better that counsel adjust to the assessor's style rather than the assessor attempting to adjust to counsel's style. The exception, of course, would be in cases where it is clear that the assessor's style would be such as to be confusing to the trier of fact.

In the course of the preparation for the assessor's examination-in-chief any weaknesses in his or her assessment report will have been revealed. Opposing counsel will cross-examine on those weaknesses. In order to reduce the effect the cross-examination might have with respect to the said weaknesses it is tactically acceptable, and appropriate, to deal with the weaknesses in the course of examination-in-chief. The areas of weakness should be identified and the assessor should offer an explanation or qualification for any such apparent weakness. If the assessor has made a mistake or in some manner the facts, data or information referred to in his or her report are incorrect, he or she should concede this in examination-in-chief with a qualifying explanation as to how it may bear on his or her opinion if at all. It is unlikely that there are major mistakes or major incorrect references with respect to the facts that may have any bearing on the assessor's ultimate opinion. Therefore, it is wise for the assessor to concede these mistakes or contradictions and to also explain that they have little bearing on the recommendations, conclusions or opinions set out in the report or given in his or her oral testimony.

4. NOTES (TO REFRESH MEMORY)

The assessor will want to know whether notes can be referred to in the course of giving testimony. A witness may refresh his or her memory for the purpose of testifying at trial from a writing made by the witness at or near the time of the occurrence of the event or matter recorded. The record or notes to which, in the case of an assessor, he or she might want to refer must have been made or verified by the assessor at or near the time that the matter recorded was observed by the assessor. By way of example, if the assessor has forgotten in the course of giving testimony what a particular child may have said, or what a parent may have said, or forgotten as to what behaviourial symptoms were exhibited by a child or parent, the assessor can ask to refer to his or her notes in this regard. As to whether reference can be made to the notes very much depends upon the assessor establishing that the notes or record was made or verified with requisite contemporaneity. It is insufficient to accept the assertions of a witness that his or her recollection was still fresh when he or she made or verified the record. This period varies depending on the circumstances of the case and the court's interpretation of what is meant by the words "at or near the time" of the events recorded.[4] An example of where a problem may present itself would be in the situation where an assessor may have interviewed a parent during the course of conducting an assessment but not made notes as to the conversation. If months later the assessor, in anticipation of the fact that the matter may proceed to a hearing, sits down and then makes notes as to what was said by the parents relying on his or her memory, it may be difficult to argue that matters were fresh enough in the assessor's mind at the time of making the notes as to meet the test of the notes having been made "at or near the time" of the conversation having taken place. Generally speaking, however, most assessors would take copious notes during the course of conducting an assessment. However, for whatever reason, and it is not uncommon, the assessor at the hearing may not recall the date, frequency of interviews or perhaps the length of time of an interview. Technically speaking, the assessor, in such an instance, would probably be permitted to review his or her notes or records kept at the time that will provide this information. Before doing so either counsel or

---

4 Sopinka, Lederman and Bryant, *supra*, note 1, at 850.

the assessor should ask the court if they may refer to the notes, in which case questions may be put to the assessor by either the trier of fact or opposing counsel as to the circumstances under which the notes were prepared. The trier of fact will then make a ruling as to whether they can be referred to or not.

5. PREPARATION OF ASSESSOR FOR CROSS-EXAMINATION

In preparing the assessor for cross-examination he or she should be told that the objective of cross-examination is not to necessarily repeat or further advocate what was said on examination-in-chief (although if given the opportunity to do so he or she should) but rather to preserve the underpinnings on which his or her recommendations, conclusions or opinions are based in the written report and during the course of examination-in-chief.

It should be explained to the assessor that once cross-examination has commenced he or she will not be able to consult with counsel, or anyone else, with respect to their testimony until after the cross-examination and reply evidence has been completed. This is particularly important for the assessor to understand prior to giving evidence so that should there be a recess or an adjournment in the midst of the cross-examination they know they will not be able to consult with the lawyer who called them as a witness. Some of the more salient points that the assessor, as an expert, should keep in mind when preparing for cross-examination, are as follows:

1. Remind the expert that the subject matter of a cross-examination is more familiar to him or her than it is to opposing counsel. Generally speaking, opposing counsel will know a small swath across the periphery of a large subject. While the expert cannot control the questions, he can often entice cross-examining counsel away from the known into the unknown, with spectacular results.

2. The expert should be told to listen to the precise question he is being asked rather than the question he would have asked had he or she been conducting the cross-examination. There is an unfortunate tendency of experts to read more into the question than is there.

3. The expert should be warned that opposing counsel play games in cross-examination. One game is to goad an otherwise convincing expert

into anger or intransigence. The expert should be told that either reaction takes a heavy toll on credibility. At the other end of the spectrum, the expert should also be on guard against disarming efforts by a sweet talking cross-examiner, whose charm should be met with stony firmness.

4. The expert should be told that long-winded answers will simply give rise to additional questions. The way to get to the end of the cross-examination quickly is to be brief and to the point. At the same time, the expert is entitled to complete the answer and should not allow himself or herself to be cut off by opposing counsel, who may not like the answer the question has legitimately evoked.

5. The expert should be told that he is unlikely to persuade opposing counsel to his point of view. Therefore, detailed explanations (except to the extent information is being fed to the fact trier on points useful to your case) are a waste of breath.

6. The expert should be told to answer the question where possible with a yes or no and then give whatever additional explanation is vital. An expert who commences an answer with a rambling discourse may appear evasive rather than thoughtful.

7. The expert should be warned against adopting the phraseology of opposing counsel's question. The phraseology may incorporate a lot of assumptions which, if accepted by the expert, will get him into trouble later in the cross-examination. The expert is better advised to restate the proposition, however harmless it seems, in his or her own terms.

8. The expert should be warned about double-barrelled questions. If you as counsel fail to object, the expert is still free to ask for clarification as to which part of the double-barrelled question he or she is expected to answer.

9. The expert should be told to watch carefully whether opposing counsel was listening to the answer. Quite often, cross-examining counsel has prepared a list of questions with whatever expert assistance is available and plunges ahead in cross-examination without adjustment or modification in light of the answers given. Counsel who don't listen don't deserve responsive answers, and the expert is free to turn a hard question into a soft lob by interpreting the question in its most innocuous light.

10. Some cross-examining counsel, knowingly or inadvertently, keep putting questions that are based on assumptions that your expert as already disputed. It is vital that the expert dispute them again, otherwise he or she may be taken to have abandoned the earlier objection. It cannot be assumed that the fact trier, any more than cross-examining counsel, grasps the full significance of a point the first time it is made.

11. Some experts are inclined to speak with perfect clarity and simplicity in chief and then retreat into technical obfuscation in cross-examination.

This approach, unless done with great subtlety, risks winning a technical knock out in the cross-examination but losing the court case. If the fact trier notices such an unsubtle change of approach, the expert's credibility will suffer, perhaps fatally.

12. Above all, the expert should be told to leave argument to the lawyer. The quickest way to be dismissed as a paid hack is to act like one.[5]

It is difficult to deal with all possible situations to which the assessor, as an expert witness, might have to adjust on cross-examination but the above referred to points are certainly fundamental. A few others that should be canvassed with the assessor are dealt with below.

The counsel who calls the assessor as a witness is there to offer some form of protection to the assessor where it is necessary such as in the situation where opposing counsel might ask a question to which objection should be made, or in a situation where cross-examining counsel may be harassing the assessor. Therefore, the assessor should really not worry about whether a proper question is going to be asked of him or her. It is counsel's job to intervene on the assessor's behalf should that occur.

Some times an assessor will not have the answer to a question in which case he or she should admit same. More often than not any question that an assessor cannot answer will relate to matters that are not significant or terribly important to the ultimate opinion being expressed by the assessor on any particular issue. If the assessor does not understand a question he or she should ask that the question be repeated. The assessor should be advised to never guess at an answer unless it is an educated guess that he or she feels they can make within his or her field of expertise.

6. CROSS-EXAMINATION OF ASSESSOR

Three purposes are generally attributed to cross-examination:

---

5 The 12 points referred to are taken from a paper presented by Binnie, W. Ian C. November 18, 1995, "Preparing the Expert Witness", Department of Continuing Legal Education, Law Society of Upper Canada, Toronto, Ontario. Mr. Binnie in the course of his paper was making reference to expert witnesses in general. The twelve points to which he made reference would apply to an assessor in a custody/access case.

- to weaken, qualify or destroy the opponent's case;
- to support the party's own case or the testimony of the opponent's weaknesses;
- to discredit the witness.[6]

If the custody/access case does proceed to trial it is counsel's obligation, even though the assessor is a neutral expert witness, to challenge and attack the basis upon which the said neutral assessor has made any recommendations or conclusions in the report which may affect one's client, particularly in such an important area as deciding which parent is to have custody or access to a child or children. One is to be reminded of the trial judge's comments in the decision of *Weaver v. Tate*:

> The report and evidence of a professional assessor . . . is just one piece of evidence which I may accept or reject in whole or in part. It is, however, such an important piece of evidence that counsel should always be prepared to test the validity of such evidence by a vigorous cross-examination of the author of such report. In an appropriate case the qualifications of the assessor should be challenged and any suggestion of bias towards mothers or fathers should be thoroughly canvassed. Many experts feel that any cross-examination of their qualifications, biases or recommendations is unwarranted and an attack on their personal integrity. They fail to understand that such cross-examination is essential to the trier of fact in order to determine the weight which should be given to the recommendations.[7]

7. CONSULTING EXPERT

One of the preliminary questions in considering the cross-examination of the assessor in a custody case is to decide whether or not to retain a consulting expert to assist in the preparation of the cross-examination. The purpose of the cross-examination is to undermine the basis for the assessor's opinion. It is probably vain to hope that the assessor's testimony will be completely discredited through cross-examination thus the reason for concentrating on the assumptions on which his or her opinion is based. This may require, in appropriate cases, the consideration of retaining a consulting expert who can assist

---

6 Sopinka, Lederman and Bryant, *supra*, note 1, at 857.
7 (1989) 24 R.F.L. (3d) 266 at 269 (Ont. H.C.J.); affirmed (1990), 28 R.F.L. (3d) 188 (Ont. C.A.).

counsel in understanding the subject-matter in question. The consulting expert can educate counsel and assist counsel by referring to authoritative texts and articles which can be read and to see if there are any inconsistent theories or statements made that can be used to impeach the assessor's testimony.

In the event that one party has retained his or her own expert (assessor) who shall be called as a witness then counsel, on cross-examination of the neutral assessor, should be careful on how he or she approaches the neutral assessor on cross-examination. Before actually attacking or challenging the neutral assessor it is probably a good idea to try to get him or her to confirm as much as possible the testimony that the privately retained expert either will give or has already given. If the neutral assessor is familiar with the cross-examiner's expert he or she will probably be prepared to admit or acknowledge the fine reputation of his adversary.[8]

The point is to have the neutral assessor agree with the assertions made by the privately retained assessor, on any particular issue in question in the custody/access case, but if the neutral assessor will not agree then to at least obtain the admission that there are other opinions of qualified assessors or other experts within the clincial community of psychologists or persons, who conduct custody/access assessments.

8. CONTROLLING THE ASSESSOR AS AN EXPERT WITNESS

Most assessors are probably experienced witnesses who have been cross-examined many times by experienced counsel. They, therefore, can probably anticipate many of the questions that will be asked of them. It is therefore important for counsel, when cross-examining an assessor, to try to control the assessor as a witness. If the assessor is allowed to go where he or she wants to go, and not where counsel wants him or her to go, there can be serious repercussions. The best way to control the witness is to make certain that questions are not asked that will simply allow the assessor to repeat his or her opinion that was given in-chief and which cannot be shaken or challenged in cross-examination. The questions should concentrate

8 Levy, J., "Examination of the Expert Witness", Chapter 3, *The Expert: A Practitioner's Guide* (Carswell, 1995).

on the weak aspects of the assessor's evidence whether that be on his or her qualifications (testifying beyond his or her expertise), methodology used (not following the prescribed procedures recommended by others in the field), lack of supportive or corroborating data regarding conclusions or the inability to provide corroborating evidence of second-hand information relied upon in arriving at an opinion. In order to control the assessor it is probably best to prepare leading questions which require a yes or no answer or require brief and concise answers. This is easier said than done. The point is counsel should not ask open-ended questions that will allow the assessor to expand or qualify any earlier testimony given.

9. CHALLENGING THE ASSESSMENT REPORT — GENERAL

It is fundamental that an assessment report be prepared in a thorough and complete fashion and that it contain and make reference to as many sources of information as possible so that the recommendations and conclusions therein can be seen as having been supported by the facts, data and information gathered by the assessor. See Chapter 5, heading 2. "The Good Assessment" and Chapter 7, heading 5. "Review of the Final Written Assessment". However, there are some areas that are deserving of comment and that should be considered in addition to the contents of the above referred to chapters when preparing for cross-examination of the assessor.

(a) Assessment Process

Depending on what jurisdiction a lawyer or assessor practices in, one will find guidelines for different associations of mental health professionals that deal with custody/access assessments. Most of the various association guidelines deal with the purpose of an assessment, the procedure of the assessment and guidelines as to what components should be included in a comprehensive assessment.[9] Reference to any

9 Custody/Access Assessment Guidelines - Ontario Psychological Foundation 1988 (published by the Ontario Psychological Foundation, Don Mills, Ontario, Canada); Guidelines for Child Custody Evaluations in Divorce Proceed-

one of these guidelines will assist counsel in preparing for the cross-examination on the issue of whether a complete and thorough process and methodology has been used by the assessor.

The more complete and thorough the investigation of the assessor then the more likely credibility and weight will be given to the accuracy of the information gathered by the assessor and the conclusions and recommendations reached by the assessor in the report. The less complete and thorough the report then obviously the argument can be made that the conclusions and recommendations set out therein are less reliable. If the process utilized by the assessor does not follow the standard procedures or guidelines commonly accepted in the particular jurisdiction where the custody/access assessment is conducted, then an assessor's report can be challenged, certainly partly on the basis that it failed to follow generally accepted practices in terms of the process followed.

(b) Interview of Adults

One of the more important components of a properly conducted assessment relates to the interview of the parties, the children and anyone else considered appropriate for the purpose of making the investigation complete. The following questions should be considered on cross-examination. Was everyone who was important to the assessment process interviewed? Did the assessor interview all persons suggested by the parties themselves? Were the parties given an equal number of interviews and given the same amount of time with respect to the interviews? Were the parties given an opportunity to express their views?

The circumstances under which the interviews were conducted should be explored in order to determine whether the adults interviewed were not in any way influenced by extraneous forces or circumstances on the day of the interview, such as ill health or extraneous stresses such as employment problems or extended family problems or any other form of stress that might have a bearing on that party's ability to provide an uninhibited and open interview.

---

ings, 1994, American Psychological Association, Washington, D.C., 1994.

If the assessor, in the report, refers to comments or statements made by the parties or any other adult, it is important to ascertain that these statements were not taken out of context. Are the statements set out in the report complete statements or only excerpts from statements? If so, why has the assessor been so selective? Has the assessor repeated the statements verbatim or has the assessor attempted to put his or her own interpretation or perception on the comments made by various people interviewed? If the assessor has referred to statements of one party has the other party had an opportunity, where it is deemed appropriate, to respond to what the other party has said? If not, why not? Does the assessor make reference to having accepted the position of one party and not the other based on allegations made by one party about the other; why has the assessor accepted the position of one party and not the other?

(c) Prior Inconsistent Statements

In interviewing the parties did the assessor review any other documents in order to see whether there were any inconsistent statements made by the parties? Has the assessor reviewed all court documents such as pleadings and affidavits and transcripts from cross-examinations and examinations for discovery, to see if there are any prior inconsistent statements made by the parties with respect to their views, philosophies or any other matter that might be significant regarding the assessment process? If there are inconsistent prior statements did the assessor attempt to reconcile them through the interview process with the appropriate persons? If there are inconsistent statements yet the assessor decides to accept the version of one party as opposed to the other, on what basis did he or she do so?

(d) Collateral Sources

Lastly, and perhaps the most important question, is whether or not the assessor considered collateral sources of information in order to corroborate any statements that may have been made to him or her by one of the parties and upon which the assessor relies in coming to a conclusion or making a recommendation in the report. The assessor, in gathering information from third parties such as schools, health care providers (doctors and nurses), child care providers, friends or extended family members, should corroborate this information by at least one other source wherever possible and appropriate.[10]

When questioning the assessor during cross-examination on the statements of others, which statements would technically fall under the hearsay rule, one is to be reminded that if the information relied upon is to form a component of the assessor's opinion, then the information relied upon should be proven if it is to be given any significant weight.[11]

(e) Children's Interviews

When dealing with the interviews of children some general comments are in order regarding the approach used and circumstances in which the children are interviewed. The issue of children's out of court statements as to their wishes regarding the custodial and access arrangement, and children's out of court statements with respect to allegations of sexual abuse are dealt with separately in this chapter. It would be impossible to consider every possible line of questioning one should employ with respect to the cross-examination of an assessor regarding same. A great deal depends upon the circumstances and the age of the children. The assessor should consider the child's comfort when interviewing the child. The assessor should be asked as to the type of language that was used in tone and whether terms were used that the child could understand. Were the child's interviews conducted in a "child-friendly" part of the assessor's office? Was there a variety of toys, games, drawing materials and doll-houses etcetera available to make the child feel as at home as comfortable?

---

10 American Psychological Association Guidelines, *ibid.*

11 *R. v. Lavallee, supra*, note 3; *R. v. Abbey, supra*, note 3. Note that Wilson J. in *Lavallee* held that not one of the facts upon which an expert opinion is based must be proven. If there is some admissible evidence to establish the evaluation for the expert's opinion, the evidence shouldn't be ignored, however the more the expert relied on facts not proven in evidence, the less the amount of weight that should be attributed to the opinion. Sopinka J., in the same decision, held that where the information upon which an expert forms an opinion comes from an inherently suspect source, such as the mouth of a party to the litigator, the lack of independent proof of the information will, as it did in *Abbey*, detract from the weight to be given to the opinion.

How much time was spent interviewing the child? For younger children clearly shorter periods of time should be used in an interview process than with older children. How many sessions with the child were there? For how long did the interviews last? Was the assessor satisfied that the child understood the issues of separation, custody and access so that when these words are used it is clear that the child and the assessor are communicating and talking about the same thing? Did the assessor vary the manner in which questions were asked so that neither parent or parties appears to be favoured in the eyes of the child? For example, if positively oriented questions are asked about the mother first, it would be difficult to ascertain whether a less positive reaction to the father was accurate or an artifact of the questioning.

(f) Are Conclusions Supportable?

Are the recommendations or conclusions of the assessor supportable on the basis of concrete evidence. This question is particularly appropriate when the assessor gives an opinion based on his or her clinical judgment as a result of observation of the parties or the children. For example, if the assessor concludes that "Mr. X has poor parenting skills and cannot adequately discipline his children" to what exact evidence can the assessor point to back this up? What was observed and stated and from whom was the information obtained?

The assessor should be cross-examined on the use of empirical data where it is appropriate to do so. For example, if the assessor concludes that "Ms. Y has poor parenting skills because she has a personality trait that makes her obsessive and compulsive" upon what empirical data base or test results is the assessor relying in coming to that conclusion? Is the fact that the parent is obsessive and compulsive really relevant to the issue of parenting in the circumstances of this case? The assessor may appreciate that nothing is known conclusively in the absence of a data base and common sense is not an adequate substitute for an empirical data base.[12] If there is no scientifically proven empirical data to establish that a parent who is obsessive/compulsive may not have appropriate parenting skills, the argument would

12 Bricklin, Barry: "Getting Optimum Performance from a Mental Health Professional" (1995), 29 Family Law Quarterly 7, at 12.

be made that this is simply a subjective clinical opinion of the assessor, which is unsupported by the evidence in the case.

A review of the assessment report should be made in order to determine whether the conclusions and recommendations therein fit the body of the report. For example, if in the report the assessor concludes that the parents have equal parenting skills, and there is nothing about either of them revealed in psychological testing that would preclude them from being parents, but the assessor recommends sole custody to one and only access to the other, the question has to be asked as to why the conclusion about the ability to parent is not consistent with the recommendation regarding custody. The assessor should be asked how and to explain this inconsistency. Why did the assessor in the said circumstances not consider joint custody or shared parenting as opposed to sole custody? Does the assessor have a bias towards sole custody as opposed to joint custody? If the conclusions regarding who should have custody or access in the report are inconsistent with the data information or other findings made by the assessor in the body of the report then one has to question the assessor's clinical judgment which point would go to the issue of credibility and ultimate weight to be given to the recommendations in the report.[13]

10. HYPOTHETICAL QUESTIONS

Hypothetical questions can be used on the examination-in-chief of an expert witness in order to establish one's case, or can be used on the cross-examination of an expert witness in order to undermine the opinion of the expert witness being cross-examined.

If an expert witness, such as an assessor, has personal knowledge of the facts or if the facts are not in dispute, he or she can give an opinion based on those facts and it is not necessary to use a hypothetical question in order to obtain the opinion.

---

13 *C. (R.M.) v. C. (J.R.)* (1995), 12 R.F.L. (4th) 440 at 448 (B.C. S.C.). In this custody case, where an allegation of sexual abuse was made against the father, the assessor concluded there was not sufficient evidence to conclude that sexual abuse had taken place, yet recommended supervised access as opposed to unsupervised access. The court ordered supervised access notwithstanding the inconsistencies between the assessor's recommendation and the finding of fact within the report that no sexual abuse had taken place.

If, however, the facts are in dispute, or if the expert does not have personal knowledge of the facts, evidence of which has been or will be led at trial, the opinion may be elicited only through the vehicle of a hypothetical question.[14]

For the hypothetical question to be effective the fact situation put to the expert witness must be clear, uncontradictory and ultimately proved at trial.[15]

An example of the use of a hypothetical question is as follows. An assessment has been ordered in a case where the mother alleges that the father has sexually abused their three year old daughter. The assessor who conducts the assessment obtains a written report from a psychiatrist to whom the child was taken by the mother prior to the assessment commencing and in which report the psychiatrist provides an opinion that there is evidence that the child was sexually abused by the father. The assessor, in the assessment report, relies upon the opinion of the psychiatrist in concluding that the child was sexually abused by the father and, therefore, makes a recommendation that there be only supervised access to the said child. Subsequent to the psychiatrist making the report and the assessor completing the assessment, the husband undergoes both a lie detector test performed by a qualified operator, and a "Sexual Behaviours Assessment" by a qualified psychiatrist. The Sexual Behaviours Assessment report indicates that there has been no past history suggestive of deviant sexual behaviour by the husband. The polygraph test concludes that the husband, in answering questions as to whether he sexually abused his daughter, was truthful when he answered the questions. He denied having sexually abused her. Notwithstanding these reports the psychiatrist attends trial and testifies that it is her opinion, based on projective tests such as pictures, play and interviews with the child, that the child presented with behaviourial responses commonly found in children who have been sexually abused.

The hypothetical questions to be put to the psychiatrist would be as follows:

Q. Doctor, assume the following facts and I will then ask you your opinion based on those facts.

---

14 Sopinka, Lederman and Bryant, *supra*, note 1, at 537–538. *R. v. Kelly* (1990), 59 C.C.C. (3d) 497 at 504 (Ont. C.A.).

15 Sopinka, Lederman and Bryant, *ibid.*, at 539.

Q. Assume that the husband underwent a Sexual Behaviours Assessment conducted by a qualified registered psychiatrist. Assume that the psychiatrist who conducted the testing specializes in the assessment of persons regarding sexual deviation behaviour. Assume further that the conclusion of the sexual behaviour assessment of the husband is that no past history suggestive of deviant sexual behaviour exists.

Q. Assume further that the husband took a polygraph test and that in the course of doing so, in denying sexual abuse, truthfully answered the questions.

Q. Using the above assumptions, doctor, would your opinion that the father likely sexually abused the child change or vary in any way?

One would think that the psychiatrist would surely have to change her opinion, however, if the psychiatrist is not prepared to do so once the evidence from the psychiatrist who conducted the Sexual Behaviours Assessment is put into evidence and once the results of the polygraph test are put into evidence the credibility of the psychiatrist and her opinion will be greatly undermined. Of course, the psychiatrist would be further cross-examined by putting the assertive literature of other experts to her which suggest that the responses of the child or the behaviourial pattern of the child, although indicative of sexual abuse, may be caused by other factors in the child's life such as stress or other factors.

11. PRODUCING NOTES AND RECORDS OF THE ASSESSOR

An issue that often arises on cross-examination of an expert, including an assessor, or any other expert witness called in a custody/access case, is whether one is entitled to production of the expert witness' entire file including notes and tests results, etc. Inevitably counsel for the party calling the expert will object to the production of the expert's file and, in particular, any instructing correspondence on the grounds of solicitor/client privilege.

It has been held in some jurisdictions that the giving of notice of intent, pursuant to the rules of procedure, to rely upon an expert's reports waives any privilege which may have attached to the report.[16]

16 *Foster v. Hoerle*, [1973] 2 O.R. 601 (H.C.J.).

It has also been held that production of an expert's report does not act as a waiver of privilege attaching to the expert's notes and records.[17]

It would seem that privilege can be waived in respect of those facts or premises in the expert's file which may have been used to base the expert's opinion, and which came to the expert's knowledge from documents supplied to the expert. For instance, if the assessor made notes with respect to interviews he or she conducted with the parties, children or other persons, surely those notes would have to be produced so it can be ascertained that the assessor's reference to them has not been taken out of context and that the said reference is whole and complete. The same thing would apply, it seems, with respect to notes made or any results with respect to psychological testing.[18]

Due to the unique nature of a custody/access case most triers of fact would likely insist that an assessor produce his or her complete file if requested so that one can be assured that the assumptions relied upon by the assessor are correct and thus that the foundation for the opinion given with respect to custody or access is sound.[19]

In order to determine whether there is privilege to any of the documents or information in the assessor's file or in the file of any other expert called in a custody/access case, one may have to request that the presiding judge or trier of fact examine the documents and

---

17 *Bronstetter v. Davies* (1986), 11 C.P.C. (2d) 289 (Ont. H.C.J.).

18 *Cacic v. O'Connor* (1990), 71 O.R. (2d) 751 (S.C.), the court ordered production of raw data and test scores used in formulating opinions set out in the report of a neuro-psychologist; the raw test data were part of the findings of that expert. In *Beck v. La Haie* (1989) 38 C.P.C. (2d) 67 (Ont. S.C.), the court reviewed the law relating to the scope of rule 31.06 of the Ontario Rules of Civil Procedure (request for findings, opinions and conclusions of an expert on examination for discovery) and concluded that raw test data resulting from psychologist testing in a personal injury action were discoverable as part of the "findings" of an expert. On the other hand, see *Kaptsis v. Macias* (1990), 74 O.R. (2d) 189 (H.C.J.) where it was held that a party was not obliged to produce expert's clinical notes and records for the expert's reports contained their findings.

19 Note, however, the decision of *Derickson v. Derickson* (1994), 93 B.C.L.R. (2d) 364 (S.C.). In that case the Master held that a court should be cautious in ordering production of a family court counsellor's file. An application for the production of the documents must establish that the documents requested are necessary and relevant to the conduct of the litigation, are not privileged and are otherwise unavailable. If there is any dispute about production the advice of the court should be sought and the documents brought to court so that they can be reviewed by a judge to decide if they should be produced.

materials prior to trial or hearing, such as at a pre-trial, or at trial or hearing where the expert witness will have to be cross-examined to determine whether all or part of the file is privileged.

12. USE OF AUTHORITATIVE WORKS

Expert witnesses will often rely upon published assertions of others when proffering an opinion. This issue was canvassed when dealing with the admissibility of expert evidence[20] and the extent to which such reliance on the opinions of others is admissible into evidence as an exclusion to the hearsay rule. In these circumstances, hearsay constitutes a component of the expert's knowledge and is admissible into evidence as an exception to the hearsay rule.

However, expert witnesses can also be used for the purpose of having authoritative works introduced into evidence. In using the example of a custody/access case involving an assessor, this technique is of particular importance when wishing to challenge the opinion of the assessor in circumstances where there are contrary opinions, theories or techniques currently in use by other members of the clinical community. The said opinions, theories and techniques may also be different than those of others relied upon by the assessor in advancing his or her opinion in the custody/access case before the court.

It is a recognized technique in challenging the assessor's expert opinion to confront him or her with authoritative works of others, or even with his or her own writings, which cast doubt on the correctness or general acceptance of his or her opinion. This can only be done if the expert witness (assessor) testifies that he or she is familiar with the work and acknowledges its authority. Once this has been done, parts of the work may be read to the witness and, to the extent that they are confirmed, they become evidence in the case.[21]

In *Marquard,*[22] the Supreme Court of Canada stated:

20 See Chapter 8, heading 5. "Admissibility of Expert Opinion Evidence".

21 Pink, J.E., Matthews, K., Tupper, A. and Wells, A., *The Expert: A Practitioner's Guide* (Carswell's 1995), Chapter 1, para. 3.4; *R. v. Anderson* (1914), 22 C.C.C. 455 (Alta. S.C.); *R. v. Marquard*, [1993] 4 S.C.R. 223, 25 C.R. (4th) 1.

22 *Ibid.*, at 20–21 C.R.

> The proper procedure to be followed in examining an expert witness on the other expert opinions found in papers or books is to ask the witness if she knows the work. If the answer is "no", or if the witness denies the work's authority, that is the end of the matter. Counsel cannot read from the work since that would be to introduce it as evidence. If the answer is "yes", and the witness acknowledges the work's authority, then the witness has confirmed it by the witness' own testimony. Parts of it may then be read to the witness, and to the extent that they are confirmed, they become evidence in the case.

The problem with this test, of course, is that the assessor, if familiar with this less than perfect criteria as to how to use authoritative works in cross-examination, may attempt to avoid penetrating cross-examination by conveniently stating that he or she does not acknowledge that a particular work is authoritative.

If the assessor or other expert witness in a custody/access case employs such a tactic and continuously refuses to acknowledge other authoritative work, it may affect the weight of his or her opinion in the eyes of the trier of fact.

Where the expert witness assessor admits to a particular writing as a recognized authority, then that part which is inconsistent with the testimony should be read to him or her by counsel. The expert should then be asked whether or not he or she agrees with the part that has just been read. Whether the witness answers "yes" or "no", he or she should be asked if he or she agrees that the statement just read was contrary to his or her opinion. The witness should never be asked to explain because he or she may do so satisfactorily.[23]

Therefore the question should be carefully framed so that, as best as possible, counsel can control the witness. It is extremely difficult to cross-examine an expert witness, particularly a well-qualified assessor in a custody/access case who has significant courtroom experience. Generally speaking it is a formidable task to cross-examine an assessor as one is usually challenging either a psychiatrist, a clinical psychologist or a very experienced social worker, on his or her own ground. It is therefore essential when challenging the expert on authoritative works to be certain one is familiar enough with not only the assessor's published works and/or theories, but also familiar with the authoritative works and theories of others being relied upon to challenge the assessor. Counsel will want to be pretty much assured that the authoritative works of others, being put to the assessor

---

23 Levy, E., *supra*, note 8, Chapter 3, para. 2.8.

witness, are generally accepted in both the clinical community and, in appropriate circumstances, by the scientific community in the field of the expertise in question.

If the assessor or other expert witness called to give opinion evidence in a custody/access case has published in the past, it should be determined whether his or her articles appeared in peer reviewed publications. Check with other experts in the field to see if the assessor witness' opinions and reviews have generally been accepted within that community of expertise.

The contents of the assessor's prior publications are, of course, extremely important. The published works of the assessor or other expert witness should be read by counsel to see if they contain opinions contrary or adverse to those expressed in the assessor's report or expert's report.

In reading the published works of the assessor or other expert witness who might be called in the custody/access trial check to see what authorities or literature is relied upon or noted by the said assessor as being authoritative on the particular issue in question. Those authorities should be read not only to determine if they contain opinions, ideas or theories that are contrary or different to those set out in the assessor's report, but to determine if they are contrary or different than those about which the expert intends to give *viva voce* testimony.

If they are, for example, it can be suggested to the assessor or expert witness that he or she, in the past has recognized other persons as an authority on the particular issue in question. The question would be phrased in such a manner as to extract a "yes" answer. That being accomplished, it would then be put to the assessor or other expert witness that the said authorities, opinion or theory on the issue in question is different from the assessor witness' opinion or theory on the same issue. Again, the question would have to be phrased in such a way as to extract a "yes" answer. In this example counsel would then have evidence that the witness acknowledges that there is another authoritative expert in the same field of expertise whose opinion or theories are generally acknowledged in the community but are at odds with or different than those opinions and theories used by the assessor witness. This may compromise the assessor witness' expert opinion evidence, which in turn, could affect the amount of weight that might be accorded the said evidence by the trier of fact.

Counsel should be very careful in using this approach, not to ultimately simply strengthen the witness' evidence. For example, if the cross-examined assessor can point out that in fact the authoritative works or other theories put to him or her do not contradict his or her opinion or theories, or point out that even perhaps the said authoritative works support his or her position, then of course the tactic will have backfired. The use of this tactic is similar to the use of statements made in previous proceedings (prior inconsistent statements) such as examinations for discovery and other trials or cases in which the assessor has previously testified and for which there are transcripts of the evidence. Counsel must be certain that the prior statement put to the witness is indeed inconsistent or a contradiction to the position currently being taken by the assessor witness. The more a trier of fact is heard to say, for example, "I don't see where the inconsistency is", or "Is that really a contradiction of what he or she is saying", or, "Isn't that really the same thing", the more likely the witness' credibility is to be enhanced.

Another means of getting contrary authoritative works before the court is by the use of the consulting assessor which concept was dealt with in heading 5. "Preparation of Assessor for Cross-examination". The consulting assessor would in fact be used to challenge the "neutral" assessor's theories or opinions and the underlying non-factual basis on which the said opinions or theories are based. Assume for example that in a custody/access case the neutral assessor on cross-examination has denied that certain works of other experts are not considered as being authoritative. A consulting assessor might be called upon to testify that any knowledgeable assessor in the field would be familiar with the writings or authoritative works on which the neutral assessor has been cross-examined. The consulting expert, if properly qualified, may also testify, of course, as to any generally accepted theories or techniques used at large by the clinical community and, where appropriate, which are deemed acceptable by the scientific community, that are different than those used by the neutral assessor and which the neutral assessor does not consider as being acceptable or to be authoritative. Of course, the consulting expert will be cross-examined and thus exposed to all of the risks that were earlier canvassed when cross-examining the neutral assessor expert witness on the authoritative works of others.

13. HEARSAY — GENERAL

Lawyers involved in custody/access cases will often find that an assessor's report, whether prepared on the consent of the parties or prepared on the order of the court, often contain statements that have been made to the assessor by persons other than the parties and to which statements the assessor makes reference in the body of the report, or which statements the assessor will attempt to make reference to while giving his or her testimony at the hearing of a custody case. These statements are considered to be hearsay statements and, on cross-examination, counsel who find the statements to be objectionable or offensive of the hearsay rule should challenge their admissibility. The hearsay rule can be stated as follows:

> Written or oral statements, or communicative conduct made by persons otherwise than in testimony at the proceeding in which it is offered, are inadmissible, as such statements or conduct are tendered either as proof of their truth or as proof of assertions implicit therein.[24]

The reason for the hearsay rule is to permit a party, adverse in interest, to cross-examine the person who made the statement so as to test the veracity of the statement made. Testimony under oath and cross-examination of that testimony have been considered to be the best assurances of the truth of the statements of facts presented.[25]

Chapter 8 deals with the issue of the general admissibility of an expert witness' opinion evidence and, more specifically, deals with the issue of the admissibility of such evidence and the weight to be ascribed to it by a trier of fact, where the opinion evidence is based on second-hand evidence, such as hearsay. A distinction is to be made between the reliance by an expert on hearsay evidence as formulating a component of his or her knowledge and reliance by an expert on hearsay evidence as formulating a component of his or her opinion.

The reliance on second-hand evidence by an expert as part of his or her accumulated knowledge in his or her field of expertise, such as reliance upon the published assertions of others or authoritative literature related to the field of expertise in question is the type of

---

24 Sopinka, John, Lederman, Sidney N. and Bryant, Alan: *The Law of Evidence in Canada* (Butterworths, 1995), at 156.

25 *R. v. Abbey*, [1982] 2 S.C.R., 24, Dickson J.

second-hand or hearsay evidence that is generally considered both admissible and reliable.[26] It is in the case of where hearsay evidence constitutes a component of the expert's opinion the problems present themselves and therefore would require the special attention of counsel when preparing for the cross-examination of an assessor in a custody case. An assessor in child custody assessment cases in particular often, gathers information which is second-hand and relied upon to provide an opinion.

For example, an assessor may speak to such persons as a child's teacher, day-care worker, former spouses of the parties, neighbours, doctors, other children and step-children, to cite only a few possible sources of information. These persons may talk to the assessor, or a staff member or representative from the assessor's office (such as a social worker) about things the child has said, the parents have said, or about things other persons have said to him or her about the child.

The sources of second-hand information that might be referred to and relied upon in an assessor's report in a child custody case are not restricted to conversations with third parties. Often there is written second-hand information, such as a doctor's report, the contents of which are referred to in the assessor's report but the medical report may or may not be attached to the assessor's report. The above examples all reflect hearsay evidence which the assessor will rely upon as facts upon which his or her opinion may be based. For the assessor's opinion to be given any weight, as an expert's opinion, the so-called facts, in the form of second-hand information or hearsay evidence should be proven.[27]

The above examples also exhibit insidious and sometimes dangerous sources of hearsay evidence in a custody assessment. Therefore the assessor should be cross-examined in order to determine whether the second-hand or hearsay evidence is indeed reliable as it may be relevant in the eyes of the trier of fact and thus have a prominent impact on the ultimate decision.

The extent to which a trier of fact will admit the hearsay statements or the second-hand evidence will to a great extent depend upon the circumstances under which the statements were made and whether the trier of fact considers them as being reliable in the context of

---

26 *R. v. Lavallee*, [1990] 1 S.C.R. 852, 55 C.C.C. (3d) 97; *The Expert: A Practitioner's Guide supra*, note 21, Chapter 1, para. 4, at 1–17.

27 *R. v. Abbey, supra*, note 25; *R. v. Lavallee, supra*, note 26.

whether or not the facts upon which the hearsay is based can be proven.[28]

On cross-examination with respect to these third party statements one will want to explore whether the persons who have made the statements are persons who have chosen sides in the separation; are persons who for some reason are biased against one of the parties; or whether the persons and the nature of their comments are considered reliable. Therefore counsel should explore the circumstances under which the statements were made or the information provided to the assessor. It is important that the assessor keep notes with respect to any conversations he or she might have had with persons who have made, to them, what are considered to be hearsay statements. Counsel might ask for production of the notes to ascertain that the notes in fact are consistent with what is repeated by the assessor in the report.[29] One might ask the assessor whether a tape recorder was used to interview any of these persons and, if so, that the tapes be produced so that counsel can be satisfied that the persons quoted have been accurately quoted or that the comments repeated have not been in any way taken out of context. Counsel may wish to ascertain whether there is one conversation or a number of conversations with the person who is being quoted. Has the assessor made reference to the complete conversation in the assessment report or has the assessor simply chosen bits and pieces which by themselves may not give proper context to the true essence of the third party statement.

It is therefore worthwhile to review some of those common and sometimes troublesome areas that may be seen in the custody/access assessment and in which areas counsel should probably give their due attention when preparing for cross-examination of the assessor.

---

28 See notes and Chapter 8; *Bruno v. Bruno*, [1984] W.D.F.L. 119 (B.C.S.C.); *Cardinal v. Cardinal* (1988), 17 R.F.L. (3d) 23 (Alta. Q.B.); *Sherry v. Sherry* (1993), 1 R.F.L. (4th) 146 (P.E.I. T.D.); *R. v. Olscamp* (1994), 95 C.C.C. (3d) 466; *Re Ammon* (1984), 47 Nfld. & P.E.I.R. 176 (Nfld. U.F.C.).

29 *M. (C.) v. M. (G.)* (1992), 40 R.F.L. (3d) 1 (Ont. U.F.C.). In this case the assessor was asked to produce her notes. The assessment report comprised 49 pages. All of the source documents for the assessment were filed as an exhibit and included four bound volumes of photocopied notes. On cross-examination various positive comments relating to one of the parties which had been omitted from the report were brought to the attention of the assessor as an example of potential bias as against that party.

Notwithstanding this tactic the trial judge held that the report was not biased.

14. PROCEDURE TO CHALLENGE HEARSAY OR SECOND-HAND EVIDENCE CONTAINED IN ASSESSOR'S REPORT

Often times the assessment report, as prepared by the assessor, and which contains hearsay statements or second-hand evidence, will find its way into the hands of the trier of fact prior to any judicial determination of admissibility of the evidence having been made. Such a scenario in effect allows the evidence to be potentially reviewed by the trier of fact, and the damage may already have been done in the context of the hearsay statements having, in essence, already been admitted into evidence and potentially having a prejudicial effect on one of the parties without the benefit of cross-examination on the circumstances under which the statements were made.

If the assessment has been conducted as the result of a court order made pursuant to any of the various permissive and enabling statutes in the country, the assessment report usually has to be filed with the court prior to the hearing and the report is admissible in evidence.[30] In the event these circumstances prevail, then counsel at the commencement of the hearing, should go on the record and advise the trier of fact that objection is being taken to the admissibility of certain statements or second-hand information or evidence which constitute hearsay that are set out in the report. The trier of fact is not likely to ignore the entire contents of the assessment report in these circumstances and, therefore, rather than ruling the entire contents inadmissible it will probably be a matter of argument at the conclusion of the hearing as to what amount of weight should be given to the offensive hearsay statements. When the assessor or any other expert is called to give his or her testimony, cross-examination will take place at that time and revolve around the circumstances under which the statements were obtained. Hopefully any damage done by the filing of the report can be undone with effective cross-examination that might reveal suspect circumstances under which the hearsay evidence was obtained and thus resulting in little weight being given to the hearsay evidence.

30 For example, see s. 30(7) and (9) of the *Children's Law Reform Act* of Ontario which stipulate that a person appointed by the court to conduct an assessment *shall* file his or her report with the clerk or registrar of the court and the report is admissible in evidence in the application.

On the other hand, if the written report of the assessor has not been filed with the court prior to the hearing and it contains statements which one party finds objectionable, counsel during the hearing, but prior to the assessor being called as an expert witness, should ask that the report not be filed as an exhibit in evidence until there has been a judicial determination as to whether the offending hearsay statements are considered admissible or not. At that point the trier of fact may conduct a *voir dire* or hearing within the custody hearing, to determine whether the statements are indeed admissible. In custody cases involving assessments, some judges will not conduct a *voir dire* and will simply pronounce that the statements are admissible into evidence, but will be subject to the exercise of discretion in deciding what amount of weight is to be attributed to the statements.[31] Other triers of fact will consider a *voir dire* and rule at that stage of the proceedings if possible, as to whether the offending statements are admissible or not. Realistically speaking, in a custody case involving an assessment report the trier of fact will likely admit the contents of the report containing the hearsay statement and allow cross-examination of the assessor on the circumstances under which the statements were obtained and then decide what amount of weight will be given to the hearsay statements.

15. AREAS OF SPECIAL INTEREST RE CROSS-EXAMINATION OF ASSESSOR

(a) Children's Statements (Out of Court) — General

In custody/access assessments it is not uncommon for an assessor to either have made reference in his or her assessment report to the statement of a child, or, while testifying at the hearing, to attempt to repeat to the trier of fact what a child may have said to him or her in the course of having conducted the assessment. A person conducting an assessment in a custody/access case will be obligated to interview the child who is the subject matter of the report. The interview would likely deal with the child's wishes regarding custody and access

31 *Re Ammon, supra*, note 225; *M. (C.) v. M (G.), supra*, note 29.

arrangements and may very will deal with more complicated matters such as allegations of sexual abuse, parent alienation syndrome, brain washing, or physical abuse.

The reference by the assessor in his or her report to statements made by the child will often occur in circumstances where the child is not going to testify and thus the said statements are referred to as "out of court" statements of the child. *Prima facie*, reference to the statements of the child who will not be testifying, made out of court, are not admissible in evidence as they are considered to be hearsay evidence unless the statements fell within any exceptions to the hearsay rule. As earlier seen, hearsay is a statement by a person, other than one made while testifying as a witness at the proceeding, that is offered in evidence to prove the truth of the matter asserted.

However, the common law has developed exceptions to the hearsay rule, including exceptions to the admissibility of statements of children made out of court.[32]

In dealing with the statements of children made out of court we intend to restrict ourselves to civil custody and access cases as opposed to criminal cases involving such statements or child protection proceedings involving such statements.

(b) Children's Statements (Out of Court) Regarding Wishes as to Custody/Access Arrangement

Courts are reluctant to have children testify in custody proceedings and prefer that a child's wishes be entered into evidence through

32 There are also certain statutory hearsay exceptions permitting the admission of hearsay evidence in particular dealing with child protection proceedings. An example is the Ontario *Child and Family Services Act* which contains two such hearsay provisions. Section 47(7) allows the court to admit and act on evidence that the court considers credible and trustworthy in the circumstances on adjournments. This credible and trustworthy language has been held to permit the use of hearsay evidence. The other section, s. 46(1) in dealing with the issue of whether a child be placed in or returned to the care and custody of a person other than the Children's Aid Society, may consider the person's past conduct toward any child . . . and any oral or written statement or report that the court considers relevant . . . which may be admitted into evidence and shall be proved as the court directs.

an independent expert such as an assessor.[33] Children are usually most uncomfortable in having to testify about any matter relating to their parents. Children can be emotionally traumatized if they have to testify about a parent regarding custodial arrangements as the children do not usually wish to be caught in the middle of the differences between the parents, and they do not wish to be seen as being disloyal to one parent or the other. Parents also usually feel that it is inappropriate for children to have to testify in a custody case as to their wishes regarding custodial access arrangements.

This reluctance to permit children to testify in custody cases has led to the appointment of assessors to conduct comprehensive assessments regarding families in some cases, has led to the appointment of an assessor with the sole restricted purpose of ascertaining the wishes of the child as to custody and access arrangements.

A child's wishes can be central to the determination of a custody case. The implied admissibility of the child's statement made out of court as to his or her wishes regarding a custody/access arrangement is seen in certain statutory provisions which clearly state that the wishes of a child, where they can be reasonably ascertained, are relevant to the determination of what is in the best interests of the child.[34]

As seen above, any statement made by a child to an assessor, or any other person regarding including a statement as to his or her wishes as to custody or access arrangements constitute hearsay and, *prima facie*, would be inadmissible. However, this is an exception to the hearsay rule re: children's statements made out of court. A child's statements out of court under the exception for then existing mental or emotional states. As such, the requirement of contemporaneity must be observed, re the wishes must be the child's then-existing wishes at the time of the statement.[35]

---

33 *Wakaluk v. Wakaluk* (1976), 25 R.F.L. (2d) 292 (Sask. C.A.); *Taberner v. Taberner* (1971), 5 R.F.L. 14 (Ont. S.C.).

34 See, for example, s. 24 of the *Children's Law Reform Act* of Ontario which provides that, the court in determining the best interests of a child, shall consider all the needs and circumstances of the child, including the views and preferences of the child, where such views and preferences can reasonably be ascertained.

35 Thompson, D.A., "Taking Children and Facts Seriously: Evidence Law in child Protection Proceedings" - Part I (1988), 7 Canadian Journal Family Law 11 at 75; *Wakaluk v. Wakaluk, supra*, note 33, at 304.

However, the amount of weight to be given to the wishes of the child in this regard still remains a function of the trier of fact even if the hearsay out of court statements are initially ruled admissible in evidence. The weight to be given to the child's statements as to his or her wishes will depend to a great extent on the circumstances under which they were given.

Thus, on cross-examination, it is essential for counsel for explore the circumstances under which the child made the statements regarding his or her wishes. For the type of questioning that counsel should consider pursuing and for the type of circumstances to be explored on cross-examination see the series of questions posed in Chapter 7, heading 5(d) "Children's Wishes".

(c) Children's Statements Made in Chambers Re: Wishes as to Custody/Access Arrangement

Few triers of fact would wish to have a child called as a witness in a custody/access case for the purpose of eliciting from that child his or her wishes or preferences regarding custody and access arrangements. Most triers of fact would prefer that the child's wishes be ascertained through the process of an assessment conducted by a qualified person.

However, there are occasions where triers of fact have in the past insisted that children be interviewed in their chambers rather than testify in court under oath.[36]

36 In *More v. Primeau*, (1978), 2 R.F.L. (2d) 254 (Ont. C.A.) the trial judge privately interviewed an 8 1/2-year-old boy in chambers over the objection of counsel. The judge advised counsel that he did not intend to question the boy regarding his wishes as to the outcome of the trial. Nonetheless in reaching a decision the judge ignored the recommendations of a psychiatrist who conducted an assessment of the parties and child. *Demiter v. Demiter*, unreported, Ontario General Division, Lawyer's Weekly, May 3, 1996. Children aged 8 and 13 had made out of court statements to third parties requesting that they reside with their father. The children were not going to be witnesses at the trial. The trial judge, at the request of the father, interviewed both children in chambers in the presence of a court reporter but in the absence of counsel. The trial judge held that it was appropriate to advise the parties in general terms as to the children's stated wishes. Both wished to reside with the mother.

To interview a child in chambers for the purpose of determining the child's preferences regarding custody or access arrangements is generally frowned upon.[37]

If a trier of fact insists nonetheless on interviewing a child in chambers in order to attempt to ascertain the child's wishes regarding custody/access arrangements, objection should be made on the record on the basis that the circumstances may be inhibiting to the child, contributing to the child's reluctance to be forthright given the pressures of the situation to be seen as pleasing his or her parents. Counsel should insist on being present and that a court reporter be present in chambers as well.

(d) Children's Statements (Out of Court) Regarding Sexual Abuse Allegations

Given the developments in recent years in custody cases, of one parent making allegations against the other of child sexual abuse, it is appropriate to visit the issue for purposes of conducting cross-examination of an assessor or other expert, as to the admissibility of statements made by children out of court regarding alleged child sexual abuse. This chapter is not intended to deal with all other issues ancillary to child sexual abuse cases such as, impaired memory, post-traumatic stress disorder, psychotic disorders, retrieval of memory, recovered memory and psychological profile evidence regarding sexual abuse. Nor is this chapter intended to deal with criminal cases or child protection cases dealing with the issues of child sexual abuse.[38]

---

37 *Jandrisch v. Jandrisch* (1980), 16 R.F.L. (2d) 239 (Man. C.A.). Thompson, D.A., "Taking Children and Facts Seriously: Evidence Law in Child Protection Proceedings", *supra*, note 232, at 76.

38 For recommended reading dealing with factors to be considered on cross-examination regarding other issues ancillary to child sexual abuse and syndrome evidence with respect to child sexual abuse, see: Cote, Isabelle, "Memory and Allegations of Child Abuse", *The Expert: A Practitioner's Guide*, Carswell, 1995, Chapter 8; Fuerst, Michel, "Syndrome Evidence", *The Expert: A Practitioner's Guide*, *ibid.*, Chapter 9; Thompson, D.A., "Taking Children and Facts Seriously": "Evidence and Law in Child Protection Proceedings", *supra*, note 232, at 11; Thompson, D.A., "Children Should Be Heard But Not Seen: Children's Evidence in Protection Proceedings", 1991 Canadian Family Law Quarterly at 1.

In a custody/access case involving an allegation of sexual abuse, one of the more common situations the court or trier of fact will be faced with is the admissibility of the hearsay evidence in the form of out of court statements made by a child (who will not likely be a witness at the hearing) to such persons as parents, other adults, a family physician, a therapist, investigators (Children's Aid Society workers), police or to the person appointed to conduct the custody assessment.

(i) Test for Proof of Child Sexual Abuse

There appears to be a distinction that should be made in the standard of proof that is to be met in criminal cases, child protection cases, and civil custody and access cases involving an allegation of child sexual abuse. In criminal cases, of course, the test is one of "beyond a reasonable doubt". The test in child protection cases as to whether there has been sexual abuse does not approach the criminal standard of "beyond a reasonable doubt", but it is higher than the proof required in civil cases of "on the balance of probabilities". In child protection cases there is a heavy onus, as set out in *D. v. Children's Aid Society of Kent*[39] where the court stated:

> The standard of proof, therefore, is not that of the balance of probabilities per se; nor is there a test akin to the onus in criminal matters. No magic formula need be derived other than the heavy onus on the director of the children's aid society . . .

In civil custody/access cases the test appears to be one of "on the balance of probabilities". In civil custody/access cases involving child sexual abuse allegations, the courts appear to be reluctant to create precedents which may have the affect of raising the standard of proof unreasonably.

However, a review of the jurisprudence of custody cases would suggest that a consensus is emerging in custody/access cases, involving an allegation of child sexual abuse, that the evidence must be more convincing than just on the balance of probabilities.[40]

---

39 (1980), 18 R.F.L. (2d) 223 at 227 (Ont. Co. Ct.).

40 Raycroft, Mary-Jo Maur, Children in and out of the Court Room, 2nd Annual Institute of Family Law, University of Ottawa, May 28, 1993, at 192. In K. (S.) v. K. (P.K.) (1988), 51 Man. R. (2d) 138 (Q.B.) a mother applied to

In summary, it would appear that in civil custody/access cases the test to prove an allegation of child sexual abuse is lower than in a criminal case or child protection case, but higher than the "balance of probabilities" found in civil cases.

The significance of this test as it is applied in custody cases involving a comprehensive assessment of the family is that there may be more sources of hearsay evidence that are considered admissible than in a criminal or child protection case.[41]

The test above referred to regarding proof that child sexual abuse took place in a custody/access case is not to be confused with the test that is to be met regarding the admissibility of hearsay statements made by children out of court in cases involving child sexual abuse allegations. However, it is important for lawyers and assessors in the case of preparation of an assessor or other expert witnesses for cross-examination and in the case of the lawyer preparing for cross-examination of the said assessor or other expert witness in a custody/access case, to be familiar with the onus of proof test so that they can be adequately prepared for cross-examination. The lawyer, in particular, must know the particular test that has to be met so that an argument can ultimately be made as to whether the facts adduced in evidence meet the said test.

---

terminate access by the father to twin daughters aged 3 1/2 years on the basis of her allegation that the father had sexually abused the children. The court stated:

> "On the issue before me, of course, the overriding concern is the interests of the children. Clearly, the more serious the allegation the more moral turpitude it involves, the more cogent must be the evidence to support it, but the liberty of the individual is not at issue in these proceedings as it would be in criminal proceedings."

In B. (W.L.) v. B. (V.L.) (1988), 89 A.R. 393 (Q.B.) the court described the evidence of child sexual abuse as overwhelming. There were five separate expert reports all of which contained hearsay statements the two children aged 9 and 4 had said in the course of interviews, and all of which concluded that the children had been sexually abused. There was no contrary evidence. Access was denied. In *H. (J.) v. H. (G.)* (1987), 81 N.B.R. (2d) 51 (Q.B.) the court denied access without discussing the standard of proof in any detail. The evidence that the father had sexually abused the children appeared in hearsay statements contained in mental health reports and was derived from witnesses who had observed the children's behaviour.

41 *R. (J.) v. I. (A.)* (1987), 60 Sask. R. 81 (Q.B.); affirmed (1988), 13 R.F.L. (3d) 44, 61 Sask. R. 225 (C.A.). In this case the court held that the practice of admitting hearsay statements by children to others about sexual abuse in custody and access cases was common.

(ii) Admissibility Test re Out of Court Statements (Child Sexual Abuse)

Having determined what test must be met to prove an allegation of child sexual abuse in a custody/access case, lawyers must also be prepared to challenge the admissibility of any out of court statements made by a child in a custody/access case involving the allegation of child sexual abuse particularly where the child would not be a witness. If the lawyer and assessors know the criteria for the admissibility of such hearsay evidence, the lawyer will be able to conduct a more comprehensive cross-examination and the assessor will be in a position to be certain that the method employed or used in obtaining out of court statements from children and in attempting to rely upon them in providing opinion evidence will be accepted by a trier of fact. Knowing the test for admissibility allows the lawyer to direct his or her cross-examination to the circumstances in which the statements were made in order to determine if a successful attempt can be made to have the statements ruled as inadmissible.

As seen in *R. (J.) v. I. (A.)*,[42] the courts in recent years have been flexible about allowing experts to interview children in custody cases involving allegations of child sexual abuse and to then repeat the statements in their testimony notwithstanding the fact that, *prima facie*, such out of court statements made by the child are considered to be hearsay evidence and thus not admissible. The courts have been admitting such hearsay statements based on a "child sexual abuse" hearsay exception rule that has developed over the years. The purpose of this exception to the hearsay rule is to permit statements made by children to other persons, regarding alleged sexual abuse, to be put into evidence by the persons to whom the statements were made for the purpose of proving the truth of the statements themselves.

The leading case on the issue of the admissibility of a child's out of court statement made to another person regarding alleged child sexual abuse is the Supreme Court of Canada decision of *R. v. Khan*.[43] In that case, a girl who was 3 1/2 years old at the time visited her doctor with her mother. Her mother did not accompany her into the examining room. Fifteen minutes after she emerged from her visit to the doctor the child told her mother that the doctor has put his "birdie"

42 *Ibid.*
43 [1990] S.C.R. 531, 59 C.C.C. (3d) 92.

in her mouth and peed. At trial the trial judge decided that the child could not give unsworn oral testimony as the child did not comprehend the significance of telling the truth in court. The only evidence therefore relied upon by the Crown in proving that child sexual abuse took place was hearsay evidence as to what the child had said to her mother. The trial judge ruled that this testimony not be admitted as it did not fall into any of the established exceptions to the hearsay rule.

The Ontario Court of Appeal held that the hearsay could be admitted. The case was appealed to the Supreme Court of Canada. The Supreme Court of Canada held that the hearsay statement of the child regarding the alleged sexual abuse was admissible as long as the twin conditions of "necessity" of the statement and "reliability" of the statement were met as in any other hearsay exception.

Although *R. v. Khan* was a criminal case the test of admissibility set out therein is equally applicable to private custody and access litigation.[44]

Thus in a custody/access case regarding the allegation of child sexual abuse, involving an assessment and where the assessor, or any other expert called, in his or her report, provides an expert opinion as to whether there was child sexual abuse, and in doing so relies on the statement of a child, counsel must determine whether the said statements will fall within the "child sexual abuse hearsay exception rule".

As with children's statements made out of court dealing with their wishes regarding custodial or access arrangements, in the circumstances of statements made out of court in a child sexual abuse case, counsel should challenge the admissibility of the statement by cross-examining the assessor or other expert, or any other person, who wishes to repeat what the child told them in order to determine if the admissibility test in *R. v. Khan* can be met. Is the relied upon out of court statement of the child "necessary" and "reliable"? If it is not and the child is not going to testify the statement of the child will not be ruled admissible.[45]

It was earlier suggested, when dealing with the issue of out of court statements of children with respect to their wishes and preferences on custody and access arrangements, that any out of court statements made by a child be challenged at the initial stages of the

44 Thompson, D.A., "Children Should Be Heard, But Not Seen: Children's Evidence in Protection Proceedings", *supra*, note 38, at 2.

45 *M. (W.) v. Director of Child Welfare* (1986), 3 R.F.L. (3d) 181 (P.E.I. S.C.).

hearing if possible. It was pointed out that this could be done by way of a *voir dire*. This practice would also be employed in launching a challenge to the admissibility of any out of court statements made by a child in a custody case regarding alleged child sexual abuse.

(A) Necessity. What did the Supreme Court of Canada in *R. v. Khan* mean in stating that the hearsay statement of the child had to be "necessary"?

Although it seems trite to suggest that the child's statement is necessary in circumstances where the child cannot or should not testify, that seems to be the foundation on which the exception rule is based.

McLaughlin J., in the *Khan* case, said that the necessity condition was met because the trial judge decided that the child was not capable of testifying. She went on to suggest that necessity was not limited to the child's inability to testify in stating:

> But sound evidence based on psychological assessments that testimony in court might be traumatic for the child or harm the child might also serve. There may be other examples of circumstances which could establish the requirement of necessity.[46]

Therefore, in conducting cross-examination of an assessor or other expert in a custody/access case counsel challenging the admissibility of the child's statements should question the witness as to why the child cannot or should not testify. A mere statement by an assessor or other witness should not be enough given the comments of McLaughlin J. regarding sound evidence that the testimony might be traumatic or harmful for the child.

If the child is not competent to testify because the child fails to understand the significance of telling the truth, as was the case in *Khan*, or if the child is mentally or physically incapable of testifying obviously meet the necessity test. However, it is more difficult to determine what might be harmful or traumatic to the child and this is one area on which cross-examination should be concentrated. Rough guidelines for what is traumatic or harmful have been suggested including the following:[47]

---

46 *Supra*, note 43, at 104–105 C.C.C.

47 Thompson, D.A., "Children Should Be Heard, But Not Seen: Children's

- Where the child is six or under a minimum of evidence will likely serve to support a finding of incompetence or harm to the child, as the court can act upon its own judgment based upon its general knowledge of children.[48]
- For children aged 7 to 13, the amount of evidence required will increase as easy generalizations disappear. Mere submissions of counsel will be insufficient.[49]

With respect to the element of the test as to whether a child would be traumatized or harmed if forced to testify one finds a rather subjective approach has been taken by the courts in this regard.

Some courts have used the test as to whether to allow the child to testify would result in serious and permanent harm to the child.[50] Some courts have used the test as to whether the child would be significantly harmed in the process of giving oral evidence.[51] Some courts have been satisfied with a test being whether it would be in the best interests of the children not to call them.[52]

Counsel challenging the admission into evidence of an out of court statement made by a child regarding alleged child sexual abuse by a parent would want to therefore satisfy himself or herself as to whether any of these tests are met.

(B) Reliability. The second and conjunctive portion of the admissibility test set out in *R. v. Khan* regarding the admission of a child's out of court statements regarding alleged child sexual abuse is whether or not the said out of court statement is reliable.

Evidence in Protection Proceedings," *supra*, note 38, at 10.

48 For examples where courts appear to accept hearsay of young children without much question about their testifying see: *H. (D.R.) v. Superintendent of Family & Child Services* (1984), 41 R.F.L. (2d) 337 (B.C. C.A.); *F. (J.K.) v. F. (J.D.)*, [1988] W.D.F.L. 799 (B.C.C.A.); *N. (A.) v. Saskatchewan* (1988), 68 Sask. R. 24 at 29 (Q.B.); *Child and Family Services of Central Winnipeg v. Q. (N.)* (1989), 59 Man. R. (2d) 247 (Q.B.).

49 For examples where courts expect that expert evidence will be necessary to support resort to hearsay: *Superintendent of Family and Child Services v. B. (M.)*, [1985] W.D.F.L. 1425 (B.C. Co. Ct.), where the appeal court upheld the trial decision rejecting hearsay from children aged 17, 14 and 12 where the agency had failed to lead any evidence on this score. *H. (G.) v. Superintendent of Family and Child Services* (1984), 44 R.F.L. (2d) 179 (B.C. S.C.).

50 *Q. (N.)*, *supra*, note 48.

51 *L. (N.)* (1986), 72 A.R. 241 (Prov. Ct.).

52 *Supra*, at 49.

Clearly the "reliability" referred to is not something for which one can provide an exhaustive list of criteria but, in the *Khan* decision, the Supreme Court did state:

> Many considerations such as timing, demeanour, the personality of the child, the intelligence and understanding of the child, and the absence of any reason to expect fabrication in the statement may be relevant on the issue of reliability. I would not wish to draw up a strict list of considerations for reliability, nor to suggest that certain categories of evidence (for example the evidence of young children on sexual encounters) should be always regarded as reliable. The matters relevant to reliability will vary with the child and with the circumstances, and are best left to the trial judge.[53]

In the *Khan* decision McLaughlin J. decided that the child's out of court statements were reliable because:

> The child had no motive to falsify her story, which emerged naturally and without prompting. Moreover, the fact that she could not be expected to have knowledge of such sexual acts imbues her statement with its own particular stamp of reliability. Finally, her statement was corroborated by real evidence.[54]

Therefore, on cross-examination in a custody/access assessment case, counsel should explore with the assessor or other expert being called upon to testify with respect to the out-of-court statement, the circumstances in which the statement was made. This is a very difficult area of cross-examination as it would appear that the test as to whether the out of court statement is reliable is very subjective based on the comments in *Khan*. Nonetheless due to the serious consequences flowing from an allegation of child sexual abuse to the parent who is accused of same, it is important that counsel and the trier of fact be satisfied that the circumstances under which the statement was provided are such that one can conclude that they are reliable and thus admissible into evidence without the necessity of the child having to testify. One would hope to eliminate any opportunities for the child to be misquoted, for the statement of the child to be distorted or for the circumstances in which the child made the statement to be such that the child was not in any way influenced by prompting, suggested answers, leading questions or the suggestion

53 *Supra*, note 43, at 105 C.C.C.
54 *Ibid.*, at 43.

being made by the interviewer that child sexual abuse may have occurred.

As suggested, in a situation dealing with the out-of-court statements of a child with respect to the child's wishes or preferences on custodial or access arrangements, one should, in dealing with out-of-court statements regarding alleged child sexual abuse, consider insisting that any such interviews be conducted with the use of a tape recorder or perhaps even a video camera. The tape recorder would reduce the risk of whether the statement made by the child was taken out of context, distorted or fabricated or in any way misrepresented. The use of a videotape allows the court to see, first hand, the circumstances in which the child made the statement including the demeanour of the child and the atmosphere and environment in which the child was asked the questions. The problem with using videotapes of a child's conversation is that it is really another form of hearsay evidence.[55] The videotape will contain statements made by the child out of court and, presumably, will be tendered as evidence to demonstrate the truth of the allegation of child sexual abuse and, therefore, the use of the videotape may be a two-edged sword in the sense that its contents may be perceived to be as more reliable than recalled statements of other witnesses. In other words they may be deemed to be more accepting and reliable by the trier of fact than out-of-court statements made to other persons.[56]

The problem in addressing the reliability component of the admissibility test of a child's out of court statements, in a civil custody case relates to the motive of why a child might falsify his or her story. (Reference is made to this motive by McLaughlin J., in *Khan*). Unfortunately, in a custody/access case the motive often is directly

---

55 See *Children's Aid Society of Metro Toronto v. S. (M.)* (1985), 34 A.C.W.S. (2d) 77 (Ont. Prov. Ct.). In this case, which was a protection case, the Children's Aid Society attempted to obtain permission to admit an audio tape of the child's statements to a social worker about sexual abuse. The court ruled that the effect of admitting the audio tape of the child's statements would be the same as having the social worker relate verbatim to the court the statements of the child. If the child is not testifying there is no opportunity to cross-examine the declarant and, hence, such statements are hearsay. The judge refused to admit the tapes. Notably this case was decided before *R. v. Khan* but nonetheless makes the point that if an audio tape is considered to be hearsay, then a videotape may also be considered to be hearsay.

56 Please note that the *Criminal Code* has provisions dealing with the use of videotape evidence in a criminal prosecution. These provisions are not applicable to a civil case such as a custody/access case.

related to the fact that one parent is so desperate to retain custody of the child that that parent may be able to successfully persuade the child to be a party to making a false allegation. Therefore, when an assessor is faced with a situation where a child makes a statement to him or her with respect alleged sexual abuse the assessor should conduct a thorough investigation as to whether there is any motive for the child to make such a statement. It is therefore extremely important when selecting an assessor, particularly in a case where one knows that there is an allegation of child sexual abuse, that the assessor be a well-qualified professional with clinical experience in the investigation and assessment of child sexual abuse cases and who is therefore skilled in interviewing child victims and interpreting their statements.

In summary, although a court may in fact rely solely upon the out-of-court statements made by a child with respect to an allegation of child sexual abuse, where the court is satisfied that the said statement falls within the exceptions to the hearsay rule, it is suggested that the lawyers involved in the custody/access case should remind any trier of fact that any such evidence should not be quickly treated as being conclusive due to the frailties of the child's statement that might effect its reliability.

Even though a qualified professional person conducting the assessment or the child interview (such as a child psychologist specializing in sexual abuse cases) may consider that he or she is well versed in how to question the child with respect to allegations of child abuse, one should, nonetheless, be cautious about accepting the evidence of the person who obtained the statement without first having explored the circumstances in which the statement was obtained. In sexual abuse cases experts may very well unwittingly induce from young victims the statement that they have been sexually abused when this has not in fact occurred. Both assessors and lawyers in a custody/assessment case should be reminded of the celebrated case that took place in Jordon, Minnesota where 23 adults were charged with sexually assaulting a large portion of the children in the town. Although there was almost certainly at least one real incident of sexual abuse, after the so-called experts in sexual abuse interviewed virtually all the children in town using anatomically correct dolls, asking leading questions and making it abundantly clear to the children the responses expected, it was impossible to tell what had happened. The Minnesota Attorney General had to drop the prosecution since it was not possible to tell what in the children's statements was a product of experience and what was the product of suggestion.[57]

(e) Behaviourial Patterns (Child Sexual Abuse Allegations)

In custody access cases involving allegations of child sexual abuse one on a more regular basis sees assessment reports wherein an opinion is given by a so-called expert that in his or her view, based on the behaviourial patterns and behaviourial characteristics of a child victim, sexual abuse has either taken place or not. One also sees on a more regular basis in custody/access cases the situation of an expert witness, whether an assessor or some other expert witness, attempting to give *viva voce* expert opinion evidence as to whether sexual abuse of a child took place, which opinion is based on the behaviourial characteristics and patterns of the child. For an expert to provide an opinion as to whether child sexual abuse took place, based on the behaviourial characteristics or patterns of a child presents a situation where one is dealing with the science of human behaviour wherein attempts are usually being made to advance a novel theory or technique regarding sexual abuse. The issue therefore requires some attention when dealing with the cross-examination of an assessor or other expert who might be testifying in this regard in a custody case.

The historic difficulty in proving an allegation of child sexual abuse (whether in a criminal proceeding, a child protection proceeding or in a civil custody/access case) has caused lawyers and judges to look to those trained in an aspect of the behaviourial sciences for assistance. In custody/access cases involving an assessment, where there is an allegation of child sexual abuse, the person conducting the assessment may very well be the person who is trained in this field. On the other hand, the assessor may rely upon the expert opinion or input or advice of yet another person who is purportedly trained in this regard, such as a clinical psychologist who specializes in child sexual abuse cases. No matter who that expert may be, one can likely anticipate that his or her opinion as to whether child sexual abuse has

57 Balla and Anweiller, J., "Allegations of Sexual Abuse in a Parental Custody Dispute: Smoke Screen or Fire?" (1986), Canadian Family Law Quarterly 343 at 372; Attorney General of Minnesota, *Report on Scott County Investigations* (Minn., February 1985).

been committed, will in whole, or in part, be based on certain behaviourial characteristics or patterns of the child, in which case, one is dealing with the science of human behaviour.

It is important for both lawyers and assessors, in custody/access cases dealing with an allegation of child sexual abuse, to appreciate the judicial perspective with respect to the use of such expert opinion evidence and a reliance upon such expert opinion evidence by the courts and other triers of fact. In the case of the assessor, a degree of familiarity with the judicial and legal perspective in this regard will assist the assessor, upon being appointed to do an assessment, or upon agreeing to do an assessment, in being better prepared to conduct a complete, full and proper assessment. It has been generally stated that the opinion of an expert witness has to be "necessary" so as to enable a trier of fact to appreciate the matters in issue due to their technical nature and without which the trier of fact would be unable to draw any inferences on a particular issue in question.[58]

There are obvious areas that come to mind where courts admit that they require the necessary assistance of an expert witness. Examples would be medicine, architecture, engineering or, in the hard sciences such as nuclear physics, to name but a few.

However, in recent years, in the jurisprudence, the question has presented itself as to whether the assistance of experts is necessary in areas of imprecise or inexact science and particularly when dealing with the science of human behaviour.

Although traditionally the courts have decided human behaviour issues without assistance from experts, the Supreme Court of Canada in *R. v. Lavallee*[59] rejected the Crown's contention that judges and juries are sufficiently knowledgeable about human behaviour and therefore do not require the opinion of an expert in this regard. Wilson J. stated:

> Where expert evidence is tendered in such fields as engineering or pathology, the paucity of the lay person's knowledge is uncontentious. The long-standing recognition that psychiatric or psychological testimony also falls within the

---

58 *R. v. Abbey*, [1982] 2 S.C.R. 24; *R. v. Mohan*, [1994] 2 S.C.R. 9 at 23, 18 O.R. (3d) 160, where Sopinka J. stated:
"As stated by Dickson, J. (in making reference to *R. v. Abby*) the evidence must be necessary to enable the trier of fact to appreciate the matters in issue due to their technical nature."

59 [1990] 1 S.C.R. 852, 55 C.C.C. (3d) 97.

> realm of expert evidence is predicated on the realization that in some circumstances the average person may not have sufficient knowledge of or experience with human behaviour to draw an appropriate inference from the facts before him or her.[60]

The above judicial attitude regarding expert opinion evidence in the field of the science of human behaviour was further evidenced in the Saskatchewan Court of Appeal decision of *R. v. B. (G.)*.[61] This case involved the sexual assault of a 7-year-old girl by three young offenders. A clinical psychologist who purportedly was a specialist in the treatment of young victims of sexual offenses gave an opinion that there were several behaviourial characteristics which are experienced by young victims of sexual offences, which included bed wetting, nightmares and anxiety. However, he also testified that these problems may be caused by other occurrences in the child's life. In the decision of the Saskatchewan Court of Appeal Wakeling J., stated:

> I do not need to resort to statistics to establish that there are many more cases now coming to trial involving sexual abuse of children and requiring a very difficult evaluation of youthful testimony. Under these circumstances, it was understandable that the court should seek as much assistance as possible from those who can be qualified as experts. They can shed some additional light on evidence that would otherwise be of negligible value, so as to assist the judge in reaching a determination of what facts have been adequately corroborated or otherwise established.[62]

The *Lavallee* decision and the *R. v. B. (G.)* decision (which was upheld by the Supreme Court of Canada) make it clear that in child sexual abuse cases, in appropriate circumstances, the courts will resort to the use of expert opinion evidence relating to the science of human behaviour. In fact, behaviourial characteristics of sexually abused children has become a common topic of expert testimony in trial courts. It is viewed as evidence capable of supporting the child's allegation of abuse.[63]

It would also appear that in private custody/access cases involving allegations of sexual abuse the courts are also inclined to rely on expert evidence regarding the science of human behaviour, more

---

60 *Ibid.*, at 111 C.C.C.

61 (1988), 65 Sask. R. 134 (C.A.); affirmed [1990] 2 S.C.R. 3.

62 *Ibid.*, at 148.

63 Fuerst, M., "Syndrome Evidence", *The Expert: A Practitioner's Guide* (Carswell, 1995), Chapter 9, at 9–6.

particularly, with respect to the theory of how a child's behaviourial patterns or characteristics in a particular case may or may not be consistent with the behaviourial patterns or characteristics of one who has been sexually abused. In the case of *C. (R.M.) v. C. (J.R.)*[64] the issue was whether a father should have access to his two-year-old daughter. The mother had alleged that the father sexually abused the girl. Pursuant to a court order a psychologist conducted an assessment to determine if there had in fact been any sexual abuse. At trial, the expert psychologist opined that there was not sufficient evidence to conclude that there was sexual abuse. This opinion was based on her own observations as well having relied upon the studies and analysis of other experts in the field of child sexual abuse. In the course of her testimony she was led through a number of "sign posts of sexual abuse" and in doing so acknowledged that the sign posts were not necessarily determinative of sexual abuse having taken place. She testified that the sign posts were consistent with the behaviourial patterns of a child under stress or a child suffering from anxiety not related to sexual abuse. The trial judge relied heavily on the evidence of the psychologist finding her to be impartial, experienced, knowledgable and wise. The evidence was given a lot of weight by the judge in deciding to grant access to the father.

Having now established that this type of expert opinion evidence is relied on by the courts, assessors and lawyers should, in the case of the assessor in conducting his or her investigation of the allegations, and in the case of the lawyer in preparation for cross-examination, consider the criteria to be met in getting such evidence before the court. As canvassed in Chapter 8, heading 5, "Admissibility of Expert Opinion Evidence" in a general fashion, the criteria for the admission of such opinion evidence is set out in the Supreme Court of Canada decision of *R. v. Mohan*.[65] The criteria are that the evidence must be relevant, necessary, not offend any hearsay rule, and that the expert must be properly qualified. The expert must be shown to have acquired special or peculiar knowledge through study or experience in respect of the matters in which he or she intends to testify.[66] Put another way, the so-called expert must be qualified to give the opinion

64 (1995), 12 R.F.L. (4th) 440 (B.C. S.C.).
65 *Supra*, note 58, at 20.
66 *Ibid.*, at 25.

and should not be allowed to give opinion evidence outside the area of his or her expertise.

When dealing with expert evidence that advances a novel scientific theory or technique, as is the case when dealing with behaviourial patterns of children in child sexual abuse cases, the said expert opinion evidence is subjected to special scrutiny to determine whether it meets a basic threshold of reliability and whether it is essential in the sense that the trier of fact will be unable to come to a satisfactory conclusion without the assistance of the expert opinion evidence.[67]

The cross-examination of an assessor, in a custody/access case, who either in his or her report, or who wishes in his or her oral testimony to provide an opinion that child sexual abuse either occurred or did not occur and which opinion is based on the behaviourial patterns or characteristics of the child should primarily focus on whether, firstly, the assessor is qualified to give such an opinion and, secondly, whether the opinion is reliable in the context of it being based on theories or techniques that are generally acceptable in both the clinical community and scientific community. The question begs itself as to whether the said theories or techniques have been scientifically approved or validated.

(i) Qualifications

The assessor should be cross-examined to determine whether he or she has the qualifications to give an opinion in the field of child sexual abuse. The procedure for challenging an expert witness' qualifications was dealt with in a general way in Chapter 7, heading 5. "Review of the Final Written Assessment". With respect to the qualifications of an expert dealing with the behaviourial patterns of a child in a case involving alleged sexual abuse the following areas which are not exhaustive, should be considered by counsel on cross-examination:

1. The field of child sexual abuse is a relatively recent one and therefore most psychologists in the field will not have obtained any formal or academic training in this regard. The assessor should be examined as to whether he or she has any such training.

67 *Ibid.*

2. Has the assessor or other expert witness done any writing or had any writings published on the topic of child sexual abuse?
3. If the assessor, or other expert witness, has published material in the field, has it been evaluated by his or her peer group, that is, by others (presumably psychologists and psychiatrists) who hold themselves out as experts in child sexual abuse cases?
4. What clinical experience does the assessor have? The concern here is not the clinical experience in general terms, as most experts in custody/access cases are *bona fide* clinical psychologists. However, to what extent do they have specific experience on the issue of child sexual abuse? How many cases of child sexual abuse have they had?
5. Has the psychologist been retained on an independent basis for the sole purpose of determining whether sexual abuse took place, or is the child victim a patient of the psychologist and undergoing therapy with the psychologist? The opinion of the psychologist in the former circumstance is likely to be more objective and acceptable than in the latter circumstance.
6. What was the methodology or assessment technique used by the assessor in trying to determine whether there was a false allegation made or whether there is any evidence of sexual abuse having taken place. Is it one that is recognized in the assessor's profession or is it a method that only this particular psychologist or assessor uses? In this regard for a review of the different assessment techniques used in child sexual abuse cases one should read Chapter 10, heading 6. "Sexual abuse allegations in the context of disputed custody".

(ii) Theory and/or Technique (Re: Behaviourial Patterns)

After having explored the issue as to whether the assessor or other expert witness in the case is qualified to give opinion evidence counsel should direct their attention, in cross-examining the assessor or other expert witness, as to whether there is in fact scientific proof or validation of the theory that behaviourial patterns of children can be relied upon in offering a conclusive opinion as to whether or not the occurrence of child sexual abuse took place. The issue to be pursued and the question to be asked of the expert witness, in general terms, is whether the present state of knowledge in the field is such that the soundness and reliability of any expert opinion purporting to characterize behaviourial symptoms as "consistent" with sexual abuse can be demonstrated. Although the courts, as we have seen, have been inclined to accept expert opinion evidence with respect to the science of human behaviour regarding child sexual abuse cases, there appears to be some question creeping into the jurisprudence, and into the field of expertise dealing with this issue, as to whether there is in fact a scientifically proven theory that can be relied upon in this regard. In *R. v. Leblanc*[68] the court observed that the behaviourial symptoms of a person claiming to have been sexually assaulted and which according to an expert were consistent with the symptoms of a victim sexually assaulted, could also arise from other kinds of psychological trauma. In *R. v. Dieffenbaugh*[69] the British Columbia Court of Appeal expressed concern about the admissibility of opinion evidence based on standards that cannot be objectively validated and concluded that the evidence had limited probative value but was of overwhelming prejudicial effect.

The American courts seem to apply this thinking to cases involving behaviourial evidence as evidenced by two cases dealing with the issue. In the decision of *Commonwealth v. Dunkle*[70] held that evidence of the typical behaviours of sexually abused children are so general as to have no probative value. The court stated:

> Clearly, drug and alcohol abuse, eating disorders, low self-esteem and not doing school work are common phenomena not solely related to child abuse. To permit the jury to speculate that they might be however violates every notion of what constitutes probative or relevant evidence. It is neither scientifically supportable nor legally supportable. Such a quandary list of possible behaviours does no more than invite speculation and will not be condoned.[71]

In the decision of *State v. Cressy*[72] the court concluded that symptoms and behaviours commonly exhibited by sexually abused children was not sufficiently reliable to be admitted into criminal trial and specifically stated:

---

68 (1992), 71 C.C.C. (3d) 527 (N.B. C.A.).
69 (1993), 80 C.C.C. (3d) 97 (B.C. C.A.).
70 602 A. 2d 830 (PA., 1992).
71 *Ibid.*, at 834–835.
72 628 A. 2d 696 (N.H. Supreme Court 1993).

> We are bound to recognize that the separate fields of behaviourial science and criminal justice are different enough in their foundations and goals that what may be considered helpful information in one may not be so valued in the other. Generally speaking, the psychological evaluation of a child suspected of being sexually abused is, at best, an inexact science...A psychological evaluation of a potentially abused child does not present the verifiable results and logical conclusions that work to ensure the reliability required in the solemn matter of a criminal trial.[73]

In the Canadian decision of *R. v. Olscamp*[74] the court considered similar evidence. In that case the accused was charged with the sexual assault of a 7-year-old girl. The expert witness, a clinical psychologist who specialized in the field of child sexual abuse victims would say in her opinion that the child had been sexually abused. A *voir dire* the admissibility of the evidence. The psychologist on cross-examination admitted that there was no existing valid profile of a sexually abused child. Various pieces of authoritative literature were put to her that suggested that behaviour assumed by some to be indicative of sexual abuse may in fact be so related, and may also be attributable to normal developmental variations, emotional or physical abuse, neglect, family conflict or parental discord. Some of the literature further suggested that there was not any specific syndrome in children who have been sexually abused and no single traumatizing process. The presiding judge in refusing to admit this expert opinion evidence stated:

> The present state of knowledge in the field is such that the soundness and reliability of any expert opinion purporting to characterize behaviourial symptoms as "consistent with sexual abuse" cannot be demonstrated.
>
> The distinction between a purely personal professional opinion and more generally accepted scientific knowledge is crucial to the trier of fact who is called upon to evaluate the validity and reliability of the opinion.[75]

All of the above cases are criminal cases and as seen earlier in this chapter in dealing with the issue of child sexual abuse, the onus of proof with respect to establishing sexual abuse in a criminal case is different than the onus of proof in a custody/access case. In a civil case generally, the onus of proof is that the allegation must be proved

---

73 *Ibid.*, at 699.
74 (1994), 95 C.C.C. (3d) 466 (Ont. Gen. Div.).
75 Ibid., at 473.

on a mere balance of probabilities. However, due to the serious consequences flowing from a decision on whether sexual abuse took place in a custody/access, one would argue that the test to be applied should be more convincing than on a mere balance of probabilities. The consequences of a trier of fact in a custody/access case relying on expert evidence based on standards not scientifically supported or validated can be extremely serious. The trier of fact has to decide whether the child victim will continue to spend more time with the alleged perpetrator of the abuse and, thus, possibly subject the child to further untold horrors and serious emotional harm or trauma. On the other hand, he or she has to decide whether the child will spend less or no time at all with the alleged perpetrator of the offence which lack of contact in the child's normal developmental process will possibly cause serious harm or trauma as well.

In summary, from the legal perspective, in cases involving a properly qualified expert, Canadian courts are mostly inclined to permit expert opinion evidence (with some exceptions), in appropriate cases, with respect to the science of human behaviour as it relates to the behaviourial patterns of persons who have allegedly been sexually abused. The courts, with some exceptions, do not appear to be concerned with the possibility that many of these characteristics are capable of explanation by causes other than abuse. This appears to be a question of weight by the trier of fact from case to case.

The most likely effective area for a lawyer to cross-examine an assessor on in a case involving behaviourial patterns and characteristics in a sexual abuse case will be on the state of knowledge in the field and whether it is considered to be sound and reliable.

The assessor or other expert being cross-examined should be questioned on that empirical data, literature and/or studies relied upon in advancing this area of syndrome evidence. The assessor should be cross-examined on the basis on which he or she feels that this theory and technique regarding behaviourial symptoms are in fact scientifically proven.

To do so usually requires counsel to put to the witness expert literature to see whether the expert witness agrees or disagrees with the opinions of others in the field, or so see whether the expert witness is attempting to testify in a field of expertise beyond his or her limits.

It has been seen that authoritative works may be put to an expert witness in order to challenge his or her opinion. In *R. v. Marquard*[76] the proper procedure in this regard was clearly set out.

Cross-examining counsel might, in the case where the testifying expert witness refuses to acknowledge another authoritative work, invite the witness to agree that in the narrow and troublesome area of behaviourial patterns relating to child sexual abuse symptoms, there appears to be legitimate differences of opinion in this regard between experts in the field. This will show that the witness is not infallible and that his or her opinion is only one of many in this particular field of expertise.

If the assessor or other expert witness will not accept that there are differences of opinion between experts in this regard then of course counsel can either call other experts to testify in this regard, or, in the course of argument can make reference to the jurisprudence that clearly exhibits that some triers of fact have acknowledged that there has not yet necessarily been determined a valid theory that supports the proposition that certain behaviour patterns of a child are or are not necessarily consistent with only those who have been sexually abused.

In having dealt with the issues of out-of-court statements made by children in alleged sexual abuse cases and with the behaviourial symptoms of children who may or may not have been victims of sexual abuse, it has been intended to simply raise the two most commonly relied upon sources of evidence upon which experts tend to rely in custody/access cases where there is an allegation of sexual abuse.

It is not intended in this chapter to exhaust all other syndromes and areas of concern with respect to child sexual abuse cases.[77]

---

76 [1993] 4 S.C.R. 223, 25 C.R. (4th) 1 at 20–21.

77 For interesting reading in the area of child sexual abuse see: Fuerst, M., "Syndrome Evidence," The Expert: A Practitioner's Guide (Carswell 1995), Chapter 9; Mary-Jo Maur Raycroft, M.J., "Children In and Out of the Courtroom" - Chapter 5 Evidentiary Problems and Expert Witnesses, Second Annual Institute of Family Law, University of Ottawa, May 28, 1993; Thompson, D.A., "Children Should be Heard, But Not Seen: Children's Evidence in Protection Proceedings", 1991 Canadian Family Law Quarterly at 1.

(f) Psychological Testing

In the majority of custody/access assessments the assessor, or somebody on his or her behalf, will resort to psychological testing of the parents and, other adults who may be involved in the children's lives. On occasion the children also undergo psychological testing. One of the first questions to be asked of an assessor on cross-examination would be why he or she did not use psychological testing in the assessment process. Not to do so could be seen as a lack of thoroughness or completeness on the part of the assessor in the context that he or she has not used all of the tools normally available to an assessor, by which to gather information and/or data that may be relevant and significant in drawing conclusions about the family in question. When used appropriately psychological testing can be invaluable in helping the court as well as the parents to understand the conflict, the child and the essential elements of the short and long term plan for the care of the children.[78]

The various types of psychological tests that might be drawn upon by the assessor in a custody/access dispute can be selected from a vast array of tests, a description of which has been provided in Chapter 5.[79]

On the other hand, many mental health professionals have been criticized for their inappropriate use of psychological testing when conducting custody/access assessments and, therefore, it is essential that when counsel cross-examines the assessor at the custody/access hearing some time be spent to assure that appropriate testing was conducted, that it was done so properly, that the results obtained are based on correct assumptions or data and, lastly, to determine that the tests, in some way, bear relevance to the issue of custody/access of the child in question and the ability of the parents in question to parent the said child.

Technically speaking results from a psychological test constitute another form of hearsay evidence in the context that the assessor or person who administers the testing ultimately shall be offering an

78 Roseby, V., Ph.D., "Uses of Psychological Testing in a Child-Focused Approach to Child Custody Evaluations," Volume 29, 1, F.L.Q. 97 at 104, Spring 1995.

79 Also for the various psychological tests that might be used in a child access assessment dispute see: Clarke, Beth, 29 Canadian Family Law Quarterly at 19, Spring 1995; Otto, Randy K. and Butcher, James N., 29 Canadian Family Law Quarterly at 79, Spring 1995.

opinion about a party or child as to their cognitive abilities, skills and personality traits which opinion will be based on second-hand information, such as, established empirical data relating to measurement norms standardization and response mechanisms built into the psychological tests, not to mention the test results themselves, which are then subject to interpretation by the assessor or other person who may have conducted the test. The person tested is likely to only be cross-examined at trial or at the hearing in a very limited manner on the testing and the testing results, as the said persons are unlikely to be in a position to explain any of the complexities involved in the administrative process regarding the tests, or for instance, with respect to the empirical background on which the standards and norms, built into the test, are based. Thus, if an assessor in his or her assessment report, provides an opinion that one of the parties not have custody or be denied access to a child, because psychological testing of that party revealed, in the assessor's opinion, a personality flaw that affects that person's ability to parent, counsel for that party will wish to extract from the assessor in cross-examination the basis upon which such an opinion is based. Can that opinion be supported by the second-hand information or facts upon which the assessor is relying? Are the test results sound? If so, how was it determined that they necessarily affect the party's ability to parent?

The criteria for the test of admissibility of expert opinion evidence as seen in R. v. Mohan[80] would have to be met in determining whether the psychological test and the psychological test results would be admissible in evidence or whether they would be given any weight and, if so, to what extent. It would have to be shown that the psychological testing meets a basic threshold of reliability[81] and that it is both necessary and relevant to the custody/access issue in question.[82]

There are probably two basic questions that judges and/or triers of fact, and lawyers should ask when considering an approach to cross-examination on a custody/access assessment which incorporates psychological testing.

First, is the assessor relying on a particular test able to document that the technique is valid, that is, that it actually measures what it

80 [1994] 2 S.C.R. 23 at 20 and 25.
81 *Ibid.*, at 25.
82 *Ibid.*, at 20.

purportedly measures? Psychological testing may provide an inaccurate representation of the individual. Reasons for potential inaccuracy include poor reliability or validity of the test, the deliberate attempt by the individual to give misleading information, the failure to administer the test in standardized fashion, and others.

Second, can the assessor or person introducing the test results demonstrate that what is measured or assessed by the test or technique is relevant to the legal question at hand?[83]

Cross-examination should focus on these basic questions. Custody/access decisions can be very "final" in the context of being difficult to modify or vary after the fact. Therefore, it is counsel's mandate to ensure that all elements to the proper administration and interpretation of a psychological test have been met. The psychological test by itself should not be the sole basis for any recommendations made by the assessor. A custody determination based solely on a clinical battery of tests, without corroborating data, would not likely stand the test of peer scrutiny, let alone the scrutiny of cross-examination. Impressions of the assessor based on his or her interpretation of psychological tĕsting are only "hypothesis", that must be verified through history, medical test and third party observations. Put another way, psychological testing is only one tool in an assessor's arsenal of methods available to assess a family in custody/access assessments. The primary tool is still the clinical impression of the assessor and the psychological testing can be used to validate or disconfirm those impressions.[84]

In addressing one's mind to whether the psychological testing is reliable and relevant to the custody/access issue, and in preparation for cross-examination counsel will want to consider those factors discussed below.

(i) Reliability

The assessor or administrator of the test should be asked whether the test employed to test the parties and children meets the "reliability

83 Heilbrun, Karl, "Child Custody Evaluation: Critically Assessing Mental Health Experts and Psychological Tests" (1995), 29 Canadian Family Law Quarterly 63. Heilbrun, Karl, "The Role of Psychological Testing in Forensic Assessment" (1992), 16 L. and Hum. Behav. 257.

84 Roseby, V., *supra*, note 78, at 105.

co-efficient" with which measuring indicia qualified assessors will be familiar. A "reliability co-efficient" greater than .80 is considered desirable in psychological testing.[85]

As used in psychometrics, the term "reliability" always means consistency. Test reliability is the consistency of scores obtained by the same persons when re-tested with the identical test or with an equivalent form of the test.[86]

The lower the reliability of a given test the lower the limit on the validity of the construct (such as intelligence) being measured.[87] Tests with a "reliability co-efficient" below .80 have been criticized for excessive error variance and thus poor validity. On cross-examination the assessor should be asked to produce the instructions for the test which should refer to or recite the "reliability co-efficient". If it does not meet the test then it should not be admitted into evidence or alternatively little weight should be given to the results.

Although one can expect a seasoned or well-qualified assessor to use a test that meets the threshold requirement of reliability, there may very well be instances where less experienced, or less qualified assessors use an inappropriate psychological test. Even experienced assessors, out of habit, may have come to rely on a psychological test whose "reliability co-efficient" may have changed over the years. Some assessors may not be able to answer the question as to what the "reliability co-efficient" is regarding the test they used, in which case the effective use of that particular test and its results could be undermined or compromised.

(A) Standardization. In the process of standardization the test is given to a large sample representative of the type of persons for whom it is designed. The test results for the standardized sample serve to establish the norm. On cross-examination the assessor should be asked as to how the particular psychological test used was standardized. The assessor should be asked as to whether the sample on which a psychological test was standardized is any different from that involved in a child custody case. For example, does the sample

85 Anastasi, Ann, *Psychological Testing*, 6th ed. (New York: McMillan 1988); Heilbrun, Karl, *supra*, note 280, 29 Canadian Family Law Quarterly 63 at 74.

86 Anastasi, V., *ibid.*, at 27.

87 Cronbach, Lee J., The Dependability of Behaviourial Measurements: Theory of General Reliability for Scores and Profiles (1990) 72.

population used in the test, against which the parties and children undergoing the assessment are compared for differences, contain a percentage population of divorced or separated families who are engaged in custody/access litigation? If not, the test standards may not fit the family undergoing the assessment. Most assessors will have to admit on cross-examination that most psychological tests are not specifically designed with custody disputants in mind.[88]

The point in argument to be used by counsel in a custody/access dispute is that the less the sample standard used in the psychological test applies or fits the family being assessed the less weight that should be given the test results.

(B) Selection of Tests. Although there do not yet exist psychological tests for child custody disputes that have been validated, there are certain tests that are considered as being more reliable and accurate than others for that purpose.

An assessor should make it clear in his or her report what psychological test has been used in the assessment.

The most frequently used is the Minnesota Multiphasic Personality Inventory - 2.[89] The second most frequently used psychological test is the Rorschach.[90]

If the assessor uses the Minnesota Multiphasic Personality Inventory it should be established on cross-examination as to whether it is the MMPI, or the MMPI-2, the latter being standardized on a more current representative sample of American society, with modifications having been made in 1989. If the MMPI was used it simply was not as reliable and its effectiveness would be questionable.

There are, however, questions to be asked regarding the MMPI-2 and its reliability when used to measure Canadian subjects as opposed to American subjects. Can it be assumed that the traits or empirical

88 Psychologists will also point out that psychological tests are currently being developed to specifically deal with custody/access litigation. However, as pointed out in Chapter 5, dealing with the interpretation of psychological tests, the validity of these tests has not yet been established.

89 Otto, Randy K. and Butcher, James N., "Computer-Assisted Psychological Assessment in Child Custody Evaluations" (1995), 29 Family Law Quarterly 79.

90 Keilin, William and Bloom, Larry, "Child Custody Evaluation Practices: A Survey of Experienced Professionals" (1986), 17 Prof. Psychol.: Res and Prac. 338.

characteristics of the American sample population used in the test are, generally speaking, the same as those of Canadians? Is the sample, for example, representative of unilingual French Canadians? If not, obviously it is arguable that if the French Canadian culture is not part of the sample representation, the test should not be given any significant weight, in appropriate circumstances.

(C) Administration of the Test. Most psychological tests have been developed with detailed instructions regarding their administration.

On cross-examination the assessor should be asked to describe the physical circumstances in which the test was conducted. Standardization is an important consideration in the accuracy of psychological testing. Many tests have been developed with detailed instructions regarding administration. All tests need a relatively quiet distraction-free setting for administration. To the extent that the instructions and conditions depart from the standard of administration in a given case, performance will be adversely affected. Since tests have been normed under the conditions described in their respective manuals, the test norms may not apply in evaluating that individual's performance under non-standard conditions.[91]

On cross-examination it would be appropriate to ask the assessor to produce the written instructions with respect to the particular test used so as to be satisfied that the instructions have been properly followed. Who gave the instructions to the person taking the test and what instructions were given? For instance, the proper instructions in the MMPI-2 test are for the subject to attempt to answer all questions and to provide a true response if it is mostly true and a false response if it is mostly false. Were those instructions specifically given to the subject? The person taking the test should also be advised to answer the questions from a perspective of the present, that is, how one feels today. Did the tester give those specific instructions to the person being tested? Was the test in fact conducted in quiet surroundings? The assessor might be asked as to who was present in order to determine whether this criteria has been met.

Other questions relevant to the circumstances or conditions under which the test was administered are whether the person had taken the

91 Heilbrun, Karl, *supra*, note 83, at 75; Anastasi, A., *supra*, note 85.

test before and, thus, may have had some unfair degree of familiarity with it. Did the person taking the test seem to be in good health or was he or she at the time experiencing poor health that might affect the ability to properly respond to the questions.

Unfortunately, otherwise valid and appropriate tests can be administered by unqualified and incompetent examiners, thereby effecting the reliability or validity of the results. The procedure used should be explored. What are the qualifications of the tester to use the test and his or her familiarity with the test limitations? Has the assessor verified that the test protocol being interpreted is actually that of the person being tested? What procedures were used in obtaining the test responses? Were the test administration procedures appropriate? Was the answer sheet processed in a standard, acceptable manner? Deviations in standard testing practices and flawed test processing procedures often result in invalid unintelligible profiles.[92]

A further problem in administration of psychological testing can occur, for example, when the assessor does not conduct the testing and refers the matter out to a third party for the purpose of having the test conducted or where the assessor may not have referred the matter out of his or her office, but may have had a member of his or her support staff within the office conduct the test. In either case, counsel would want to cross-examine the assessor to determine that the person conducting the test was properly qualified, followed the proper procedures and gave the proper instructions to the subject being tested.

If someone other than the assessor doing the evaluation of the family conducts the psychological tests then there could be a lack of continuity and/or lack of communication in that the testing was not conducted by the same pair of eyes, the same mind, the same sifter and sorter as the person who conducted the balance of the evaluation.

This poses a problem particularly with respect to the relevance of the testing and its results, to the custody/access question and how it may confirm or disconfirm a final conclusion by the assessor. For example, how does the assessor know that the proper instructions were given? Does he or she have a written report from the administrator of the test describing the instructions that should have been given? How can the assessor be assured that the test carried out was carried out in the proper conditions as prescribed in the test manual. Did the assessor simply assume that this was done? How does the assessor know

92 Otto and Butcher, *supra*, note 89, at 95.

whether the test administrator properly interpreted the test results? Does the assessor have the actual test results, scores and working papers of the test administrator in his or her possession so that they can be reviewed by counsel? If none of these questions can be satisfactorily answered by the assessor on cross-examination then the test results could be compromised.

(D) Response Bias. In a custody/access case the parties undergoing the assessment process will wish to present themselves as the ideal candidate for obtaining custody and/or access of their child or children. They will tend to exaggerate their good qualities and down play or deny any less than perfect qualities which, in the situational context of a custody/access dispute, is certainly understandable. In other words, the parties may not be as truthful or honest about themselves or others when undergoing a psychological test as part of the assessment process, in an attempt to be seen in the best possible light.

It is understood that all psychological test subjects are instructed to answer questions as truthfully as possible. For example, on the MMPI-2 test they are to provide a "true" response if the answer to the question is mostly true and a "false" response if the answer to the question is mostly false.

Mild distortions (or mildly untruthful answers) may not invalidate the results but the more extreme the form of deception or unwillingness to become involved in the testing process, the more likely such responses could render the test results meaningless.[93]

There are generally four response styles to be assessed in a psychological test:

1. Reliable/honest. This is where a sincere attempt is made to be accurate in responding, with factual inaccuracies attributable to poor understanding or misperception.
2. Malingering. A conscious fabrication or gross exaggeration of physical and/or psychological symptoms, distinguished from factitious disorder in that the motivation for malingering goes beyond the desire to assume the patient role and is understandable in light of the individual circumstances.

93 Heilbrun, Karl, *supra*, note 83, at 77.

3. Defensive. A conscious denial or gross minimization of physical and/or psychological symptoms distinguished from ego defences, which involve intra-psychic processes that distort perception.
4. Irrelevant. The failure to co-operate in the evaluation process; responses are not necessarily relevant to the question content and may be random.[94]

In the MMPI-2 psychological test there are contained several scales measuring response bias or test taking attitude that can identify subjects as being excessively defensive and "faking good" or excessively maladjusted and "faking bad".

In a custody/access dispute, given obvious influences involved, assessors should probably pay particular attention to the possibility that a defensive style may be used by one or both parties to the dispute.

When a response appears to be malingering, defensive or irrelevant rather than honest/reliable, the results of psychological testing may need to be discounted or even ignored and other data scores emphasized to a greater degree.[95] Therefore, on cross-examination it should be determined from the assessor as to whether appropriate response biases are built into the testing; which of the appropriate response biases are applicable to the person having been examined and if that response bias is other than reliable and honest to attempt to have the assessor admit that the results may be compromised and that, therefore, meaningful interpretation may be impossible.

In a custody/access dispute, as in all forensic disputes, there is frequently an induced motivation (custody/access to one's child) to distort one's traits or characteristics. Therefore the responses may affect the validity or reliability of the test.

(E) Clinical Interpretations. Once counsel, on cross-examination, has worked his or her way through the selection of the tests, the standardization and response biases, attention should then be directed to the issue of whether or not the results of a particular test as administered to an individual was properly interpreted by the assessor or any other person who may have administered the test.

Most interpretations of psychological testing involves whether or not the person or persons tested fall within norms or normal ranges of

94 Rogers, Richard, "Towards an Empirical Model of Malingering and Deception" (1984), 2 Behav. Sci. and L., 93–111.

95 Heilbrun, Karl, *supra*, note 83, 63 at 77.

scales developed for psychological tests. The person administering the test therefore has to determine what range the parties to the custody/access dispute or the child fall into if they have been tested. For instance in the MMPI-2 psychological test the normal range for all scales is between the 50th and 65th percentile. Scales are most clearly interpretable if they are above the normal limit or below it. Therefore, on cross-examination, counsel should ask the assessor or person who administered the test whether the scale elevation in fact exceeds the normal limit or is so low as to also be clinically significant. This is important as interpretations will often be made even if a scale approximates clinical significance or if it is the highest scale overall in the overall profile. There appears to be a major difference between a profile elevation well into the pathological range, and one that hugs the upper limit but still remains within normal values. The assessor should be cross-examined on the ranges of scales, but the point to be made on the said cross-examination is whether a party's test results will fall above or below the normal range and, thus, whether the scores may have an impact on the party's ability to parent children.

If the assessor has used a computer-based interpretative report by which to measure the test results and on which is based his or her opinion then the assessor should be asked whether all of the descriptions given in the computer report actually describe the subject of the assessment. For instance, if a psychological test identifies the presence of a disorder in a parent on the basis of a computer interpreted test one should ascertain whether this diagnosis was confirmed or supported by other sources of information such as interviewing, observation or other circumstances in the person's life such as documented difficulties with the child that may have caused the problem. In other words, did the assessor or members of his or her support staff interview other persons in order to determine whether the diagnosis was consistent with other data or information collected in this manner. The main point to be made on this aspect of the cross-examination of the assessor is whether the test results as measured by the assessor or other person having conducted the tests are consistent with other sources of information or data or evidence that would be led in the course of the hearing or trial and, thus, raising the question as to the reliability and validity of the said test results.

(ii) Relevancy

Once the psychological results have been measured by the assessor, the question presents itself as to whether the test results, regarding what has been measured or assessed by the test, are relevant to the legal question at hand. In other words, in what way do the test results or the diagnosis from the test results exhibit any relevance to the parenting issue, that is before the trier of fact.

It seems clear that currently there are no psychological tests that have been validated for the purpose of directly assessing parenting ability and, thus, in that context psychological tests are irrelevant when clinicians attempt to use them in a straightforward fashion to measure legal concepts. For instance, if psychological testing is done in order to measure a person's intelligence or the emotional functions of a person, such as whether they are less prone to depression, their relevance or causation to their capacity to parent must be justified. A justification can be made on theoretical grounds however if there is no research with which to evaluate the accuracy or strength of the connection in a psychological testing result and the test subject's ability to parent, then the test results may not be relevant. However, the causation between the test results and the issue of a party's capacity to parent should also be justified on the basis of whether information and data were gathered by the assessor from other sources. Once again, if testing result shows that one party suffers from "depression" but all other evidence gathered from other sources by the assessor would suggest that has been no evidence or history of depression then one would have to question the accuracy of the test results and whether they are in any way relevant to the legal question of who should have custody or access to the children.

10

Special Clinical Problems in Family Assessments for Custody and Access

1. INTRODUCTION

When we enter the realm of special problems in custody and access, in many ways we depart from the primacy of the best interests principle and, rather, look for guidance in the principle of least detriment. These situations represent those minority of cases where psychopathology and character disturbance are severe and where the assessment must disentangle a child as best as possible from harmful impact or influence. Such complicated scenarios represent a special challenge for the assessor quite apart from what is normally faced in the health system. For one, custodial disputes are often initiated by parents who are unlikely otherwise to seek psychiatric or psychotherapeutic help and this seems even more true in those special cases which tend to be more destructive and pathological. Secondly, the assessor's task is twofold; to identify abnormality if it exists as well as to pose recommendations that will favour the adaptation prospects of the child. There is usually no doubt in these situations that an assessment is required to make sense of the clinical complexities involved. Finally, these special situations are often litigious, explosive and more likely than typical custody matters to be settled in court. They often involve the efforts of the office of the child's lawyer and child protection services and the assessment may occur in the context of parallel developments in terms of the police and criminal courts. Hence, the assessor must be especially prudent and perceptive in order to protect children from the almost certain harm that these problems can cause.

Although difficult cases are of different sorts and varying severity as well as representing different clinical problems, there are certain scenarios commonly observed in many of these cases. The following psychological types come to mind as representing common constellations in which these special problems arise:

- Pathological blame is often the dominant motif and there is a lack of balanced perception. There is a blinding inability to allow the other parent a legitimate place to stand. The depth of animosity is like a wall that poisons the post-separation adjustment. One or both parents will describe a deep sense of betrayal that almost certainly has earlier roots in their family history.
- Fearing depression and deeply injured, the ex-spouse demands vindication and wants the other parent brought swiftly to justice. They will insist that the assessor and the court "nail" the offending parent and expose their painful conduct and betrayal. The clinical picture will be dominated by rage, either overt or covert, and vengeance. Success is measured by how little access the offending parent receives and how many roadblocks can be stood in the way.
- One parent insists that their love is special and the only love their children need. They idealize their contribution alone and irrationally devalue the other parent and often his or her family of origin. They seem incapable of self reflection and self knowledge. The other parent is seen as crazy or completely at fault while the parent in question claims total normality which they defend like a fortress. Their capacity for insight and common sense is minimal. MMPI profiles are frequently invalidated due to an inability to admit even minor faults or inconsistencies.
- The relationship will likely have been short term and chaotic and there may well have been substance abuse during the course of the

marriage. One spouse will treat the other as totally worthless and the children may well be poisoned against this parent. The blaming parent will place all the "bad" qualities and blame in the lap of the denigrated other parent whom they seek to exclude.

In general, all of the above situations preclude parents speaking or thinking in terms of their child's best interests. On the other hand, the experienced family lawyer will also recognize some of these traits in many cases. In other words, the severe cases are not so much new entities than pathological extensions of more commonly faced divorce and custody conflicts. In this respect, blame, denial, vengeance and even episodes of violence are not uncommon in contentious divorce although most often these factors do not override all capacity to act for the well being of children. Sometimes, the separation itself can bring out such maladaptive traits even in people who have no obvious prior history. In the long run, though, healthier emotions usually prevail and some balance and redefinition of roles is achieved often within the first three years. In the special cases under consideration, though, such restoration does not occur and the pattern can be chronic.

In these special cases to be discussed, the reader will observe that all represent examples of abuses of power of one type or another although in different spheres. Hence, the expression may be intimidation (e.g., stalking), physical violence (assault), exclusionary (parental alienation) or sexual (incest), but the underlying motives are most often aggressive and represent attacks on others in the family. There are clear gender differences with men more likely to physically attack or sexually exploit while women are more likely to alienate or brainwash children. Aggression, in general, however, is not simply a male problem and the vicissitudes of aggression in both sexes run the gamut from covert provocation to unprovoked assault. In this regard, the combination of the emotional rupture and conflicts of separation along with substance abuse always adds an explosive factor to the mix and heightens the risk of antisocial behaviour.

For the assessor, the important factor may not only be whether a certain abnormal behaviour occurred but whether it is likely to represent a recurring trait that requires special recommendations in order to protect the child. We have all witnessed that divorce may well bring out extreme reactions in parents who perceive it as a serious emotional threat and trauma that undermines coping skills at least temporarily.

On the other hand, it is a further minority whose character disturbance or psychopathology is so profound that these abnormal behaviours represent entrenched ways of handling life tensions. Here, maladaptive behaviour is more typical than situational. Deficits in how the parent relates to others will permeate the assessor's findings in areas other than the marriage.

There are a number of cardinal traits or qualities that need to be assessed when these special cases arise. First, the assessor will need to determine whether the parent is capable of viewing the other as independent with his or her own experience and valid point of view. Although mature love is associated with a deep identification with the lover, desire is not expressed to the detriment of reality. In pathological cases, on the other hand, boundaries become diffuse and the ex-partner refuses to acknowledge the autonomy of the lover especially at the time of divorce. In such cases, any individuality or separateness is seen as a grievous assault worthy of intense counter-attack. Love is completely supplanted by hate which can be extraordinarily strong. The marriage breakdown is experienced as a tearing apart or hemorrhaging that seems to have no end or closure.

Secondly, the assessor must come to understand what the subject expects from the world of others and whether they hold to a benign supportive world view or one dominated by the anticipation of pain, negligence and even violence from others. It is not uncommon in these more intractable cases for one parent at least to be quite paranoid of the other and deeply fearful of their motivation and dishonesty. Even in less obvious cases, masochistic attitudes and an expectation of pain may represent a subtle but pervasive theme.

Thirdly, can the parent in question honestly and morally invest in human relationships or are people simply a means to an end in a need gratifying cycle? Here, the assessor must recognize those people whose entire psychology may be oriented to the manipulation of others for self serving ends. These people do not love and invest in others as much as hiring and firing when the situation changes. Yet, there may be an arrogance and sense of superiority that is undeniable and, when coupled with sophistication and intelligence, can be formidable adversaries in a custody conflict. Their loyalties to others depends heavily on the extent to which needs are being met and this same pattern observed in the marriage may also characterize their relationships to lawyers who represent them.

Fourth, can the subject accurately and logically appraise the motivation, thoughts and feelings of others in a psychologically minded fashion or is understanding highly distorted and illogical and full of misattribution? In certain cases, one may be struck by the inability of a parent to interpret what happens in any reasonable and balanced form. This is seen most clearly in those false sexual abuse allegations which seem based more on distortions of reality than fact.

With this introduction, we can now consider specific clinical problems and their implications for custody and access assessments.

2. PARENTAL ALIENATION

Parental alienation is a term describing a particular set of interpersonal dynamics in which one parent in conscious or unconscious collusion with a child succeeds in having that child repudiate the involvement of the other parent in their life. The phenomenon has been elaborated by Richard Gardner, an American child psychiatrist and psychoanalyst who has worked extensively in the custody dispute arena.[1] The reader will notice at the outset that this description implicates the child in the alienating outcome. No doubt, this is far different from the usual view in legal circles that children are only unwitting participants and solely open to the manipulation of adults. Although the latter also occurs, it does not preclude the fact that in certain circumstances some children, overtly or covertly support the excluding parent. This is usually the mother who will absolutely refuse to have anything to do with the apparently loathsome other parent, usually the father.

The tell-tale sign of parental alienation is that the condemnation and accusations against the excluded parent will be extreme and far in excess of anything that the parent actually deserves. There is often

1 Gardner, R.A. (1989), *Family Evaluation in Child Custody Mediation, Arbitration and Litigation*, Cresskill, N.J.: Creative Therapeutics; (1987) *The Parental Alienation Syndrome and the Differentiation Between Fabricated and Genuine Child Sex Abuse.* Cresskill, N.J: Creative Therapeutics; (1986) *Child Custody Litigation: A Guide for Parents and Mental Health Professionals.* Cresskill N.J.: Creative Therapeutics.

a shrill air of irrationality as the child may describe beatings, torture, and other gross abuses without any reality based support for these accusations. In other cases, the child may attribute enormous implications to minor failings. For example, the child may say that the father will not permit going to the store alone and this explains why they refuse to visit. The child may even become hysterical when visitation is mentioned as a possibility and when the "threat" is withdrawn the child will return to peace and calm. The child will automatically reject anything that father provides be it a gift or a letter and the degree of animosity is always surprising to the observer. What is noticeable is that the child has no qualms or struggle and the hatred is total and is offered without any hint of doubt. The alienating parent in these cases will disclaim any instigating role and the observer will sense a degree of hopelessness that there can be any progress without resorting to extreme measures.

From the parent's point of view alienation is always about winning exclusive care and control over a child. The child becomes enmeshed in the parent's thinking and adopts an image of the "hated" parent that is congruent with the parent's view. The defining feature, though, is that the targeted parent is by all standards a reasonable and caring parent who has provided appropriate love and care. Consequently, it is the gross exaggeration of failings that is the hallmark of the disorder as well as the severity of the child's negative response towards that parent.

The relationship between parental alienation and brainwashing is a complicated one. Brainwashed children who are programmed against one parent do not necessarily forsake all visitation with that parent. They may demand certain limitations or conditions but their hostility will not be transformed into a complete rejection of the relationship. The alienated child, on the other hand, wants nothing to do with the parent no matter how positive the relationship was in the past. The difference between parental alienation and brainwashing may lie in the motivational differences between the parents. The brainwashing parent seeks to undermine the relationship with the ex-spouse while the alienating parent attempts to kill it altogether especially in the minds of the children. It is the difference between theft and murder — the former being aimed at stealing all the goodness and parental worth from the other while the latter is aimed at extinguishing the very existence of the hated adult as a viable parent in the child's mind.

Moreover, parental alienation often occurs independent of the quality of the prior relationship with the targeted parent. Although this does not appear to have been researched, there may even be a tendency for alienation to occur when the prior relationship with the excluded parent has been quite strong and positive. For instance, a man with teenage daughters opposed his daughters moving to another city with their mother to share the home of her new lover, a man well known to the family prior to the break up. The daughters seemed alarmed and distressed that they would be unable to accompany their mother. Litigation led to the beginnings of parental alienation and it was clear that the children would have sacrificed their relationship with their father if it had meant remaining with him in the family home. From the assessor's point of view, the father was articulate, mature and persuasive although persistent to the point of being mildly obsessive. Although the girls preferred the care of their mother and wished to share in her romantic journey, it was not because they had not enjoyed the care of a good father. The mother maintained that he was very controlling and critical, an allegation that seemed mainly tied to her choice to leave the marriage than any specific problem between them. The assessor's recommendation that the children move with their mother with appropriate visitation to the father managed to settle the problem for the family and the paternal relationship survived unscathed. On the other hand, there was no denying that the girls would have gone to the limit of excluding their father from their lives, with their mother's tacit approval, if the assessor or the court would have chosen the status quo for them. In this regard, brainwashing can slide into the territory of alienation if the right circumstances are present.

Because there is no absolute preference for mothers over fathers in the role of primary parent, parental alienation will arise in order to buttress one side over the other.[2] It is by all experience highly successful and treating families with such a disorder is never easy. Gardner advises that the court should intervene in such a case and remove the child from the grip of the alienating parent.[3] Such a court ordered transfer of care, if done in the early stages, might in fact work.[4]

2 Idem, at 94.
3 Idem, at 102.
4 See case example 4 for the description of such a case.

But if this is tried in extreme cases after the alienation has set in, then the cure can be worse than the disease.

In one family, for example, the mother had been convicted of abduction of her two school age children and still claimed that they "hated" their father and desired no contact with him. Both offspring told grossly exaggerated tales of a mean and brutal father and when shown photos reflecting warm and affectionate times with him claimed that they were "faking" out of fear. The mother totally denied any attempts to influence the children and described it as a coincidence that a daughter from a first marriage had also been alienated from her father. Although the mother asserted that "no one loves you like your mother", the reality was not so simple. At best, her love was highly conditional, the assessor suspected deep underlying hostility and rejection and there was much trauma in her background which she addressed with little sense of connection or emotion.

The children, it seemed, alienated their father in order to salvage the relationship with their mother. The assessor perceived that the children had followed her lead in ascribing only badness to the father and goodness to herself. The assessor observed that the older child, a daughter, was steadfast in her refusal to visit or correspond with her father. The younger child, a son, was seen as more flexible and slightly less rigid in his views. The judge ordered a transfer of care for the son and a therapist was named to intercede if necessary and assist with the transition. The first two weeks proved very difficult. Contact with the mother was suspended but the child had "attacks" of hysteria and on one occasion had to be sedated. Yet, by the end of the second week he was doing surprisingly better and father and son appeared to have re-found their old relationship. After three months of psychotherapy, the son became better able to think for himself to have a space for two parents without need to rid his mind of either. Visits with the mother were re-started without repetition of the alienation. The daughter, however, ceased all contacts and never recovered her link with her father.

In the above example, the motive for the alienation seemed to lie in the mother's own fragile alliances with the children based on her underlying relational disturbance. The children's collusion with the mother's agenda was strictly aimed at reinforcing the brittle link with her and the father was mostly incidental to the problem. This is a common theme in parental alienation. The children's identification with the alienating parent's negation is a defence against the real threat of losing her love.

One can also observe this pattern in situations where the mother is so emotionally injured by the breakup that the children reject their father in order to help salvage her emotional balance. In one instance, a couple with three children became separated after the father had begun a serious relationship with one of the children's music teacher. The mother had been the oldest child in her family and was forced to look after her siblings following the death of her own mother. Although a striving and motivated parent, she was also very rigid, moralistic and unyielding. She reeled from her husband's betrayal and her hemorrhaging of emotions spilled over to the children. Their oldest child, an adolescent daughter, became deeply hostile to her father and would verbally attack him if she accosted him even in public places. Sadly, she had to be hospitalized briefly for a reactive psychosis. The second child, a son, sporadically visited for about a year with his father and then stopped visits altogether.

Communication with the children ceased despite the father's many efforts. Only the third child felt free enough to continue visits with the father as if the mother's ante had stopped at two. Her stated position was that the children could make up their own mind as regards visits with their father and she neither encouraged nor stood in the way of them. Underneath, though, she communicated that she was the only parent to be trusted and that he had forsaken his role as parent when he undertook the affair. The deeper truth was that she had almost psychically collapsed under the terrible strain of this rupture and that her hatred, soothed by the children's alienation, had bound her together. It would be an underestimation, however, to assert that the mother had simply programmed these two children or that they in fact hated their dad. Although her contempt was well known to them, the children's fear for her psychological survival was foremost in motivating the alienation and functioned to shore up her battered emotional reserves.

In treating this disorder, the hated or targeted parent often benefits from some counseling aimed at helping him understand and restore even minimal contact with the child. The preferred strategy in such a situation is to go slowly, for rushing matters often leads to backlash and a further hardening of alienating attitudes. The hated parent must be counseled not to retaliate and further entrench the child in the parental conflict. Lawyers are wise to distinguish for the targeted parent between what is right and what is possible and not to zealously anticipate that right will quickly prevail. It is usually worthwhile to help the alienated parent find some means of contact with the embroiled children even if this is rudimentary and inadequate in the long run. Cards, letters, small gifts, e-mail or any acceptable opportunities for linkage should be accepted as a baseline on which to build.

Referring the alienating parent for psychotherapy rarely works. Either the parent will deny that they own any part of the problem or, and this is borne out often, they will seek counselors who validate their perceptions as compared to exploring their propensity to polarize and exclude.

The best opportunity to restore relations, though, lies with helping the child gain some sense of autonomy and capacity to think independently.[5] The therapist can help the child distinguish between a blanket negative stereotyping of the hated parent versus a view that is more realistic and balanced. Stressing moments where the child and the alienating parent differ helps to ground a child in a reality that is separate and rational. This helps gradually to separate the child from the parental morass and encourages the growth of a much needed neutrality. In milder cases, this is possible from the outset.

In more extreme cases, especially where litigation has intensified conflicts, there can be little recourse as children and the alienating parent may not even be willing to undergo therapy. Moreover, assessors may be concerned that suggesting a radical "parentectomy" where the child is removed from the custody of the alienating parent may be risky especially if the alienating parent is otherwise providing adequate care.

In cases where the alienating parent is emotionally maladjusted to the degree that they are unable to provide appropriate care, court action to alter care and control is often the preferred route. A hiatus period of no contact is often necessary before gradually introducing monitored reconnection with the alienating parent.

5 Garrity, C.B. and Baris, M. A. (1994), *Caught in the Middle: Protecting the Children of High-Conflict Divorce*, New York: Lexington Books.

3. BRAINWASHING

Although most parents are guilty of trying to influence children during divorce disputes, some parents engage in covert or overt campaigns to program their children against the other parent. These can be conscious or unconscious and the impact on the children can vary. We are concerned in this section with the extreme examples of such negative programming that arise in certain custody disputes.

This should be differentiated from occasional comments made in states of exasperation by a frustrated and grieving parent as well as from the tendency that some children have in using the other parent as a reference in passing judgments. Hence, for example, one young boy took pleasure in telling his mother that, "Daddy says that you are too mean", whenever she denied him what he desired. This led to a hasty supplementary affidavit condemning the father for his brainwashing of the child. That children may play one parent off the other is certainly not restricted to children of divorce although when parents have split in any case, the child may see no additional harm in exploiting these differences.

In serious brainwashing campaigns, the culpable parent is obsessed with the need to denigrate and demolish the image of that parent in the children's eyes. These parents waste no opportunities in hammering home to the child how immoral, worthless or unreliable is the targeted parent. For example, one man sought to convince his young adolescent son and daughter against the evidence that their mother had surreptitiously slept with her new friend behind their backs and had made a mockery of family ideals. He referred to their mother as a "slut" on numerous occasions and organized his campaign around the theme of her unsuitability to parent. He encouraged the children to view her as the epitome of the infidel who was not worthy of respect. Additionally, he was very indulgent of their wishes and made it worth their while to side with him against her.

Gardner is of the opinion that mothers are more likely to brainwash children than fathers due to the increasing opportunities for men to win custody in disputed cases.[6] This seems quite unclear, though, as the same logic could be used to suggest that there is more reason for fathers to fight dirty if they have a chance of winning. In any case,

6 Gardner, R. (1986) *supra*, note 1 at 80.

the bottom line for brainwashing is that it serves to vanquish over the other parent and to deliver their just desserts. Although it is rationalized as an attempt to secure what is best for the children or to expose them to the naked truth about the other parent for their self protection, the real motivation lies in the desire to demolish the reputation of the targeted parent. One also sees this in certain false allegations of impropriety that serve to put the other parent on the defensive and in the position of having to prove not only their worth but their virtue. These could be of a sexual nature but may be more vague and generally damning in contrast to anything actually specific.

There are common themes in brainwashing and it is not unusual for children to parrot their parent's accusations. Several examples may suffice to illustrate these points that all experienced family lawyers will recognize:

- "Your father has left us broke and I don't know how we are going to manage — you'd better get used to Kraft Dinner."
- "Your father is late again — you'd think that his children would be enough to make him behave a little better than usual."
- "Your mother takes every penny I have and then asks for more — she wants me to starve so she can have the lifestyle she thinks she deserves."
- "Your father thinks he can just dump us and go off and have the good life while we go without."
- If you feel uncomfortable with your father, call me any time of day or night — Mom will be waiting for you to return and I won't budge until you're back home."
- "Don't worry about me — you just go and have a good time; I'm sure I will be OK until you get back."
- "You think your Dad is so great — Well then why is he taking us to court and trying to give us as little money as possible."

Because brainwashing always occurs as a negative campaign, the offending parent will use subtle as well as obvious means to influence the children. As an example, there is the father who implies that the mother is egocentric, irresponsible and solely interested in her own pleasure because she tries to take one night out per week for a modicum of social life. Then there is the mother who instructs the father to remain in his car and honk to announce his presence because he is far too aggressive to ring the door bell when picking up the children. Some parents will go so far as to stage reactions like fear in front of the children in order to highlight how threatening their parent can be.

This campaign may not only be directed at the children but also at their own lawyer in order to gain support for an exclusionary agenda. For instance, the father may buy the children with gifts and advantages (e.g., tickets for the child and all their friends to a concert!) while he undermines the mother's discipline. But in front of his lawyer, he will speak of the meaningful and even spiritual bond between himself and the children that transcends the divorce. These parents will amplify the shortcomings of the ex-spouse and seek extraordinary measures to protect themselves or their children from the ill effects. For example, a mother of a four-year-old boy may seek supervised access because the child is rambunctious or unsettled after infrequent visits.

Perhaps most subtle is where one parent attempts to compromise the other by taking advantage of their personal weaknesses. In one instance, the father was a vulnerable man who had great difficulty coping with the breakdown of his marriage and the loss of daily contact with his three-year-old son. The access was very infrequent and the mother had succeeded in painting the father as a volatile figure who could not be trusted. She had achieved in obtaining a restraining order with a supervised access provision at the outset of the conflict. Knowing the father frequented a donut shop in mid afternoon, she arrived there unexpectedly and surprised him in front of his friends. Overcome with emotion, he fled the shop quickly. This was dutifully described in an affidavit. Here, the motive was less to brainwash the three-year-old than to secure her own legal position as the one parent stable enough to provide reasonable care.

Many of the most successful techniques in brainwashing will never be apparent directly to assessors although the basic strategy is always apparent. How the parent calls a child to the telephone when the targeted parent calls or how that parent greeted at transitions carries a powerful message for the child. The qualifiers and facial gestures also communicate images and "truths" to the child that can be distorting and influencing. This can be amplified when the parent casts a certain shadow over access or a relationship with the targeted parent. For instance, the mother who says that, "visitation is strictly between you and your father and doesn't concern me", is conveying the message that father is a pariah who is expendable. This same message follows if the custodian allows or even encourages the child to cancel an access visit because of some arbitrary scheduling conflict. Often this meshes with developmental issues. Hence, for example, a seven-year-old boy and, perhaps eldest sibling, will pick up on negative messages about the father as this might fuel his fantasies of taking his father's place with his mother. An eleven-year-old girl may be inclined to be influenced against her mother as she is already angry that her mother has abandoned poor daddy to fend for himself.

Brainwashing has its origins in the fury of rejection and the battle for children's loyalties that arise in divorce. Although these emotions are ubiquitous in most severed relationships, the majority of parents can keep one eye on the fact that this is their issue and not their children's. They struggle to balance their own emotions and reactions to the divorce with their children's needs now and in the future. This functions as a stabilizer and helps to maintain perspective. In a minority of cases, the goal of resolution and mourning becomes replaced by a wish to destroy the relevance or worth of the ex-spouse in the eyes of the children. Aggression of this magnitude precludes mourning and, sadly, these parents cling in their negativity and find it most difficult to get on with their lives.

4. VIOLENCE IN THE CONTEXT OF DISPUTED CUSTODY

It is well recognized that when children are exposed to ongoing parental hostility and conflict that they are altered by that experience. Consequently, research confirms that although frequent or liberal access is preferable in most post-divorce families, it is not beneficial in the presence of sustained parental hostility or when a parent is emotionally impaired.[7] When hostility erupts into violence then the negative impact on families increases. Boys and girls raised under the cloud of such violence often end up mirroring the worst aspects of

7 Johnston, J., Kline, M. and Tschann, J. (1991), "Ongoing post-divorce conflict in families contesting custody: do joint custody and frequent access help?", in J. Folberg (ed.), *Joint Custody and Shared Parenting* 2nd ed. at 177–184, New York: Guilford Press.

these impulse problems later become victims of abusive relationships.[8] Not only do such parental behaviours undermine a child's sense of safety and trust, they also harm the child's emotional and social development and predispose the child to identify with the aggressive aspects of the parents as a primary means of defence. Not surprisingly, one study observed in the sample studied that in 45 per cent of cases, violence between spouses eventually widened to include children.[9]

Understanding violence in families is a broad and complex topic and there are numerous sources for its occurrence. This discussion will be limited to the problems that face assessors and lawyers in the resolution of custody and access disputes. In itself, this is a sizable problem and one that consumes a great deal of court time in resolving. There are two major categories of violence met in this context: the first involves couples where violence was at issue prior to the breakup, while the second comprises those couples where violence breaks out during marital dissolution and as a response to it. In some cases, as well, a spouse may allude to a violent episode in the past, less because of current fears regarding the ex-spouse, than to highlight that the other adult is unfit to be primary parent and should be restricted in terms of access to their child.

In any case, the assessor must determine the nature of the aggression within the family and investigate its causes and long-term implications. This requires an assessment of the parent's capacity for impulse control and willingness to change plus an accurate appraisal of personality structure and potential for mature and empathic responses that can put a child's needs ahead of the parent's.[10] As well, the assessor must address the type of interaction and couple dynamics and the ability of both parties to disengage and re-define their interaction. Moreover, the assessor must also look to the external stresses on the family when the violence occurred, the chronicity of violence as a habitual mode of handling frustrations and tensions and the veracity of allegations especially in those situations where exaggeration seems possible or when other exclusionary tactics are observed. In reviewing these sources of violence, the reader will note that they

8 Wallerstein, J. and Blakeslee, S. (1989), *Second Chances*, New York: Ticknor & Fields.
9 Emery, R.E. (1989). "Family violence", *American Psychologist*, 44:321–328.
10 Garrity, C.B. and Baris, M.A., *supra*, note 5 at 60.

arise from internal, interactional and contextual origins and the assessor should be prepared to balance all three in determining how this should be understood and treated in terms of custody and access recommendations.

It seems likely that separation and divorce stresses may precipitate violence in predisposed individuals and either worsen an existing problem or initiate violent behaviour in separating couples even where it was not an issue in the marriage itself. Betrayal, deep emotional dependence, fears of abandonment, loss of control with overwhelming feelings of impotence and paranoid or sociopathic reactions, are all common scenarios in the violence associated with divorce.

As well, the violence can be mild (yelling, throwing and breaking objects), moderate (biting, kicking. slapping, hitting) or severe (brutal beatings).[11] Yet, classifications are not always completely sensitive to the realities of such violence. Stalking, for example, can be extremely violent as measured by its impact on a terrified ex-spouse although there is no actual contact. Intimidation may be psychologically terrifying as are false allegations and their impact can be extensive on an individual or family's well being.

In an excellent preliminary study on violence in high conflict divorced or divorcing families in custody disputes, Johnston and Campbell derived four characteristic profiles.[12] These were identified as: (1) ongoing or episodic battering by males, (2) female initiated violence, (3) interactive violence controlled by males, (4) violence engendered by separation and post-divorce trauma, and (5) a subgroup from the first two types where violence stems from mental imbalance. It should be pointed out that in two samples studied, the ex-spouses had been separated for an average of 2.25 and 3.25 years, respectively. These comprised 140 San Francisco Bay families referred by the family courts for counseling and mediation. Johnston and Campbell's categorization provide a useful framework for discussion.

---

11 Straus, M.A. (1979), "Measuring interfamily conflict and violence: The Conflict Tactics (CT) Scales," *Journal of marriage and the Family,* 41: 75–86.

12 Johnston, J. and Campbell, L. (1993), "A clinical typology of interparental violence in disputed-custody cases." *American Journal of OrthoPsychiatry,* 63:190–199.

(a) Male Battering

Briefly, this first group represents those severe cases where the man, due to personal dysfunction, reacts to any perceived threat or frustration with violence against his spouse and possibly his children. These men need little excuse to beat their wives who, in turn, fit the description of "battered wife syndrome". The women are not implicated in initiating the violence although they may defend themselves. At some point, with help, they may overcome their helplessness and depression and escape the marriage. Such extreme cases do not often lead to assessment as much as they are channeled into the family and criminal courts or provoke child protection authorities. Less obvious or extreme cases may present for assessment especially if the man denies or greatly downplays the violence or rationalizes that his wife in some way deserved it.

A woman from a Moslem country had precipitously left her marriage after seeking assistance from a local community health centre. She described a pattern of verbal and physical abuse that occurred on a regular basis. The frequency was increasing according to the wife due to the frustrations faced by her husband who had been humiliated and slapped by his wife's brother who suspected him of mistreating his sister. He blamed his wife for their marital problems and fumed over his conviction that she loved another. The wife was a simple person but made it clear that this did not explain why he was so controlling, jealous, thin skinned, violent and possessive. The couple had two preschool children who were at this stage kept mostly free of the conflict although the mother was somewhat flat and depressed. The husband for the most part denied or downgraded the history of emotional and physical abuse as inconsequential. The assessor recommended sole custody for the mother and limited access to the father to occur apart from the domicile of the mother and without contact with her.

(b) Female Initiated Violence

In this second category, the woman attacks the man due to her state of intolerable internal tension and distress. These women become furiously angry and harangue, pursue and even scratch or hit their husbands in the vain hope of rousing him to meet their emotional needs. These explosions of anger may occur throughout the marriage and will intensify at separation. The man is often characterized as passive-aggressive, intellectualizing, sometimes depressed and obsessive. Many of these men are frightened of their wife's aggression and ashamed of being drawn into conflicts with them. If the man does retaliate, the violence can quickly escalate and become extreme.

In one example, the woman was a very volatile, histrionic person who abused alcohol especially when under stress. She had few career aspirations and after the marriage ended became less functional and less independent. The husband, trained as an engineer, was very passive but a man who suffered psychological as well as vocational problems that were quite limiting. They had one child, a daughter, one year of age when their marriage failed. On numerous occasions, the husband would react with severe anxiety and in his distress he would seek comfort from his wife. She, in turn, would try and soothe him but with every passing minute would become more and more furious. She berated him as a weak and spineless person and demanded that he be a man worthy of her dreams. She would lash out giving him black eyes and a scratched face. He rarely retaliated but when he did he would cause damage as in one instance where he broke one of her fingers. His colleagues at work could not help but notice the scarred and bruised face and no amount of makeup quite hid the reality from view. The care provided the child was adequate in the most basic sense but the psychological ambiance was perverse and sadomasochistic. It was obvious that any prolongation of the marriage would expose the child to a pattern of violence that would have cause certain psychological harm. The assessment highlighted their individual problems and recommended psychotherapy. a custody and access formula was suggested that emphasized mutual autonomy and minimal interaction with transitions occurring through a neutral caregiver.

A second example may also be worth mentioning as it implicates the important variable of past history and its impact on marriage adjustment. Mr. C felt very deeply for his wife and yet trembled in the face of her anger. His own childhood had led to sexual inhibitions with conflicts around guilt ridden incestuous desires. Mrs. C had been sexually violated by her mean spirited and denigrating father and although she clearly loved Mr. C she feared both her husband's sexual assertion which reminded her of her father and Mr. C's intense anxiety and sexual fears which made her feel abandoned and unloved. Although they were excellent and thoughtful parents to their son and daughter as well as bright and creative people, the chaos they produced together was alarming and violent. Mr. C suffered a broken rib and numerous bruises and he was forced to separate from his wife in order to avoid greater harm and destruction. The happy ending at least in this case is that both undertook individual psychotherapies as well as couple counseling and found a way to overcome this negative interaction.

(c) Male Controlled Interactive Violence

In the third category, one sees a pattern of escalating aggression that revolves around disagreements between the spouses. Although the aggression may be initiated by either the man or the woman, the man usually takes control and dominates the woman physically. The man feels absolutely justified in so doing as he views his role as managing the situation and putting the woman in her place. These men are not inclined to beat up their wives but they use sufficient force to subdue them. In particular, these cases are marked by the minor issues that begin the altercations and the inevitable escalation to violence.

In one example, a man and woman attempted therapy but decided that their emotional pathologies were simply too intertwined to rescue their union. Each had grown up in stormy families where harsh and critical treatment was common place. They had met through work contacts and each was a motivated successful employee in their own right. Yet, they spoke of silly, meaningless arguments that would erupt for apparently no reason. What was characteristic, however, was the chronic pattern of escalation that took these small disagreements and magnified their intensity. Inevitably, they ended in violence where hitting and slapping would occur. It was always the husband, though, physically much larger, who terminated the argument by subduing his wife. Although he expressed remorse for having to play the role of "enforcer" there was an underling sadomasochistic theme that drove the interactive system. Curiously, each seemed aware that while striking out at the other, they demanded that the other show reason and self-control. Their two preschool children had witnessed several episodes but the parents took solace in the fact that they avoided these confrontations until the children were asleep!

(d) Separation Induced Violence

Violence in this group is uncharacteristic of either spouse during the course of the marriage. It usually occurs due to the strain just before or after separation. This can be initiated by the woman or the man and is often in response to some shock, betrayal, or inability to accept a turn of events leading to the break up of the marriage. Although the violence may not be a repetitive pattern, it can still be severe in intensity. The perpetrator is usually upset and ashamed and it is unmistakably an extreme response to an extreme stress.

As an example, a father was observed in his car scanning the family home on several days in succession. On one occasion, he entered the house without permission while the mother and children remained upstairs obviously aware of his presence and frightened. There had been no history of violence during the marriage and the father historically had a significant role in caring for the children when they were young. On the other hand, he was described by his wife as exceedingly moody and forlorn and this had been one reason that she had finally given up on the marriage. Prior to the stalking allegation, he had become very emotional when one of the children called her mother expressing insecurity and discomfort. When the mother came at the child's request to bring her home, an unnerving altercation occurred between the parents. A restraining order was obtained with supervised access until an assessment could determine matters more thoroughly. The assessor reasoned that the father's behaviour was of traumatic origin and that it would be unlikely that such behaviour would be repeated in the future. The children had sensed that their father's acute reaction had passed and that they were free to resume their old relationship with him. Regular liberal unsupervised access was recommended and adopted by the parents without delay.

(e) Paranoia and Mental Instability

Finally, there are a small number of instances where the violence is triggered by a paranoid reaction to separation or is generated due to disordered and even delusional thinking. This is likely due to mental illness but could be relate as well to substance abuse, especially drug induced brain syndromes. These people are motivated by internal psychic images of the ex-spouse as an enemy who means them harm or is harming their children. Such individuals view their violence as self protection and feel absolutely justified as a result. The spouses of these perpetrators are helpless to control events and are often passive in the face of it. They do not usually initiate nor encourage the violence. There is a subgroup of this category who harbour delusions of sexual abuse and rape and who accuse their spouses of both.

As an example, a mother's lawyer arranged for a psychological assessment of the father of two young sons due to acts of violence. The man was clearly sincere and motivated to see his sons but his behavioural controls over aggression were decidedly weak and had been so throughout the marriage. He accosted a man whom his ex-wife dated well after the marriage ended and lifted him by the collar while threatening to kill him. The mother spoke of numerous holes in the walls and damage to the house caused by his explosive loss of temper during the marriage. He had never actually struck her nor the children, however, and in the incident of assault, he let the man down and instead hit his hand on a wall with sufficient force to break a bone. He could express deep remorse but it was only operative after the fact and did not prevent these episodes. The assessment revealed a manic disorder mixed with paranoid ideation. The mother was observed to be a responsible and reasonable person who was well able to represent her sons' need of their father despite her intense anxiety regarding his aggression and bizarre behaviour. Yet, she also noted that he was stalking and obtained a restraining order against him. The assessor recommended a series of steps including parenting training, stress management therapy, psychiatric follow up, and brief supervised access once weekly to take place in a community setting. It was not anticipated, however, that the man would ever be more involved in his sons' lives due to the limitations stemming from his emotional disorder.

Although most early researchers looked for answers regarding family violence solely in the corridors of psychopathology, it is now evident that this single dimension is inadequate to explain the multiple causes of this problem which include intrapsychic, interactional and situational variables.[13] Moreover, as there is no single profile that characterizes an abused child, so there is no specific personality type that reflects abusive spouses or parents. It seems to be a complex issue and very much affected by marital instability, separation and divorce stresses. One can conceptualize that aggression can be deflected outwards into the adult sphere as in interparental violence as just discussed or deflected inwards as in sexual abuse of child. In fact, when child sexual abuse occurs in a family solely after a separation, it generally represents a pathological response to the marital rupture. In all circumstances, though, the presence of alcohol abuse exacerbates the potential for harm. The effect on families of violence is well documented and children as young as 12 months of age have been found to respond with crying and distress to violence even when the aggression is not directed at them.[14]

The assessment of violence within a custody/access dispute may be complicated by the divergent view of events and behaviours offered by each parent. In one instance, for example, a young separated woman in her twenties insisted that she had been raped by her husband when he had returned from a party in a drunken state. He completely denied that it had ever occurred and he blamed his ex-wife for contriving allegations in order to suspend access with their son. In fact, the woman he had met and was cohabiting with a new boyfriend whom she saw as clearly superior to her son's actual father. She also alleged that the father was inept as a parent and that the aftermath of the visits was too hard on their son.

From an assessors' standpoint, the accusation of rape in any situation is serious and, although this couple both had a history of drug use, such an act of alleged violence would surely interest the court. Yet, in this case, the usual signs suggestive of poor controls over aggression were not apparent to the assessor. The man was in fact quite passive and although well meaning was also clearly outshone by his ex-spouse who had moved beyond him socially and vocation-

13 *Ibid.*, at 190-191.
14 Cummings, E.M. (1987), "Coping with background anger in early childhood," *Child development.* 58: 976–984.

ally. Yet, he was capable of empathy, seemed to treasure his child, and did not show any evidence of poor emotional control or continued substance abuse. Also relevant, he was working hard to better his life and had recently completed preliminary training at a trade school.

The assessor concluded that the rape episode could not be confirmed but that this did not absolutely mean that it did not happen. On the other hand, what was reassuring was that the father did not bear the stamp of a man who characteristically used aggression and abuse of power to get his way. Equally relevant was the exclusionary motive of the mother who had engaged a new father figure for her son whom she believed would be a better role model. She emphasized this repeatedly during the assessment and viewed the loss of the biological factor as no loss at all to her son. The assessor concluded that she would have to make a place for the biological father for the sake of her child and that history could not be swept away as readily as she desired. Otherwise, he would exist so powerfully in fantasy for the son that resolution of that relationship would be impossible and the son's emotional development could be adversely affected.

Further complications in assessments where violence is alleged arises from the tendency for it to occur in the midst of separation when feelings of guilt, blame, outrage, disillusionment, betrayal, low esteem and hopelessness are at a pitch. These become festering wounds for some divorcing spouses and can alter the perception of the other for time immemorial. That is, instead of remembering the spouse in the days of love and hope as well as in the days of anger and disappointment, the spouse may become fixated on the negative image of the other and carry it to their grave. It has been estimated that 25 per cent of divorcing couples never get past this stage of intense fury and upset which becomes a permanent feature of their interaction.[15] Needless to say, many of those 25 per cent end up in complicated litigation that requires the intervention of skilled family law lawyers and mental health assessors when children are involved.

What adds to the entanglement for the assessor is that such people often enlarge their conflicts to include extended families and even therapists and other support systems. We can note a propensity for such people to find validators for their cause instead of pursuing the type of support that aids conciliation, openness, self reflection and

---

15 Maccoby, E. and Mnookin, R. (1992), *Dividing the Child,* Cambridge: Harvard University Press.

new beginnings. If there was any history of violence at the end of the marriage, it is likely that one or both warring parents will magnify its significance and demand that the other be viewed solely on the basis of this end stage conduct. It is up to the assessor to get beyond this restricted view for violent outburst is not in and by itself an abnormal event and many people are capable in certain circumstances, under high stress, of being driven to extreme behaviour. This should not be read as an apology for every man or woman's violence in divorce. Rather, it should be seen as a context in which violence within divorcing families can be more fruitfully understood.

When violence remains an issue or potentially so and high conflict characterizes the relationship of the separated parents, parenting plans should be adjusted to reduce the likelihood of an altercation as much as possible. Contact between the parents should be kept to an absolute minimum and transitions are best made in a neutral setting such as school or a relative's home. Having each parent drop off a child as compared to picking up the child is also a better strategy when conflict is high. If the parents appear unable to handle their feelings towards each other in any reasonable way, then access may best be minimized, sufficient to ensure contact between the children and the non-custodian but clear in its demarcation of one parent as primary caregiver. Providing an alternate means of dispute resolution to the courts such as a forced arbitration clause within the separation agreement can provide an outlet for tensions and prevent impasse. Finally, the parenting plan put in place should leave little room for arbitrary interpretation and is best thorough in its detailing of arrangements.

Parental couples who are prone to exceedingly high conflicts, irruption of violence and impasse tend to be those people who are unable to communicate in any way with each other and likely refuse to talk even about the children. If they do attempt to discuss concerns regarding the children, this will quickly devolve into ranting and attacks on each other. In other cases, any contact can become an excuse to denigrate and dominate the other to the point that the victimized parent cannot bear any contact without suffering emotionally. The second major feature characteristic of this group is a profound denial of responsibility for problems and a rigid, moralistic and blaming personality style. Such people lack a meaningful capacity for self reflection and their vulnerability is extreme. Lawyers and mental health professionals can become drawn in by such individuals for they tend to polarize settings and aggravate splits. One is either with or against them and neutrality may not be an option. Although their style initially conforms with the adversarial model, they quickly exceed its intentions and use the legal system as an extension of their aggression. Hence, they seek to pummel, punish and not resolve.

5. SUMMARY

This concludes our discussion of interparental and family violence in the context of high conflict custody/access disputes. Lawyers and assessors will face a broad array of aggressive behaviour in divorcing couples ranging from acute, uncharacteristic actions stemming from desolation and helplessness to a prolongation of bullying and sadistic behaviour that also characterized the marriage. In the context of custody disputes, allegations of aggressive behaviour may arise that are difficult to clarify and implicate the strained interpersonal relations between the separating spouses. These accusations may form the mainstay of one party's case against the other used to justify why the other parent's role should be down graded or denied altogether. Whenever antisocial behaviour is suspected or involved, then the related subjects of emotional balance and substance abuse can also come into play. This will be discussed further in the following two sections which concern sexual abuse allegations and mental illness.

6. SEXUAL ABUSE ALLEGATIONS IN THE CONTEXT OF DISPUTED CUSTODY

Of all the problematic areas related to divorce and custody disputes, none has proven more thorny or explosive than has the issue of sexual abuse. The reasons are complex but are certainly linked to the checkered record of society in exposing the sexual exploitation of children. Doctors, teachers, clergy, parents (mainly fathers and stepfathers) and others in positions of trust have been implicated and the fate of their child victims have been well chronicled in the professional literature and public press. In this regard, there is definitely an aura of crisis surrounding the topic of child sexual abuse. It is not surprising, then, that Gardner in his book on the subject of true and false sex abuse allegations introduces the topic with a historical look at the phenomenon of "hysteria" and compares the current furor over child abuse with the Salem witch trials![16] Although certain high profile cases have taken on the hue of hysteria, others have proven to be quite real. The real issue, therefore, is not only whether sexual abuse occurs, of course it does, but whether we have the appropriate objective and responsible mechanisms in place to accurately assess the merits of each accusation on its own terms.

With an urgent need to clean house and with some cases stemming from decades ago, behavioural science has been brought to bear on these problems with some success. Yet, the continued high incidence of reported child sexual abuse underlines the importance of further understanding and progress in this area within a strictly scientific format. In many ways, therefore, the lifting of repression on sexual abuse has coincided with a more general willingness on the part of society to acknowledge the enormity of the impact on victims. In part, this is reflected in mandatory reporting laws, greater public awareness, proactive education for children in the schools, more available therapeutic resources and hefty research initiatives with increasing sophistication.

On the other hand, communities must trust that their health and social service providers have kept pace with these changes and are neither biased in their approach nor reliant on unproved techniques such as anatomically correct dolls. On this score, the track record is variable which has added a further complexity for lawyers and the courts. Mixed with the power of suspicion and the caution of judges faced with determining the veracity of allegations, child abuse claims can seem to take on a life of their own.

When we narrow the focus and look specifically at those child sexual abuse allegations that arise in custody and access disputes, the soup thickens. The factors of loss, trauma, helplessness, conflict and anger can both lead to transient sexual abuse or be a source of false allegations. Although false claims are a minor issue over all, in divorce disputes they become a major concern with over one-half of

---

16 Gardner, R. (1992), *True and false Accusations of Child Sex Abuse*, Cresskill, NJ: Creative Therapeutics, p. xxvi-xxvii.

all reported cases remaining unverified or revealed as untrue.[17] It is not uncommon, therefore, for alleged child sexual abuse to become a flash point in a custody battle. The allegations may be loosely stated, vague and primarily intended to create doubt about that parent or explicit enough to raise serious concerns for the assessor and the court. In between are a spectrum of complaints that may not ever be clarified by child protection or law enforcement services and which will never be proven or disproved.

(a) Routes of Disclosure

When sexual abuse has occurred in a family, exposing it will lead to divorce in about 50 per cent of cases.[18] There are usually three routes for such an occurrence: (a) the abuse is discovered by a third person, often a school authority or health professional who informs the family; (b) the abuse is discovered by the mother who then divorces the husband; and (c) the abuse is long-standing and well known to the mother but is revealed only at the time of marriage breakdown. Although well-documented cases are not usually referred for family assessment due to custody conflicts, these may be ordered if the man continues to deny the impropriety by contesting custody of the children. It will also become relevant when the issue of access, future risk or remediation potential is deliberated by the court.

When the abuse is discovered by the mother, she will have either uncovered it herself or will have been told by a child victim or another party. She may then seek divorce and move to have access denied or to have it supervised. The abuse itself may only come to light when the issue of access to the father is raised by the woman's lawyer. In other instances, the woman may choose to call police, therapists and/or child protection services to confront the sexual abuse perpe-

17 Awad, G. and McDonough, H. (1991), "Therapeutic management of sexual abuse allegations in custody and visitation disputes", *American Journal of Orthopsychiatry*, 45: 113–123; Green, A. and Schetky, D. (1991), "True and false allegations of sexual abuse", in. D. Schetky and A. Green, *Child Sexual Abuse: A handbook for Health Care and Legal Professionals.* New York: Brunner/Mazel; Mantell, D. (1988), "Clarifying erroneous child sexual abuse allegations", *American Journal of Orthopsychiatry*, 58: 616–621.

18 Faller, K. (1991), "Possible explanations for child sexual abuse allegations in divorce", *American Journal of Orthopsychiatry*, 61:48–58.

trated by her husband. Whether it is the authorities who learn of the abuse and inform the mother or the mother herself who contacts authorities, professionals may have a major influence in encouraging the woman to divorce. As noted above, the man may accuse the wife in theses instances of using the accusation of sexual impropriety to win custody or restrict access. When social services or health authorities have a strong case for abuse, denial and counter accusation will be less likely. But as many cases are less certain, it is not uncommon for men to defend themselves by disputing its truth.

Sometimes the abuse may not precipitate divorce but is itself revealed during the divorce process. A child, for example, may report it only after the abusing parent has left the family home and the child feels safer. In other cases, the mother may only consciously acknowledge what she has always known after the separation has occurred. Finally, the mother may reveal the abuse only after the marriage ends because it is no longer expeditious or beneficial in terms of keeping her marriage to conceal it from view.[19]

Another major group of sexual boundary violations occur during the early phases of the divorce itself. These are most likely to be perpetrated by men although very occasionally women may abuse as well. Abuse in this context stems from the traumatic aspects of the divorce experience on the parent's judgment, reality testing and frustration tolerance. It is similar in some respects to a transient psychosis resulting from the role and structural disintegration of the family and its impact on psychological functioning. In this instance, the divorce process may precipitate an emotional regression in which the incest is linked to self soothing while reality and moral appraisal as regards what is actually happening is suspended. Lawyers will recognize examples of such displaced grief in criminal law when, for instance, a woman with ample cash and credit cards is caught shop lifting following a serious psychological stress in her life. Such previously uncharacteristic behaviour further destabilizes the family at a vulnerable time.

Yet, in the case of incest, the parent, usually the father, may have had tendencies prior to the marriage breakup to cross boundaries during otherwise tender moments and the abuse may not surface entirely from no where. Besides, there may have been an underlying latent sexual attraction to a child that emerges at the time of catastro-

19 *Idem*, at 88.

phe. The absence of the other parent as a control factor may also allow more leeway with aberrant impulses that can culminate in abuse. In certain cases, as well, the sexual abuse may represent an attack on the ideal of the family and a denigration of what the other spouse holds as sacred. Here, the wish to hurt is primary and overrides the parental demand to protect.

The final important category met in the course of family law concerns false allegations of sexual abuse. These will tend to be made by adults and not children although in practice the actual source of the complaint may be obscure. The impetus or momentum of the allegation, however, will usually arise from a parent and not a child. Most false allegations of incest stem from emotional factors in the accusing parent but occasionally they can represent conscious deliberate lies. There are also cases in which a child has been abused and a parent is blamed while the actual perpetrator is another adult. Finally, there are cases where the child will claim abuse for their own reasons in order to win some advantage or leverage within the family order.

False allegations can be a potent means to discredit a parent and are most likely leveled by a woman against a man. In a small number of cases, the allegations arise from psychotic delusion and is explained by the emotional illness of the accuser. Mainly, though, the accuser finds in the label "sexual abuser" an apt description of the morally depraved and despicable ex-spouse who has shattered their life and dreams. The term has a widening meaning and appeal to the bitter parent who finds sure revenge and legal advantage when she raises the cloud of suspicion. "If he could do this to me," she ponders, "then he is surely capable of anything." The man must then channel his energies and legal resources to deflect the accusation more than asserting his own valid point of view. False allegations almost always poison the post-divorce relationship and represent a serious attack on what remains of the neutral ground between the parents. This encroaches on the emotional space required by children to adjust to marriage breakdown while maintaining healthy links to both parents.

Parents who claim sexual impropriety from flimsy evidence are often seeking to exclude the other parent from the children's lives or to incisively devalue their parental status. Such accusing parents will be prepared to see signs of sexual abuse in their children based on vague findings that become increasingly obscure as the assessment proceeds. For example, a little boy tugs once too often at his penis, a little girl has too many nightmares following visits with her father, a three-year-old girl is observed smelling her fingers after exploring her vagina, a four-year-old boy has a small abrasion on his penis, or a five-year-old tells her wary, jealous mother that daddy "hugs me, kisses me and tickles me all over before I go to bed".

In a mind-set prepared to expose the former spouse's sick depravity, such signs become absolute proof of the evil they know lurks in their former spouse. In other situations, it is less depravity that is at issue than a need to incur legal or moral advantage or to neutralize some perceived superiority that might exist if the allegation was not made. For example, if the accusing parent feels very guilty for leaning heavily on paid baby care for her own convenience then this could motivate an allegation to counter guilt and the possibility of being seen in a negative light. More commonly, if a parent had a sexual affair during the marriage, the allegation may arise as the great moral equalizer. It is as if the accusing parent is saying, "I may be sinful because of what I did, but you did it too." Acknowledging and coping with guilt can be extremely taxing for some people and failures of judgment can occur in order to escape excessive moral incrimination in those who cannot bear their own guilt.

Additionally, anxious, traumatized parents may be under the influence of "therapists" or others who are themselves ready to pounce on any suspicion of child abuse. One employee assistance counselor, for example, precipitated a messy and destructive legal dispute when she told her wary client that if her husband was "abusive" to her, he could well have been inappropriate with her sons. The mother rushed home and confronted her children (not her husband) and the frightened boys told her what she feared (wanted?) to hear.

Unfortunately, the availability of willing and seemingly qualified validators makes this area especially vulnerable to supporting or enabling false sex abuse allegations. This may include child protection authorities or counselors who equate being supportive with being validating. These professionals may implicitly believe that where there is smoke there must be fire and they are always persuaded by the power of suspicion. They would never accept that children fabricate, exaggerate or distort truth in collusion with or under the subtle pressure of a parent.

(b) Assessing the Allegation

Having sketched the various categories of sexual abuse allegations, it is clear that the two most relevant types, common to the context of assessments, will be those alleged but difficult to verify cases where the abuse occurred just before or after the separation as well as false accusations. Those cases that are grossly apparent and either trigger a divorce or are revealed at the time of separation will be generally handled by child protection and law enforcement services and they do not tend to become custody disputes for obvious reasons. It will fall to the courts and assessors to sort out those less obvious and often obscure cases where front line protection workers have least to offer. These most often comprise cases that either cannot be substantiated but seem plausible and those that are most likely false.

In the light of the increasing report of sexual abuse and the probability that an allegation in the context of custody disputes could well be a veritable source of trauma for a child, standards must exist for a clear handling of such matters by assessors. Even among mental health specialists, there is a wide variation in how such allegations are handled or interpreted and diagnostic precision has proven elusive.[20] This seems particularly true at the margin between child protection and child custody resolution which defines the territory occupied by family psychological assessments where endangerment to children or spouses is alleged.

In this regard, one must distinguish the task of a child protection worker employed by a mandated agency and the task of a mental health expert who undertakes to see all concerned and recommend on the care and control of children. The duties of a child protection examination versus the task of a child custody assessment overlap but represent different approaches with distinct perspectives. Each has its own vantage point although neither must be confused with the role of therapist which is again a different hat with very different coordinates.[21] It is of little relevance in evaluating these matters whether one is a psychiatrist, social worker or psychologist as long as a clinical

20 Horner, T., Guyer, M. and Kalter, N. (1993), Clinical expertise and the assessment of childhood sexual abuse, *Journal of the American Academy of Child and Adolescent Psychiatry*, 32:925–931.

21 The issue of "dual roles" is an ethical one and is discussed in the chapter on the ethical infrastructure of family law.

method is followed that is acceptable to the mental health field as a whole and addresses the issues posed by the family in question.

The following factors come to mind in distinguishing child protection from child custody evaluations:

- Child protection is an investigation of a specific and limited issue, the culpability of someone accused of the exploitation or maltreatment of children, and represents a form of law enforcement. Child custody, on the other hand, is an evaluation of a family unit, its mandate is predictive and is aimed at proposing a parenting formula that will best serve the needs of the children in a post-divorce environment. In this regard, child custody work is based on a careful clinical scrutiny of the relative psychological merits of the parents and the emotional/social needs of the children. Child protection work is restricted to the sole investigation of an aberrant behaviour and its impact.
- Child protection assessments are resolved on behavioural and physical criteria and represent a form of risk assessment focusing on whether a specific adverse behaviour occurred; child custody evaluations, on the other hand, are primarily psychological and focus on gaining a clinical appreciation of the aptitudes, relationships, personal qualities, and levels of commitment among the parents and the needs and dispositions of the children.
- Child protection investigators must also employ psychological acuity to clarify the indirect, unverbalized, and qualitative factors that are vital to a responsible investigation; the child custody evaluation must also take heed of behavioural, social and physical findings that might well clarify the question of whether sexual violation of a child has occurred. This describes the necessary area of overlap although one type of investigation should not be mistaken for the other. Nevertheless, it is quite possible that a careful custody assessment may reveal findings that would support an allegation of sexual impropriety. Likewise, the custody assessment may reveal family dynamics that diminish the probability that abuse has occurred. In this sense, the custody assessor works indirectly from a deeper understanding of the family, and hypotheses are tested against a growing knowledge of the history, personalities and family system involved.

The method taken by the assessor in child custody work is vital. This raises the issue of "clinical method" which, in the case of possible sexual abuse, is fundamentally different from the investigative method employed by police or child and family services. Clinical method describes the process used by the mental health professional to give "meaning" to data gathered during the course of the assessment. From a discussion of the psychological qualities of the parents and children, an explanation of the interpersonal dynamics of the parents both during the marriage and since the separation, and from an appraisal of parental aptitudes and parent-child relationships, the assessor constructs a parenting plan that best fits the findings and conclusions. Hence, the child custody evaluation may address an abuse allegation but it is not its *raison d'être*. Moreover, it must transcend the investigative issue in order to look broadly at the best interests of the children.

There are three acceptable clinical formats or methodologies available to an assessor and the custody report should be based on one of these models:

1. The information is gathered from the background history of the parents, the history of the marriage, present conflicts, personalities, parent-child relationships which is then viewed through an appropriate clinical model such as family systems or psychodynamic theory.
2. A primary focus is placed on the parent-child relationships as observed and measured by the assessor. This method highlights the use of observation and participant-observation. Questions are posed related to how well the parent knows the child, the nature of parent-child interaction, parenting aptitude, or whom the child most depends for comfort, reassurance and conversation. From such a detailed analysis emerges the assessor's recommendations, based on clinical judgment, as to the specific parenting formula likely to best serve the developmental needs of the children.
3. Either (1) or (2) buttressed by psychological test data which, by tradition, employs the Minnesota Multiphasic Personality Inventory (MMPI-2) but may include other assessment tools including projective techniques such as Rorschach, Human Figure Drawings, the Thematic Apperception Test, or recently developed

psychological assessment batteries designed specifically to answer custody questions.

The failure to employ a clinical method in a custody assessment always represents a major handicap and may invalidate a report. It could unfortunately lead the assessor to interpret statements at face value or simply group or list them without properly interpreting their meaning in the context of the subjects involved and the family in question. In the case of a sexual abuse allegation, assessors lacking a proper clinical method will remain fixated on proving or disproving an allegation of molestation for without a clinical methodology there can be no perspective or ability to see the broader picture. This could prove spurious especially if neither parent's version reflects an accurate understanding of the family milieu. A proper clinical method, however, seeks a more complete sense of the family dynamics and the parent's personalities. This, then, permits the assessor to discuss the question of abuse from a vantage point that is both novel and neutral to the premise of either parent. It must, in the end, add a dimension that was not available before the evaluation began. In a nut shell, in the complex and less obvious cases where abuse is alleged, the assessment transcends a strictly behavioural vantage point and, as a result, gains a higher magnification.

It is beyond the scope of this book to provide an exhaustive review of how an abuse allegation is appraised and each situation is to some extent unique. Yet, there are certain guidelines and basic information that may assist the practising lawyer on two fronts. First, to become aware of those sexual abuse accusations that will likely be interpreted as false and, secondly, to evaluate the competence and thoroughness of an assessor's approach to a specific allegation. This will be considered in respect to five aspects: (a) the accusation, (b) the accused, (c) the accuser and, (d) the child.

(i) The Accusation

In all cases, the accusation will be attributed to a child or children who have told someone of sexual impropriety by a parent or other care taking adult who had the opportunity to abuse them. On closer inspection, however, it is important to verify that the report of abuse in fact emerges from tensions within the child and that it is not spearheaded by a parent eager to pin abuse on the ex-spouse. In valid cases, the child is often deeply affected not only because of the violation but because of the adults' serious response to it and the degree of coercion that was employed by the abuser. In any case, the child often suffers from the affects of the abuse and the assessor's knowledge of the sexual violation will be communicated directly from the child. In false allegations, it is often the parent who fills in everyone on the serious impact of the abuse and the symptoms, as described, are often flagrant and exaggerated. In this regard, the momentum of the case is carried by the parent while the child remains basically in the background. This may be glaringly apparent, for example, in joint interviews where the child "checks" with the accuser and seeks approval for their responses. When seen with the accused, the child may also seek permission from the assessor to include the accused or share something as if the accused is suspended from their parental role.

In the case of a pre-verbal or very young child, the accusation of abuse cannot stem simply from the child and they will not have the cognitive means even to judge the abuse as wrong. It will be therefore always be reported by a caretaker or parent. It is usually a very disturbed and often drug or alcohol addicted parents, however, who would willfully abuse an infant or toddler child. Because of the degree of character disturbance involved, abuse of a very young child will most likely be supported by physical findings.

It is important to place the allegation or disclosure in the context of the marriage, divorce and custody dispute that forms the main focus of the legal intervention. Usually one can identify some major event or catharsis upon which the allegation turns. In valid cases, signs and symptoms of distress in the child are present prior to the alleged abuse which may itself clarify the nature of a child's turmoil. In false cases, evidence of distress only emerge after the complaint of abuse is made and there is no hint in reliable records that the child's behaviour was a prior concern.

A further point of discernment concerns qualitative factors. For instance, in validated cases, the mother may have come to sexual abuse both reluctantly and as a last straw. She may struggle to know that it is not true and may have problems accepting that it could occur. When she uncovers it other than through direct observation, she will demand an explanation from the father first before seeking assistance from child and family services or police. Even then she may look for ways to reject the conclusion that the child was abused and acceptance may only come slowly and reluctantly. She will remain maternally protective and, understandably, will be cautious about exposing the child to stressful examinations or interviews. She will not have demonstrated any prior motivation to exclude the father from the life of the child nor will she reflect an over-reactive, competitive or suspicious character style ready to denounce the father at every turn.

In false cases, the quality of the accusation is very different. These parents seize on the allegation as a *cause célèbre* and do not for one moment doubt its veracity. As one mother noted, "In your house it is an allegation, whereas in mine it is a truth." They rarely ask the father for an explanation and immediately complain to police or child protection services. They can be quite angry if and when authorities question the veracity of the claim. They are keen to have the child questioned and examined as often as they can arrange and show little empathy for the impact this is having on the children. Yet, the parent who promulgates a false accusation will at the same time describe the child as suffering serious emotional trauma and they always seek to have the father banned from access or to have visits supervised. When doubt is cast on the allegation, they may show bitterness rather than relief and blame the assessors or police for insensitivity and incompetence. They gather as allies those individuals who will support their cause and they reject any that will not. This tends to include lawyers and mental health providers. They may be vengeful and retaliatory and yet have little insight into their own aggression. They often show impaired capacity to protect children and think nothing of exposing them to multiple examinations and interviews.

Fictitious reports of sexual abuse will often be characterized by lack of detail, use of language that is in excess of a child's linguistic or cognitive skill, and vague, inconsistent or contradictory details that may well be logically impossible. Further more, the emotional tone may well be inappropriate to what is being described. The child may only repeat the allegation in the presence of the accusing parent but will otherwise show disinterest. Sometimes, although this is rare, what the child communicates is plainly memorized and is spoken by rote. Confusion or non-response may occur if questions are posed that go beyond the learned script. The children may well be in considerable conflict and show signs of emotional burden.[22]

22 Jones, D. and McGraw, J. (1987), "Reliable and fictitious accounts of sexual

(ii) The Accused

Perpetrators of incest are not necessarily evil monsters but in all cases it represents a serious breakdown of the protective parenting role. Moreover, the cases that arise for assessment are not usually committed pedophiles whose sexuality is habitually devoted to the pursuit of children. Most often in the cases met in family law, pedophilic behaviour may be either transient, circumstantial and triggered by regression or mixed with higher level, more mature functioning that is also present. Often, they are men who have not come to terms with their own depriving and traumatizing pasts and who suffer from inadequate emotional resources. Some psychodynamic clinicians believe that pedophilia represents a reaction against unconscious hostile, murderous impulses towards children.[23] This is an important observation as it underlines the aggressive, coercive aspect to sexual molestation that is often apparent to child victims who then show reasonable fear, mistrust and confusion in the face of that person.

To focus discussion, a clinical example is in order. A man whose own father had died when he was a teenager was then left at the mercy of a brutal elder brother who was severe in disciplining and controlling him. The family of origin was very poor. Following a 10-year army career in which his technical abilities shone, the man married and studied architecture. Faced with long hours of study, a growing family and financial strain, he would on numerous occasions enter the bedroom of his daughter and molest her. It may have begun when she was four and stopped when she was ten. It would begin with kissing and end with oral sex. There was never a word shared between daughter and father in these terrifying visits. The child at one stage appealed to her mother who remained impassive, fearing that a confrontation would end her marriage. The child was terrified that her father might kill her to erase the record of his crime against her. After age 10, the incest ceased. Later it was learned, though, that the victim's younger brother as an adult had molested his niece. The father in this case was, in general, a congenial, hard working man but emotionally shallow and unable to work through complex feelings

---

abuse to children," *Journal of Interpersonal Violence*, 2: 27–45.

23 Arlow, J. (1991), "Derivative manifestations of perversions", in G. Fogel and W. Myers, *Perversions and Near Perversions in Clinical Practice*, New haven: Yale University Press, at 73; Stoller, R. (1975), *Perversion: The Erotic Form of Hatred*, New York: Pantheon Press.

states. The mother was in one sense determined and involved but also self centred, superficial and insensitive. She believed that her hardships outweighed whatever ordeals was faced by her daughter. Characteristically, she minimized what her daughter had experienced.

In this example, we see many of the qualities that characterize abusers of numerous ilk.[24] They are either victims of sexual abuse themselves or have faced deprivation and family violence in their youth. Almost always, they come from families we would label as dysfunctional and this impairs their capacity to cope. Psychological adjustment is fragile and coping skills are in short supply. In the example given, a brutal oldest brother who beat the perpetrator as a child also became the model of an overseer and totalitarian who brooks no refusal. By identifying with the cruel brother who terrified him as a child, he must have unconsciously gained some measure of false control. Often times, the perpetrator uses coercion and is by nature a demanding, dominant and forceful personality. Nevertheless, in this example as well as in other cases, the offender is best described as passive, constricted and unassertive. Although not true of this example, substance abuse and alcoholism often occur together.[25] One will often observe a history of poor judgment and emotional immaturity in the perpetrator. They may well suffer from other perversions and have a history of voyeurism or fixation on pornography. If the perpetrator denies the accusation, it is usually feeble, avoidant and unconvincing.[26] Moreover, they will often refuse diagnostic testing whether this be a blood test for a sexually transmitted disease that was passed to the child victim, phallometric assessment or a lie detector test.

Unlike male child molestation, female pedophilia occurs in the form of incest, that is almost entirely from within the family and with her own children.[27] In some bizarre cases, the woman participates in the incest at the behest of a dominant and often controlling and sadistic man whom she blindly follows and wishes to please. In these instances, the woman's erotic excitement is aligned with surrender to

24 Abel, G. and Rouleau, J. (1995), "Sexual Abuses", *Psychiatric Clinics of North America*, 18: 139–153.
25 Yama, M., Fogas, B., Teegarden, L. and Hastings, B. (1993), "Childhood sexual abuse and parental alcoholism: Interactive effects in adult women," *American Journal of Orthopsychiatry*, 63: 300–305.
26 Gardner, R. (1992), *supra*, note 16, at 63.
27 *Idem*, at 75–91 and 75–79.

the dominant, powerful male and not necessarily to the perversion itself.

Again, as with the male perpetrator, the female molester comes from a seriously impaired family background with an obvious history of violence, substance abuse, divorce, and/or mental illness. In certain cases, the woman may show signs of severe depression, character disorder or even psychosis. Loneliness and severe deprivation will have led to aberrant expressions of the need for affection. Their marriages are often chaotic and extremely unhappy, frequently ending in divorce. They turn to their children for compensatory warmth and take them to their beds. In one example, a woman described a depriving bleak childhood that led to her leaving home at 15 years of age. She married a man who used violence to control his children and was well known for his abuse of power and brutality. She had six children and, along with her elder two daughters, treated the youngest sibling, a boy, as if he was a personal teddy bear. The mother and daughters stroked, masturbated, cuddled and molested him until he could build enough strength and muscle to protect himself. Predictably, the mother first denied the incest although when it was confirmed by a repentant sibling she sought professional help. She was seen as extremely immature, highly self centred, unempathic and manipulative. Not surprisingly as an adult, the boy victim struggled with threatening violent impulses and fears regarding women that limited his capacity to tolerate closeness.

Turning to cases that are believed false, it will be all too apparent that the major portion of these criteria will not be met and the thrust of evidence will point away from perversion or boundary disorders. Looking for an explanation and source of tension within the family will point more meaningfully at other sources usually in the purview of the accuser. Although problems may be observed in the accused, as well, these will not readily predict sexual abuse.

Yet, there may well be an observed aberrant sexuality but it will be situated in the marital relationship and not simply the husband. Highly instinctualized marriages where conflict is sexualized can lead to allegations of incest following marriage breakdown. Children in these families are chronically exposed to the erotic battling between their parents who keep their sex life at the forefront of their divisive interaction and within listening range of the children. When a child apparently alleges sexual abuse, the same terms and phrases used by the parents are re-issued by the child or children in question. Those supporting the accusation of abuse will observe that no child could invent such language on their own which of course is true but has nothing to do with the actions of a perpetrator. Assessment will reveal overstimulated, aroused children whose parents have inundated them with their eroticized struggle. Further, the alleged crime against the children will be a direct extension of the allegation connected with the marital relationship. On the other hand, neither parent will be the victim of the other and they will be very much an even match.

These are the same types of families that typically embroil their children in their conflicts and make loyalty a key issue of their struggle. The parents may well be defective in their capacity to protect children and free them from the repercussions of mutual aggression. This is often a long-standing pattern which was apparent to an observer prior to any allegation of sexual abuse.

Considering other scenarios that can lead to accusations of abuse, the possibility exists that a parent may have violated a boundary in a minor way without any intention of abuse. After marriage breakdown, for example, many children ask to sleep in the same room as the accessing parent during visits. A child reporting this to a suspicious and angry mother may lead to a charge of sexual meddling without any substance at all. In the climate of a contentious divorce, many behaviours that were once quite acceptable can become interpreted from a different vantage point. Mother's interested in establishing that only they can truly protect the children will also find that such allegations may well bear fruit in a custody war. Minor indiscretions like a father showering with a four-year-old daughter can be turned into a sexual orgy and bedtime games can be revealed as surreptitious seductions just as easily as an evening martini can be reinterpreted as a pattern of chronic alcoholism. The one explanation that should never see light of day is that such accusations arise out of a disturbed sense of overprotectiveness. False accusations are never about protecting children and are strictly engineered to fulfill a plan beneficial to the accusing parent. Ironically, a child who is exposed to police, medical and child protection interviews for no good reason may well experience the arduous process as deeply abusive.

(iii) The Accuser

False allegations are either made by a parent on their own or through the manipulation and undue influence of children. Although they can arise from vindictive as well as delusional motives, false allegations are also a powerful means of controlling a custody suit. As already mentioned, the courts are often reluctant to take chances that abuse is occurring and the power of suspicion is often enough to hijack a custody battle and reshape its focus. Mothers are far more likely to allege abuse than fathers although the latter situation is also occasionally met.[28] Such false accusations in the context of custody disputes ride the coattails of the many legitimate cases that communities face daily in their newspapers. Basically, they are made to measure for a parent who views the other as lascivious and evil as well as those who seek to derail any chance of losing custody or who wish to wreak havoc on the life and reputation of the ex-spouse even to avoid their own guilt.

In part, experience conveys that these accusations are most often multi-causal and are rarely simply the conniving manipulation of a competitive parent who wishes to win at all cost. There is a gradient between the parent who consciously deceives and the one who is deluded in belief and whose accusations are built of several elements: personal history projected onto the present relationship; shock and betrayal turned into malevolent mistrust of the other; aggression and hatred; fears based on regressed violent moments at the termination of the marriage; comments made in emotional turmoil; suggestibility enhanced by outsiders who are keen to find sexual abuse in men; wishes to denigrate, humiliate and punish the ex-spouse; distortion in thought processes in mentally vulnerable parents who view their overreactions as protectiveness; and finally, a fervent desire to win a custody case and be rid of that person forever.

Often, there is some historical issue that predisposes the accuser to formulate a false allegation. They may have themselves suffered sexual abuse or were witness to family violence and other serious disappointments in early life. They may also struggle with a guilty conscience and see their guilt reflected in the other parent whom they

---

28 Newberger, C., Gremy, I, Waternaux, C, Newberger, E. (1993), "Mothers of sexually abused children: trauma and repair in longitudinal perspective", *American Journal of Orthopsychiatry*, 63: 92–102.

are accusing. Such parents, mainly mothers, may be very sensitive to their children's safety needs and are prone to see a betraying husband as a threat. Perhaps contrary to her own experience as a child, she may assert that she will never leave her children unprotected and in harm's way. Hence, when suspicion is raised, these mothers will be quick to sound the alarm and seek validation from authorities. There is none of the ambivalence and caution of the reasonable parent who must be convinced even beyond a reasonable doubt that abuse actually happened and then, once again, that it was the father who was the likely perpetrator. Where accusations prove unfounded, rational parents are truly relieved that their children have not been harmed through abuse. In contrast, the falsely accusing parent can be paradoxically distraught and may cling to their convictions as unshakable truths. One can observe therefore that false accusers are often angry and disappointed as compared to glad and assuaged by the negative findings. It is as if the negative finding itself is a further betrayal of their child or children.

Although there is not a standard profile of a falsely accusing parent, several features are commonly observed. One notes a strong tendency to think and act in black and white terms. Others may be perceived as either good or evil and there is little sense of subtlety in interpersonal relations. One is either with or against them. The accusing parent is most often the mother and is likely highly moralistic. She will emphatically portray herself as the upholder of what is virtuous and good for her child. She has no use for the father and will likely perceive him as irrelevant to the children as well. There will be little regard for the consequences of actions and, although she will be quite aggressive in her pursuit of "justice", there may be no self awareness or understanding of the potential destructiveness of her actions.

In the course of events, the sex abuse allegation may become the *coup de grace* or finale of a series of actions intended to expunge the father from the children's lives. Although the allegation may be without foundation, it can stem from a kernel of reality. Misperception, confusion, as well as desires to deliberately falsify can augment a display of affection or caring into a major assault on a child. For example, in one case, a recently separated father who had always kissed and hugged his children at bed time, was unaware that his pre-adolescent daughter was increasingly uncomfortable with this ritual due to her natural physical and emotional development. The girl told her mother who had remarried and relished any opportunity to alienate the father from the children's lives. She preferred her new husband as a father for the children and was influencing them to follow her lead and make the switch. Hence, exclusionary motives were paramount prior to the allegation and had in fact already led to ongoing litigation and a court ordered assessment. Without contacting the father, though, the mother complained to the child protection service and the police even though the custody assessment had just begun. She cancelled all further visitation much to the chagrin of the father and his lawyer. The assessment revealed a long suffering and basic man who needed guidance in terms of expressions of affection with older children.

In contrast, in the face of real sexual abuse, the non-abusing parent often suffers extensive emotional distress following disclosure that a child has been sexually molested.[29] Although other antecedent and concurrent emotional stresses may well be involved especially if revelation leads to divorce, it is apparent that these mothers are initially at least secondarily traumatized by what has taken place. Although hostility and mistrust may develop within the first year following the revelation, it will not have been present prior to the exposure of the abuse. These parents will tend to become withdrawn, avoidant and overwhelmed by what has happened. Although they may defend against the full realization of what occurred, this will gradually improve. They will seek and benefit from psychotherapy that helps separate their feelings from their children and aids coping with self blame and secondary traumatization from the experience. These parents most often remain empathic to their children's needs and will seek to protect them even from police and child protection personnel. There will be evidence of shock, depression, helplessness, especially at the outset, more than fury, vilification and singular blame of the father. The mother may even discount the child's perception or blame a third party other than the other parent. Denial and minimizing of the event are not uncommon at least when the sexual abuse is first discovered. Even though abuse occurred, the mothers of truly abused children may not lose sight of the importance of the child's relationship to the father and may well mourn the loss for their child.

29 Green, A. and Schetky, D. (1988), *supra*, note 17, at 117–118.

(c) Child Abuse Syndrome

As there is no established syndrome that typifies perpetrators of sexual abuse, likewise there is no specific child sexual abuse syndrome. Experts in child abuse may be called upon to give opinions as to whether abuse occurred or whether there is a further risk of harm. Trying, however, to match a child's symptoms to a supposed expected abuse profile would be far too open to error and distortion. First, distress is ubiquitous to many childhood disorders as are signs of trauma. Secondly, precocious sexual awareness may be a result of real abuse or it may occur innocently when parents misjudge the needs for privacy and modesty and expose the child to sexual overstimulation through parental nudity, group bathing and other "liberal" behaviours.[30]

Further, although children who show abnormal concern about sexual intercourse and other adult sexual acts may well have been exposed to it through direct experience, abused and non-abused children do not necessarily differ in their knowledge of gender and sexuality. On the other hand, abused children will often respond in a qualitatively unusual manner, expressing affective distress, that will catch the attention of the assessor. Here again, though, it is the qualitative dimension that is central to a careful reading of what a child is trying to communicate.

It is essential for the family lawyer, therefore, to understand that assessors cannot rely on a proven test or clinical/demographic profile that will validly predict sexual abuse in children. In fact, abused children may be quite asymptomatic in some cases or they may suffer from severe post-traumatic symptoms in others. Indications commonly noted in the literature are anxiety, avoidance, specific fears and phobias, distress in the presence of the abusing parent, depression, withdrawal, hygiene problems and academic difficulties. On the other hand, such symptoms are also observed in non-abused children who suffer from other concerns, some of which are developmental and will

30 Gordon, B, Schroeder, C. and Abrams J. (1990), "Children's knowledge of sexuality: a comparison of sexually abused and nonabused children", *American Journal of Orthopsychiatry*, 60: 250–57.

likely pass naturally with time and family support. As was discussed previously, divorce and family conflicts in themselves can cause the same constellation of signs and symptoms. Consequently, the diagnosis of child sexual abuse, especially in those gray area cases that frequent custody and access work, is a difficult matter and the prudent assessor will build a broad multisource picture that might then point to sexual impropriety as a likely cause for a child's symptoms.

In a study done in 1984 at Tufts New England Medical Centre and reported by Weissman, 17 per cent of 4 to 6-year-old children who had been abused or had their abuse revealed within the prior six months, met the criteria for major clinical impairment.[31] Forty per cent of 7 to 13-year-old children were also seriously affected which suggests that older children, perhaps abused longer, are more disturbed. On the other hand, paradoxically, adolescent victims of sexual abuse were found to be relatively free of serious impairment. In this regard, therefore, one should not automatically expect that each and every abused child will show serious emotional deficits. On the other hand, even those who do not demonstrate observable emotional damage may suffer more subtle mood, self esteem and self concept problems that will clearly affect their later adjustment.

In the same vein, not every child that reacts seductively or anxiously should be suspected of child abuse without many other supporting indications that inexorably point to this factor. We might add as well, in this respect, that minor alterations in peri-anal and genital anatomy or condition may be due to normal variation, hygiene factors, or causes other than sex abuse. It is unfortunately not uncommon for these to be blown up and used as sure evidence in litigation without any reference to normative data, caution or common sense.[32]

These qualifying and limiting issues bear upon the caution that assessors must use in approaching sexual abuse allegations in custody matters. Assessors must not only be aware of the strength of their evidence and findings but also its limits. This includes negative evidence and the limitations of procedures used in analyzing the issues. As there is no classic profile for any of the protagonists in an

31 Weissman, H. (1991), "Forensic psychological examination of the child witness in cases of alleged sexual abuse", *American Journal of Orthopsychiatry*, 61: 48–58.

32 *Idem*, at 53; Emans, S., Woods, E., Flagg, N. and Freeman, A. (1987), "Genital findings in sexually abused, symptomatic and asymptomatic, girls", *Pediatrics*, 79: 778–785.

alleged scene of incest, the assessor must be prepared to weigh the many factors that can lead to false conclusions.

(d) Child Competency

Assessors of custody issues faced with children who may have been sexually abused face several obstacles, one of which is the fact that the child may have undergone several interviews regarding the abuse prior to the assessor's involvement. Additionally, there may be a considerable interval between the alleged event and the time of the assessment and memory decrements and distortions due to secondary factors may influence recall and self report. Finally, the question of competency of the child to meaningfully relate what has been learned must also be established.

Generally, a child's testimony is acceptable to the court if the child can perceive the facts accurately, can remember what occurred, can appreciate truth from falsehood, and can communicate what happened as well as answering simple questions about it. In practice, the child's competency is not simply a measure of cognitive maturity but must take into account how much interference and pressure has been endured as well as the child's developmental and emotional status.

Moreover, and this is crucial, children are extremely vulnerable to how they are interviewed and the approach and attitude of the examiner. An assessor that is intrusive and leading will likely distort a child's recount of events. For example, if the examiner says to a child who ventures towards the toys, "Now we have to talk about what you told your mother about what your father did to you", the conclusion is already decided. In contrast, an assessor who spontaneously allows the child to fill the interview with his or her own thoughts and feelings is more likely to hear in return genuine and reality based experience. Hence, the skilled assessor watches the child as he or she ventures to the toys and plays. The assessor seeks elaboration but does not add content nor direct the child's associations. If the child seems to reveal abuse, then the assessor can calmly seek further details and hence can learn much about the child's construction of reality and what has occurred. If the report describes events and details that are very plausible and the child's affective response is appropriate to that situation, then the chances that abuse has occurred increase dramatically. In some situations several sessions or meetings are required but the method does not change. In many unsubstantiated and likely false cases where the allegation is actually made by a parent, the child may never actually allude to abuse and this in itself is significant.

Children are similar to adults in that they will find some way to tell the assessor if they are worried or have been hurt through sexual assault by a parent or other adult. On the other hand, and this is worrisome but unavoidable, a child who was genuinely abused may fail to report it no matter how facilitating and sensitive the assessor. This is why experienced clinicians utilize a multisource perspective that does not rely totally on the admission or absence of disclosure made by a child.

In a clear indictment of validators who disguise themselves as authentic assessors, King and Yuille observe that assessors with a preconceived notion of the "truth" will implicitly demand that the child concur with their conclusion.[33] Hence, the neutrality and receptivity of the assessor to allow the child to relate their true self feelings and concerns is the only viable method for approaching these complex matters.

The research on children's memory is complicated and not always consistent.[34] Most psychological researchers would agree, though, that very young children before age five are most susceptible to distorted recall and ineffective memory retrieval.[35] Their testimony can be highly influenced by post-event suggestions including misinformation. With each intervention, new information, some of it misleading, can thus be introduced. This is why cautious child protection professionals are extremely concerned with repeated questioning and examination of young children. Although answers are still forthcoming, researchers must also differentiate between actual recall and what is communicated by the child due to compliance to authority. When combined with emotional factors, fantasies and lack of knowledge,

---

33 King, M. and Yuille, J. (1987), "Suggestibility and the child witness", in S. Ceci, M. Toglia and D. Ross (Eds.). *Children's Eyewitness Testimony*, New York; Springer-Verlag.

34 Doris, J. (ed.) *The Suggestibility of Children's Recollections,* Washington, 1991, American Psychological Association.

35 Ceci, S., Ross, D. and Toglia, M. (1987), "Suggestibility of children's memory: psychological implications," *Journal of Experimental Psychology*. 116: 38–49.

very young children are the most difficult group to interview and can be easily programmed to elicit false accusations.

Studies of older children reveal considerable memory skill that can approach the level of an adult where memory impairment is a minor factor. Yet, adult memory and eyewitness testimony can be highly influenced by contextual and motivational factors and both children and adults forget over time.[36] Experimental psychological research, as well, does not easily simulate the web of fear, arousal and threat that may compromise a child's perception or willingness to relate or recall. Coupled with the fact that many children will lie in order to ingratiate themselves to a caretaker to gain affection or not to lose it, the situation is certainly complex.[37]

Because children can be persuaded to give a false report does not mean that they perceive the action as harmful or abusive. Consequently, a child may be induced to report that her father touched her private parts but will be quite relaxed and happy in her father's presence. This underlines the fact that although children's response are modifiable, their inherent beliefs may be much more resistant to change. As well, accuracy is often greater for events that fall within the scope of their comprehension and although younger children may be less accurate as to person, place and time, they are quite able to describe repeated abuse more than a single incidence.[38]

Although there is some support for the value of free recall over specific questioning, the down side is that children may fail to disclose what is not prompted. On the other hand, asking a child for specifics routinely would certainly increase the rate of false reports. This is where the skill of the assessor comes in to enlarge, facilitate and open a space for the child's experiences and recollections without leading the child towards appeasement or compliance. The literature is very consistent, however, in demonstrating that biased interrogators of children will strongly affect children's responses to even the most central aspects of what they have observed.[39]

---

36 Fitzpatrick, G, Reder, P. and Lucey, C. (1995), "The child's perspective," in. P. Reder and C. Lucey, *Assessment of parenting: Psychistric and Psychological Contributions*. New York: Routledge, p. 65.

37 Gardner, R. (1992), *supra*, note 16, at 102.

38 Weissman, H. (1991), *supra*, note 31 at 51.

39 Goodman, G. and Clarke-Stewart, A. (1991), "Suggestibility in children's testimony: implications for sexual abuse investigations", in Doris, J. (ed.), *supra*, note 34, at 92–105.

These studies underline that obtaining accurate testimony from children about sexual abuse can be a complex task. Like abuse itself, the more insistent and intimidating the interviewer and the longer the delay between the event and the interview, the more likely that young children at least will accept suggestions and alter their report. Most research on the suggestibility of memory, it appears, is limited to one-time events. In actual life, however, sexual abuse is most often recurrent and children may be examined and questioned by a parent and many strangers before even getting to the stage of a custody evaluation. Consequently, the opportunities for distortion, misperception, and fabrication remain high. Gardiner, in an excellent review of the literature from a pragmatic clinical perspective highlights that across the broad range of studies up to 20 per cent of children will give false-positive responses. Supporting this observation, in one research paradigm, children falsely declared four years after an experimentally induced event that they were hugged or kissed by an adult when in fact they were not.[40] Accordingly, the forensic implications of such findings are very significant.

(e) False Allegations Made by a Child

Children who falsely accuse a parent of sexual abuse in the context of custody and access acrimony do so for a number of possible reasons.[41]

(i) They may be coerced or brainwashed by a vindictive parent, usually the mother, who finds in incest the perfect crime to demolish the reputation and custodial position of their former spouse.

(ii) They may be under the influence of a delusional mother who intrudes her psychic reality into the children and compels them to adopt her perspective and interpretation of events. Such mothers are highly controlling and deeply disturbed. Their love is very conditional while at the same time they insist that the children only need their love. Often, in severe cases, any legitimizing of

40 Gardner, R. (1992), *surpa*, note 16, at 107.
41 Green, A and Schetky, D. (1988), *supra*, note 17 at 108–109.

the father's relationship and status in the children's lives is met by a further accusation of abuse.

(iii) The allegation may be based on sexual fantasy fueled by separation and developmental factors. As an example, a seven-year-old girl whose parents had recently separated bragged to her mother than she slept with Daddy on mother's side of the bed and that Daddy "humped me". This sexually precocious and competitive child viewed herself as her mother's successor in her father's life and viewed this "disclosure" as a personal triumph. It is also warded off latent fears that her father had rejected her as well as her mother. Now the actual event was quite different in as much as both she and her younger brother had fallen asleep on their father's bed watching television and he had returned both to their own beds later in the night. When asked to explain what "humping" was, she could not elaborate other than to say that everybody knows that! In family drawings, she placed herself beside her father followed in sequence by her brother and mother. In a play situation, the seven-year-old depicted a family with a grumpy father who lost patience with his son (not his daughter!) and left on a long journey. Happily, he realized how much he missed everybody and returned to a joyous reunion.

(iv) The accusation may be based on a child's vindictiveness and hostility. A 12-year-old girl, in one example, had been hopeful that her new stepfather would fill a major gap in her life. She was the eldest of three daughters, the youngest being a product of the union between her mother and stepfather. Her mother, who had been sexually abused over time by a relative as a child, had drifted from man to man in a series of unhappy alliances. Much to this child's chagrin, her mother and stepfather began to fight viciously with one another. The fights even became physical and the police became involved. The mother, in turn, leaned heavily for support on her 12-year-old who grew to despise her stepfather for failing to bring harmony to the family. Although she had enjoyed positive private times with her new dad, she now felt guilty and compromised by the relationship and blamed him intensely for all that had gone wrong. Following a playful scuffle, when they were alone, she told her mother that he had touched her inappropriately through her clothing. This led to a great crisis and the mother fled the home with the children. She resisted all efforts to permit access or any continuing contact with the girls. In the assessment, the elder daughter insisted that people like him belonged in jail. Revenge was the only emotion she could express on the subject.

(v) False allegations can arise from the intervention of third parties who misinterpret findings or have insufficient training to appreciate the complex nature of certain cases. In one example, two young girls, two and four years, respectively, were brought by their mother who when being bathed by their mother apparently spontaneously claimed that their father "poked them". The girls were physically examined and non-specific irritation were noted vaginally and anally.

On the basis of these findings, a physician determined that sexual abuse had likely occurred. What the mother did not make clear, however, was that she had questioned the daughters for the prior three days which included videotaping them demonstrating how their father "poked" them in the anus and vagina. This could easily have accounted for the redness and irritation apparent in the medical examination. To further the children's admissions, the mother had also knit anatomically correct dolls to improve the accuracy of their disclosure. The police, however, were dubious and when they would not proceed legally against the father, she became quite angry and questioned their methods. "Do you think that I have nothing better to do than shove a banana up them," she was quoted as saying.

Another physician continued as the children's therapist and treated them and the mother for distress and parenting effectiveness. As with many child protection units of this type, the accused father was never interviewed and he was perceived and judged solely through the mother's eyes. Yet, the suspicion of abuse, backed strongly by the assessor/therapist, proved sufficient to convince the court that interim access should be supervised and an assessment ordered. The paternal grandfather was chosen as the supervisor and following the first access visit, the mother alleged that the children had made a "disclosure". They were immediately rushed to the therapist/assessor's office who interviewed them and took note of the few lines muttered by the four-year-old that indeed Daddy had "poked" them. Several days later, the mother added that the children had elaborated the scene to include the grandfather. The children, according to the mother's report, described being strung up by ropes and sodomized as well as having their vaginas enlarged to tolerate the adult penis.

In the one and a half years it took to finally resolve the case, the mother's delusion of sexual abuse and the doctor's collusion maintained a powerful hold on the courts and child and family services. Despite clear indications that the mother suffered from a serious paranoid disorder and was infecting her children with delusional beliefs, the physician/therapist remained a powerful validator in an influential role. Initially, the courts and protection authorities accepted the therapist's conclusions and did not question the objectivity, methodology or the right of the father to present his side of the story. This though changed as the mother's obvious pattern of illogic became more evident to the courts. Clearly, this therapist relied on extremely limited data to make her determination. Moreover, she made no attempt to interview the father or have him psychologically assessed. Thirdly, she was not trained as a child or family therapist despite being well qualified as a physician. Lastly, she was evidently inadequately trained to differentiate an emotionally ill, delusional parent from a normally protective one. The most striking parallel between accusing parent and validator is that neither can accept a negative conclusion. "What ever you say," notes such a person, "we know that he really did it and is probably doing it right now with YOUR consent !"

(vi) Finally, the misinterpretation of physical findings can also lead in certain mind-sets to allegations of abuse. In one example, an assessor concluded that an eight-year-old boy who seemed to be forever pulling at his penis was showing precocious sexual arousal. This was offered as one sure indication that his separated father had sexually abused him. The description of this behaviour, however, suggested that it was mainly absent minded and had no link to seductive behaviour associated with the father or other adult men. Moreover, it was learned that the boy had undergone surgery for an overly tight foreskin which, along with residual discomfort, might have better explained such a preoccupation.

(f) Methodology in Evaluating Sexual Abuse Allegations in the Context of Custody Assessments

In our judicial tradition, it would not fall to a mental health expert to determine the ultimate truth of an allegation such as one concerning sexual abuse. This would be left to the trier who has a one-time opportunity to hear from all sides and to cast judgment on the matter. Nevertheless, from necessity has arisen an opportunity for the court to be assisted by expert testimony that is relevant, valid in its premises, and of probative value. In order to better meet this challenge, the health professions have encouraged their members to fully appreciate the risks their interventions hold for people in litigation and to protect the legal and civil rights of those who are the subject of evaluation. Hence, the health professions have placed ethical standards at the forefront including the requirement to be competent as well as knowing the limit of one's expertise. Within these limits, though, and with prudence and restraint, a well executed family psychological evaluation can shed much light on the matters before the court. In the case of sexual abuse accusations, this would not only address the probability that abuse occurred but other possible explanations that might be equally relevant.

The assessor in a custody conflict will not usually begin interviewing the family until late in the dispute when other reports are available. The child or children involved will likely have been interviewed by numerous professionals including pediatricians, nurses, police, social workers and lawyers for the Official Guardian. Furthermore, the alleged event may have occurred months and sometimes more than a year before the assessment begins when the child was at a developmentally different stage. Often in those ambiguous cases that are most difficult to substantiate, it may be next to impossible to ensure the credibility of what is reported. This becomes even more problematic when there is a history of the accusing parent prejudicing the child's discourse through interference and pressure. Lastly, in the most contentious, litigious and difficult cases, there may have been a prior custody evaluation that either failed to adequately address the concerns or was superseded by new allegations and continuing familial strife. All of these factors complicate the process for the assessor due to a layering of actions and interventions that bear on the validity of a child or parent's report.

From the other side of the coin, the custody assessor has a distinct advantage if only for the fact that everyone in the family will be seen and a psychological construction of the family and its workings will expose their mode of relating or "doing business" with each other. What was likely not clearly observed before hand can now be brought into focus and this goes along way to shedding light on the issues, including sexual abuse. Not all assessors will be comfortable nor sufficiently experienced to handle the most complex cases and the referring lawyers should be confident that the expert selected has a track record of handling these cases adequately.

Because it is not the habit of most child protection teams to interview the whole family, especially the accused, the custody assessment may also be the first occasion for the accused parent to actually be heard on the matter.[42] The balanced in-depth psychological assessments of both parents as well as observing how the child interacts with each parent and during transitions is central to clinically determining the veracity or likelihood of an allegation. In this regard, the assessment must be comprehensive and should rely on the assessor's knowledge in diverse areas including child development, child abuse, psychopathology, personality theory, and diagnostic/forensic assessment. It is vital that the assessor employs a multifactorial approach that builds conclusions from numerous vantage points including historical analysis of the parents, diagnostic assessment, review of records and prior reports, a detailed chronology of events including the complaint of abuse, child and parent-child observation and, when applicable, psychological testing.

It is through a close inspection of the family as a relational or interactive unit, that a deeper understanding is obtained. Children are expressions of their parents' desires and they are imbued by their parents with personal meaning. Consequently, they may stand for what is most cherished in the parent or, conversely, what is bad and worthless. Again, the child has little control over this outcome and victimization may take many forms, not just physical and certainly not just sexual. The assessor through the prism of observation has an opportunity to perceive this dimension of meaning that is often a reflection of the parent's background, attitudes and concerns. In the

42 Conte, J., Sorenson, M., Fogarty, M., Rosa. J. (1991), "Evaluating children's reports of sexual abuse: results from a survey of professionals," *American Journal of Orthopsychiatry*, 61: 428–37.

example of delusional abuse noted above, the mother's own father had died when she was three years old. Yet, she informed the assessor that his death was fortuitous for he was such a rogue that he would have surely abused her when she became older. From a psychological standpoint this was powerful evidence that the premonition of the abusing father had a prior existence and significance for this woman and fueled her perception and motivation in the divorce context. When she added that she had been emotionally abused by her mother who was described as unempathic and even sadistic, the possibilities for unconscious projection received much support. With such vulnerable people, internal psychological reality may become confused with external events while the past is also collapsed into the present. This understanding was strengthened when she anxiously admitted to a social worker that she had anticipated her husband's abuse of the children but not until they were older!

Yet, in other situations, it may become evident that a child has been used in the past by the parents as a scapegoat for unresolved tensions or even as an intermediary because they cannot tolerate closeness with each other. Knowledge of these pre-existing family relations help to interpret later events and contextualize the abuse investigation in the wider assessment of the family as a unit. Although this may be difficult to describe, sexual abuse does not occur out of nowhere and there is no behavioural outcome, abuse included, that does not, at least in retrospect, fit some pattern in terms of personalities, propensities and interactions. By assessing these features, a deeper insight can be obtained that throws essential light on whether sexual abuse was a likely occurrence.

It is important to observe that there are two separate components that will interest the assessor and the court. The first is the suspected abuse itself whereas the second is the allegation of abuse. Hence, the same careful analysis must also be applied to the abuse allegation and to its place within the scope of the parents' conflicts. For example, in one case a woman became convinced that her husband has abused their two sons at the same time that she had become convinced that the marriage should end. The husband apparently resisted her initiative and wished to persevere in joint couple therapy. It was the allegation of abuse, in fact, that propelled the breakup of the marriage and freed the wife from the enmeshed union. It also became clear that sexual excesses had been a constant theme in their struggle and the wife had accused her husband of being oversexed, sexually controlling, sexually rejecting, and unfaithful. Furthermore, she was also convinced that he was autocratic and abused power with her and the children. In this respect, the child abuse allegation was a slight shift from what she had always purported rather than a new phenomenon. When it came to the examination of the two boys, details and appropriate affect were entirely lacking and there was no contextual realism to the complaint. It never took form during the assessment as an actual event but remained an expression of the mother's distrust and enmity towards her ex-husband. In fact, the only real "disclosures" had occurred when the mother questioned the children on the same day as she told them of the immanent separation and hastily arranged for them to be interviewed by the police and child and family services. The fact that the accusation had occurred first in the mother's mind and not in the children's psyche was also an important element. From the assessor's point of view, in order to be treated as a valid event based on actual history, the allegation would have to find its way into the authentic discourse of the children as an essential communication either through word, sign or symptom. Another way to state this is that in cases where abuse is most likely, the allegation recedes to the background whereas the actual abuse events become more central and the focus of the assessor's evaluation.

Besides, the interactive and intrapsychic levels of analysis, the assessor may also have available an accurate account of the initially recorded accusation made by the child. Here, the underlying issue will be less whether the child is capable of accurate reporting but whether in the real life context of the family breakdown there are reasons to misrepresent and misperceive. In other words, is the account credible.

In cases that are substantiated and obviously true, the child will often be reticent to discuss the abuse even with the non-abusing parent, usually the mother. The child may be quite frightened of the father and refuse a joint interview. If the abuse was "gentle" and non-threatening, the child may accept to meet with the father and yet act quite inappropriately and even seductively with little sense of borders or limits. Assessors must be prepared for the uncomfortable possibility that although the weight of understanding will favour one conclusion or the other, there are often residual doubts or cautions that cannot be totally set aside or resolved. These can and should be stated in the report although the assessor should make every effort to conclude either way. If anyone is prepared finally to err in the direction of caution despite findings that are 90 per cent opposed to the reality of abuse, for example, then it should be the judge and not the assessor.

In substantiated cases of abuse, the mothers will most often be depressed and sorrowful and the child will likely demonstrate some cardinal features associated with sexual abuse. The abusing parent will often suffer personal inadequacies or character flaws that would predispose them to such actions. The allegation of abuse will not in itself have a profound function or meaning but, rather, the assessment will turn more to the behavioural patterns and personal styles that have long characterized the family. In contrast, in false cases vengeful, hateful, alienating and devaluing attitudes of the accusing parent may well be prominent. The child will discuss the abuse on cue and the directing function of the accusing parent will be evident. Often the child will behave very differently towards the father when the mother is present or absent. At transitions, the child may act stone faced and sullen until beyond the sight of the mother and only then flash a smile.

Sorenson and colleagues in a survey of 212 professionals involved extensively in child protection investigations, listed the most important criteria employed by this diverse sample in assessing suspected cases of child sexual abuse.[43] In order of importance these were:

- physical indicators such as genital trauma, enlargements and sexually transmitted diseases
- age inappropriate sexual knowledge
- a consistent report of sexual abuse over time with idiosyncrasies in the reporting that clearly add to its credibility
- a progression of sexual activity (almost all actual incest follows an escalating pattern)
- sexualized play during the interview
- the child's description of the abuse reflects pressure or coercion
- seductive behaviour
- responses to anatomically correct dolls typical of an abused child
- the child is able to distinguish real events from fantasy
- the child's story is logical

43 *Idem*, at 431.

- excessive masturbation
- preoccupation with genitals

True to experience, 90 per cent of the respondents to the survey also indicated that the presence of a custody dispute was a major indicator of false allegations. In addition, they would apply similar caution if the family was characteristically overstimulating with lack of boundaries, if the child was emotionally disturbed, or if there was a strong punitive motivation in the attitude of the accusing parent or child.

One promising approach in terms of children's testimony regarding sexual abuse by Raskin and Esplin has been to deconstruct these statements of abuse and look closely at their structure according to specific criteria.[44] The authors underline that the statement should be obtained in as free a narrative as possible without the assessor imposing unwarranted structure on the account. In this regard, direct questions should only be asked at the end of the interview and, then, only when necessary. Their criterion based method was applied to a sample of 40 sexual abuse cases involving children between 3 and 18 years of age who were divided into a group of 20 highly substantiated cases of intrafamilial incest and a group of 20 very doubtful cases. As to the likely false cases, the researchers determined that the alleged perpetrator had never admitted abuse, there was no corroborating evidence, and the allegation was either recanted or dismissed by the court with the specific finding that abuse had not occurred. In contrast, in the confirmed cases, 16 of 20 included physical evidence and 14 of the perpetrators had confessed their guilt along with there being physical evidence of anal or vaginal trauma apparent.

The results, in general, revealed little overall overlap between the two groups on the 19 content variables measured. Focusing on those criteria that were most often present in the substantiated cases and almost never present in the doubtful ones provides an interesting perspective on differentiating between true and false cases. In the unsubstantiated group, the following criteria were almost never or infrequently present:

---

44 Raskin, D. and Esplin, P. (1991), "Assessment of children's statements of sexual abuse," in Doris, J. *supra*, note 34, 153–64.

- The child (in true cases) could recall the conversation and words of the perpetrator in its original form including specific phrases and unfamiliar terms.
- There is some report of complications or unexpected interruptions or other happenings during the abuse that are noted by the child.
- The child in true cases may mention unusual but realistic details regarding the person, objects or events that add an element of realism to the narrative.
- The child in true cases may describe incidental details that are irrelevant to the abuse but related to the situation or context.
- In true cases, the child may make some mention of the mood or mental state of the perpetrator.
- The child may make spontaneous corrections or additions that add to the credibility and realism of the account.
- Sometimes the child in true cases will criticize themselves or point out some aspect of their own behaviour that may have been wrong or inappropriate.
- In substantiated cases, the child may make excuses for the perpetrating parent, may pardon the parent, or will fail to blame the parent when it would be appropriate to do so.

There was a more moderate difference apparent between the groups on four other variables:

- In valid cases, the report is embedded in a spatial and temporal context where events are connected to the daily life of the child.
- There may be reports of actions or reactions that add to the realism of the account.
- The child may describe feelings or thoughts that took place during the abuse or in its aftermath.
- The child in the true account may admit to lack of memory or lack of knowledge of some aspect of the experience.

Although the determination of these matters remains an imperfect science, such research represents a major step forward. First and foremost, it pertains directly to the real life complexities that face assessors in child abuse and child custody assessments. Secondly, it transcends the behavioural signs and symptoms method that is so vulnerable to misperception and false determination. The deconstruction of a child's description of what happened to them opens the way to a more subtle and sensitive evaluation that meshes well with an in-depth clinical approach.

(g) Conclusion

Nowhere in the custody arena are the skills, integrity and objectivity of assessors tested as in cases of alleged child abuse. Unlike child protection workers, the assessor's mandate is usually broad and advisory and what qualifies as clinical decision making may not always perfectly suit the legal discourse of the courts. Furthermore, diagnosis in such situations is complicated by the obscurity of many allegations, the time delay from the alleged event, the age, cognitive maturity and motivation of the child, the skills and attitudes of interviewers, the number of times the child has been questioned, the child's experience of these interviews and examinations, the underlying agenda of the accusing parent and finally, the general ambiance of acrimony that settles on most divorce disputes.

By the time the custody assessment is under way, therefore, there is often a complex historical underlay that itself shapes as much as it informs the assessor about what has happened or is happening in the family. Although a nurse or pediatrician may be instrumental in initiating a complaint, the assessor and finally the judge may have to finally determine its merits. In this complex web of factors, the custody assessor's contribution is directly related to the extent that they can create a new perspective, a novel vantage point, that builds upon a model of the family and its protagonists. The assessor's method should not be altered by an abuse allegation for its strength lies in the breadth and depth of the analysis that allows the assessor to uncover the essential dynamics of the parents, children and their interactions. Only by explaining the family and how it works can more specific questions be profitably addressed including those related to sexual abuse.

7. PSYCHIC TRAUMA

Since its introduction into psychiatric nomenclature in 1980, the label post-traumatic stress disorder (PTSD) has been applied to many contexts and events and to all age groups.[45] It has not, however, melded easily with jurisprudence although in certain cases it has had a tremendous impact in terms of both criminal and civil matters.[46] In the most appropriate applications, there is usually a temporally defined event that is life threatening or extremely frightening and distressing leading to high physiological arousal and overwhelming helplessness. The syndrome was first defined in the context of war where severe battleground experiences led to emotional and mental disability as a result of the horrifying experiences faced by soldiers. This had been well observed in every war of the 20th century but became better understood due to the Viet Nam experience when the modern label PTSD was first utilized. It is also known to occur as a reaction to natural disasters including man made ones such as being a victim of a violent crime through rape, torture, hostage taking or severe assault.

The defining symptoms of PTSD all reflect an organismic fixation on the trauma and although the sufferer wants nothing more than to be able to leave it behind they are haunted by its chilling terror. Hence, the subject suffers from hallucinatory flashbacks, recurrent nightmares of the trauma itself, intense psychological distress associated with any hint of the experience, severe anxiety and unremitting tension, and withdrawal and emotional blunting so that life has no leisure nor reprieve. In this regard, PTSD is a psychophysiological disorder and it is not meant to be equated with psychic stress that in itself can be severe and disruptive.

The closer a traumatic event resembles what has been described, the more appropriate is the label of PTSD. Often though, in many life contexts, the objectivity of the supposed causal event is illusory and the term causes more problem than it solves. Moreover, the subject

45 American Psychiatric Association (1987), *Diagnostic and Statistical Manual of Mental Disorders, Third Edition, Revised* (DSM-III-R). Washington, DC: American Psychiatric Association.

46 Stone, A. (1993), "Post-traumatic stress disorder and the law: critical review of the new frontier," *Bulletin of the American Academy of Psychiatry and the Law,* 21: 23–36.

may suffer from psychic stress without suffering from actual PTSD. By trying to bend this very specific disorder to fit so many different contexts and conditions, lawyers and mental health experts have lost sight of its real meaning and place in the spectrum of disorders. This is not to imply that both children and adults do not suffer from PTSD but usually there is a clearly demarcated provoking stress such as a vicious attack or violent sexual abuse. It should not, though, nor was it ever intended to be used as a defence for the impulsive, unwise and excessive reactions that may characterize certain people in the midst of domestic crisis.

Adding to the confusion about what constitutes PTSD, the label may also be misused to validate a subject's victim status. For example, a man seeking joint custody of his two sons was accused by his ex-wife of being physically abusive. Although there was little to corroborate her claim, the police, whom she had summoned on several occasions, suspected her of being more tactical than threatened. Yet, she attended a counseling and advocacy service for battered women who reported that she indeed suffered from PTSD due to the husband's alleged abuse. The implication was, of course, that if she suffers the disorder then her account of events must be accurate.

Along the continuum of reactions that one does observe in family matters, though, it is possible for a child or adult to suffer from an actual PTSD. The evidence is clear across many studies that given a big enough traumatic event almost no one will escape a PTSD. Sometimes, for instance, it can even be difficult to shake the feelings of a frightening but relatively minor motor vehicle accident so it is certainly understandable that a war, natural disaster, witnessing a murder, being raped or assaulted in a dangerous out-of-control encounter, could well induce such a syndrome. The presence of PTSD always marks a failure of recovery which is why it can easily become a permanent condition. Because coping resources are overwhelmed and not just seriously strained, the biopsychological functioning of the person becomes incapacitated. Hopefully, this conveys the extreme dysfunction and helplessness associated with PTSD and explains why it should not be used as a synonym for high stress.

In terms of family law, a lawyer may claim that the erratic and unfit behaviour of their client can be attributed to PTSD that was operative at the time. They may even find medical support for the supposition based on the self report of the client. If the diagnosis is accepted by the court, then the corollary supposition is that the ex-spouse is responsible for the victim's dysfunction. Hence, the implications can be significant. Determining the accuracy of the diagnosis is important. There must be some defined stress or event and not just an impression that the victim was mentally or physically assaulted by the ex-spouse. Alleged sufferers who do not have PTSD will retain a capacity for leisure even though they may claim that their life has been practically ruined. They will also demonstrate amazing stamina in pursuing their cause. The supposed deficits will be viewed as problematic in the past and only germane to the behaviour to be excused. They will embrace every opportunity to vilify the ex-spouse rather than shirking from any recall or association as in valid cases. Further, they will show considerable motivation to exclude and negate the other parent in the lives of the children. There may well be signs of evasion and a tendency to overstate their adjustment and quality of life prior to the marriage. The symptoms are often vague and inconsistent and there is often a prior hint or record of emotional or character problems as well as a history of dysfunction in the family of origin. Psychological testing such as on the MMPI-2 will reveal extreme defensiveness in contrast to valid cases where the profile more likely resembles subjects with true organic pathology and stresses inefficiency, feelings of impotence and high tension.[47]

Having placed PTSD at the extreme end of a continuum of possible reactions, we are on safer ground to describe as psychically traumatic all those experiences that are associated with helplessness and the individual's inability to adapt or master an experience at the time that it occurs. Consequently, someone can suffer from the emotional injury of psychic trauma, and this is very common, without suffering from the psychiatric condition known as PTSD, which is far rarer in a family context. As a brief example, a young man described being seduced at age five by his adolescent neighbour and engaging in mutual fellatio. Although the seduction was obviously significant for the patient, the depth of his emotional trauma focused on the failure of his parents to protect him. This lack of a needed protective shield had seriously compromised his sense of trust and was associated with intense suppressed rage and depression.

---

47 Chaney, H., Cohn, C., Williams, S. and Vincent, K. (1984), "MMPI results: a comparison of trauma victims, psychogenic pain, and patients with organic disease", *Journal of Clinical Psychology*, 40: 1450–54.

In another example, a woman of 65 came for psychotherapy after she could no longer suppress her turmoil regarding sexual abuse that had occurred so many years before. Raised on a farm, and four years of age, she was playing in the hayloft and being supervised by an older cousin, a young man at the time, who was helping her father stack the in-coming hay bales. Between unloadings, the cousin grabbed and digitally raped her in what became a series of assaults that occurred until she was old enough to run away from him. Although a librarian, wife and successful mother who had raised four children, there was a core in her that was deeply traumatized and she often felt that she was "shattering into pieces". True to the nature of psychic trauma, she had recurring fears of being killed and felt a stabbing pressure in her mid-back — a flashback to the cousin's erection when he would grab her from behind. Again, although sexual abuse was certainly responsible for damaging psychic trauma that had impacted on her emotional development, her symptoms did not approximate that of PTSD.

Faced with psychic trauma, it is not unusual for children or adults to ward off intrusive emotions through denial and avoidance. People with PTSD, of course, do not have this luxury and become fixated to their pain, but for others, often those seen in custody assessments, such avoidance may represent an adaptive mechanism. It allows the traumatized person to retain control until they can gradually work through problems manageably and in smaller doses. In one example, a six-year-old boy who had been exposed to a deeply bitter and vindictive mother who insisted falsely that he had been sexually abused by the father was viewed by his teacher as exemplary and surprisingly adapted. When custody and residence was awarded to the more neutral and protective father, the boy became quite depressed. The therapist who treated the child observed that the psychic strain of coping with his mother's vituperations had taxed his coping resources to their maximum and the depression could be seen as restorative. Moreover, although the boy would have been alienated from his father if left in his mother's care, he nonetheless felt the loss of her far apart from her complicated depression, there was a sincere and loving core to her care. A gradually ascending access regimen within the more balanced context of the father's custody assisted his adaptation measurably.

Summary

Although this discussion has been brief, it hopefully conveys that psychic strain, psychic trauma and the organismic failure associated with PTSD are different concepts with different meanings. Although we do not often see PTSD in parents or their offspring in custody disputes, psychic strain and psychic trauma are important complicating elements to many family assessments.

(a) Substance Abuse and Custody Assessments

The overriding goal of a custody assessment is to provide for the best interests of children when their parents prove unable to resolve matters between them. Misuse of alcohol or drugs can impact on the capacity of a parent to provide consistently and to maintain the child's interests in focus. In extreme cases of child abuse that come to court, there is a much higher likelihood of alcoholism than in a matched sample of non-abusers. Famularo observed a 43 per cent level of alcoholism in an abuse sample and only a 12 per cent level in a control group.[48] In another review of 206 court cases of child abuse, Murphy and colleagues again noted that 43 per cent were substance abusers.[49] Clinically, alcohol is known to have a disinhibiting effect and otherwise latent or controlled tendencies or patterns can be expressed much more easily under the impact of mood altering drugs or alcohol. Hence, the presence of alcohol, drugs or both adds a factor of credibility to sexual abuse allegations and accusations of violence. In the presence of an impulsive and undercontrolled individual who is, as well, under the pressure of marital dissolution, the adverse impact of substance abuse on behaviour can be potentiated.

On the other hand, it is not uncommon for people to drink alcohol and it can be difficult to determine if a parent is underestimating their real consumption. Many of the better alcoholism screening instru-

48 Famularo, R., Stone, K., Barnum, R. and Wharton, R. (1986), "Alcoholism and severe child maltreatment", *American Journal of Orthopsychiatry*, 56: 481–5.

49 Murphy, J., Jellinek, M., Quinn, D., Smith, G., Poitrast, F. and Gashko, M. (1991), "Substance abuse and serious child mistreatment: prevalence, risk and outcome in a court sample", *Child Abuse and Negelect*, 15: 197–211.

ments require an openness and honesty which may not be readily available when people are trying to promote a positive image. There is a scale included in the MMPI supplementary measures that assesses the potential for addictions but this may not actually predict consumption which either has to be witnessed by an objective, neutral observer or accurately self reported. Besides, recreational use of soft drugs is not a rare occurrence and both parents may have indulged to varying degrees. Often, in custody assessments, as well, such excesses are ascribed to the past and parents may try and demonstrate to the assessor that there is no further risk of substance excesses or abuse. A final complication to assessing this dimension is that the other spouse is often motivated to grossly exaggerate the bad habits of another, including alcohol.

Where substance abuse is a significant problem, though, it is usually mixed with poor parenting and/or a disordered personality. Often people who chronically abuse alcohol or drugs demonstrate low frustration tolerance, chronic resentment and impulsivity. They may have trouble establishing a daily structure and reliably meeting commitments to their children. As already noted, there is a greater risk of adverse behaviour including sexual and physical abuse of children, interparental violence, accidents (including motor vehicle accidents), illness and even premature death. It is wise to ask parents in a custody dispute whether they have been charged with impaired driving in the past as this is often a useful indicator of alcohol abuse. Another question concerning charges for antisocial behaviour such as assault, theft or disturbing the peace may also be useful. As a verification, if such substance abuse is suspected, the assessor should not only ask the parent in question about this history but also the ex-spouse.

In the final analysis, it is always the child's needs that should take precedence in a family assessment and some degree of substance abuse may not preclude a parent from providing decent care. This is especially the case when drug or alcohol misuse has been episodic and stress generated. It is always a positive sign when the parent accepts referral for treatment or, on their own, has taken the problem in hand. Regular involvement in Alcoholics Anonymous is a positive sign and the social support provided by this exceptional self help organization is often a substantial resource in many life contexts.

(b) Perversion, Pornography and Antisocial Behaviour

It is natural when advising on the interests of children that assessors and the courts promote an approach to sexuality where intimacy and human sharing prevails. In this regard, sexual perversion is clearly at deviance from this model as it focuses on conscious erotic excitement stimulated by unloving, anatomical and often aggressive aspects of sexuality.[50] It should be noted, however, that this practical description of what is perverse would not pertain to homosexuality which is simply a change in sexual object and not a degradation of the loving dimension in erotic life. Homosexuals can be as loving and intimate as heterosexuals or as perverse. In this sense, heterosexuality has no primary claim on healthy erotic expression.

Perverse behaviour may be limited to a masturbatory fantasy shared between two consenting people, or acted out in ways that create public mischief. They may exist along side a healthier sexual adjustment or dominate and determine erotic life. From a psychoanalytic perspective, perversions are best described as erotic rituals, compulsively enacted, which evolve as an individualistic solution to coping with certain types of early childhood trauma.

Perverse behaviour comes in a myriad of forms and fixations that are as diverse as the human imagination but fetishism (inanimate object), exhibitionism, voyeurism and sadomasochism are more commonly known. Although all sexuality contains minor variants of these perverse themes, the pervert substitutes this element for the whole of their sexual response. From a clinical standpoint, these are complex pathologies although it should be said that most perversions do not deserve the reprisals they attract.

In terms of custody and domestic disputes, perversion may be vaguely alleged but it is rare that a true perversion will be noted in a parent. In one example, though, a man contested custody of his three-year-old daughter although he seemed more intent on overcoming the restrictions that his ex-wife had imposed on the visitation. When she refused to allow him access until he obtained and installed a car seat, he fumed with rage and expected the assessor to join him in outrage. This man's own adjustment was questionable and it was

---

50 Stoller, R. (1975), *Perersion: The Erotic Form of Hatred,* New York: Pantheon Books.

hard to pin down his actual work or source of income. The mother was employed as an administrative assistant and could not rely on regular financial support from her ex-husband. He was particularly glib and facile and although energetic and loquacious, also untrustworthy. On the other hand, he seemed interested in his daughter and regular visits and he could not understand why he would not be considered as a candidate for co-parenting.

During the assessment, the mother produced a box full of letters and pornographic magazines that emphasized homosexual fetishistic cross dressing and sadomasochistic submission. He had a secret correspondence, it seemed, with a host of like minded people who responded to various personal advertisements placed in newspapers. Although he denied any activity in this regard beyond meeting his "curiosity", the issue for the assessor was how to take this erotic deviance into account in the context of access and the implications for the father-daughter relationship. The man rejected any idea of seeking psychotherapeutic help and he denied that this interest represented a problem. He was incensed that this would be given any weight and he viewed it as an injustice that the assessor took it seriously. On his own, following the release of the report, he contacted numerous other assessors hoping to find someone to condemn it for considering the implications of this perversity in terms of the child's best interests. The assessor's essential conclusion was that this father's psychosocial stability was in question and the perverse interest was simply a further expression of these unresolved identity issues that undermined the extent of contribution to his daughter's life. On the other hand, he had never shown any proclivity to include his daughter in his erotica and his basic care was adequate.

Apart from perverse sexuality, which is uncommonly observed in this context, it is more likely that assessors may be confronted with men who keep stashes of pornographic videos or magazines but who see this a totally independent of their aspirations as parents. Again, the issue is less a moralistic one than a matter of judgment and tact in the face of children's real needs. Assessors should make it clear to such parents that if pornographic material is in the home then it will eventually find its way to children's eyes. This is not an issue of probability but one of inevitability! It is best for the assessor to approach this matter in respect to the overall character of the parent and not as a moral breach related to badness or sinfulness. That is, if the parent disposes of the pornography and understands the implications for the child who might otherwise view it, then this does not have to be an ultimate decisive factor. If the parent becomes defensive and views it in terms of their rights and freedoms, then this resistance suggests tunnel vision surely bearing on child care. Because of the popularity of pornography, this is not an uncommon occurrence or factor in a custody assessment.

The presence of antisocial behaviour in the context of a custody dispute must always represent a special concern for the assessor. These are parents who aim to win and who cope by pressuring and manipulating the system, including the assessor, to meet their needs and desires. Truth for such people is a relative term that is shaped according to the desired goal which in turn justifies the means of attaining it. One sees a spectrum of manipulative and controlling people in custody work from transparent and unsophisticated bullies to highly intelligent and skilled manipulators who can be surprisingly successful in the legal arena. These are often litigious people who, faced with the prospect of an undesirable outcome, will think nothing of dissimulating a version of their experience during the assessment to make the assessor appear biased and hostile. Because such adults are not sensitive to the social ideals of the court process, they do not surrender to its good will in the hope that the best interests of their children will be served.

By referring to antisocial traits, it may appear that this is a homogeneous group when in fact it represents many different types of people. In general, though, they all strike fear or anxiety in the other parent who will emphasize how helpless they are to ward off the intrusive and bullying conduct they experience. Hence, these antisocial types induce a sense of panic and impotence in the spouse as they do not abide by the rules of the game. Both experienced lawyers and assessors learn to be cautious of such people for they can just as easily re-direct their aggression against the professional if the situation suits them.

As an example, an order for an assessment was obtained in a case involving a family with three children. The couple had married when the wife was 18 and the husband was 25 years old. She had remained submissive for most of the marriage although the husband was unfaithful and controlling during the relationship. On assessment, she appeared brittle, easily rattled and mistrusting. A businessman, he had found numerous ways to hide funds and used this skill to avoid paying appropriate child support and alimony when the marriage ended. His new girlfriend with whom he began a relationship before his marriage ended, accepted his distorted version of events and colluded with his many attempts to bribe and coerce the children into supporting his side over their mother's. He lied to the assessor concerning when he entered into the new relationship although this was discovered much to his chagrin. An older son, especially, became locked in the parent's struggle and suffered greatly in the impasse that developed. The husband simply blamed this mounting pressure on the mother's poor parenting and maintained a frightening pressure on his ex-wife including threats and intimidation. Although the assessment suggested the mother as custodian, the father retained some access. The mother feared, however, that this was simply a first gambit and that he would not ease the struggle until he had triumphed over her.

In assessing antisocial pathology, moral vacuity may be difficult for all assessors to perceive and such people have a knack for soliciting support and slyly organizing their case. This may exceed even what the assessor expects from parents in custody disputes. Such parents do not only try and control the ex-spouse but they extend their efforts to the legal process and the assessment. In some cases, though, such controlling traits may be more subtle and the assessor may perceive very clearly what is occurring although this may not be as evident to others who might be surprised by the assessor's findings. Of course, there are also those situations where the character pathology is well known to all concerned and the assessment, although balanced, will take this factor into account.

In approaching these problems, it is important for the assessor to evaluate the parent's capacity for loving investment with children and not simply to become absorbed by the history of manipulation. Can the adult in question think about the needs of others or are all people simply treated as an extension of their own needs? There is a continuum that exists. On one end are people who employ mild degrees of manipulation whose distortions are solely in the service of winning a court battle regardless of whether it concerns their children or not. These are very different, though, from the overtly sadistic and hurtful parents on the other end who are either callous or paranoid and generally vengeful. Loving investment in a child is a complex quality and should not to be simply equated with knowledge of a child's life or whether the adult attends parent-teacher meetings. Antisocial parents may espouse the greatest respect for their children but underneath they cannot help but exploit them to serve their ends. They treat their children well, therefore, to the degree that the child confirms the parent's needs and aspirations.

8. CONCLUSION

This concludes the discussion of special clinical problems faced in the context of custody disputes. Although this overview does not by any means exhaust the subject, it hopefully provides the practising lawyer with the essence of these concerns and the challenges they impart to the family legal system. Depending on the complexity involved, these cases are best handled by experienced assessors and are not appropriate for "teeth cutting" work. Many of these examples represent adults who would be unlikely ever to seek therapeutic help. As most assessors begin their careers as therapists, it takes time and additional experience to understand and work effectively with this subset of the population. On the other hand, assessors must be prepared to deal with many different manifestations of conflict, dispute and personality and these are often the types of cases that will benefit most from the expert's interventions.

11

Ethics and Custody/Access Assessments: An Assessor's View

The custody assessor is constantly faced with ethical issues to a degree not often met in usual clinical practice. Perhaps this has to do with the mediating role played by assessors who function equidistantly between the courts, the lawyers and the parents. Reports must satisfy various tests for objectivity, neutrality, adequacy, comprehensiveness and relevance to the issues at hand. Furthermore, the assessor is doubly accountable, first to a professional college or governing body in term of standards and procedures and then to the courts which have their own requirements, perspective and rules. In this complex domain, then, the assessor's actions must bear an ethical stamp and be judged by all parties as fair and moral. This presents a formidable challenge to the mature assessor to understand how to balance these concerns while contributing freely and meaningfully to the legal system and family law.

In structuring this discussion, it may be helpful to consider the dimensions of the assessment process as they bear on specific ethical concerns. The intent is not only highlight moral issues but also to familiarize the family law lawyer with the thought processes and challenges faced by the assessor in providing a worthwhile assessment.

From the outset, an ethical dimension is set in motion and is apparent from both sides of the equation. The parents must relate to their own needs and interests as potentially separate from their children's. Similarly, the assessor must arrive at conclusions and recommendations without absolute criteria for any recommendation over another. Clinical judgments, moreover, are based on the assessor's particular way of organizing the psychological facts of the case as they are experienced and understood. Hence, the assessment situation is by nature complex. By examining the ethical texture and situating it within its professional framework, we can hopefully learn more about it.

1. THERAPEUTICS VERSUS ASSESSMENT

The risks of consulting in family law are not lost on assessors as college disciplinary reports often document the problems that face ill prepared or unethical colleagues who tread in this difficult area. Sticking to psychotherapy or other patient-oriented services carries far fewer risks to the health practitioner. Apart from serious breaches of procedure or conduct, most health professionals can usually attend to patients throughout their career without ever facing formal questioning of their actions. The emotional climate of custody disputes and its adversarial tone, however, have little in common with therapeutic relationships. Although the assessor is trained and prepared to make a valid and independent contribution to the family's post-divorce adjustment, this may well be lost on the litigant/parent who is unlikely to view themselves as a "patient" in any sense of the word. In fact, many parents in custody/access disputes might never step foot in a psychologist or psychiatrist's office if it was not for the assessment. This distinction between therapeutic and forensic intervention is an essential difference that all assessors must realize irrespective of their home discipline. Although assessors should always aim at helping the family in question, the two areas bear only moderate resemblance in the light of what is demanded of both the provider and the client.

There are other differences, as well, that bear on the ethical texture of custody assessments. For instance, therapy is based on a mutual although asymmetrical relationship that aims at improving the emotional health of the person receiving help. In contrast, the custody assessment, although not without its therapeutic potential, is focused on decision making and socio-legal aims. If it serves to enhance emotional health, this is a by-product and not a primary goal. In a nutshell, the assessment acts as a consultation to the court stemming from the parents' inability to agree on a solution regarding the care of their children following divorce. In this regard, the parents cede their ethical responsibility to the courts who act in their stead.

Herein lies another major distinction, then, between psychotherapy and court-ordered family assessments. In therapy, the patient is linked personally and directly to the interpretive cause and participates in a to and fro process. The therapist is part of the dialogue and the process is collaborative. The patient experiences relief and psychic change by working with the understandings gained within the interaction of the therapeutic relationship. In the assessment context, however, the relationships are short lived, immersed and less collaborative. The assessor remains in the tradition of the scientist who observes, collects an array of clinical data, organizes this information according to clinical theory and arrives at a pertinent conclusion.

Consequently, the role of therapist and the role of assessor require a different perspective although the same professional likely performs both functions. It is imperative, though, that any mental health professional who undertakes such assessments be fully aware of these differences. Yet, as in psychotherapy, there is always a degree of selectivity in the process and even after a thorough evaluation there remains a degree of uncertainty that always opens the door to other possibilities. This should not be read though as meaning that assessment data is by nature arbitrary or weakly founded. In fact, there is likely to be healthy agreement between assessors within an acceptable range. Although theories and specific training may vary, most assessors would agree on the broad fundamentals of what to look for and how to understand what they see. On the other hand, the very complexity of the task, the varying skills and knowledge of assessors, and the breadth of recommendations available, add an element of uniqueness to each assessment.

Accordingly, if a lawyer in cross-examination risked posing the question of whether another assessor might arrive at a different conclusion with the same data, an assessor could answer "no", not because this is guaranteed but because the question is essentially irrelevant. The issue is not whether hypothetically another professional faced with similar findings could arrive at other recommendations but whether this assessor proceeded reasonably and ethically in arriving at the conclusions articulated in the report. Obviously, there is a direct parallel to the judicial appeal function where the test is based on procedural factors and not whether another judge might arrive at a different conclusion.

Such a personal and intimate process as family assessment will preclude ever standardizing the task completely and this is probably a good thing. Often, the more uniform a process is, the more rigid, insensitive and less attuned it can be to individual nuance and needs. What the practising lawyer requires, then, is not the only assessment possible but simply a good one. A good enough assessment will carry a measure of conviction and will be persuasive even in the face of cross examination. It will not, however, say all that might be said about the family nor will it exhaust other options that could apply. There will be though a rational balance between the analysis and its conclusions so that the former supports the latter. In comparison, the inadequate assessment will fail to convince and moreover it will often add to the discord. This should be differentiated though from the risk of strong disagreement which is always a possibility quite apart from the merits of the assessment.

In the inadequate assessment, there is often a lack of balance and either the body of the report will not support the recommendations or the recommendations will be at odds with the body of the report. For instance, lawyers may find it unsettling to work with a report that suggests custody and access to one parent while seeming to prefer and support the psychological characteristics of the other. Likewise, occasionally one will see a report where the parents are locked in paralyzing non-communication and the assessor incongruously calls for joint custody. By the same token, if a report is mediocre and yet the analysis and recommendations remain in balance, it may well prove acceptable despite its other limitations.

2. SCOPE OF PRACTICE

Ethics are always at the heart of our aims and outlook and they both determine and regulate what we do. When thinking of ethics, we begin to ponder the basis for judgments and how one determines that a process is both responsible and just. This leads to the question of how the assessor goes about the task of studying the family and formulating recommendations. Obviously, a proper procedure is essential to a good result although there are differences about what that procedure might be. In this regard, assessors must clearly define their scope of practice and stay close to their real expertise. For example, some assessors will invite the parents to enter into an agreement based on the findings and will act as a mediator in implementing a final parenting plan. Although fine in theory, this may backfire if the assessor underestimates the recalcitrance and depth of conflict between the parents. Furthermore, it begins to slide into dual roles that is always a potential source of problems when the primary purpose of an intervention is assessment. Hence, although therapeutic ideals are met when the role is stretched beyond pure assessment, ethical concerns may arise especially if the assessor overstates the flexibility and problem solving potential of the parents. It seems, in fact, that how a report is handled or what use is made of it is as important as the strength of its analysis and conclusions.

This touches on the issue of what can reasonably be remedied through custody assessments. Divorce is by nature fragmenting as is human conflict in general and no assessment can retrieve a lost unity that may have always represented an ideal in any case. What an assessment can achieve is a plan that hopefully distributes the energies and capacities of the parents to best meet the needs and desires of the children. Although a good assessment works with what is beneficial and healthy in both parents and children, it must also take into account the undesirable and reckon with limitations and deficits. Although the families are often seen at a low point when psychological resources are most strained, it remains a common error for assessors to expect too much in terms of post-divorce cooperation. Parents who showed little if any capacity to cooperate in raising their children are then asked to do more on this score than they ever managed before. This overestimation of the parents' capacities arises not only from the assessor's wish to bear good news but also from the pressure exerted by lawyers who measure their success in terms of the client's satisfaction with the result. Assessor's who are unused to managing such pressures may find it difficult to remain as autonomous or objective as possible. They may succumb to a mediation of pressures and resort to appeasement rather than assessment.

As an experienced family lawyer once commented in respect to a certain assessor: "Why is it that everyone is always so wonderful in ____'s eyes, just perfect parents and everybody is just perfect." The purpose of an assessment cannot be achieved in this regard if the assessor refuses to acknowledge or state what is known. This is not an invitation to forfeit either tact or balance but stresses the need for frankness from the assessor's side. Unfortunately, as in medicine, some practitioners may become intimidated by the professional risks in custody work and as a result operate too defensively to the detriment of what can be done. Such assessors fear that frankness will increase the probability of complaints and they become more invested in self protection than in the candid evaluation of the family's issues. As noted above this is a major departure from the domain of psychotherapy where unhappy patients tend to go elsewhere rather than lodging complaints that can impact on the assessor's reputation and standing.

In this regard, assessors who are not members of regulated health professions are obviously less vulnerable although their credibility in court and general accountability to the public are also less as well. This counselor group can include pastoral, educational or Adlerian counselors but could also include those with more indistinct qualifications such as in sociology. In general, the lawyer should bear in mind that family assessments in custody matters are an onerous task that require a high level of clinical sophistication and it is important to choose an assessor who can handle this demand and, if need be, establish their qualifications as well as defend their findings in court.

3. CLINICAL FACTS

Clinical facts are facts that arise in the clinic where the aim is to provide timely help. As facts are compiled in the courtroom and lead to judicial decisions, so clinical facts are accumulated and lead to clinical opinions. In common usage, fact pertains to material reality or historical truth. A fact is something that actually exists and is often used as synonymous with reality. In a more general and less restricted view, however, we might also say that fact concerns what has taken place or happened. In this latter definition, the location and form of the fact are not specified. As such, it might be a perception as well as an event as both could be said to have happened. Hence, for example, pain is very much a fact in life at one time or another although it cannot be verified or externally observed. When reported within the health care context to a health professional, it assumes the status of a clinical fact. Pain, of course, can also be of the emotional variety and in a psychiatrist's or psychologist's consulting room, for example, it too would be considered a clinical fact. In the mental health area, such clinical facts are often relational and subjective. By viewing the clinical domain in this way, we can avoid the misconception that all facts must belong to the field of material reality. Shortly, we will note the direct relevance of such distinctions in the domain of custody/access assessments.

One way to understand the nature of clinical facts, then, is to see them as something more than empirical observation. They help explain or give meaning to why something occurred as well as the relationship between facts. In a psychotherapy, these clinical facts can be honed to ever more clarity through a process of clarification and interpretation. In the context of custody assessments, there is usually more indeterminacy and the assessment must often be satisfied with more general themes. Nevertheless, assessors can through their evaluation link clinical facts into clusters that describe and infer. Clinical observation is used to deduce important parent and child variables as well as relational factors that suggest a course of action in settling a child care dispute.

Consider the example where a woman accuses her ex-husband of belligerence and emotional abuse and strongly holds that this negative trait should preclude his receiving a major role in the care of the children. The assessor's task will be to address this issue not as much to confirm or refute it but to understand its meaning in the light of the personalities involved and the marital relationship. In this regard, the compilation of clinical facts may lead to numerous possible explanations (clinical judgments) that will go beyond whether it is a valid accusation or not. For purposes of discussion, several possibilities might be relevant: (a) he is emotionally abusive as she suggests, (b) she perceives him as such for other reasons particular to her own character and background; (c) she is actually the emotionally abusive partner but attributes this negative aspect of herself as belonging to her husband; (d) the allegation of emotional abuse functions as a rationalization to alleviate guilt for the failed marriage; (d) within the couple interaction, he responded aggressively although this may not be an enduring character trait; and (e) he does have character problems that may be best described in other terms.

The assessor's exploration of the clinical facts would be directed at explaining what happened (or is happening) between the ex-couple in a way that is plausible and revealing of their potential as parents. It is actually a construction of the assessor that is formulated through numerous clinical observations and sources of evidence. It is informed by theory and past knowledge, aided by the collaboration of the participants, and leads to the assessor's conviction of certain truths. In the example given, if the husband was truly controlling and domineering, we might observe a denial of aggressiveness and yet be struck by his resentment or cavalier dismissal of others who disagree with him. We might identify as well a dominating authoritarian personality, a disturbed family background, and attempts to intimidate or control the assessor. The point is that in the process of doing the assessment, clinical facts converge to support one hypothesis over others. There is a gradual process of information gathering, synthesis and revision that slowly clarifies the assessor's thoughts. Because it is a process, one shot assessments that collapse the exercise into a single extended session often fail to satisfy the parents' or the court's expectations and often prove unsatisfactory even they are in the end accurate.

Not all data available to the assessor, however, is in the form of clinical facts. School records, reports from other professionals, affidavits and other collateral sources also regularly add to the assessment. How the assessor works with such information is also an important issue. The supposed facts of a case often prove to be highly subjective and a source of dispute. What is absolute fact for one parent can be hog wash to the other. Such variance over the most elemental facts can be quite startling and some ex-couples may disagree on just about everything. Such discrepancies reflect the polarization of the relationship and discordant motivations of the parents as well as their relative capacities for accuracy and integrity. Besides conflicting narratives, parents may consciously distort what is said to amplify their virtues and detract from the rival parent. Hence, the assessor may be ill informed if relying mainly on the attestations of a parent without seeking confirmation in the clinical data.

The task of the assessor, as we see it, is to remain true to the clinical perspective where the assessor's strength lies by steering a path by way of numerous perspectives from different vantage points and with divers procedures. What is finally concluded is usually a fresh outlook that integrates the various versions and inputs and lends new meaning. In this sense, it is not beholden to any one rendition and is not restricted to agreeing with either participant. The assessment should, though, alter the terms of the conflict and provide a more reasonable and balanced way of comprehending the capacities of both parents in the context of their children. Traits that are important are repeated or seen often during the assessment and are observed from individual interviews, psychometrics, collateral sources and through the narrative and observations of the child. These major traits connect and provide deeper meaning to the events and conflicts behind the dispute. More than other factors, they best predict the fate of the post-divorce adjustment. Recommendations are then posed to take into account the assets, liabilities, availability and relational capacities of the parents in order to improve the chances of a satisfactory adjustment.

One can imagine a cross-examination where counsel requests that the assessor explain why, what they deem to know of the parents and children, is actually true. Although the assessor as expert is perfectly entitled to rest on the merits of a well formed clinical opinion, such a question touches on a thorny and complex problem. At the nub of the issue is the distinction between a truth and the whole truth. The assessor is fully capable of reflecting certain truths that are verifiable through repetition and explanatory relevance. Such truths when integrated with recommendations promote a healthier process and aid the legal cause. Nevertheless, the assessor cannot capture the whole truth nor should this be the measuring stick in evaluating the merits of the exercise. Most lawyers who have had experience with assessments can easily speak to their consequence and because they address the more elusive psychological domain does not detract from their value to the legal system. However, we should keep in mind that assessments can only be partial in scope and can never claim absolute certainty. This should not be interpreted as a special limitation, though, but only as a statement of the human fallibility we must all endure.

4. METHOD

It stands to reason that the means used to obtain knowledge and to form judgments must be ethically based. In this regard, they should be professionally acceptable, scientifically sound, logical, common sensible in terms of how people and families actually function and, finally, accurate. It is unethical, for example, to infer sexual abuse solely on the basis of a child's drawing without any strong, reliable collaborative data. It would be equally unethical to make presumptions regarding the custody of a child based on the good word provided by a neighbour or relative who was obviously partial to the cause of one parent. It is acceptable practice, however, to interview neutral professionals who may be able to offer an independent and useful contribution to the assessor's task. In this regard, teachers, doctors, police and social workers, among others, may be important collateral sources and add to the depth of family assessment. Such procedures, although hearsay, are professionally acceptable, sound and logical and can add to the overall accuracy of the assessment. Still, though, such information should be considered secondary and would not replace primary clinical data based on the direct experience of the assessor. This does not imply that such information is unnecessary for it can often be highly instructive and relevant. It is up to the assessor, though, to determine what value to give it.

Breaches in method are common errors in custody assessments which often become the subject of peer discipline. In one example, Dr. X, a psychologist, conducted an assessment for custody in which a principal issue was an allegation of sexual abuse.[1] The College took issue with the lack of detail noted in the report and that personal histories were not taken on any family member. Moreover, some very pertinent information to the allegation was ignored by Dr. X who also failed to observe one of the parents with the children. Based on

---

1 Bulletin of the College of Psychologists of Ontario, December, 1995, 22: 9–10.

inadequately obtained conclusions, Dr. X reported his findings to the police and was instrumental in having a criminal charge laid against a parent who was later acquitted. The College of Psychologists aptly ruled that Dr. X failed to provide services that were in accordance with the profession's accepted ethics and standards. Among the conclusions was that the method employed by Dr. X was neither fair nor objective and that Dr. X had failed to actually provide a custody/access assessment.

Because custody disputes are settled in line with the best interests of the children, it is natural that the methods employed should be oriented to elicit relevant and sufficient data. For example, family relationships, emotional stability, the ability to guide and make good decision and the capacity of each parent to provide a permanent and stable home environment are obviously important in determining custody and access issues. On the other hand, a long list of traits, some of dubious relevance, and others unrelated to the main issues would not be seen as a proper process. Equally, an assessment that simply reflected a child's preference without exploring the actual willingness and ability of each parent to meet the child's needs would also be lacking. There must be a balance between the method employed and what the assessor hopes to address in the assessment; the former has to be the equal of the latter. When the method is faulty either through omission or commission, it is unlikely to garner the support needed and will often become a focus for further conflict. In our experience, an inadequate assessment is often worse for the family and the courts than the lack of one altogether.

For example, in one case a psychiatrist/assessor provided a seven-page report regarding custody of a male child of four years of age. The assessor concluded that there were no "psychiatric contraindications" to either parent assuming the custodial role but the mother was far more in tune with the child. Access of three of every four weekends per month was recommended with the rest of the detail to be left to counsel to devise. The upshot of the evaluation was that the lawyer for the father successfully argued for a re-assessment after a prolonged period of further discord. There was little to recommend the report. It was seven pages long and lacked detail. Basically, it was unworthy of the serious task it undertook.

In this case, the father had raised with the assessor the question of his ex-wife's alcohol abuse and partying habits. She, in turn, referred to his poor treatment of his first wife and lack of honesty in dealing with her. The assessor seemed to assuage both parents by appealing to their essential virtue without exploring these issues or the broader question of their merits and weaknesses as people and parents. Despite reference to a profound stutter, there was also no in-depth discussion of the child. Finally, when the conclusions were offered, one could not tally these with the body of the discussion.

5. COMPLAINTS AGAINST ASSESSORS

Richard Gardner, a well-known psychiatrist and author recalled the day in June 1988 when he finally stopped performing custody assessments.[2] Among reasons cited including the adversary system, client rage and problems with payment, he included the numerous complaints to ethics bodies that he had endured over the years. Although patients will rarely lodge formal complaints, litigants are much more likely to do so. This is especially relevant in cases of custody dispute.

There seems to be at least four major causes of such complaints. First, with the considerable demand for family assessments, some mental health professionals accept to do assessments without any clear understanding of what is involved and will be required of them. Putting all ills into one pot, assessment skills may be marginal, knowledge of custody options meager, methodology superficial, understanding of the legal process inadequate and the final report unconvincing. Depending on professional affiliation, these professionals may be exposed through the complaints process and end up having their names and actions laid before peers in disciplinary actions. Needless to say, it can be a messy business which is unfortunately why the broad majority of mental health professionals avoid doing this type of work.

Secondly, parents who become the subject of assessment may not be those most open to new learning and most adroit in working with compromise. The atmosphere can be coercive especially when the assessment is unwelcome or viewed as based on the other parent's initiative and legal strategy. Such parents may then equate a desired

2 Gardner, R.A. (1989), *Family Evaluation in Child Custody Mediation, Arbitration and Litigation.* Cresskill NJ: Creative Therapeutics.

result with a competent assessment. In fact, they may complain no matter how thoughtful or thorough the assessor has been although this would represent a very small minority. Assessor's must be very careful to ensure that they are operating with the full consent of the parent even if the assessment is court ordered or supported by their lawyer.

Thirdly, even if tendencies to blame are not extreme, litigants may not understand the psychological frame of reference of the assessor and can perceive the assessment in terms of a trial. Perhaps the assessor may not have conveyed the perspective of the assessment nor made available any written information to allay anxieties and increase trust. The assessor may be seeing far more patients than litigants in their daily work and take for granted that the parent comprehends the health professional's benign and impartial point of view. Experience teaches us, though, that parents may well identify the assessor with the adversarial system and wonder whether the assessor has taken sides. Although serious bias is anathema and a grave breach of ethics for assessors, litigants may assume that it is the most likely scenario. When the lawyer is also unsure of an assessor's neutrality and professional attitude, persecutory anxieties may heighten outside of the assessor's awareness and can eventually lead to complaint.

Finally, assessors may err in procedure due to oversight or poor practice and this may in certain situations also lead to complaint. A common example is where an assessor accepts to see one parent with the children and make recommendations for custody and access without seeing the other parent. It is now common practice that both parents must consent to participate in an assessment. Yet, assessors unfamiliar with the process and standards set by most professional groups may become confused if asked, for instance, to evaluate a client who is unhappy with the opinion rendered in a prior assessment. Even though a lawyer may assure the assessor that they can avoid any comments about custody and simply focus on the strengths and weaknesses of the individual, the college or licensing board may view this as a one sided assessment if a complaint is made. The Ontario College of Psychologists, for example, makes this explicit: "If the psychologist makes any recommendation or provides any opinion that could affect these issues, then the report will be viewed by the Board as having been a custody assessment."[3] Lawyers are often surprised by the hard line of such a policy as it may limit an avenue of response in dealing with an unfavourable report. Yet, from experience, the health disciplines have learned to steer a more neutral course that is ultimately respectful of the rights of both parents.

Hence, the best way for lawyers to handle reports that seem grossly inadequate is through a motion seeking re-assessment. If the report is simply unfavourable to their client's view, then the proper recourse is cross-examination during a trial. Mental health experts have learned to shun the role of "hired gun" and any hint of this legacy in domestic legal matters is likely to be viewed as slanted and unethical.

Another frequent cause of complaint occurs when recommendations posed are inadequately supported by the report. Anxious and easily threatened parents may react badly and complain when they see recommendations that seem suspended in mid-air and not grounded to the basic substance of the report. Hence, if an assessor praises the virtue and strengths of both parents and then recommends meager access to the father without any reasonable explanation, the aggrieved parent may reject the report altogether. Parents are more likely to accept a report if it can explain the reasons for the approach taken. If these are inconsistent and especially if not supported by the broad thrust of the findings, then the parent may well conclude that the recommendation is wrong or that the assessor was biased or insensitive.

Besides procedural problems and extreme tardiness or procrastination in preparing a report, perhaps the most frequent complaint is that the assessor was biased from the outset and made his or her determination entirely on fallacious grounds. The assessor may be described as hostile, insensitive, critical or other such adjectives that justify the parent's contempt for a perceived unacceptable result. It is of course very difficult to prove unprofessional bias which is always possible although infrequent. This is different from the intellectual or social inclinations such as whether the assessor approves of joint custody or whether there is an innate preference for mothers. These latter predilections may well be based on a certain reading of the literature as well as professional and even personal experience and are unavoidable. The notion of the perfectly objective assessor or judge

3 Bulletin of the Ontario Board of Examiners in Psychology (now College of Psychologists), July 1990, 17:3.

for that matter is likely an illusion. What is more important is the assessor's philosophy is openly stated so that the court can better evaluate the testimony. It is rare, though, in our experience for an assessor to disqualify a parent simply because of some inherent dislike or prejudice. As lawyers are well aware, professional training and its inherent ideals build safeguards against such an occurrence. On the other hand, there has always been a place in psychoanalysis, for example, for disruptive "countertransference" problems in the analyst which can interfere with the analytic function. This refers to unconscious elements of the therapist that become activated within the interaction with the patient. Hence, it would follow that the same phenomenon is possible in the assessment situation and may contribute to a poor result.

It is obviously no light matter to assess and recommend on the best interests of children when parents are separating, feuding and unable to resolve issues on their own. Assessors generally belong to professional disciplines that view themselves as neutral and scientific and a "patient", for example, would not typically question their therapist's bias. Yet, even when it is unlikely that an assessor based their findings on other than the clinical facts, the allegation of bias may be considered a perfectly legitimate legal tack. Whatever one may think of this strategy, the assessor's mindset seems to be fair game in the cross examination of the report. This approach can be used to cast doubt on the credibility of the assessor as compared to elucidating substantive weaknesses in the content of the report. In some cases, in fact, ethical issues may dominate the focus of scrutiny and each assessment (and assessor) must be prepared to face this test within the adversarial system.

As a final comment on this topic, lawyers may justifiably ask when a formal complaint against a mental health assessor might be warranted in the aftermath of custody litigation. Although it is impossible to indicate all situations, some of the more obvious include: (1) accepting referrals where there is clear lack of specialized knowledge in the areas required to complete a custody/access assessment; (2) accepting referrals where prior relationships or conflicts of interest would prevent necessary objectivity and neutrality; (3) failing to provide a custody assessment that is fair, two sided and comprehensive in pursuit of the issues in question; and (4) failing to report on the findings so that the parties can meaningfully understand the reasons for opinions, interpretations and conclusions. We would hope that this recourse, although open to any member of the public, would be taken only in the more extreme situations. Nevertheless, lawyers are very familiar that such vulnerability is the necessary trade off for the entitlements enjoyed by regulated professional groups. It helps ensure public confidence and ultimately supports the public good.[4]

6. ETHICS AND RECOMMENDATIONS

To introduce this section, we might first look at an example. Mrs. M, a woman of European extraction, was glad to be rid of her husband whom she saw as "old world", rigid and unsuitable for this modern age. She had remarried and it was clear to the assessor that she saw little merit in having the father actively present in the children's lives. She seemed to take delight when any of her three children complained about him and was quietly supportive when they chose to visit less and less often. In contrast, she encouraged their link with her new husband whom she saw as a preferable role model. On the other hand, Mrs. M. was not without her virtues as a parent and the children, the youngest of whom was eleven, were content with her care and quite vocal about their preference. They implied that their negative feelings about their father were earned by his intransigence and insistence that they do chores when visiting. In brief, they also found him rigid and insensitive to their needs. The father, in turn, was bewildered and heart broken and viewed his children as brainwashed. The assessor recommended briefer but regular access and suggested that the children and their father engage in a family therapy to work out these problems. By freeing the children to talk with their father without their mother's direct influence, the assessor hoped to bypass the mother's alienating tendencies and assist the father in adjusting to the children's perspective. The father's lawyer expressed consternation that the assessor would go so "easy" on the underhanded behaviour of the mother. Why should she be allowed to alienate the children with impunity, he queried. At what point, he asked, would she actually lose care and control of the children. Now the assessor was well aware that these were not young children and the feasible options were limited. Fur-

4 Pettifor, Jean L. (1996), "Ethics: virtues and politics in the practice of psychology," *Canadian Psychology,* 37:1–12.

thermore, although the mother was definitely alienating, the children were contributing significantly to the current of indifference towards the father and had little patience for his more awkward ways. Wisely or not, they were making choices and within the family, each reinforced this common sentiment in the other.

In exploring this common dilemma, mental health assessors must adhere to a legal framework where recommendations must not only be moral but applicable to the real situation. It is pointless for a family to undergo the rigorous demands of an assessment which concludes with suggestions that could never be actualized in the circumstances that exist. In this case, for example, if the assessor took the position that the children must visit their father and that it was the mother's task to ensure their compliance in order to keep the custodial role, the likelihood of even greater intransigence would be extremely high. If there was a trial, the children may well be psychologically induced to oppose visitation altogether. It could deepen the alienating structure and finally work against the father's right to have any relationship with his offspring. It is this demand for realism that adds a measure of complexity to assessments and can create a tension between what is just and what is possible in a given family system.

This example also highlights the necessary limits of assessments in the family legal system. It is the prerogative of a judge to hold people responsible for their actions and to reinforce the rules of conduct and fair play. The assessor, therefore, must stop short of acting in a judicial fashion or infringing on the responsibility of judges.[5] The role of the assessor is rather one of expert with the obligation to educate, inform and furnish a uniquely clinical perspective. Moreover, as it is the court's function to ultimately determine these matters, experts play an advisory role. Yet, mental health experts are often quite comfortable addressing these ultimate issues with the emphasis on providing cogent reasons on the advisability of following a certain path. The focus of the assessment should, however, remain in the realm of clinical fact and opinion as compared to the wider scope of evidence available to the court. It is this clinical orientation that sustains the often weighty impact of an assessment on the resolution process. Hence, evaluations that are primarily based on second-hand sources lose this critical focus and inevitably dilute the value of

5 Weissman, H.N. (1991), "Child custody evaluation: fair and unfair professional practices", *Behavioral Science and the Law*, 9:469–476.

the report. We can speak, therefore, of a report's gravitational centre which is best kept close to the assessor's own primary focus. In this respect, the more the gravitational centre of the assessment is removed from the real skills and expertise of the assessor, the less convincing the findings are likely to be.[6]

Another important factor concerns the relationship between lawyer and assessor during the assessment process. It stands to reason that the process must occur free of any personal influence from lawyers or other sources. Hence, assessors prefer to have as little contact with the lawyers while the process is ongoing. There may be need for administrative contact in order to obtain relevant documentation, for example, but in general there should be no unilateral communication as regards the thoughts or opinions of the assessor. Experienced lawyers routinely respect the assessor's responsibility not only to maintain neutrality but to avoid even an impression of bias. In this regard, we are reminded of a case where a lawyer suddenly discovered in the latter stages of an assessment that the opposing lawyer in a previous career had once been employed by the assessor. Needless to say, the assessment was instantly "dead in the water" for its objectivity could no longer be assured.

As a further variable, clinical opinions should be based on a grasp of all the relevant information that bears on a specific case. Consequently, it is important that the lawyer provide all documents and records that the assessor may need to complete a thorough evaluation. If the lawyer or client believes that a certain record should be obtained in order to meet the standard of completeness, then this should be communicated in advance to the assessor. It profits the assessor and the assessment if the clients and their lawyers are satisfied that the assessor has access to all the relevant facts and history.

Having applied an accepted assessment methodology, the mental health expert is then able to formulate clinical opinions to respond to the issues raised in the initial referral and statement of the problem. This may simply relate to the best interests of the children but it might also address parental fitness, special needs of a child, substance abuse, parental alienation, violence or sexual abuse. Hence, the questions to be answered in the assessment can be complex and multivariate. In this regard, it benefits all concerned that the referral issues are clearly

6 Diamond, B.L. (1973), "The psychiatrist as advocate", *Journal of Psychiatry and the Law*, 1:7–19.

spelled out and not left to the chance of miscommunication. Sometimes this is obvious but on other occasions it may be less clear cut. For example, what appears to be vague allegations of interparental violence or alcoholism may, if not spelled out as a focus for evaluation, appear after the fact as a major oversight in the assessment. In other situations, it may be unclear whether the issue is custody/access or simply access that is under consideration. It is very important that in correspondence with the assessor that the lawyers indicate what issues should be specifically addressed in the assessment. Assessors should not undertake a psycholegal evaluation unless there is full agreement among the parties as to what are the germane problems or questions to be answered in the report. It is an issue of full disclosure and full compliance with the aims of the assessment that bear on its eventual success.

7. THE MORAL COMMUNITY

Assessors, lawyers and parents share a common ethical responsibility to protect the psychological interests of children and families. There is good reason to believe that when such a perspective is kept at the forefront, children do better than expected in adjusting to the strains of divorce.[7] This brings to mind that recommendations must be good for children and not simply suited to the demands and needs of their disputing parents. Here the courts and lawyers must also prove their integrity in the process by walking the fine line between pursuing a client's case and protecting the right of the client's children to receive a developmentally beneficial outcome. This is where psychological research has much to offer the legal system and can provide a scientific base on which to discuss these factors.

What are required, then, are good recommendations that reflect what we know of human development. For example, for very young children, prominence should be given to stability, attachment to the custodian(s), and continuity. Look for frequent but shorter access to the non-custodian. For preschoolers, emphasis should be on routine and an atmosphere of acceptance to both parents. For school age children, look for longer periods of time with the custodian and

7 Wolman, R. and Taylor, K. (1991), "Psychological Effects of Custody Disputes on Children," *Behavioral Sciences and the Law:* 9: 399–417.

parents who can control their hostile sentiments and not expose the children to chronic strife. The emphasis needs to be on school and peer adjustment with supportive parental environments. By adolescence, children need to individuate beyond the family circle. Yet, parental support is still important and adolescents need to be kept away from parental worries as much as possible. Look for parents who have the psychological autonomy to adjust to their life change or crisis without leaning so heavily on their teenage child that it thwarts development.

As part of this moral commitment, as well, is knowledge that children grow and change and parenting plans should be adjusted accordingly. Recommendations need to be detailed enough to take this into account rather than limiting the scope and forcing the parents in a few years to face again the same procedure. At the same time, it is fruitless to provide vague and open ended suggestions that leave too much scope for endless debate. Children and families, in this regard, need stability and a feeling of permanence. Clinical experience would hold that an agreement that was slightly unsatisfactory in terms of access would be easier for a child to bear than one that left the parents with endless opportunities for dispute.

Part of this moral commitment, then, is the recognition that parents, lawyers and assessors, although assuming different roles, are linked in a common cause. The moral community is an expression of this common conscience and awareness that we are links in a chain of responsibility with the welfare of children at the heart of the process. When parents are seen in the context of custody disputes, currents of splitting, blame and despair can engulf the very action that is trying to sort matters out. It is vital that lawyers encourage parents to keep an observing eye on the broader moral issue and not be totally consumed by their experience of disappointment and hurt.

8. CONCLUSION

Ethics is a powerful and compelling topic that has taken us deeply into the core of legal and mental health work. We have hopefully seen the merit of expanding the notion of ethics to where it can be used as an insightful guide in decision making and not simply to represent standards of practice that must not be breeched. Whenever we attempt to intervene in the passions of human life, and family law does just that, we are invariably faced with ethical dilemmas and complexity that require a clear eye and a rigorous format. Hopefully this chapter has emphasized this requirement in the context of custody/ access work.

12

Case Studies

In this chapter, we hope to familiarize the family law lawyer not only with examples of reports, which they may already have in abundance in their own files, but more importantly with the thinking leading the assessor to the conclusions reached. Of course, this is somewhat individualistic and would differ depending on the experience, methodology and clinical orientation of thc assessor. Hopefully, though, a review of several cases will communicate more of the actual flavour of these assessments and the difficult issues they pose for the assessor, the lawyers and the court.

CASE 1

We begin with a hotly contested case where two experienced family lawyers represented two vibrant and well educated parents with two young children.[1] At the time of the assessment, they both remained in the family home awaiting a legal outcome as regards custody and the sale of their house. Although it appeared that the matter was court bound, the lawyers skillfully managed to resolve the matter along the lines suggested in the report. Of significance from an assessor's view was to determine what combination of custody and access would provide the scope that the children and parents needed from each other. This had to be weighed against their conflicting

1 See Chapter 13, "Analysis and Commentary of Case Study".

styles that threatened to create an impasse that could ultimately stymie the family's adjustment. This touches on the difficulties faced often in these matters when both parents are capable, devoted and very involved with the children but cannot get along nearly well enough to enjoy the fruits of joint custody. Consequently, such a case example is chosen for the very reason that neither parent has a clear advantage over the other and the assessor cannot easily discern a direction to follow.

We have chosen to reproduce the report in most of its entirety in order to give the thread if its argument and to give one full example of an accepted style of reporting. The parents were seen over five sessions each as well as being administered the MMPI-2, a clinical personality inventory. The children were seen once in the office with each parent and once in a home visit. There were several collateral consultations that were also obtained and discussed in the report. All names, of course, are fictitious and details have been altered to protect confidentiality.

Reason for Assessment

The initial session with each of the parents reflected their very different personalities and dispositions. Mr. A was succinct and to the point: "Since Tanya was born five years ago I have taken the exclusive role of caring for the children." He is confident that he is the primary parent for the children and that he should be granted sole care and control when he and Mrs. A physically separate. He believes that his wife's non-involvement in the care of Tanya and Sean has been apparent since the children were born.

Mrs. A, from her side, focused on the relationship between her and Mr. A. She referred to the two attempts at marriage counseling and her own psychotherapy with Dr. B, a local psychiatrist. She summarized that the marital relationship reached a "stalemate" and that her husband informed her on May 4th that he had contacted a lawyer. She described herself as shocked that his demands for the children were as excessive and that she has to fight for her presence in their lives. "I am not going to give my children away," she explained. Although she had expected a demand for joint custody, she rejects her husband's position as reflective of the "emotional abuse" which she believes permeated their relationship.

The assessment, therefore, was undertaken to clarify the nature of this interaction, to investigate the relative aptitudes of the parents, and to harmonize these findings with the best interests of their two children, Tanya, five, and Sean, three years of age.

Mr. A

Mr. A, 35 years of age, joined the Acme Company when he was 24 and has spent the last 11 years with this employer. His description of the couple's parenting record emphasizes his dominant role in the care of the two children. Despite his five day per week work schedule, he claims that he cared for Tanya "almost exclusively" during the weekend. Mrs. A, he suggests, disliked cooking and "never prepared a meal." His portrayal leaves no doubt that in his perception he and the family's nannies raised the children with only marginal and inconsistent support from Mrs. A. He relates that it has been he who cared for the children during the evenings and that he "got up exclusively at night" beyond the short duration when the children were breast fed.

When he turns to his wife's general sense of responsibility, he remains equally unflattering. "Mrs. A has a great appetite for spending," he advised, and this has created a major financial problem for them. In part, he believes, this has been fostered by an unnecessary reliance on hired caregivers. He believes that his wife's failure to manage responsibility has been a major contributor to their present financial woes. He explained that Mrs. A has avoided being alone with the children and her reliance on external help is excessive and unnecessary. He suggests, that his wife's unilateral dismissal of their nanny after the breakup to become a "full time homemaker" has no precedent and occurred in consort with her lawyer. Mr. A feels that the children have suffered from the absence of their mother and in his judgment she has failed to adequately respond to the children's needs.

Mr. A is frank that the couple's marriage has been "on the rocks" for some time. When they began marriage counseling, the theme of Mrs. A's lack of responsibility was one of the major issues. He admits that the first counselor they saw viewed him as "emotionally abusive".

He feels though that this became a convenient label for his wife to discount what she did not want to hear. "She is accustomed to having her way," Mr. A noted, implying that designating him as abusive may be an attempt to avoid her own responsibility for what transpired. In any case, Mr. A did not feel comfortable with the counselor's approach and he was not aware that the referral emanated from his wife's psychiatrist, Dr. B, whom his wife was seeing without his knowledge.

Mr. A felt more compatible with the approach of Dr. W, the second marriage therapist attended by the couple. Mr. A considered the social worker to be "biased" towards his wife's point of view and that Dr. W was "neutral". Dr. W clarified for Mr. A that he was feeling "emotionally blackmailed" by his wife. "She would threaten me with something," he noted, "if I disagreed." He recalled Dr. W as telling Mrs. A, "at your age, you must take responsibility for your actions." He feels that Dr. W viewed him as open and direct in contrast to his wife whom he offered to see individually as she was unable to open up. "I am not perfect", he concluded, "but she could not accept constructive criticism". Although the couple dealt with their conflicts within these sessions, he does not recall that they addressed any problems in child rearing at that time.

Mr. A's general impression of his wife is that she is often unrealistic and unable to face the difficult realities of life. Money seems especially important to his sense of grievance. When his wife wanted to attend a concert in another city this past March, he felt that he had reached the end of his tolerance. He sought legal counsel at this stage as he believed that she would never be the responsible person he needed in a spouse. In comparing himself and Mrs. A, Mr. A observed: "I have been there every step of the way without exception." As to his wife, he states, "she abhors responsibility." As is clear from these remarks, he has little respect for Mrs. A's autonomy or maturity as a wife and parent. Despite an 11 year marriage, he appears to discredit her as negligent and wasteful. He also emphasizes that she is very dependent and requires someone on whom she can constantly rely.

Mr. A feels misunderstood and undermined in this process. He sees himself as someone who, although born with a loud voice, has made every effort to be a good husband. He conveys that he bears a strong sense of responsibility for others and that he felt he had to provide Mrs. A with what she desired. He feels that this may explain why he agreed to the debt that now saddles them. Although he is a successful employee at Acme, he tries to maintain a balance between family and business concerns. Although ambitious, he accepts that this may limit his ultimate rise in the company.

Mr. A contends that he often felt insecure with Mrs. A and feared that, "she would up and leave if she didn't have her way". He questions whether she has really made "genuine efforts" and states that did not sense "good will." Expressing the broader picture, he maintains that many people were shocked by their separation and that his reputation as "a caregiver" is well known.

It is important to note that Mr. A views his wife and her family as trying to drive him from the home. They behave as if Mrs. A must not be alone with him lest she be hurt. In this regard, he feels manipulated by the consistent effort to depict him as aggressive and abusive. His sense of being treated unfairly is pronounced. "I was giving my all", he noted, "and Mrs. A said I was 100 percent at fault". Besides these injustices, he also questions the objectivity of others who have taken the side of his wife.

Mr. A expressed often in our interviews that he feels unappreciated and misperceived in a cantankerous legal process. He is concerned that his wife's "charm" and vulnerability will mislead others into seeing her as a victim of his abuse. He adds that he too was prone to protect Mrs. A and that this may explain part of the reason why they are at the edge of financial ruin. In this regard, he emphasizes that their debt is onerous and they are still living with a budgetary deficit. His plan is to remain with Acme and if awarded custody to carry on with "business as usual."

History of Relationship

Mr. A was first drawn to Mrs. A's obvious allure and the two shared several common interests. He was already working for Acme and she was pursuing a chemistry degree. As he was facing a move related to his job, the couple made a choice to be married and move together.

This was the second longer term relationship for Mr. A. He had one other during the latter two years of university but ended it when he did not feel an intellectual compatibility. With Mrs. A, however, he felt that he could talk freely and be understood.

Apparently, problems started between the two families during the planning of the wedding. Mr. A believes that his wife focused entirely on her parents and ignored his who wished to be equally involved. Despite these cracks, though, he recalls the relationship with Mrs. A as positive and their thoughts soon turned to having a family. At the time of Tanya's birth, there is no report of fighting or dissension.

Following Tanya's birth, the couple incurred expenses that later on proved burdensome. The financial implications of certain decisions may not have been fully reconciled with their resources and it is at this juncture that Mr. A remembers conflicts beginning. In defence of his own contribution, he noted that Mrs. A had fundamentally different views and that, "Mrs. A always had an answer to things." He recalled that Mrs. A would refer to him as obsessive regarding money but he is now aware that these problems were genuine.

The fate of the marriage and their financial circumstances seem to go hand in hand in Mr. A's narrative. At the end of the marriage, he noted, they were spending more than their income. "I am at the brink of insolvency," he stated. He felt caught in a bind with his wife who referred to him as emotionally abusive when he raised these contentious issues whereas he feared bankruptcy if he did not. Despite these problems, he contends that he "went along with all of it".

The couple attempted to find worthwhile investments to support their lifestyle. He recalls financial problems as beginning as early as two years into the marriage and attributes them to Mrs. A's greed. "Mrs. A would want that piece of jewelry or that piece of furniture," he related. He claims that Mrs. A was never able to save to buy and that he was unable to say no to her. In this regard, he observed, "I had to keep her happy." He attributes this motivation to his love for his wife and to his confidence that he would do whatever, "if this is what it takes to make her happy." In this vein, he agreed to expenditures that he now realizes were excessive in terms of their real financial situation and they learned to live on an expanding line of credit.

Two years after Tanya was born, Mrs. A gave birth to Sean. They moved from an apartment to a town house and the extras they requested added financial strain at that time. Mrs. A's characteristic way of dealing with difficult issues, he recounted, is to avoid and that his is "to address issues and go on." This pattern, he feels, is partly responsible for the poor collaboration between them. Their conflicts came to include life style. Mr. A noted that he enjoyed socializing as families and preferred child oriented activities while his wife favored a more active social life on their own. He alleges that she considered him "a dead beat" and he felt frustrated by their lack of common values.

Psychological Findings

The accuracy of Mr. A's MMPI profile was diminished by a defensive response bias. He seemed unwilling to admit minor flaws and claimed unrealistic virtue. Despite these tendencies, though, the profile would also suggest that he can be effective in many normal situations; yet, it also reflects a pattern of inflexibility and moral rigidity that may undermine his capacity to work his way through complex interpersonal issues. He can be counted on to be socially conforming and naturally gravitates to a leadership role. Yet, he may overestimate his capacities and he can turn to blame when events oppose or frustrate him. Such people may not always have the insight or knowledge of consequences that their actions bring. Overall the profile is typical of someone who wants very much to be a competent and responsible person and who makes this a priority. Yet he does not seem to always handle inadequacy feelings well and he may tend to deny them. This limits needed flexibility and can narrow the opportunity for new learning.

As he suggests, Mr. A has no problems with anxiety and he is very much in control of his tension. He does not suffer from excessive guilt or depression and he can be relied upon to be an active, vigorous and alert man who values success and achievement. The profile is strongly reflective of a competitive personality and someone whose desire to achieve should stand him in good stead. Such people create a very positive impression and appear to be as capable as they are confident and persistent. On the other hand, when problems become straining, they may become less tolerant and can be seen by others as critical and blaming. Mr. A, then, is open with his resentment and anger but he may not as readily see his own contribution to interpersonal difficulties.

What is most positive on the profile is the extent to which he is likely to be responsible, efficient and dependable. He is a practical person and someone more at home with concrete details of life and living. When not threatened, he can be cheerful and very friendly. He is by nature very sociable, talkative and engaging. He can take advantage of opportunities when they present but he may not always anticipate the consequences of actions or the effect they may have on others. This is especially true when interpersonal conflicts ensue and he may become aggressive as a way of coping. This is the unfortunate negative side to a personality that can otherwise be resourceful, stable and determined.

Conclusions

Mr. A said numerous times that he is an open person who speaks bluntly and to the point. I found no evidence to suggest that he is not caring nor concerned about his children. Mrs. A raises the issue that the children can become afraid of his aggression and this may be true in certain circumstances. This would be more a question of style than representing any real threat to their person. On the other hand, the interview material and psychological testing reflect his tendency to be categorical and extreme in his judgments. He had a tendency in the interviews to control the content and to endeavour to influence how Mrs. A was to be seen in the evaluation. Unfortunately this detracted from his many positive features and added this element of rigidity and control that is emphasized by his wife. I concluded that Mr. A very much wants the best for his children and views himself as best able to provide for them. In his perspective, he has assumed the role of exclusive provider with Mrs. A as the secondary parent. Obviously, this is unacceptable to Mrs. A who shares the home and duties with the children. Of course this implicates the couple dynamics that are in the end likely more telling than a description of either one in isolation.

Mrs. A

In this transition period, Mrs. A is not now employed outside the home. She began our discussions by recounting the couple's attempts to repair their marriage. It was her psychiatrist who referred them to a social worker and when this did not work out, Mr. A requested that he find someone of his choosing. They saw Dr. W then for six to eight months but the marriage and her essential unhappiness remained unaltered. They then sought the help of a mediator and the focus shifted to one of separation. Mrs. A indicates that although she anticipated a difficult separation, she never considered that he would request sole custody. She now views their relationship as polarized and at an impasse whereas before she would have listened to proposals for shared parenting. In this sense she fully acknowledges Mr. A's role as a parent but cautions that his deficits and personal style are daunting and limiting.

Mrs. A's reason for consulting the psychiatrist revolved around chronic feelings of sadness, loneliness and upset. It was the social worker's identification of her husband as emotionally abusive that provided a turning point and crystallized her motivation to leave the marriage. Apparently the counselor warned Mrs. A that if he acted this way to her he may well respond in a similar way to the children.

Mrs. A does not negate the fact that Mr. A has been an active father but she resists his portrayal of her as irresponsible or non-involved. She worked part-time when the children were young and a live-in nanny assisted with the care when she was not around. Yet when she was home she fully attended the children's needs. She feels that much of his ammunition against her stems from the fact that she was forced to find part-time work at odd hours in order to increase their cash flow. This was a mutual decision and they both did not anticipate how disruptive it might be. This took her away from the children at inopportune times but it was certainly not of her choosing. "Mr. A was pushing me to work and make money," she reiterated, "and he told me I had to and I felt responsible to do that."

Mrs. A related that money pressures were significant but that she has never had a full accounting from Mr. A. It was evident that she was more than willing to work and that she had provided income to the family for the majority of their years together. Yet it was also apparent that she deferred to Mr. A on financial matters and felt that he exerted a final say in most of these concerns. Hence, she is surprised that he now blames her for all their troubles as if she was solely instrumental in incurring their present debt load.

The general tenor of her comments reflects the distress she feels in the marriage. "I told him repeatedly that he scares me," she observed, "he has hit me, is very controlling and I don't love him - I have some concerns that he hits the children and screams at me that I don't know how to discipline the children." She views herself as a more "laid back" person than Mr. A whom she says imposes himself on the situation. She underlines that her contribution to their lives is substantial and that the image Mr. A convey does not reflect her real input. Further, she feels that his style is limited to activity and that it is she who talks to the children and works with their feelings and emotions. She believes that Mr. A takes every opportunity to re-write situations so that they emphasize his righteousness while making her look bad in the eyes of others. She is aware, as well, and he has told her, that he will prove her unfit during this assessment. Underneath she feels that it is her growing personal strength that has proven most unacceptable to her husband and has led to the breakdown of the marriage.

Mrs. A has been seeing a psychiatrist for approximately one year with the focus being on her marital problems. She noted that at the outset, "I wasn't myself" and that she found herself crying and unwilling to spend time with Mr. A. She alluded to a pattern of withdrawal and escape from the marriage and noted that this had begun early in their union. Mrs. A observed that she often blamed herself for these actions and considered herself the cause of their problems. "Why would he tell me that I am a bad mother", she contemplated. Mrs. A described what she felt was a pattern of constant undermining and criticism that had a seriously negative impact. Because she felt that he would be uncomfortable, she never told Mr. A that she was being treated by the psychiatrist and he has only recently learned of the intervention.

Mrs. A sees Mr. A as results oriented and always focusing on activity. Rather than say, "how are you," for example, he will say "what are you doing." She can understand how he might impress others as he involves himself directly and needs to be visible. "He is a doer," she added, "and I am more laid back, more emotional; I am the one who talks to the children." Mrs. A asserts in no uncertain terms that her relationships with her children are strong and that she does not take a back seat to her husband.

History of the Relationship

Ms. A met her husband when in her late teens. During the early stages of the relationship, her father, with whom she is very close, was injured in a serious car accident. She feels that this event was a turning point not only in that it changed her father but that it may have precipitated her marriage as a defence against the distress of the event. She spoke positively of Mr. A prior to the marriage and felt drawn by his outgoing and apparently strong nature that she found appealing. She felt that he, "would take care of me." The couple dated for two years before marriage.

Predicting the divisiveness that followed, Mrs. A outlined that the families did not get along well and that divisions were prominent from the outset. Mr. A's parents apparently became the focus of arguments and she recalls that he struck her during one of these disagreements. Yet, she also recalls that Mr. A was very supportive of her schooling and credits him with help in the final two years of her chemistry degree. They also enjoyed common leisure interests such as golf and swimming. The romantic element, so prominent prior to marriage, quickly receded, however, and she never felt particularly desirous of intimacy with him. The gist of her comments suggests a rapid decline in her sense of trust and closeness and she quickly shifted into a pattern of avoidance and disavowal. Underlying this, Mrs. A now believes that she became diminished in the relationship and changed from being a leader and a positive person to someone more inhibited and intimidated. "I felt that he was always right," she described, indicating that she was more inclined to surrender than to relate. "I have the feeling that I have been dead a long time," she offered in summary, again outlining the extent to which she sees the marriage as a deleterious experience. This extends in her mind to her in-laws who also shared a denigrated view of her as did her husband. She feels that Mr. A conveyed a negative image of her and that this influenced how his parents as well as friends might view her. In a more positive tone, though, Mrs. A added that, "now I am beginning to believe that I am not that person."

Mr. A worked long hours but they were able to travel together with Tanya on occasion. She continued to work part time and arranged for a part time nanny. She recalls that Mr. A would often enhance his image as a parent and took pride that he also got up with the children at night. She noted that she resented his exaggerations of the truth and his need to bolster his contribution. She agrees that he was a morning riser and she was a night person and that he would get up with Tanya on Saturday mornings but her general attitude was non-competitive.

Mrs. A views Mr. A as promoting his positive image and always findings ways to undermine her influence or participation. "I have faults," she noted. "and I am not near perfect but he blames a lot. . .". She tolerated her husband's need to see himself as the family mainstay but views this as an expression of his emotional need more than a reality.

From the earliest stages of the marriage, finances were an issue, according to Mrs. A. She feels wrongly judged by her husband and defends her track record. "I am not trying to bankrupt the family," she observed, "I am just as concerned as he is." This theme whereby she defends herself against his criticisms seems important. Mrs. A describes Mr. A as very controlling. For instance, during most of the marriage he would telephone from work "5 or 6 times a day" to "check up" on her. She did not view this as his fear of infidelity as much as it was a need on his part to know where she was and to maintain control. This general level of surveillance escalated at their worst times into a pattern of badgering where she would be blamed for their problems.

It is also evident that despite her psychiatric help, Mrs. A finds it difficult to stand up to her husband. On several occasions she observed that she continues to be intimidated by his assertiveness and easily prone to self doubt. She feels that there has been little acceptance of her in the marriage although now she is beginning to resist his efforts to convey reality in his self serving terms. As to what transpires when she makes suggestions, she noted, ". . . if I suggest it, he won't hear me, unless it comes from him."

Family History

Mrs. A notes that she has excellent relationships with both of her parents. She considers her father to be an objective and supportive person and she appreciates his assessments of situations. He has always been close to her and is a helpful person. Mrs. A notes that she is also close to her mother and that they speak on the telephone daily. She describes her mother as extremely giving and caring and that she would go to any length to help her children. Mrs. A notes that Mr. A has never liked her mother although her mother tried and was attentive.

She describes the atmosphere growing up as exceedingly positive with no serious problems. She considered herself to be a popular and healthy child and observed that the family enjoyed many activities together.

Her father's accident when she was a teenager shattered the innocence of her life and her fears of losing him seem to have been especially traumatic. Apart from this incident, however, Mrs. A describes little in the way of detail that would texture her life and deepen its meaning for her. She seems to have been good at school and had no difficulties making friends. Outgoing, she had many boyfriends although none were particularly serious. Yet, when she met Mr. A she seems to have welcomed his leadership and looked to him to fulfil a role equal to her father's. It suggested an innocence and an expectation of an ideal protective relationship.

Psychological Findings

Ms. A's MMPI-2 profile pointed to some degree of denial as well as difficulties obtaining deeper self-understanding and insight. Such people may not be resilient under stress and pressure and this may lead to feelings of inner confusion. She seems to be hesitant about close emotional involvement and she may not be in as much control of herself as she would desire. On the other hand, she can be creative as well as versatile and she does seem to enjoy challenge. There is evidence of healthy ambition and a capacity to engage in life with a high degree of interest.

When more relaxed, we could expect Mrs. A to convey a good impression and to be likable, outgoing and friendly. She reports considerable social interests, confidence and an affable spirit. The profile suggests spark and enthusiasm as well as considerable psychic energy and vitality.

As might be expected, Mrs. A's profile also reflected some tension and agitation. This is coupled with underlying hostility that is poorly expressed within her personality. This underlying anger and resentment leads to bodily tensions and diminished self esteem. Although she suffers from inadequacy feelings, there are no major indications of depression evident. Yet, she obviously feels deflated by what has happened in her life and she can be overwhelmed by her self doubts and self criticism. Although she has considerable energy and can be both persistent and reliable, she feels guilty when she falls short of her goals. This is typical of someone who is emotionally burdened and dissatisfied. Lack of ease in expressing herself verbally and a lack of overall efficiency seem characteristic. The more tense she becomes, the more constricted and yielding she can be, despite a competent nature. This is the down side to an otherwise sensitive, modest and idealistic person who tends to think the best of others while fearing the worst about herself.

Although many of these problems have been intensified by the marital discord, they are not entirely due to this factor alone. It seems that despite Mrs. A's apparently positive family background, she does not always bear up well under stress and she has had difficulty coping with complex problems. She is an internalizing person who is best suited to a cautious and supportive environment. I think it clear that she needed more emotional support that was available in the marriage and the lack of it filled her with tension and uncertainty. One can recall Mrs. A's observation that the crisis of her father's illness propelled her into an alliance with Mr. A whom she perceived as strong and as someone able to take care of her. The issue of emotional reliance is highlighted here as well as a difficulty in handling stress and pressure.

Conclusion

I can certainly agree with Mrs. A that she is now making those individual steps that will surely reinforce her personal adjustment in the future. One has the sense that her psychotherapy and even the marriage breakdown are for her liberating experiences that are essential to her life as a mature woman. The years of her marriage to Mr. A did not offer those integrating experiences that are so necessary in that transition between adolescence and adulthood. She seems to have yielded to a model of dependency that did not serve her well. In this model, the dependency is weakening rather than helping her to forge her own resources. Her flight from the distress of her father's car accident and its link in her mind to the marriage emphasizes this vulnerability. I could certainly see the effects of this emotional dependency on Mrs. A's personality as well as her struggles to lift away from it. She is working very hard now to gain autonomy and emotional maturity and in this aspect one can commend her efforts. I appreciated her flexibility and capacity to acknowledge her husband's contributions as well as her caution in jumping to conclusions.

Integration of Findings

The combination of their personalities was likely to exacerbate matters for both Mrs. A and Mr. A. There was little capacity to work together and pursue common goals. Rather, each phase of their marriage split them further while Mr. A blamed Mrs. A and Mrs. A blamed herself. On the other hand, one can appreciate Mr. A's complaint that Mrs. A evaded the tough realities and took refuge behind a wall of innocence. One can see a problematic if not vicious circle developing whereby Mrs. A would defer to Mr. A and trust in his leadership while Mr. A would blame Mrs. A for the financial and lifestyle problems they were experiencing. In the end, each feels bereft of the real strength and partnership they needed from the other and what remains is a struggle to see whose shoulders will bear the blame.

Mr. A is action oriented and an excellent organizer but it is unfair for him to suggest that all their problems are Mrs. A's doing. Mrs. A, on her part, is a sincere and tender person but it would be unjust for her to attribute all her adjustment problems to the behaviour of her husband. No doubt, though, Mr. A has not matched his professional achievement with success on the marital front and Mrs. A has yet to achieve the emotional independence and strength befitting her years. Unfortunately, as well, the marriage likely amplified their weaknesses rather than attenuating them. In this sense, each appears at their worse in interaction with the other which furthers their polarization.

As people, however, both parents are likable and motivated. It is obvious that they love their children and are extremely interested in providing for them. They are dedicated parents whose own parents were dedicated to them. This is a positive finding and one that should aid the family in the events that follow. Despite their personal virtues, though, their grievances against each other are notable. It is may not be surprising as well to discover that there is some merit in each one's condemnation of the other. Hence Mrs. A may have been too passive, yielding and dependent and Mr. A may have been too overbearing and too willing to control their lives. Unfortunately, a marriage founded on themes of dominance and dependence may easily regress into a destructive encounter where complaints of abuse and victimization arise.

Collateral Consultations

Dr. B (Psychiatrist for Mrs. A)

Mrs. A has seen Dr. B in once weekly psychotherapy. As his letter indicates, she has certainly earned his unequivocal support in this matter. Dr. B concludes that his patient suffers from stress due to a marriage he concludes to have been "physically, verbally and emotionally abusive". He highlights that Mrs. A has always kept the well being of the children foremost in mind and places her own needs secondary to them. Dr. B observes that many incidents described by Ms. A convince him that she has been victimized by the control and aggression of her husband. Dr. B believes that Mr. A systematically undermined the individuation of his patient through emotional and physical means. He suspects that Mr. A is explosive and denigrating and he questions his capacity to control his temper. Dr. B feels that Ms. A is at risk if she were to continue to reside with her husband and he believes strongly that she is not prone to exaggeration or is by nature easily intimidated.

There is much in this report that would correspond to my perception although I have a certain advantage of seeing all parties in a context of neutrality. If I err in these assessments it is likely to be in the opposite direction of Dr. B; that is, giving too much benefit of the doubt. As a therapist, advocacy is no sin and Dr. B is clearly alarmed by what he has consistently heard about Mr. A. We can also understand, though, that Mr. A may feel disadvantaged by being judged by a health professional whom he has never met. Interestingly, Dr. B's letter says much more about the character of Mr. A than it does about Mrs. A. I suspect that Dr. B is aware that his view is one sided but feels that there is sufficient support for this side to purport its truth. I would provide two notes of caution. The first is that I have too much respect for psychic reality to draw conclusions about a complex relationship from the perceptions of only one spouse. By psychic reality I am not referring to fantasy versus reality but rather to the inflections, unconscious motivations and subjectivity that colour how we interpret events. I would have felt more at ease if Dr. B had concentrated on Mrs. A's personality where his knowledge would have been on firmer ground. Secondly, relationships are usually not one sided and it is difficult in my experience to fully grasp a relationship from seeing one spouse. This is especially true when the relationship is conflictive and disintegrating and where violence or control is raised as an issue.

Dr. W

Dr. W, a psychologist, saw the couple in couple therapy with the hope of saving their marriage. His general point of view reflects an appreciation of their interactive dynamics rather than focusing on either party as responsible for the marriage failure. Dr. W observed that Mr. A could "come across" as controlling, aggressive and powerful" but that underneath he was emotionally "needy" and required much recognition. Mrs. A, Dr. W felt, seemed overly dependent on her family and had looked to Mr. A "to take charge of her". He felt that she was initially content with Mr. A assuming the dominant role but when her own needs for autonomy increased the marital problems ensued. Dr. W views Mrs. A's assertions of abuse as her "presentation". It is his view that this reflects a means to control the relationship as was Mr. A's "external" efforts which included taking over as well as projecting blame. Dr. W underlined that there is more of a power struggle than might be obvious at first glance.

Ms. M (Social Worker)

Ms. M was the first couple therapist to meet with the A's at the request of Dr. B who was then treating Mrs. A. Her efforts with the couple did not meet with success in part she feels because of the lack of insurance benefits for her services. Further, she observed a deep and incompatible pattern between the two that made any resolution very difficult to achieve. As people, they were like "apples and oranges" with very different ways of responding. Ms. M believes that Mr. A wanted to fashion Mrs. A in the image he desired and that her resistance led to the marital distress. Wanting matters to go his way, he was disinclined to accept Mrs. A's self determination. As parents, though, she never had any reason to suspect inadequate parenting from either although she could imagine that their styles would be quite different. In fact, her sense is that each on their own may be more effective than any attempt to work together. She concluded that the A's are a "grossly incompatible couple".

Ms. M's view of Mrs. A is that she is a reasonable person who may have become exhausted living under the pressure that Mr. A was applying. In the sessions she would tend to be quieter than her husband but when she spoke it was usually with logic and rationality. Ms. M's problem with Mr. A seemed to revolve around his inability to see matters differently and to revise his views. She found him very tense during sessions and this limited his flexibility and openness. Ms. M also recalled his "obsession" about money which seemed excessive and tended to be controlling. In the end she supported their seeing a therapist where his insurance would apply to limit the financial strain the treatment may have been causing.

Recalling that Mrs. A had referred to the therapist's help in labeling Mr. A's behaviour as emotionally abusive, Ms. M confirmed its deleterious effects on Mrs. A. She underlined that he would criticize her for being a "bad mother" and that comments such as this were very detrimental to Mrs. A's self esteem.

Home Visit

I visited the family home and met Tanya and Sean prior to seeing them at my office. The children appeared relatively relaxed and although Tanya did seem to be somewhat reticent, both parents felt that this was characteristic of her. Sean seemed to be bright sociable child developmentally ahead of his chronological age. Tanya sought comfort equally from her mother and father. Sean, as well, seemed involved with both parents and was also comfortable engaging me in play. He had none of the hesitation apparent in his older sister.

The town house is tastefully and well furnished and the children have an excellent physical environment. There are many toys and activities and they have the love and involvement of both adults. On the surface, there was no indication of problems although Sean made it clear that father's bedroom was different from mother's. Under the surface, there was some competition as might be expected but both Mr. A and Mrs. A handled the visit well.

Unfortunately, Tanya and Sean had not been told of the marital problems and that eventually mother and father would be living separately. I suggested that the parents tell them less because the children will truly understand the reality but that at least in the case of Tanya, she can begin to put some label to the tensions she has been experiencing. I recommended that the parents speak to their children together prior to the office visit. Apparently, this was received well by the children and Mrs. A noted that Tanya seemed less burdened as a result.

Children's Visits

Both Tanya and Sean were seen together with each parent respectively in accompaniment. They had been told of their parents' dilemma and Tanya could now connect my presence to the vague implications of what had been related to her. During both office visits, however, she was unwilling to discuss any matter and was unwilling to be separated from either parent. My sense of Tanya is that she is functioning well within normal limits and is bright, curious and creative. She has a sense of humor and initiates humor. She related well to both parents although often in whining and querulous tone that seemed somewhat immature for her age. There was little differentiation as to how she related to either her mother or her father. My sense was that she looked to them to provide for her and was used to their input into her play. On the other hand, she was able to construct her own play which expressed themes typical of a little girl her age. Tanya's drawing were also age appropriate and, perhaps typical of a slightly intolerant streak, she refused to draw her brother in a family portrait. Nevertheless, she was able to play beside Sean although not with him which suited Sean as well. Instead she drew her maternal grandmother who is obviously an important part of her life and has spent time with the family during this crisis.

Tanya's attitude towards me was one of caution and both parents alluded to her shyness with strangers. Tanya was clearly unwilling to meet alone but I also felt that this had something to do with the anxiety generated by the assessment. Mrs. A and Mr. A both indicated that Tanya had asked questions related to her parents' conduct and sharing of duties. Hence she has been very aware of the tensions existing in the family.

Sean is a self contained, alert and cheery three year old who is very interested in his life. Language and social skills seemed somewhat in advance of his age. His play was age appropriate and, for the most part, unaggressive. His mother noted that he can amuse himself for hours whereas Tanya is more dependent and needy of her parent's involvement. An unusual moment occurred during the father's visit with the children when Tanya grabbed a toy that Sean had taken. Mr. A suggested that Tanya play with it for a while Sean objected strenuously and took the opportunity to beat on Tanya's back with surprising force. Mr. A allowed Tanya to achieve her end although cautioned her about her methods while chiding Sean for his behaviour. Mrs. A noted that Sean does tend to hit often and she wonders whether it may relate to Mr. A's use of hitting when the children misbehave. On the other hand, both parents commented on how loving a child Sean is and how easily he conveys affection.

Mrs. A, though, has noted that if a mishap occurs, Sean may say, "Dad will be mad at you." She adds that both children are wary of their father's anger and can be intimidated by him. Further, she believes that Mr. A is more likely to hit Sean than Tanya.

It is very hard to judge parenting in the limited and often strained atmosphere of a custody assessment. I am also aware that children have the power to make any parent look good or bad. Yet my impression of both parents was that they are more comfortable facilitating and stimulating their children's lives than in restraining and disciplining them. Both seemed overly accepting of Tanya's moods, for example, which could in the future present some concern. On the other hand, I have no hesitation in commending the affection and interest each showed in their children which is evident in the children's affectionate response to them.

Tanya's kindergarten teacher completed a Teacher's Report Form that documents the child's progress and general adjustment. Tanya is said to be performing above age expectancy and is obviously a bright and curious little girl. Although her progress is above average, her general behaviour is average. The teacher feels that Tanya is unhappy and she underlines certain symptoms of stress and depression. She notes that Tanya tends to cry often and demands attention. In particular, she frequently complains of stomach aches and other physical problems that seem unrelated to physical illness. Tanya can also be difficult to motivate and demonstrates shy, withdrawn and secretive traits. The teacher views her as worrying, whining, often unhappy and observes that she tends to sulk. She is concerned for her pupil's unhappiness and describes Tanya as doing more clinging than typical for her age. On the other hand, she underlines that this is a well mannered and polite child who is also very affectionate. "Tanya is a great person," the teacher wrote, "she enjoys athletics and is always eager to run and play in the school yard." Yet, she also added that, "Tanya is quiet and it is often necessary to coax her into participating verbally."

Although there are developmental issues also present and I suspect a certain moodiness, Tanya was clearly pressured by the split between her parents and the interminable tension in the home. The fact that it was unclarified or unexpressed as well for such a long time further augmented her tension. Mrs. A observed that Tanya seemed better after she was told although she was not thrilled by having to attend my office. In fact she was wary of my presence and would have quite possibly been unable to participate in the assessment if I had not permitted her parents to be present.

For the most part, have no long term concerns regarding Sean or Tanya. The fact that both are developing well suggests that each parent likely does better on their own with the children than together. Whatever negative episodes occur between them, they are not prone to put their children in the middle. This is a further positive sign in a family where affection for the children is seemingly off limits from the conflicts that have divided them. If I have any immediate concern then it is for Tanya who I feel is most likely to suffer some trauma from these events. She is already stressed and any further escalation could prove detrimental to her. This is most obvious to her teacher but was also evident in this assessment.

Conclusions and Recommendations

This is one of those assessments where neighbours, relatives, business associates and friends all have been enlisted to support one side or the other. Although I am aware of their problems together, I found no reason to criticize either one's efforts, regard, love or commitment to their two children. I have tried to be open as regards their personal weaknesses but I would also add for their benefit that each makes a sizable contribution to Tanya and Sean's life and it would be incorrect to assert that either towers over the other on the parental scale. Hence, Mrs. A is not redundant to her children as Mr. A implies and Mr. A is not just an activity father who does not otherwise relate to them.

Ms. M spoke of Mrs. A as "driven" which is hardly the description given by her critics who view her as either shopping or catching up on sleep. No doubt, though, the strain and money pressures must have weighed heavily on both adults and Mrs. A, in particular, was driven to balance her efforts between earning extra money and caring for her very young children. This took Mrs. A away from the family at key times and Mr. A filled in with aplomb. Sadly, like all the strains they faced as a couple, this cooperative effort is not highlighted as a triumph but is discussed in terms of neglect and control. I would add, though, that I cannot see how Mrs. A can be judged against this predicament as if either parent felt that they had any alternative. I agree with her that it is prejudicial to use her attempt to reduce their debt as further cause for blame.

Perhaps it is also clear from the above discussion that I consider both parents to have some problems in their individual adjustment. Mr. A is more intransigent than he may appear and I suspect that he would have been severe with Mrs. A who did not feel recognized or supported. Mrs. A, despite clear eagerness to contribute, was too willing to yield control and saw her marriage in dependency terms. This led to a progressive weakening of her position and left her feeling dominated and controlled. In this sense, she was not able to give Mr. A the emotional support he needed despite his veneer of adequacy and control. The images of a negligent, spoiled Mrs. A and a denigrating, belligerent Mr. A are the result of this interaction but hopefully do not express the full potential of each on their own. In this regard, both are talented people with many personal assets.

In this examination, neither Mr. A nor Mrs. A excelled above the other as parents. Both were able to engage with their children and to enjoy the pleasures of the interaction. Neither was intrusive nor seriously inappropriate in any way. If their personality profiles can be used to predict their parenting styles then Mrs. A would be more likely to be conciliatory whereas Mr. A would tend to react and quickly draw a line or take a stand. Both qualities in their right proportions are useful ingredients to any parenting model. The major concern for the future is that they have a poor track record in pulling together when faced with a common purpose. Unfortunately, I know of no way of improving on this situation other than to note that they have demonstrated some capacity to rise above their own conflicts for the good of their children and this should remain a primary goal.

For purposes of clarity, I have noted the following factors as relevant when considering who might assume the custodial role:

Mr. A

1. a sentimental, structured, highly motivated person who would try very hard to be what his children want;
2. not always open to new learning on an emotional level — tends to be justifying versus self examining;
3. Active, committed but perhaps somewhat rigid which may become a source of difficulty as the children develop and are less likely to comply with his leadership or direction;
4. tends to be perceived as aggressive when frustrated with some support on psychological testing for this trait;
5. as custodian, he might be so clearly in charge that it would perpetuate the unhealthy interaction between them;
6. as custodian, he might be too powerful and the system between the parents could be imbalanced for the children, marginalizing the mother, and putting most strain on Tanya;
7. conciliation may not be a strong point in the future for their relationship and it is probable that his custodianship would amplify this problem more than resolving it.

Mrs. A

1. a warm, engaging parent who is genuine and caring;
2. as custodian, she would be less likely to be dominated and balance of power would be more equal;
3. an emotionally dependent person who has not adequately matured in the scope of the marriage but is making strides with professional help;

4. may not provide as good a structure as does Mr. A but is his equal in the provision of care:
5. tendency to avoid and deny in the face of conflict which may continue in the future;
6. more likely to facilitate access and to be less judgmental in the application - more live and let live than the father;
7. has demonstrated less than optimal fortitude in coping with extremes of stress - this could have implications for child rearing if too much on her own.

I would add as well that Tanya is somewhat at risk as evidenced by the strain, vulnerability and moodiness. For her sake, freedom from interminable conflict will be essential. The question arises as to what relationship should be fostered to best protect her emotional status at this juncture and in the years to follow. My impression, in this regard, is that the maternal link should be strengthened due to Tanya's age and phase specific needs. A devalued mother would be most stressful on this child as it would weaken a vital link for her development and add a further risk factor for future problems. Furthermore, a protected maternal link should nullify any undue competition with the mother for the father's affections that would certainly undermine her identity. It would also protect her from the necessity of taking sides, a reflection of the father's inclination towards polarization. Considering Tanya's best interests, therefore, I cannot envision sufficient advantage in asking the father to assume primary care whereas there would certainly be some added risk. Sean, I suspect, is a more hardy individual as well as young enough to make the transition as long as father contact is well maintained. From the children's point of view, therefore, mother as custodian might well be the best alternative while a strong father presence should mitigate against any long-term build up of emotional tensions and aggression.

My overall sense is that we are contending with two parental styles that are disparate but not uncomplimentary. The question is less who deserves custody than what combination of parental involvement would maximize the resources available to the children. My major concern, in this regard, is that a father centred custody would lead to a negation of the mother's presence whereas a mother centred arrangement would allow for the ample presence of both. It is not that Mr. A would purposefully act to minimize Mrs. A's input for he is a well meaning person. Yet in the service of exercising control over the structure, he would likely be too dominant as has been the pattern in the past. Again, I would say in Mr. A's defence, that this is not simply a function of his character but a measure of the interaction between both.

Consequently, due to the above, my suggestion would be that the mother assume the role of custodian while the father's role, strengths and major input be acknowledged through generous access:

I would recommend the following details as to access:

1. Mr. A should have access for what is essentially two of every three weekends. On a rotational basis, Mr. A should care for his children from Thursday at 4:00 pm until Monday morning for the first weekend; Friday until Monday morning for the second. After a weekend with the mother, Mr. A should then spend Thursday to Monday morning beginning the cycle again. On the relevant Monday mornings, the children should be taken by their father to school. If Monday falls on a statutory holiday then the return time should be extended to Tuesday morning.
2. Mr. A should also have overnight access on the Thursday evening prior to the mother's weekend from 4:00 pm until Friday morning when the children should be delivered to their schools.
3. The summer holidays should be equally divided with frequent turnabouts while the children are young to achieve maximum continuity of relationships. Each parent should have the option of spending two weeks outside of the city without providing access to the other. Arrangements should be made by June 1st of any year. As long as they are in the city, however, the rotational schedule should apply.
4. The winter holiday as defined by the school calendar should be equally divided with Mrs. A spending the first half of the holiday with the children. The pattern should alternate in the years following.
5. The March Break as defined by the school calendar should again be equally divided with Mr. A providing care for the first half of the holiday.
6. Mother's Day and Father's Day should be spent with the respective parent no matter on whose weekend the special day falls. If visitation is required, it should be from 10:00 am until 7:00 pm.

7. Halloween should be an alternating responsibility beginning with Mr. A .
8. Telephone access should be open and unrestricted.
9. Each parent should have some access on the children's birthdays even for a minimum of one hour.
10. If a dispute arises as to major issues in child care and where Mr. A refutes a decision made by the custodian and no compromise seems possible, then they should submit to binding arbitration in order to resolve it. Agreeing to a mental health professional as arbitrator, they should submit their views and agree to abide by the decision reached by the arbitrator. Mr. A would be responsible for the fee.

With these suggestions, I can now conclude my assessment of this family. I hope that the report will help to resolve their issues and I appreciated their cooperation and good will during the process. Please contact me if I can offer further information or clarification as required.

CASE 2

The next example touches on several issues that arise frequently in custody and access assessments: suitability, sexual abuse and children's wishes. Furthermore, in the prior example, the parents were both high functioning and participatory whereas in this case we confront serious limitations that enter into the child protection realm. Although the parents in the first example might hurl accusations of inadequacy at each other, the evidence of two bright and lively children portray a different reality that puts their allegations in perspective. In this matter, the problems and dangers run much deeper.

There were two children, a girl of 8 we will call Helen and Tony, a boy of 13. Helen and Tony were living with their father and had done so since the parents' separation six years previously. It was a chaotic marriage and Mrs. G, the children's mother, had been hospitalized for suicidal gestures, emotional inadequacy and an immature personality disorder. At the time of the assessment, she had no access to Helen although she did see Tony on a monthly basis. While in hospital, she met Mr. H, also a patient, and when her marriage disintegrated she immediately moved in with him.

The circumstances that led to Helen not seeing her mother arose in the context of this new relationship. Mr. H, an active alcoholic, had been previously married and this marriage had ended when there were strong suspicions of incest. Apparently, he gave up all rights of access in order to avoid possible criminal charges. It was not long after visitation began for Tony and Helen that Helen, then but a toddler, was diagnosed with chlamydia, a sexually transmitted disease. At age 2½, she was forcing nursing bottles between her legs and medical examination revealed signs of vaginal laceration as well as the presence of pubic hairs. Although all the men associated with Helen were tested, Mr. H took some two weeks before his results were submitted and he avoided the official health authorities that he was instructed to consult. After police, hospital and Children's Aid Society involvement, the court ordered supervised access for Mrs. G apart from Mr. H plus telephone access. Without more definite proof, though, criminal charges could not be laid.

Minimal access did not resume for three years and when it did, it only involved Tony. Mr. G, Helen's father, refused to extend access to Helen due to her fragile emotional state and behavioural problems. Helen was receiving ongoing psychiatric treatment during this time. Mr. G, who was having his own adjustment problems but was a sincere and caring man, professed that Tony only visited under duress as he feared that his mother, supported by Legal Aid, would return over and over to the courts and drain the family of funds and energy. In fact, Mrs. G had maintained intermittent but unsettling pressure on the father and children during the six years of separation. During the assessment. Mr. G made it clear that he loathed Mrs. G and remained disgusted by his memories of her maltreatment of the children, her emotional instability and poor hygiene. He recalled that she was fundamentally irresponsible and remembered returning home to find Helen in her crib with a soaked diaper and curdled milk. Tony had also recalled how Mr. H and his mother would forcibly hold Helen on the toilet against her will while Helen screamed to be released.

Psychological testing of Mr. G confirmed that he was a practical, modest person who had certain passive traits. On the other hand, there were no indications for psychopathology and the test profile suggested that he was both sincere and reasonable.

The evaluation of Mrs. G, then 35 years old, proceeded in greater detail. She focused on Mr. H who seemed to occupy her thoughts. She referred to him as a "gentleman" but also confessed that, as of recent, he was tending to be violent towards her. Although he received a disability pension which supported them, his tendency was to drink the money away leaving them short of funds and food as well as behind on their rent. The hostile-dependent nature of the attachment became obvious for she also spoke about his dire health problems and her concerns for his mistreatment of himself through alcohol. As she had done in the marriage to Mr. G, her way of influencing the situation was to leave and seek respite in a women's shelter, just long enough for Mr. H. to temporarily mend his ways. As to the molestation of Helen, Mrs. G did not dismiss Mr. H's probable guilt. In fact, she described him as forcing himself sexually on her as well. Although it was clearly unreasonable for Mrs. G to remain with this odious man, it was also evident that she was totally submissive and dependent on him and would accept his terms whatever they may be.

Mrs. G was three months pregnant with Tony when she married Mr. G. Although she had known him during primary school, they became reacquainted following her discharge from the hospital after a bizarre suicide attempt following the breakup of another relationship. The medical records indicated that it was likely an impulsive action aggravated by the acute intake of 15 ounces of rye whiskey. She was diagnosed as having a passive-dependent personality and it was noted that she adjusted very well to the ward environment.

Three years after she married Mr. G. she was again hospitalized in an agitated and angry state. She felt coerced by her husband and his family and accused Mr. G of pushing her down some stairs. The social worker who interviewed the couple concluded that their problems were likely insurmountable. The diagnosis during this admission was changed to passive-aggressive personality. It was during this stay in hospital that she first met Mr. H who was also a patient having played "Russian roulette with a 38".

When building a house on a lot next to Mr. G's parents, their problems worsened and Mrs. G again fled to the woman's shelter. She accused her husband of being mentally and physically cruel and recalled that on one occasion he had tied her with nylons and prevented her from calling the police. However, in her version, his apology encouraged her to return home and try once more. Yet, disagreements became more intense and the marriage quickly ended. Although she expected to be the custodian of the children, her lawyer informed her that this had been switched. She never fully understood exactly how this happened but she knew it was connected to the likely molestation of Helen by Mr. H.

During the assessment, Mrs. G stressed that despite all her faults and poor choices that she was still very much committed to her children. She insisted that her children's welfare preceded her loyalty to Mr. H although in practice it was apparent that she was profoundly dependent on him even if it jeopardized her relationship to her children.

The MMPI-2 profile revealed a person who was more likely pleading for help than someone intent on creating a positive impression, The test profile suggested profound ineffectiveness along with deep dissatisfaction with life. There were signs of very low ego strength and evidence of chronic adjustment problems. In general, she was seen as a passive, dependent person who can easily be led by others. There were indications that she would have trouble initiating or handling responsibility and she seemed to be motivated primarily by needs of attention and support. Her capacity to handle negative emotions also seemed weak and she appeared to be the type of person who blames others.

Based on her behaviour during the assessment, the history and the test findings, the assessor concluded that despite her resolve to find her way back into her children's lives, one should not underestimate her inadequacies, She showed a surprising degree of inconsistency that made one question whether she could be responsible for a child in her care. Moreover, the serious allegations against Mr. H and Mrs. G's total surrender to his control seemed a further negative factor.

The meetings with the children were useful in clarifying the situation further. Helen spoke with an affable frankness about her feelings of uncertainty and fear. Her teacher referred to her as a "dear soul" who appears at times to be "a little waif". She was also described by her teacher as naive and good natured. Helen's school adjustment was being affected by specific learning problems and she had been troubled by a bed wetting problem that worsened when she was under stress. Helen seemed very invested in her father and brother and made it clear that she did not want her world altered. She had shown no inclination to speak to Mrs. G when she would call to speak with Tony. She was unsure exactly what her feelings were regarding Mrs. G but she spoke of the fact that Mrs. G had "harmed" her. Helen was also aware that her father opposed her seeing her mother and that Mrs. G was off limits in her father's eyes.

Helen's pencil drawings showed simplicity and immaturity and on a story telling task her elaboration lagged behind her chronological age. Yet, on a measure of general word knowledge, she scored well in excess of her chronological age. Hence, the problem was certainly more than lack of intelligence. The assessor underscored the impact of early psychic and physical trauma and her tendency to withdraw into a sheltered world of innocence where she could be protected from harm. Needless to say, she was a vulnerable child who could ill afford further abuse or stress on the frail adjustment she had managed to attain.

Tony, 13 years of age, was in the eighth grade and was progressing normally. He was relaxed, open and expressive during the interviews with him. He referred to his mother by her first name and viewed her as a nuisance and obstacle. He was very negative about continuing monthly visits with her and explained that he felt like a hostage. He was relieved when the visits did not occur which happened whenever Mrs. G's life was under stress, usually tied to her relationship with Mr. H. Moreover, Tony perceived these visits as serving his mother's needs and not his own and he disliked her personal questions. The assessor was aware that Tony was influenced by his father's views and he shared his father's fears that the courts would enforce his mother's rights in spite of his wishes. In this regard, he perceived the access to his mother solely as a restriction but that by complying in a physical sense he was saving his sister from further pressure. It was the plight of Helen that drew the most concern and reaction from Tony. He feared that she could not survive if his mother played "her mental games" and "screws everybody up". A review of the records on the family revealed that Tony's message had remained the same over the years. In fact, Tony was the first to raise concerns about their safety while in the care of their mother and Mr. H. This confirmed for the assessor that Tony also spoke with his own voice and had formed an opinion similar to his father's and not a simple parroting of it.

Although the assessor fully acknowledged the importance of parental relationships, even with inadequate parents, this situation seemed fraught with complications. Although there was no doubting Mrs. G's sincerity, the history of her ability to protect her children or to contribute to the children's lives was dismal. Her impulsivity, poor judgment and submission to a man she considered her daughter's attacker did not support her case for access. As to Tony, at 13 years of age, his right of choice seemed earned for he had tolerated the visits mostly against his will. In regard to Helen, the risk that even supervised visits might place her too close to the trauma she had suffered as a toddler precluded a recommendation for access. As her father was also opposed to such visits, this would surely destabilize the family and further imperil this vulnerable girl's adjustment. Hence, the increase in family tensions along with feelings of threat could not have served any benefit in the child's life.

In order to settle the matter for the long-term, the assessor suggested that Tony be given control over visits and that Helen be given the same privilege when she reached 16 years of age. Until then, the assessor did not see any merit in recommending access, supervised or otherwise. The assessor went further in suggesting that telephone access also cease and that Mrs. G be asked to communicate with Tony by letter and to inform him of changes in address if this would arise. Additionally, the assessor recommended a more extensive examination of Helen's learning problems and coordinated with the family's general practitioner a referral to a pediatric urologist. Finally, the assessor suggested to the court that continued Legal Aid financing of the mother's claims was clearly adverse to the family's equilibrium and, hence, represented a further affront to Helen's already fragile adjustment. What took precedence in this case was the right of children to be safe and secure even if this meant that a parent's access would be denied.

CASE 3

The following case may be typical of many of the sexual abuse allegations that arise in custody disputes that upon assessment prove false. Generally, the accusation is made at the outset of the separation or at some point during the process of resolution. The accusation may dramatically escalate the conflict or may add further complexity to an already entangled divorce. Unless there is tangible evidence of penetration or other physical findings, police intervention may be limited and child protection services may favour supervised or no access until the matter can be settled within the scope of an assessment.

Although lawyers are familiar with the usual method of seeking truth from an intelligent inquiry of the issues and facts, the more indeterminate allegations met in many custody cases remind us that there is a less known tradition which seeks truth through the method of facing an ordeal. The late French philosopher Michel Foucault defines this route to virtue as based on *l'épreuve* (the test).[2] Such a method is quite at odds with science or law and shares more in common with medieval jousting or the more sinister trials by torture. Here, one's virtue is not as much discovered as it is proven in the triumph over adversity.

Although seemingly farfetched, we can perceive such a trial or ordeal in many of these custody related false abuse allegations. The mother and father face off in a bitter duel where the powerful weapon of abuse allegation is chosen, often unconsciously, by the mother. If the father can weather the ordeal, often including penile plethysmography, defending his record as a parent and non-pervert, only then can he claim to be a virtuous parent who deserves a role in his child's life.[3] In many of these case, the mother comes to view herself as the only true parent and protector of her child. Such mothers may devalue the father not simply because they fear loss of custody but because they fear loss of their distinction and self image as the parent of merit.

Although this description sketches the framework of such false allegations, the exact motivation or dynamics will be individually determined. The assessor's task, when faced with allegations of this nature, is to distinguish between those cases where a child may well have suffered harmful sexual interference from those where accusations of abuse take the father out of the "we", leaving only the mother and child. The following case reflects this tendency and is included,

2 See Miller, James (1993), *The Passion of Michel Foucault*, New York: Doubleday, at 270.

3 The plethysmograph is an instrument used to measure a man's sexual response to visual and auditory stimuli, some of whwhich are likely to encourage arousal in a pedophile. Among other physiological measures, a the changing circumference of the penis is measured through a pressure sensitive ring.

as well, because it advocates joint legal custody as a novel means of sustaining the father's relevance in the child's life.

These were the facts of the case. Mr. and Mrs. B were in their early thirties and divorcing after a ten-year marriage. Mr. B's career in sales had been meteoric since leaving university where he had met his wife. The couple had one child, a daughter we shall call Virginia, seven years of age and in the second grade at the time of the assessment. The link between mother and daughter was very close. The allegation of impropriety arose approximately three months after the couple separated although the actual behaviour in question had been known to the mother for some time prior to the separation. This apparently involved tickling or patting of Virginia's buttocks in a playful way that had apparently begun in Virginia's early childhood. At the time of the assessment, Mrs. B had retained a second lawyer who had wisely advised her based on the details of the case to tone down the accusation of sexual molestation and to view the assessment simply as an opportunity to put the matter to rest. Hence, the original affidavit material portrayed a more strident tone than the later documents. Yet, both counsels and Mrs. B agreed that the father should undergo sexual behaviors testing as a part of a comprehensive screening.

The episode began when Mrs. B contacted the Child and Family Services who in turn made arrangements for the police to videotape an interview with Virginia. The child was also seen for abuse counselling by a social worker with a local hospital with a child protection mandate. Later the father's lawyer sought an order suspending that counselling as it was based on the premise of an abuse that had not been substantiated. Hence, although the actual sexual nature of the alleged behaviour seemed vague, the authorities still proceeded under the assumption of sexual meddling.

Mr. B, although mystified and caught by total surprise by the allegation, did admit that he would tickle his child's buttocks when she dawdled in order to prompt her to move. He was aware that she did not like this approach and had protested to him previously. Otherwise, he completely denied the allegation that he had infringed on his daughter's privacy either sexually or otherwise. Mrs. B agreed that there was no evidence of penetration and that Mr. B was apparently content to touch Virginia's peri-anal region without any apparent escalation of the sexual content of the gesture. Her hand gestures, however, suggested a more substantive and erotic touching than described by Mr. B.

There were other complicating factors that were important in clarifying the matter:

1. Mrs. B had taken a lover prior to the end of the marriage; although she suggested that she met this man only four months before the marriage ended. Yet, it was obvious that this behaviour was of deep moral concern in a woman who had been raised in a religious Catholic family. Mrs. B confessed that the worst aspect to her brief affair was having to inform her mother whom she knew would be sadly disappointed. A counselor who briefly saw the couple prior to the break up related that Mrs. B had telephoned in distress one day to confess the affair even though the couple were no longer seeing that counselor.
2. Mr. and Mrs. B had allowed Virginia to sleep in their respective beds following the separation. The court ruled that Mr. B's access must be supervised until the matter was clarified and this prohibited Mr. B from being alone with Virginia including lying down with her in order for her to fall asleep. Hence, Virginia proved unable to sleep at her father's residence for access visits when this restriction was imposed.
3. Mrs. B stated that her husband did not satisfy her needs and that this problem had become worse in the final two years. She implied that this was approximately when her husband began to tickle or pat their child's buttocks. It was at this time as well that she became active in personal pursuits and sought more contacts outside the marriage. It was also when Virginia began kindergarten and closely followed on Mr. B's completing a post graduate degree. Hence, this period in their lives seemed very important for all three family members.
4. In her narrative, Mrs. B delineated the many disappointing and disillusioning experiences she had experienced during the marriage. She had clearly not shared his work goals and viewed him as a "workaholic". He, in turn, stressed that he had been satisfied with his marriage and although he understood the marriage had problems, he was fully prepared to work toward their resolution. He did not fault his wife's parenting and insisted that until the allegation was made he would have considered her "a great

> mother". He hoped that this was an aberration created by over-protectiveness and not a deeper plot to undermine his role in their child's life. He insisted that he was prepared to do whatever to clear his name and reputation "although the damage is already done".

Mr. B's lawyer took the initiative to ensure that the assessor had access to the tape of the interview conducted by the police and social worker. The interview followed each strand of the child's narrative seeking signs or evidence of sexual misconduct by the father. Virginia seemed to focus on two issues. First, her father placed his whole hand on her "bum" in a manner she did not appreciate and that this had happened on several occasions at which time she always protested to her mother. Secondly, her father insisted that they visit "scary" parts of the house in the basement where she was not happy going. The interviewer tried to link the sexual issue to the basement fear but no link was made and this part of the allegation remained obscure. Nevertheless, Virginia specified on several occasions during the interview that she did not like to go to the basement of the family home and she objected to her father "touching me on spots I don't like him to." As to the latter issue, the expressed affect was more annoyance than threat. Moreover, both grievances were placed on the same level of gravity. Hence, she referred to her dad as "bugging" her but was also able to speak positively about him at other moments. It also seemed apparent when the social worker questioned the anatomical specification that "bum" meant the buttocks and not the vagina.

There was no mistaking the conclusion that Virginia was upset with certain actions of her father although the sexual nature of these behaviours was obscure. It also seemed that this was not a new issue for Virginia and that she had protested before to both her parents. The implication was that her mother did nothing about it until the context changed following the marriage breakup. Perhaps this was why she had spoken to her grandmother on the topic. The basement issue was more obscure and the interview failed to clarify the nature or source of this complaint.

In general, Virginia appeared as a loquacious and friendly seven-year-old with excellent communication skills reminiscent of her parents. There were no signs of psychic trauma evident in her behaviour nor were there indications of precocious sexuality. The interview was skillfully performed by the police officer although its agenda was clear and not open ended. Hence, Virginia was not asked about positive aspects of her relationship with her father nor was she asked if her mother ever does things that bother her. When the rigorous interview finally concluded to the obvious relief of the child, Virginia showed a certain political astuteness by expressing trust and confidence in her mother as well the two authorities in front of her.

As the assessment proceeded several other points became clarified concerning the personalities of the parents:

1. Mr. M proved to be a stable, reliable and sincere man although heavily invested in his work. His personal skills and sense of adequacy had not kept pace with his professional development which was, to say the least, extraordinary. Personally, though, he was seen as insecure and inhibited and the assessor could perceive that this factor may well have been instrumental in inducing the separation.
2. Mrs. M, although very energetic and resourceful, was also highly competitive and achievement oriented. This was exemplified on the MMPI-2 profile which revealed more than a small measure of opportunism. Despite vim and vigour, she seemed personally unfulfilled and had not been able to meaningfully focus her efforts.
3. Sexual behaviours testing of Mr. M, conducted by a forensic psychiatrist, was negative for the cognitive distortions and sexual interests typical of pedophiles. There were also no indications observed of problems with hostility or substance abuse.
4. Although Virginia had experienced problems sleeping at her father's house following the allegation, there was no report of problems in this regard previous to the accusation. Hence, what seemed imperative was less the "abuse" by the father and more the allegation that had been lodged. On the other hand, it was also clear that Virginia disliked this infantile game and that at minimum her father had underestimated her dislike of it.

In the assessment interviews, Virginia took pains to let the assessor know that the "game" was no longer an issue. She expressed positive feelings about both parents and was comfortable with both when seen by the assessor. The school reported satisfactory performance and no significant signs of emotional tension or stress. The basement fear that was featured in the police interview was never reported again either to the social worker Virginia saw at the hospital or the assessor and both parents could not relate this complaint to anything they knew or had heard from Virginia. Moreover, a home visit revealed that the rooms to which she referred were well integrated into the craft room where she enjoyed much of her play.

Virginia's facile mind led to an intriguing drawing of her family which is reproduced in Figure 1. The drawing indicates the family members who are depicted from left to right include herself, her mother and then her father. The father is obviously dressed as a woman and Virginia related that in the picture he is very mad. Her mother's arms are outstretched and she seems to be holding father and daughter apart. Curiously, her mother appears to be wearing pants. Even more curiously, father's hands are drawn quite differently from her mother's and her own hands. One would not be far wrong to note that these most resemble claws. The assessor saw in this dream a pictorial representation of what the child might not be able to explain in words: "Mother and I have negated (castrated or emasculated) father's strength in the family and mother wears the pants and keeps father and I apart."

Based on the broad array of data collected, the assessor concluded that although Virginia had clearly objected to the touching even prior to the separation that this was likely re-interpreted by her mother due to the changing circumstances created by the marital breakdown. As the sexual basis of the allegation seemed unwarranted and there had been no escalation nor genital involvement or hint of such violation, there seemed to be no reason to suppose that her father represented a risk to her well being.

In intrafamilial sexual abuse of a child, there is most often an escalation that inevitably leads to genital contact. In this regard, a man driven to sexual molest his daughter over a two-year span will find a way to really do it. In this sense, the sexual nature of the interference would come plainly to the fore and might itself lead to the separation. In this particular circumstance, the mother knew of the behaviour for some time but did not stress its importance or inappropriateness until the politics between the parents had altered.

Further, the assessor reasoned that the time frame in which the allegation was made coincided with Mr. B's awareness that Mrs. B

Figure 1

had indeed had a sexual affair prior to the end of the marriage. Guilty regarding her own conduct, the allegation allowed Mrs. B to evade her own remorse which was clearly displaced onto the father. Through the allegation, she was able to reclaim her sense of lost virtue while he had to fight to retain his.

The question that arose for the assessor was the issue of custody. In this case, there was no doubt that only Mrs. B had the time or involvement to be residential parent and their division of labour had followed traditional lines. Mr. B, in fact, never wanted more than standard access as he knew that the demands of his employment precluded more involvement. Further, his aims did not change due to the assessment and remained modest. On the other hand, the assessor felt that the adverse momentum instilled by the allegation impaired Mrs. B's capacity to represent Virginia's needs for her father over the long-term. Although residence and access was not an issue, the assessor outlined that joint legal custody, although unlikely prior to the allegation, might be an important assurance that Mr. B would be accorded a necessary validity as a parent. This suggestion was also seen as important for Virginia so that she could experience her father in a less emasculated and more credible role as well as facilitating the emotional separation of mother and daughter which seemed somewhat in jeopardy. Although the litigation had eroded their sense of trust and collaboration, both parents retained an ability beyond the immediacy of the conflict to communicate regarding their daughter. Whether this would be sufficient to support a joint legal arrangement was juxtaposed against the assessor's belief that the father's role would otherwise continue to be diminished. Not surprisingly, joint custody was not the first preference for the mother or her legal counsel. They took the position that the allegation was strictly initiated by Virginia with Mrs. B acting only as a conduit and representative of her daughter's rights and needs. Consequently, the suggestion of joint legal custody was initially interpreted as a punishment rather than a means to ensure that Mr. B's credibility as a parent would be maintained in Virginia's eyes and that she would be spared any further complicity in marginalizing her father's role. Joint custody, therefore, although in this instance a less typical application, was viewed as potentially helpful in restoring the integrity and balance of the parents, especially in their child's eyes.

CASE 4

The subject of parental alienation is currently topical in family law circles and the reader can refer to Chapter 10 where this special clinical problem is addressed. Although it can be observed in pure form, in many cases described in this book one can denote elements of this syndrome. The following case is very illustrative and is included for this reason. In this example, there were two children, a girl we will call Beth, age 12 at the time of the assessment and a boy Joel, 8 years of age. Due to a series of events, Joel was forcibly removed by the court from his mother's care due to the determination of parental alienation and was required to live with his father. Although there was apparent distress at the outset, Joel responded to removal and to psychotherapy and became better adjusted. His development then proceeded more smoothly. He was gradually reintroduced to visits with his mother who cooperated with the efforts of the therapist. Although the problems did not cease with this intervention, they became far more manageable as a result. They would likely have been irretrievable if this action had not been taken.

Mr. and Mrs. Q were married for 10 trying years and when they first separated they discussed the possibility of joint parenting. In retrospect, this was obviously idealistic and the post-separation adjustment was marked by increasing tensions. In spite of this, a prior assessment recommended that they adopt a joint parenting arrangement with two week intervals. Instead of solving the problems, the strains became more evident and the children became hopelessly enmeshed in the parents' conflicts. Mr. Q found it increasingly harder to achieve the access to which he was entitled. A crisis quickly evolved and took the strange form of child abduction.

Ostensibly taking the children for brief trip to a neighbouring Ontario city, Mrs. Q telephoned to say that she was in British Columbia and had applied to the court to allow her to remain there with Joel and Beth. Mr. Q took legal and police action and Mrs. Q was subsequently charged and convicted of abduction and the children were placed in the custody of Mr. Q. With time, however, Mrs. Q was again allowed access that gradually increased to include a two-week summer vacation. Mr. Q recalled that at this time telephone calls between mother and children noticeably increased and the children were often "tied in knots" following what appeared to be manipulative conversations.

This came to a head when the 12-year-old, Beth, complained about her father to her guidance counselor who in turn contacted the school social worker who then made contact with the office of the children's lawyer. Beth convinced these professionals that she was being mistreated by her father and subsequently the children were removed from his care. When the father defended himself legally, a re-assessment was ordered and the son was returned to his father's care.

The assessment revealed that there was little substance to the accusation that Mr. Q was abusive and whatever negative comments were made by the children related to minor issues and matters of style. Although he was somewhat obsessive, emotionally dependent and defensive, he was also a warm and engaging person who did not merit the attacks of the children, especially that by the daughter Beth. The assessor concluded that Mr. Q felt deeply for his children and had the aptitude to be a decent parent. The assessor also observed that he was reliable, responsible and dependable.

This had been Mrs. Q's second marriage and she had a son by her first husband who was then 20 years of age. She spoke of her marriage with reluctance and sadness but stressed Mr. Q's unpredictable nature. She was quite open about the dysfunctional nature of her own family of origin and felt that Mr. Q was attributing all his problems with the children to her because of this background. Although Mrs. Q was hesitant about discussing her family history in any depth, it was obviously highly traumatic and was characterized by severe psychological abuse, alcoholism and physical violence. She described herself as a woman who has been victimized by her parents, her first husband, and now by Mr. Q. It was evident that she felt powerless in the custody dispute and was deeply bitter that the courts would further victimize her.

When Beth and Joel refused to continue visits with their father, Mrs. Q denied having any influence on her decision. She referred to her children's moods as "Jeckyl and Hyde", seemingly composed at their father's but deeply distressed and upset when they returned to her care. She also noted that Joel was very angry and picked needless fights with his sister. Mrs. Q viewed herself as solely protective of their well being and considered that their wishes were being ignored by the court.

An interview was arranged with Mrs. Q's 20-year-old son from her first marriage who was now living on his own. He had, however, spent time living with the Q's and considered Mr. Q to be his stepfather. This young man was forthright in his views. Although he considered Mr. Q to be somewhat domineering and strict, he never knew him to be abusive. On the other hand, he described being encouraged by his mother to avoid his natural father and it was only of recent that he was able to know his father better. In this regard, he discovered that his father was a very different person from the man portrayed by his mother. He noted that he and his mother are now estranged and that she could not tolerate his contact or rapprochement with his biological father. He described his mother as jealous, manipulative and stressed that when he was growing up she demanded total loyalty in his relationship to her.

The psychological test data on Mrs. Q was equivocal. Although she had an adaptive and friendly side, she could also be competitive and hostile. There were no obvious signs of psychopathology evident on the testing although the assessor made the comment that in her case the pathology seemed to be externalized on the stage of her life rather than being represented in her mind.

Beth was unequivocal in her desire to live with her mother and she was proud of her efforts to contact the social worker and to achieve her desired goal. She added that she had felt this way for a long time and was distressed that no one would listen or take her views seriously. Beth complained that her father did not understand or care about her feelings. She recalled that when she would express her sentiments that he would "treat me like dirt" or "lecture me for hours". At the same time, she felt that her father spoke meanly to her while he denied his anger. Beth concluded that because of his conduct, she hated her father and she had thoughts of running away or killing herself or him if she was forced to return to his care. Yet, she refused the idea of meeting him with a mediator and could not envision telling him of these feelings directly. The assessor noted that Beth did not make any positive comments about her father and remained in tight control of her message.

Joel was much less outspoken than his sister and he was clearly disturbed by the family situation. During the home visits at his mother's, Joel was unable to talk to the assessor. He hid behind a chair and curled up with his "fur". At the second home visit at his father's, however, he spoke a little more but was mainly sullen and highly stressed. When seen in the office after two home visits, he was able to say that his mother was "perfect" but beyond this he was tongue tied. As to his father, he noted that his father was rarely angry and did not force or lecture him inappropriately. On the other hand, he felt that he should only see his mother so he would not feel as split. The parents description of Joel were contradictory and revealed the extent to which he felt pulled apart by the conflict. Mrs. Q described a child who trashed his room and remained curled in a fetal position. Mr. Q, on the other hand, described a happy, active boy who seemed to enjoy his life.

The assessor concluded that Beth was caught in a situation where loyalty to her mother was the only way to avoid being abandoned. Joel seemed on the way to the same conclusion and he took his cue from the powerful influences of his mother and sister. The assessor suggested that Joel reside with his father and visit his mother much less frequently and for short period of time. As to Beth, the options seemed limited due to her age and the depth of her conviction. She proved very hardened in her views against her father and it seemed a risk to try and intercede. Although it was evident that the child was being held hostage by the psychological needs of the mother, Beth's collusion was also apparent. She sought an exclusivity with her mother that would pit mother and daughter against the world. There was some room to manoeuver with Joel, however, although leaving him in the sole care of his mother would most certainly lead to total alienation from his father. Therapeutic intervention was recommended with the therapist having some control over how the visits with the mother would be re-introduced. The assessor concluded, finally, that the only real solution would be for Mrs. Q to take responsibility for her own emotional problems and to free her children from the legacy of her troubled childhood years.

Conclusion to Case Examples

The examples cited are simply four cases from an abundance of possibilities that populate the landscape of family law. Notice, though, that each has its own inherent logic and blend of psychological forces that require the assessor to convey considerable detail to give the flavour and nuances of the case. Doing an assessment is an immersion experience in the lives and psyches of the protagonists. Interestingly, assessing an assessment is also an immersion experience and most lawyers report reading these accounts several times to absorb their meaning. Hopefully, the effort is worthwhile and although such reports cannot be successfully utilized to settle all cases, they should at least offer the trial judge both information and perspective that is not available otherwise. Although the conclusions reached and the recommendations made in assessments can be controversial in certain instances, as long as they emerge from the clinical data and can be shown to be logically and psychologically sound, then they will have served their intended aim. In the forays of human conflict, so personified by custody and access disputes, we must ultimately conclude that our goals must indeed remain modest.

13

Legal Analysis and Commentary of Case Study

This analysis is being done of Case 1.[1] The analysis is being done from the perspective of husband's counsel. The recommendation of the assessor is that the wife should have sole custody, care and control of the children, but that the husband have, what has to be described as liberal and generous access. Both parties were seeking sole custody. It is therefore assumed, for the purpose of this analysis, that counsel for the wife will be calling the assessor as a witness and that during his examination-in-chief his assessment report was filed with the court as an exhibit. Therefore the husband's counsel will be conducting cross-examination of the assessor. If the wife's counsel was going to cross-examine the assessor many of the same points in the approach used below would be equally applicable.

Assessment Report	**Comments**
Qualifications: No reference is made in the body of the report to the qualifications of the assessor. Nor is there a curriculum vitae attached although it is presumed that the assessor would probably attach one to the report that is to be filed with the court.	A complete and up-dated curriculum vitae should be attached to the report that has been served on opposing counsel and that has been filed with the court. The assessor should be cross-examined on formal education, clinical experience, continuing education and publications.

1 Found at page 411.

Assessment Report	Comments
	Years of experience and number of occasions on which he has testified in a custody access case should be explored. Counsel, presumably, will know whether he has testified in previous cases and will know whether his opinion evidence has been accepted. If it hasn't reference should be made to the cases in which his testimony was not accepted by the court. If the case is dealing with syndrome evidence or circumstances that involve a theory or technique the assessor should be cross-examined to determine whether or not he is testifying beyond his scope of expertise and whether the theory or technique being relied upon by him is in fact generally accepted by the clinical community of which he is a member and whether it has been accepted as valid by the scientific community regarding the particular field of expertise in question.
Terms of Reference and Reasons for Referral: No mention in the report is made of the terms of reference or the circumstances that caused the matter of the assessment to be referred to the assessor. Reference is made to the reason for the referral in the context of the parties not being able to agree on what custodial arrangement should be put in place for the children.	The assessor should set out a description of the circumstances under which the matter was referred to him. Was it done by court order? Was he selected on the mutual consent of the parties? Is the report in fact a unilateral assessment or private assessment involving only one party? Are the terms of reference that this is to be a comprehensive assessment or is the assessment one that is restricted to a narrow issue such as, for example, access only, or to determine what the

Assessment Report	Comments
	wishes of the children are with respect to a custody access arrangement. Once the terms of reference have been determined one would look to see whether or not the question referred to the assessor has in fact been dealt with in the assessment and to be assured that other unrelated issues or matters are not dealt with. The assessor makes it clear in this case that the reason for the assessment is to clarify the nature of the interaction of the husband and wife and to investigate the relative aptitudes of the parents and to harmonize these findings with the best interests of their two children.
Sole Custody versus Joint Custody: Reference is made to the wife having expected a demand from the husband for joint custody but being surprised by the husband seeking sole custody. There is a suggestion that the wife was not prepared to consider shared parenting given the husband's request for sole custody. There doesn't seem to be any reference in the body of the report to the issue of whether joint custody would be appropriate as opposed to one parent or the other, having custody.	The question to be put to the assessor at some point in the cross-examination would be whether or not he at any time considered recommending that the parties have joint or shared custody of the children. One should determine whether there is an element of bias on the part of the assessor with respect to whether he believes in the concept of joint custody. In this regard, prior to cross-examination, counsel should probably read any published works of the assessor to see if he has expressed an opinion one way or the other with respect to joint custody and whether it is a form of parenting regime that he adopts or generally rejects.

Assessment Report	**Comments**
Husband's History: In dealing with the husband's history the assessor makes reference to comments that the husband purportedly made about the wife and comments that the husband made with respect to his involvement in caring for the children over the years. The assessor on page 413 refers to other equally unflattering comments the husband makes about the wife. At page 414 the assessor makes reference to the husband as having little respect to the wife's autonomy and maturity as a wife and parent.	Throughout the report dealing with husband's history the assessor in making these comments, at least on the surface, seems to be showing a preference to the wife as opposed to the husband. Therefore the question presents itself as to whether there is an element of bias here. Counsel will want to determine whether the quotes the assessor has attributed to the husband are in fact accurate, complete and not taken out of context or given an interpretation that is unsupported. Therefore counsel should ascertain whether notes were kept by the assessor regarding conversations with the husband and they should be reviewed to determine whether the husband in fact made any flattering or positive comments about the wife which he almost surely did at some point about something. If it is learned that the husband did make flattering or positive comments about the wife in respect to any issue raised in the course of the assessment such fact should be highlighted to undermine the assessor's possible bias. Why have they not been referred to? In addition to bias of course the issue of thoroughness and completeness of the report would be raised.

Assessment Report	Comments
On pages 413 to 417 in making reference to the husband's history the assessor makes reference to the husband's perspective of what factors contributed to the breakdown of the marriage. For example, the assessor refers to the husband as having claimed that the wife was never able to save to buy and that he was unable to say no to her. The assessor would then use a very specific quote such as "Mrs. A. would want that piece of jewellery or that piece of furniture". "I had to keep her happy."	The structure or methodology used by the assessor in generally making reference to the position of the husband and then specifically highlighting or selecting certain quotes raises the question as to the purpose of using such a structuring method in the report. What is the purpose for highlighting certain things that the husband has said, but not others? Is the assessor being selective in order to accentuate the negative feelings or attitude of the husband towards the wife or is he attempting to accentuate the negative characteristics of the wife? In this assessment one gets the feeling that counsel should again ask for production of the assessor's notes and ask him to point to the area from which these quotes are taken to make sure they are full, complete and accurate and not taken out of context. The purpose of this exercise is also to make certain that not too subjective an interpretation is put on any comments made not only by the husband but by the wife.
Wife's History: The assessor uses the same structure or methodology in taking the history of the wife as he does in taking the history of the husband.	The same course of investigation should be pursued with respect to why only certain comments of the wife are highlighted in the report and a determination should be made as to whether they are complete and accurate and not in any way taken out of context.

Assessment Report	Comments
Wife's History of Employment: The report is not clear as to whether or not the wife was working full time as of the date that the assessment was conducted. Reference is made in her history to her working at least part time. It is not clear however whether the wife continued to work and whether she was working at the time of separation and at the time of the assessment.	It is an important factor as to whether or not the wife was working full time or not. The conclusions of the assessor with respect to the personality profiles and strengths and weaknesses of the husband and wife as parents will reveal that there is little left to chose between them as parents being capable of caring for these children. In recommending that the wife have sole custody, one therefore has to wonder whether the assessor was influenced by the fact that the wife was not working and therefore was available to be a "full time homemaker". The husband has alleged that the wife dismissed the nanny so that she could be seen as a full time homemaker. The question presents itself as to whether she gave up a position of employment for the same reason. The assessor should be asked whether in his view the wife being available to be a full time homemaker impacted on his decision. If the negative and positive attributes of the husband and wife as potential custodial parents are equally balanced and the argument can be made that the real basis for the assessor's recommendation as to custody is the fact that the wife is at home full time, it would be argued that the expert opinion of the assessor isn't really necessary in this regard as the trier of fact should be able to decide without any

Assessment Report	Comments
	assistance from the assessor as to whether the wife's availability as a full time homemaker is relevant or not to the ultimate issue in the case.
Psychological Testing: Response Bias. The husband was given the MMPI-2 test. The assessor says that the husband's MMPI profile was diminished by a defensive response bias. The wife's MMPI-2 profile pointed to some degree of denial.	The assessor should be asked whether or not, generally speaking, a defensive response bias is such that one should totally ignore or discount the psychological testing as it may be deemed invalid or unreliable. The assessor should also be asked questions about the wife's psychological testing regarding her response bias. It is interesting to note that the assessor in dealing with the wife's response bias doesn't use the same strong language that he does for the husband even though they seem to be talking about the same type of response bias, that is denial. With respect to the husband he states that the husband's profile was diminished by a defensive response bias. In referring to the wife he simply says that her MMPI profile pointed to some degree of denial as well as difficulties obtaining deeper self-understanding and insight. He does not suggest that the wife's profile should be diminished in any way as he did in the husband's case. Most authoritative works would suggest that "denial" and "defensive" are the same thing. Does the assessor's failure to discount the wife's MMPI profile in this respect reflect an element of bias?

Assessment Report	Comments
Psychological Findings: In his report, the assessor in dealing with both the husband's and wife's respective psychological test results makes reference to both negative aspects and positive aspects of their profiles.	The idea here is to have the assessor admit that the psychological testing results of the husband and wife are a wash in the context that neither appears to have scored any better than the other. It should be put to the assessor that in his conclusions with respect to the husband's testing he described the husband (page 418) as a person who very much wants the best for his children and that there is no evidence to suggest that the husband was not caring or concerned about his children. Have the assessor admit that he seems to dismiss the wife's concern that the children might become afraid of the husband's aggression. The assessor suggests that this aggression is more a question of style than representing any real threat to the children. The assessor suggests in the report that the husband can be dominant and attempt to be controlling. Have the assessor admit that the wife's psychological testing reveals a number of problems and that in fact it appears to the reader that he identifies more problems with respect to the wife than the husband. For instance (see page 423) he identifies the wife as having difficulties that require deeper self-understanding and insight and that such a person may not be resilient under stress and pressure and this may lead to feelings of inner

Assessment Report	Comments
	confusion. More importantly he suggests that the wife seems to be hesitant about close emotional involvement. Surely this is not a feature to be overlooked when dealing with what is in the best interests of the children. If the wife is hesitant about developing a close emotional involvement with the children then one has to question whether it is in the best interests of the children that they be in her sole care, custody and control. The assessor also, in dealing with the psychological test results of the wife identifies that she has an underlying deep hostility that is poorly expressed within her personality. It should be suggested to the assessor that this hostility seems to reveal itself in the wife's position that she will not consider joint custody given the fact that the husband is asking for sole custody even though she stated that she would have previously considered a shared parenting arrangement. This seems to suggest that her hostility is preventing her from considering what is in the best interests of the children. Does this hostility not cause the wife to appear to be vindictive and to focus on same as opposed to focusing on the issue of what is really in the best interests of the children? Lastly, in the wife's psychological testing, the assessor has suggested (page 424) that despite the wife's positive family background she

Assessment Report	**Comments**
	does not always bear up well under stress and has had difficulty coping with complex problems. The assessor should be asked whether he considers that there is a fair amount of stress in raising a five year old and a three year old, particularly in that period immediately following a separation or divorce and he should further be asked whether in his view complex problems can arise in the normal course of raising children. Assuming that the answer to these questions is yes one has to question whether the wife's inability to bear up well under stress is a feature that should be disregarded when deciding what is in the best interests of the children.
Administration of Test and Selection of Test: Reference is made to an MMPI psychological test having been conducted of the parties. No reference is made to how it was administered, who administered it and in what circumstances.	It should be determined whether the MMPI-2 test was used as opposed to the MMPI. The MMPI-2 is the most up to scale and progressive form of the test. This goes to the issue of the examination of the procedure invoked by the assessor and whether it was complete and thorough in all regards. No reference is made to who conducted the test and it should be determined whether the assessor himself did it or whether a member of his support staff did it. If some else did it, did they do it correctly? How do we know whether it was or wasn't done correctly?

Assessment Report	Comments
Conclusions: After dealing with the history of the parties and after having reviewed their psychological test results the assessor makes certain conclusions, in the case of the husband at page 418 and in the case of the wife at page 424. In dealing with the husband at page 418 the assessor in the conclusions makes reference to the husband's concern for his children and his wish to do his best for them. However, in the conclusions with respect to the wife no reference at all is made to the issue of how the test results in any way are relevant to her ability to care for the children.	It is interesting to note that the assessor in drawing conclusions with respect to the wife's psychological test results and family history focuses entirely not on how the history and the test results relate to her ability to parent but more on how they relate to her growing as a person. In fact the assessor refers to the wife's psychotherapy and her marriage breakdown as a liberating experience for her that are essential to her as a mature woman. Two points should be made on cross-examination here: 1. In dealing with the husband's conclusions the assessor accentuated both positive and negative aspects of the psychological testing vis-a-vis the husband's ability to care for the children. With respect to the wife's conclusions, the assessor does not make reference to the negative aspects of her psychological test results (of which we saw there were many) in his paragraph dealing with conclusions. It is therefore suggested his report is somewhat incomplete and somewhat biased in this regard. 2. In the conclusion paragraph the assessor deals with the wife's liberating experiences and commends her on her efforts to gain autonomy and emotional maturity. The question has to be presented as to whether the focus of the assessment and the psychological testing is to determine whether the wife is growing as an individual or rather the object of the exercise is to determine what is in

Assessment Report	Comments
	the best interests of the children. The wife's liberation and growth may or may not necessarily be what the focus of the assessment ought to have been. The focus of the assessment should be what is in the best interests of the children.
Integration of Findings: In this section of the report once again it would appear that the husband and wife score evenly.	The assessor's findings in this regard should be highlighted. The assessor points out that both parties have to share the blame for the marital breakdown. Mr. A. blamed Mrs. A. and Mrs. A. blamed herself. On the other hand the assessor points out one can appreciate the husband's complaint that the wife evaded the tough realities and took refuge behind a wall of innocence. Have the assessor admit, as he does in the body of the report, that both parents are likeable and motivated. Have him admit that they both love their children and are extremely interested in providing for them and that they are dedicated parents. The point to be made here is that both parents cannot simply blame the other for the marital breakdown and that both otherwise are fit, capable and loving parents.

Assessment Report	Comments
Report of Dr. B: Dr. B is the psychiatrist who the wife saw alone for psychotherapy. Dr. B provided a written report to the assessor and the assessor at page 426 makes reference to the comments of that report. Dr. B concludes in his report that the husband was physically, verbally and emotionally abusive.	The assessor refers to having received a letter from Dr. B. The letter's contents clearly constitute hearsay evidence. Counsel should object to the assessor being able to make any reference to the contents of Dr. B's report. The argument should be advanced that Dr. B's report should not be put into evidence and that none of the contents from it should be referred to by the assessor. The report is incomplete in the context that Dr. B only heard one side of the story. The assessor, justifiably so, comments that the husband did not have an opportunity to present his side of the story. However the assessor does not unequivocally state as to whether he puts any weight on the report or not. One is left with the impression that he does because he uses the expression "there is much in this report that would correspond to my perception". An admission should be obtained from the assessor that there are no collateral sources (other than speaking to the parties) that were used to corroborate the conclusion that Dr. B came to in his report. The assessor should admit that the only evidence that Dr. B seems to have relied upon in coming to his conclusions was what the wife told him. The assessor would likely

Assessment Report	Comments
	admit that in conducting psychotherapy of the wife as did Dr. B, where only one side of the story was told, it is likely incomplete as the husband was not given an opportunity to present his side of the story, and therefore that Dr. B's conclusions are not objective. An attempt should be made to get an admission from the assessor that for the above reasons the conclusions of Dr. B should be ignored and should not be relied upon in formulating a conclusion or recommendation that the husband was physically, verbally or emotionally abusive. The assessor would likely have to admit same given that nowhere in his findings does he come to a similar conclusion. In particular have the assessor admit that when he states "There is much in this report that would correspond to my perception" he is not suggesting that the husband was abusive in any way. Should the assessor disagree with that conclusion then he could be cross-examined further on the comments of Dr. W which would seem to suggest that assertions that the husband was abusive were simply "her presentation".
Report of Dr. W: Dr. W saw the parties in conjoint psychotherapy at one point.	The assessor should be asked whether he received a written report from Dr. W and if so it should be produced in its entirety. The assessor refers to quotes that are attributed to Dr. W such as Mr. A.

Assessment Report	Comments
	could "come across as controlling, aggressive and powerful". The assessor should be questioned as to why he emphasises this portion of Dr. W's report. The assessor in dealing with the psychological findings of the husband and the conclusions regarding same (page 418) does not use such words as "controlling", "aggressive" or "powerful" to describe the husband. The only time the word control was used was when the assessor described the husband as having a tendency in the interview to control the content. The point to be made here is to get the assessor to agree that he did not come to the same conclusions as Dr. W in this regard. The assessor should be asked whether he was able through collateral sources (other than his personal observation of the husband) to determine if the husband was controlling, aggressive or powerful. He should be asked whether any of the husband's family or friends that he interviewed described the husband as such. Were there any independent sources to whom he spoke, such as fellow employees, school teachers or children's coaches who may have had similar observations. Did anyone else to whom he spoke use any such descriptive language in describing the husband? Dr. W also states that in his view the wife's assertions of abuse are simply

Assessment Report	Comments
	her presentation. An admission should be obtained from the assessor that Dr. W clearly has not come to that conclusion himself and that it is simply the perception of the wife. Attempts should be made to have the assessor admit that Dr. W did not in any way make a recommendation as to which of the husband or wife should have custody of the children or what type of parenting arrangement should be entered into regarding the children. An admission should be obtained from the assessor that Dr. W did not attribute more negative features to the husband than to the wife and that in essence Dr. W's results and conclusions are a wash vis-a-vis whether the husband or the wife is better suited to have custody of the children.
Social Worker: The assessor makes reference to the social worker's comments that the husband wanted to dominate and control the wife. The social worker also identified the husband as being abusive of the wife.	As with the case of Dr. B the psychiatrist, the comments of the social worker are clearly hearsay evidence and the argument should be made that they are inadmissible and that no reference should be made to them. The assessor should be asked as to whether or not the social worker has a written report. It appears that the assessor spoke to the social worker. He should be asked whether he took notes of the conversation and to produce them so as to verify that what the social worker told him is complete, accurate and not in any way taken out of context.

Assessment Report	**Comments**
	If the comments of the social worker as set out in the assessor's report are determine by the trier of fact to be a matter of weight the assessor should be asked on what basis was it that the social worker identified the husband as being abusive of the wife. What collateral sources were relied upon by either the social worker or by the assessor in attempting to corroborate anything that the social worker may have relied upon in coming to her conclusion. The assessor should be reminded that neither he nor Dr. W concluded that the husband was in any way abusive of the wife. In argument the point will be made that no reliance should be put on any comments made by the social worker. Is there any empirical date that the social worker has relied upon in coming to her conclusions the husband was abusive. What is it that the husband said that supports her conclusions that he is abusive. Have the assessor admit that the conclusions of the social worker are inconsistent with the conclusions of Dr. W who, as seen above, has suggested that the wife's allegation that the husband was abusive was the wife's presentation. An admission should also be obtained from the assessor that the social worker's comments were made in the context of entering into marriage counselling with the parties and not in the context of conducting

Assessment Report	Comments
	an assessment regarding custody and access. This is important because the recommendations by the social worker that the husband wanted to fashion the wife in the image he desired, and thus, led to the marital distress may not be terribly relevant to the issue of whether the husband should have custody of the children. As a matter of fact the assessor seems to have obtained from the social worker an admission that as parents the social worker had no reason to suspect inadequate parenting from either although she envisioned that their styles might be different. The point to be made here is that the conclusions of the social worker are hearsay and based on facts that cannot be corroborated in any way and that they are in no way relevant to the husband's ability to care for the children and that the social worker's comments reflect a subjective opinion as opposed to an objective clinical judgment that one might expect from a properly qualified person.
Home Visit and Children's Visits: In his report the assessor makes reference to the children with respect to a home visit and visits the children had with the assessor.	The point to be made in cross-examination with the assessor is that neither child has either directly or indirectly, it appears, exhibited a preference to be with either parent. Tanya specifically showed little differentiation as to how she related to either parent.

Assessment Report	Comments
Conclusions and Recommendations: The assessor at page 432 states that it would be incorrect to assert that either the husband or the wife towers over the other on the parental scale. He found no reason to criticize either one's efforts regarding love or commitment to the two children. He considers both parents to have some problems in their individual adjustment with the husband being more intransigent than he presents and with the wife being too willing to yield control. The assessor is faced with the very difficult task in this case as it would appear that both the husband and wife are capable of caring for the children. The assessor therefore in feeling that a decision has to be made one way or the other concludes that the wife should have custody and seems to rely predominantly on two factors, one being that he finds the husband to be somewhat more rigid than the wife and a little more controlling than the wife. Secondly he makes reference to the fact that he is concerned about Tanya's emotional status and that it is him impression that a maternal link is required at her age and current phase of development.	It will probably serve no purpose to cross-examine the assessor specifically on the recommendations he made as he is unlikely to change his mind in any way. The point to be made in argument, however, is that the conclusions and recommendations appear to be inconsistent with other findings made in the report regarding both the husband and the wife. In other words, the conclusions and recommendations may not "fit" the other positive findings of the husband made by the assessor and the negative profile traits of the wife. For example nowhere, elsewhere in the report, does the assessor use such strong language as he does in recommendation No. 6 that the husband might be too powerful or as he did in recommendation No. 6 that the husband's rigidity may become a source of difficulty, or as he did in recommendation No. 5 that as custodian he might be so clearly in charge that it would perpetuate an unhealthy interaction between them. The point should be made that although some reference is made to the controlling aspect of the husband's personality, nowhere else in his findings in the report does the assessor suggest that this is necessarily a negative trait or one that might affect the husband's ability to parent.

Assessment Report	**Comments**
	Counsel might consider retaining a consulting expert in this case. The parents appear, at least from a laymen's perspective to have equal qualities and abilities that they could bring to the responsibility of having the children in their respective care and control. There is little to choose between the positive and negative tendencies of the parents. It would be interesting to see if another psychologist would be able to assist counsel in preparing to cross-examine this assessor particulary when to use the assessor's words, "neither parent towers over the other on the parental scale".
Recommendations and Conclusions Regarding Wife:	In dealing with the recommendations and conclusions regarding the wife (that she have sole custody) at page 433 the assessor makes reference to a couple of factors on which he should be cross-examined. In factor no. 2 he makes reference to the fact the wife would be less likely to be dominated and the balance of power would be more equal. Factor no. 3 makes reference to the wife being an emotionally dependant person who is not adequately matured in the scope of the marriage but is making strides with good professional help. Factors 4 through 7 all have a negative connotation to them and point out the shortfalls in the wife's ability to cope.

Assessment Report	Comments
	The question that presents itself for cross-examination is whether or not, once again, the focus of the recommendations in the case of the wife are on her liberation and voyage to becoming a more independent person rather than what is in the best interests of the children. The fact that she may less likely be dominated and that there would be a greater balance of power if she had custody seems to suggest that the recommendation is made so as to allow her to improve herself and grow as a person rather than being based on what is in the best interests of the children. Lastly, on cross-examination one would try to obtain an admission from the assessor that the 7 factors listed with respect to the husband when considering custody, as compared to the 7 factors listed for the wife in considering who should have custody, do not to any great extent differ from one another. The positive factors of the wife do not tower over the positive factors of the husband. The negative factors of the husband are not necessarily worse than the negative factors of the wife. The assessor will obviously disagree with this in order to be able to support his conclusions, however he should be asked as to whether in the circumstances of this case in deciding that the negative factors of the husband outweigh the negative factors of the wife, it is simply a subjective view or opinion. The ultimate point to be made in

Assessment Report	Comments
	argument is that another person conducting the assessment and obtaining the same information could just as easily have come to the conclusion that it would be in the best interests of the children that they be in the care of the husband as opposed to being in the care of the wife.

The above analysis and commentary is simply meant to act as an outline for preparation of cross-examination of the assessor. The idea is to, firstly, demonstrate to the trier of fact that the assumptions on which the recommendations are based are possibly incorrect or that they could be shaken in some regard and that thus the conclusions in the report can therefore not be relied upon and, secondly, to show that in this case, in particular, the conclusions and recommendations of the assessor are so subjective that any other person upon reviewing the same information and data could easily come to a different conclusion.

Epilogue

Both authors had occasion over the years to work together on cases that arose for assessment but it was the opportunity provided by the publisher that brought two working professionals together in this much larger collaboration. Looking at the result, we hope that this represents a unique contribution for the practising lawyer who broaches the demanding and difficult business of family law.

The book has represented two very different perspectives as must be the case in such a cross disciplinary endeavour. Mental health professionals and lawyers are apt to think very differently and to approach family conflicts in divorce litigation from their own unique vantage points. Yet, it is the synergy created by this very difference that accounts for the value of family assessments. In the most contentious or confusing of matters, the assessment ensures a vital focus on the child's needs. This can assist the courts in bridging the gap between adult client and dependent child and to maintain a real working commitment towards the child's best interests. It is by way of this final common aim that both assessors and lawyers achieve common ground. Hopefully, this spirit that enjoins our differing approaches and perspectives is as evident to you as it has been to us.

Having spoken so favourably about the role of assessments in family law, it is still worth noting that neither of us would favour the blanket use of assessments in custody disputes as the only means to achieve settlement. We would in fact agree with those who criticize the indiscriminate use of such evaluations simply because custody is in dispute.[1] At the same time, it is spurious for the court to imply that it has sufficient expertise to determine those cases where "clinical" issues predominate. The most efficacious use is probably in those cases where special problems arise or where an assessment is likely to turn the tide and assist the court in making a reasonable determination in an otherwise mired controversy. Yet, if divorcing parents agree that they wish to be guided by an assessor's opinion then this should also be reasonable grounds to proceed. The fact remains that when family lawyers are sensitized to the advantages of good assessments, then they are likely to want them. Although difficult to apply in practice, we would support a balance between the routine use of assessments in custody disputes and those cases where they are likely to make a significant contribution and not just an additional one.

We hope that you have found our two portions complementary and interactive and that they meet your broad professional needs. At all points, we have tried to make the book practical and although it delves into some thorny theoretical issues, it hopefully has not swayed too far from its mandate which is to assist the practising lawyer in the judicious use and handling of clinical assessments in family law.

1 *Linton v. Clarke* (1995), ODC 1435-006. Also see "Child custody assessments ordered too frequently?", The Lawyers Weekly (January 27, 1995), 14:35, 36.

Appendix I

Custody Booklet: Preparing the Client for Assessment

Onc of thc principal problcms faccd by asscssors is that clicnts who present for family assessments may have many misconceptions about the assessor and the process. Such misunderstandings can interfere with a reliable and accurate outcome. The assessor is often a mental health professional who is accustomed to be seen as a "helping" person and who may underestimate the adversarial dimension of the legal process even in the domain of family law. Hence, the client may wonder if the assessor is partial to one side or likely to be biased if considered the other side's choice. If the client is prone to see bias or simply very anxious that the assessment be just and balanced, fears may arise that can negatively impact on the assessment.

Because of the prevalence of such confession and doubts, a preparatory booklet that explains the process is often extremely helpful. In our experience and those of lawyers who have used it, the following information can be reassuring, as well as orienting the client to the frame of reference of the assessor. This will almost always serve to facilitate the process and improve the rapport.

The reader is free to copy the following guide and to distribute it to clients facing custody assessments.

A Parent's Guide to Custody and Access Family Assessments

by

Arthur Leonoff, Ph.D., C. Psych.
Psychologist/Psychoanalyst

Introduction

This booklet is intended as an introduction and guide for separating or divorcing parents who are facing an assessment to determine custody and access provisions for their children.

An assessment involves a study of the family. These family studies are commonly requested by the lawyers representing the parents or ordered by the court to provide an impartial basis of evidence upon which to make these vital and sensitive decisions. The assessments are only conducted when court ordered or when mutual consent of both parents and their lawyers has been attained.

The assessor providing the evaluation is a mental health professional with special training in personality and human development who lends his or her expertise to assist you in making these decisions with the least stress and trauma to your children and to yourselves.

If you are now in the position where an assessment has been recommended or ordered, it is very important that you are familiar with some of the basic principles and procedures that the assessor will use in evaluating yourself and other family members or significant others. This is the intention of this booklet. Hopefully, with this overview, you will feel more informed about the assessment, more comfortable with the process, and more aware of what it can accomplish.

The Assessment and the Assessor

Divorcing parents, in conflict over the proper route for themselves and their children, face many losses and disruptions. No loss is more feared, however, than that of children. We all experience our children as part of ourselves and we may be concerned that the other parent may not appreciate how precious a bond they represent to us. In this burdened atmosphere, custody and access assessments can feel like the edge of a slippery slope. How will the assessor view the process and what should you, as a participant, know in order to further the aims and progress of the evaluation?

1. The Assessor

The assessor is trained to be "therapeutic" and he or she will try to be so in your case. Although the legal system works within a conflict model, mental health assessors do not. Rather, the assessor will look at what each parent can bring to the new family system, the strengths and weaknesses along side special needs and capacities of the children, in order to propose a post-separation arrangement that will best fit your children's emotional and social requirements. This framework will include specific recommendations as to residence, legal responsibilities, and visitation schedules. The assessor will be interested in whom you are as people as well as the personality, needs and attributes of your children. Having collected much information from the evaluation, the assessor will then harmonize and integrate what has been learned in order to tailor make a parenting formula that will be most relevant and useful not simply in the present but for the years to follow.

The assessor will look at strengthening bonds, avoiding further losses, healing emotional wounds, and finding ways to avoid creating new ones. Of course, the assessor is being asked to make judgments and this is unavoidable for the reality of the divorce conflict or concerns demand this. Yet, all research shows that it is chronic unresolved conflict between parents that is most harmful to children in divorce no matter what arrangement is in place, and the assessor is most interested in helping you prevent this.

2. *An Atmosphere of Dispute*

When a divorcing family is referred for a custody and access assessment, there has often been a great deal of prior conflict and negative feelings likely prevail. Understandably, parents may feel misunderstood and even blamed by the other parent for what has happened to their relationship and they are anxious that the assessor understand their point of view and work with their concerns and worries. Because marital breakdown and divorce result in a very stressful time, it is natural for self esteem to suffer and for people to be drawn into a fighting stance.

Having lawyers to represent you in this conflict and to provide access to the courts is one way to help resolve disputes. Family assessments are another because they can get beyond combat and look at the longer term interests of the children and their parents. The atmosphere and aims of an assessment are best seen as an objective study and not as a battle. It is important to remember that you will have many years to parent together long after these urgent matters are settled.

3. *"Best Interests of the Children"*

During litigation, the courts often ask the assessor to consider what custody and access provisions will be in the best interests of the children. This determination is never easy to make and, although it is made after much thought and study, it remains an opinion. The assessor is asked to assist your lawyers and the courts but is not there to replace them. The assessor is not a judge but his or her expertise in human behaviour should allow a special insight into what will likely work best for all concerned in the future. In the case of a trial, judges will generally rely on the results of the evaluation in reaching a decision.

4. *Might the Assessor be Biased or Prejudiced Against Me?*

It is the lawyer's role to represent and defend your legal rights and to effectively present your position. In this sense the lawyer is professionally "biased" and must be in order to protect you. Unlike the lawyer, the assessor is not a court officer but is, rather, a mental health advisor or consultant to the legal system. In this sense, the assessor must be accepted as a neutral health professional whose goal is to psychologically evaluate the family and arrive at an appropriate course of action which is set forth in a series of detailed recommendations. Conclusions arrived at by the assessor will only be on psychological grounds which is the nature of the assessor's expertise.

Before the assessor is chosen to provide expert advice, your lawyers will have determined that the assessor is experienced, professionally competent, and able to provide a useful assessment. Further, your lawyers will have confidence that the assessor is a neutral professional who has neither reason nor desire to impose on your particular family situation any pre-determined conclusions. Like all professionals, mental health assessors have their own ideals and aspirations and the thought of prejudicing a family based on prior judgments is contrary to an assessor's ethics and standards, be they a psychologist, psychiatrist or social worker.

5. *On What Basis Does the Assessor Decide Upon Recommendations?*

It is difficult to list all the factors that are considered when such an assessment is done. Each family situation is unique and requires a special investigation of the merits and issues that divide the parents and impede resolution. The following, however, are some of the important factors that are well described in the psychological literature:

a. The relative strength and health of relationship between each parent and child.
b. The personality of the parents and what each can bring to the benefit of their children during the growing up process.
c. The developmental stage and needs of each child both now and in the future.
d. The extent to which each parent knows their child and can be sensitive to the child's developmental needs while separating these needs from their own.
e. The capacity of each parent to facilitate the children's links to the other parent and to acknowledge the other's parenting role in the lives of the children.
f. The willingness and ability of each parent to cooperate and resolve issues concerning the children.
g. The potential of each parent's life style to provide socially and emotionally for their children on a consistent and realistic basis.

6. *Common Anxieties and Concerns During Custody Assessments*

Because these assessments are done at a time of conflict, disruption and uncertainty in the life of the parent, anxieties may run high, especially when one has to face the scrutiny of such an assessment.

The following are common concerns often raised or faced by parents during these family studies:

a. Can I question the assessor and raise my concerns or will the assessor hold it against me?" — By all means tell the assessor or otherwise you may not feel confident to be open and facilitating and the assessment will suffer as a result. When you do speak of these concerns, it is up to the assessor to deal effectively with your concerns and to allay your anxieties. Because assessors are often trained in psychotherapy, they are generally very used to being questioned and consider this a natural part of any healthy relationship. Psychologists are also aware that this is of vital importance to you and that you must be assured that the process is an objective and reasonable one.

b. "Should I discuss these concerns with my lawyer?" — Absolutely, for your lawyer's role is to protect your rights even as regards the assessment. It is very important, though, that you discuss fears, doubts, and criticisms first with the assessor who is the proper person to address these matters. If the assessor fails to allay your concerns then you have every right to request that your lawyer communicate with the assessor on your behalf. In almost all cases, this will suffice to resolve your concerns so that the assessment can proceed normally to its conclusion.

c. "Why do I feel that the assessor does not accept what I am saying?" — This is a very natural feeling and almost everybody seems to experience it, especially at the outset of an assessment. Naturally, you are anxious to be well received and to have your views acknowledged; likewise, the assessor is motivated to know you as well as possible in the time available. Towards this end, the assessor will ask questions and perhaps question you further on a certain issue. This probing might leave the impression that you are being disbelieved when, in fact, the assessor is simply trying to deepen an understanding and know you better.

d. "Can I be open and honest or should I be strategic and on guard with what I say or don't say?" — Naturally, parents want to put their best foot forward and not to tarnish their image in the assessor's eyes. The assessor, on the other hand, can only do the job best if he or she can develop a rapport and a strong working alliance with each parent. It is in each person's best interest to be open, especially for the sake of the children. There is no better strategy, then, than to be yourself in all your dimensions and not be concerned that this will condemn you in the assessor's eyes. It is in fact the opposite. Parents who remain closed, defensive and overly guarded limit the evaluation from being as meaningful and healthy as it might be and are rarely satisfied with the result.

e. "If I have personal problems or have needed therapeutic help in the past, will this be used against me?" — Having undergone psychotherapy, psychiatric treatment, or help for addictions and other personal problems does not preclude anyone from having an important role in the life of their child.

Assessors, in their everyday practice, work with people with emotional and behavioural problems and know this to be a very common occurrence. Because of their work and training, assessors are highly respectful of people who seek mental health treatment and are likely to see this as an asset and not a liability. It takes definite courage and self responsibility to face one's problems and get to the bottom of what troubles us.

f. "Will the assessor morally judge my past conduct and my decisions?" — None of us are absolutely free of moral judgments and neither are assessors. Yet, assessors are trained to go beyond these simple notions and to try and understand people in their depths. As it is our chosen work, we are very motivated to put forth recommendations that will further the health and adjustment of the family at this most difficult time. Alleviating tension is an assessor's first responsibility as we know that it is this factor that can lead to psychological symptoms in children and adults. Hence, what the assessor does is totally opposite to judging, blaming or accusing. This type of behavior may, however, occur between ex-spouses during divorce and participants may worry that the assessor will act in kind.

g. "Will the assessor ask my children with whom they would rather live?" — There is substantial research evidence to support the conclusion that children have a wish to love and be with both of their parents, and it is unnatural for them not to express such a desire. Many years after separation, children will still harbour wishes that their parents will someday reconcile and live together as one family. It would never be appropriate, therefore, for an examiner to place such an ill suited choice on a child's shoulders and such questions will not be asked. Yet, older children, especially of adolescent years, will sometimes take sides and act in a very judgmental way. They may want someone to take the blame for this harsh imposition on their lives. Occasionally, though, for reasons specific to the family, a child of sufficient age may offer some opinion as to the type of arrangement they desire. This may include the notion of living with one parent or the wish that the parents would share the time and responsibilities.

Even when a child spontaneously expresses a preference, however, the assessor will always explore the underlying reasons behind this preference to determine its meaning and motivation.

h. "How should I explain the assessment to the children?" — Naturally, this will vary somewhat with the age and maturity of the particular child. Generally, however, it is important to explain that mother and father have asked an assessor to help decide where the children should live and how the family should function now that there is a separation. It is also useful to explain that the assessor will be meeting with all concerned including them. Children are most often very willing to participate in these evaluations and seem to weather the process quite well. The assessor is very sensitive to children's fears of being placed in the middle between their parents and will design the activities and questions to avoid unnecessary stress.

Younger children may have tendencies to blame themselves for the marriage breakdown and it is worthwhile for both parents to reassure their children on several occasions that this is not so. Older children and adolescents may want to lay blame and side with one parent against the other. They are at an age where moral judgments are important and are often made in very concrete terms such as "all good" or "all bad". Although it may be soothing in the short term to gain an alliance with a child especially when we are angry with the other parent, in the long run this will only further a harmful split. Parents should support each other's legitimacy and encourage children to express their negative feelings of anger, betrayal, or shame while not cutting off relationships.

7. *How Will the Assessment Proceed and What is Involved?*

The assessment will consist of several different activities and procedures, each designed to provide a certain part of the overall picture. The assessor works by gathering as many observations and insights as possible concerning the parents and children through each of these means. Conclusions and recommendations, then, emerge from the analysis of all that has been learned. Each assessor will tend to emphasize certain procedures over others depending on their particular training and approach. The following represent the procedures most commonly used in completing an assessment:

a. Interviews with the parents
b. Interviews with the children
c. Interviews of each parent together with their children
d. Interviews with additional significant adults such as new spouses and grandparents when necessary
e. Home visits where appropriate
f. Psychological testing of the adults and children
g. Consultation with teachers, physicians and others who may have important reliable information to offer
h. A careful reading of all documentation provided by the lawyers in support of the parent's position.

8. *Protecting Children During this Transition*

Separation and divorce are hard on children and they may have problems adjusting to it. The most stressful period seems to occur in the first 18 months after separation but problems can continue especially if there is a high level of conflict between the adults. What can parents do to offset these strains and tensions and allow children to make the best and quickest adjustment possible?

a. It is important to maintain parental control by trying to parent as you did prior to the separation. Because it is an upsetting and disruptive time, you may feel less able to parent and less patient to meet children's complex needs. Yet, it will pay dividends for parents as well as children to try and keep the familiar routines, rituals and style of discipline of which you and the children are most accustomed. Children need to feel that the parents can still provide for them and support their development despite the separation.
b. Resist involving the children in the conflict with the other parent. Children can least cope with the stress of divorce when they feel in the middle between their disputing parents. Make it clear to your children that these conflicts are for the adults to solve and that they should feel free to love and be

loved by both their parents. Do not ask the children to pass angry notes or otherwise convey messages that are likely to upset the other parent. This will serve to create unwanted guilt and anxiety. It is vital to remember that children need more support and nurturing during separation and divorce than they do during normal times.

c. Ask children of sufficient age to take some household responsibilities which will allow them to feel useful and part of the re-adjustment process. Separation leads to the formation of new households which can be a challenge to all concerned. Children respond to being useful and responsible and this enhances their self control and self esteem.
d. If you cannot easily talk to the ex-partner, use a note book to communicate details regarding the children's lives and any concerns that you may have.
e. Notify the school that there has been a separation and ask them to contact the custodial parent(s) if the need arises. Ask the school if they have a program to help children from separated families and whether your child may benefit from it.
f. Remember that transitions from one home to another, particularly at the outset of a separation, are difficult especially for younger children. They are likely to miss the parent they are leaving and may be reluctant to part. This calls for reassurance and support rather than in assuming that this as an expression of their real preference.

9. The Ingredients of a Good Assessment

This is a very important issue and one that is difficult to quantify. One measure that should not be applied, though, is that the family assessment recommends exactly what was wanted. This may or may not occur which is why one must keep in mind that the goal is to provide as secure and enabling an environment as possible for your children despite what has occurred between the parents. Maintaining this frame of reference will help to absorb the conclusions and suggestions of the examination and will facilitate working with your lawyer towards finalizing this part of the settlement.

Having been through an array of interviews and evaluation techniques, you should definitely feel that there has been a serious attempt on the part of the examining assessor to understand you and to address your issues, concerns and the needs of your children. What this means is that the assessor has explored with you aspects of your personality, background, the history of the marriage or relationship, your understanding of your children, your aspirations and plans for them in the future, your concerns regarding the other parent, along with other issues that may be important in your particular situation.

You should also feel that the assessor has given you the opportunity to express yourself and to relate matters and concerns that are of relevance to you. Of course, there is a limit as to how long the assessment can be extended and at some point it must end. Nevertheless, each parent should feel that they have more than an adequate opportunity to express themselves and that their concerns and issues have been well communicated and understood. It is common for parents to request one more meeting, more to be sure that they have been heard than to convey new information. This is a natural experience and the assessor will help you determine whether there is need or not for additional meetings. The assessor will also be willing to discuss the conclusions with you before the results are conveyed to your lawyers. This is an important ingredient to a good assessment and often provides a last occasion to fine tune the specifics of recommendations so that they will be most applicable.

As the family study is completed, you should also have the impression that the examiner has considered your children carefully and taken steps to review their personalities, progress and any special concerns that they may have.

Finally, everyone involved recognizes that divorce has consequences that none of us can entirely defer. The assessor is very aware, as you are, that both parents cannot always be pleased for this is the sad reality and limitation with which we must all contend. Yet, a good assessment paves the way to accepting a result that may not be at all favoured or may not provide for all that we had hoped. In the end, though, we all share a common goal which is to provide for offspring who must keep pace with our changes and who must adapt to changing circumstances that are stressful and not of their own choosing.

Appendix II

Guidelines for Child Custody Evaluations in Divorce Proceedings*

INTRODUCTION

Decisions regarding child custody and other parenting arrangements occur within several different legal contexts, including parental divorce, guardianship, neglect or abuse proceedings, and termination of parental rights. The following guidelines were developed for psy-

---

† These guidelines were drafted by the Committee on Professional Practice and Standards (COPPS), a committee of the Board of Professional Affairs (BPA), with input from the Committee on Children, Youth, and Families (CYF). They were adopted by the Council of Representatives of the American Psychological Association in February 1994.

COPPS members in 1991–1993 were Richard Cohen, Alex Carballo Dieguez, Kathleen Dockett, Sam Friedman, Colette Ingraham, John Northman, John Robinson, Deborah Tharinger, Susana Urbina, Phil Witt, and James Wulach; BPA liaisons in 1991–1993 were Richard Cohen, Joseph Kobos, and Rodney Lowman; CYF members were Don Routh and Carolyn Swift.

Correspondence concerning this article should be addressed to the Practice Directorate, American Psychological Association, 750 First Street, NE, Washington, DC 20002-4242.

chologists conducting child custody evaluations, specifically within the context of parental divorce. These guidelines build upon the American Psychological Association's *Ethical Principles of Psychologists and Code of Conduct* (APA, 1992) and are aspirational in intent. *As guidelines, they are not intended to be either mandatory or exhaustive. The goal of the guidelines is to promote proficiency in using psychological expertise in conducting child custody evaluations.*

Parental divorce requires a restructuring of parental rights and responsibilities in relation to children. If the parents can agree to a restructuring arrangement, which they do in the overwhelming proportion (90%) of divorce custody cases (Melton, Petrila, Poythress, & Slobogin, 1987), there is no dispute for the court to decide. However, if the parents are unable to reach such an agreement, the court must help to determine the relative allocation of decision making authority and physical contact each parent will have with the child. The courts typically apply a "best interest of the child" standard in determining this restructuring of rights and responsibilities.

Psychologists provide an important service to children and the courts by providing competent, objective, impartial information in assessing the best interests of the child; by demonstrating a clear sense of direction and purpose in conducting a child custody evaluation; by performing their roles ethically; and by clarifying to all involved the nature and scope of the evaluation. The Ethics Committee of the American Psychological Association has noted that psychologists' involvement in custody disputes has at times raised questions in regard to the misuse of psychologists' influence, sometimes resulting in complaints against psychologists being brought to the attention of the APA Ethics Committee (APA Ethics Committee, 1985; Hall & Hare-Mustin, 1983; Keith-Spiegel & Koocher, 1985; Mills, 1984) and raising questions in the legal and forensic literature (Grisso, 1986; Melton et al., 1987; Mnookin, 1975; Ochroch, 1982; Okpaku, 1976; Weithorn, 1987).

Particular competencies and knowledge are required for child custody evaluations to provide adequate and appropriate psychological services to the court. Child custody evaluation in the context of parental divorce can be an extremely demanding task. For competing parents the stakes are high as they participate in a process fraught with tension and anxiety. The stress on the psychologist/evaluator can become great. Tension surrounding child custody evaluation can become further heightened when there are accusations of child abuse, neglect, and/or family violence.

Psychology is in a position to make significant contributions to child custody decisions. Psychological data and expertise, gained through a child custody evaluation, can provide an additional source of information and an additional perspective not otherwise readily available to the court on what appears to be in a child's best interest, and thus can increase the fairness of the determination the court must make.

GUIDELINES FOR CHILD CUSTODY EVALUATIONS IN DIVORCE PROCEEDINGS

I. Orienting Guidelines: Purpose of a Child Custody Evaluation

1. The primary purpose of the evaluation is to assess the best psychological interests of the child. The primary consideration in a child custody evaluation is to assess the individual and family factors that affect the best psychological interests of the child. More specific questions may be raised by the court.

2. The child's interests and well-being are paramount. In a child custody evaluation, the child's interests and well-being are paramount. Parents competing for custody, as well as others, may have legitimate concerns, but the child's best interests must prevail.

3. The focus of the evaluation is on parenting capacity, the psychological and developmental needs of the child, and the resulting fit. In considering psychological factors affecting the best interests of the child, the psychologist focuses on the parenting capacity of the prospective custodians in conjunction with the psychological and developmental needs of each involved child. This involves (a) an assessment of the adults' capacities for parenting, including whatever knowledge, attributes, skills, and abilities, or lack thereof, are present;

(b) an assessment of the psychological functioning and developmental needs of each child and of the wishes of each child where appropriate; and (c) an assessment of the functional ability of each parent to meet these needs, including an evaluation of the interaction between each adult and child.

The values of the parents relevant to parenting, ability to plan for the child's future needs, capacity to provide a stable and loving home, and any potential for inappropriate behavior or misconduct that might negatively influence the child also are considered. Psychopathology may be relevant to such an assessment, insofar as it has impact on the child or the ability to parent, but it is not the primary focus.

II. General Guidelines: Preparing for a Child Custody Evaluation

4. The role of the psychologist is that of a professional expert who strives to maintain an objective, impartial stance. The role of the psychologist is as a professional expert. The psychologist does not act as a judge, who makes the ultimate decision applying the law to all relevant evidence. Neither does the psychologist act as an advocating attorney, who strives to present his or her client's best possible case. The psychologist, in a balanced, impartial manner, informs and advises the court and the prospective custodians of the child of the relevant psychological factors pertaining to the custody issue. The psychologist should be impartial regardless of whether he or she is retained by the court or by a party to the proceedings. If either the psychologist or the client cannot accept this neutral role, the psychologist should consider withdrawing from the case. If not permitted to withdraw, in such circumstances, the psychologist acknowledges past roles and other factors that could affect impartiality.

5. The psychologist gains specialized competence.

A. A psychologist contemplating performing child custody evaluations is aware that special competencies and knowledge are required for the undertaking of such evaluations. Competence in performing psychological assessments of children, adults, and families is necessary but not sufficient. Education, training, experience, and/or supervision in the areas of child and family development, child and family psychopathology, and the impact of divorce on children help to prepare the psychologist to participate competently in child custody evaluations. The psychologist also strives to become familiar with applicable legal standards and procedures, including laws governing divorce and custody adjudications in his or her state or jurisdiction.

B. The psychologist uses current knowledge of scientific and professional developments, consistent with accepted clinical and scientific standards, in selecting data collection methods and procedures. The *Standards for Educational and Psychological Testing* (APA, 1985) are adhered to in the use of psychological tests and other assessment tools.

C. In the course of conducting child custody evaluations, allegations of child abuse, neglect, family violence, or other issues may occur that are not necessarily within the scope of a particular evaluator's expertise. If this is so, the psychologist seeks additional consultation, supervision, and/or specialized knowledge, training, or experience in child abuse, neglect, and family violence to address these complex issues. The psychologist is familiar with the laws of his or her state addressing child abuse, neglect, and family violence and acts accordingly.

6. The psychologist is aware of personal and societal biases and engages in nondiscriminatory practice. The psychologist engaging in child custody evaluations is aware of how biases regarding age, gender, race, ethnicity, national origin, religion, sexual orientation, disability, language, culture, and socioeconomic status may interfere with an objective evaluation and recommendations. The psychologist recognizes and strives to overcome any such biases or withdraws from the evaluation.

7. The psychologist avoids multiple relationships. Psychologists generally avoid conducting a child custody evaluation in a case in which the psychologist served in a therapeutic role for the child or his or her immediately family or has had other involvement that may compromise the psychologist's objectivity. This should not, however, preclude the psychologist from testifying in the case as a fact witness concerning treatment of the child. In addition, during the course of a child custody evaluation, a psychologist does not accept any of the involved participants in the evaluation as a therapy client. Therapeutic contact with the child or involved participants following a child custody evaluation is undertaken with caution.

A psychologist asked to testify regarding a therapy client who is involved in a child custody case is aware of the limitations and possible biases inherent in such a role and the possible impact on the ongoing therapeutic relationship. Although the court may require the psychologist to testify as a fact witness regarding factual information he or she became aware of in a professional relationship with a client, that psychologist should generally decline the role of an expert witness who gives a professional opinion regarding custody and visitation issues (see Ethical Standard 7.03) unless so ordered by the court.

III. Procedural Guidelines: Conducting a Child Custody Evaluation

8. The scope of the evaluation is determined by the evaluator, based on the nature of the referral question. The scope of the custody-related evaluation is determined by the nature of the question or issue raised by the referring person or the court, or is inherent in the situation. Although comprehensive child custody evaluations generally require an evaluation of all parents or guardians and children, as well as observations of interactions between them, the scope of the assessment in a particular case may be limited to evaluating the parental capacity of one parent without attempting to compare the parents or to make recommendations. Likewise, the scope may be limited to evaluating the child. Or a psychologist may be asked to critique the assumptions and methodology of the assessment of another mental health professional. A psychologist also might serve as an expert witness in the area of child development, providing expertise to the court without relating it specifically to the parties involved in a case.

9. The psychologist obtains informed consent from all adult participants and, as appropriate, informs child participants. In undertaking child custody evaluations, the psychologist ensures that each adult participant is aware of (a) the purpose, nature, and method of the evaluation; (b) who has requested the psychologist's services; and (c) who will be paying the fees. The psychologist informs adult participants about the nature of the assessment instruments and techniques and informs those participants about the possible disposition of the data collected. The psychologist provides this information, as appropriate, to children, to the extent that they are able to understand.

10. The psychologist informs participants about the limits of confidentiality and the disclosure of information. A psychologist conducting a child custody evaluation ensures that the participants, including children to the extent feasible, are aware of the limits of confidentiality characterizing the professional relationship with the psychologist. The psychologist informs participants that in consenting to the evaluation, they are consenting to disclosure of the evaluation's findings in the context of the forthcoming litigation and in any other proceedings deemed necessary by the courts. A psychologist obtains a waiver of confidentiality from all adult participants or from their authorized legal representatives.

11. The psychologist uses multiple methods of data gathering. The psychologist strives to use the most appropriate methods available for addressing the questions raised in a specific child custody evaluation and generally uses multiple methods of data gathering, including, but not limited to, clinical interviews, observation, and/or psychological assessments. Important facts and opinions are documented from at least two sources whenever their reliability is questionable. The psychologist, for example, may review potentially relevant reports (e.g., from schools, health care providers, child care providers, agencies, and institutions). Psychologists may also interview extended family, friends, and other individuals on occasions when the information is likely to be useful. If information is gathered from third parties that is significant and may be used as a basis for conclusions, psychologists corroborate it by at least one other source wherever possible and appropriate and document this in the report.

12. The psychologist neither overinterprets nor inappropriately interprets clinical or assessment data. The psychologist refrains from drawing conclusions not adequately supported by the data. The psychologist interprets any data from interviews or tests, as well as any questions of data reliability and validity, cautiously and conservatively, seeking convergent validity. The psychologist strives to acknowledge to the court any limitations in methods or data used.

13. The psychologist does not give any opinion regarding the psychological functioning of any individual who has not been personally evaluated. This guideline, however, does not preclude the psychologist from reporting what an evaluated individual (such as the parent or child) has stated or from addressing theoretical issues or hypothetical questions, so long as the limited basis of the information is noted.

14. Recommendations, if any, are based on what is in the best psychological interests of the child. Although the profession has not reached consensus about whether psychologists ought to make recommendations about the final custody determination to the courts, psychologists are obligated to be aware of the arguments on both sides of this issue and to be able to explain the logic of their position concerning their own practice.

If the psychologist does choose to make custody recommendations, these recommendations should be derived from sound psychological data and must be based on the best interests of the child in the particular case. Recommendations are based on articulated assumptions, data, interpretations, and inferences based upon established professional and scientific standards. Psychologists guard against relying on their own biases or unsupported beliefs in rendering opinions in particular cases.

15. The psychologist clarifies financial arrangements. Financial ar- rangements are clarified and agreed upon prior to commencing a child custody evaluation. When billing for a child custody evaluation, the psychologist does not misrepresent his or her services for reimbursement purposes.

16. The psychologist maintains written records. All records obtained in the process of conducting a child custody evaluation are properly maintained and filed in accord with the APA *Record Keeping Guidelines* (APA, 1993) and relevant statutory guidelines.

All raw data and interview information are recorded with an eye toward their possible review by other psychologists or the court, where legally permitted. Upon request, appropriate reports are made available to the court.

REFERENCES

American Psychological Association. (1985). *Standards for educational and psychological testing.* Washington, DC: Author.

American Psychological Association. (1992). Ethical principles of psychologists and code of conduct. *American Psychologist, 47*, 1597–1611.

American Psychological Association. (1993). *Record Keeping guidelines.* Washington, DC: Author.

American Psychological Association, Ethics Committee. (1985), *Annual report of the American Psychological Association Ethics Committee.* Washington, DC: Author.

Grisso, T. (1986). *Evaluating competencies: Forensic assessments and instruments.* New York: Plenum.

Hall, J. E., & Hare-Mustin, R. T. (1983). Sanctions and the diversity of ethical complaints against psychologists. *American Psychologist, 38*, 714–729.

Keith-Spiegel, P., & Koocher, G. P. (1985). *Ethics in psychology.* New York: Random House.

Melton, G. B., Petrila, J., Poythress, N. G., & Slobogin, C. (1987). *Psychological evaluations for the courts: A handbook for mental health professionals and lawyers.* New York: Guilford Press.

Mills, D. H. (1984). Ethics education and adjudication within psychology. *American Psychologist, 39*, 669–675.

Mnookin, R. H. (1975). Child-custody adjudication: Judicial functions in the face of indeterminacy. *Law and Contemporary Problems, 39*, 226–293.

Ochroch, R. (1982, August). *Ethical pitfalls in child custody evaluations.* Paper presented at the 90th Annual Convention of the American Psychological Association, Washington, DC.

Okpaku, S. (1976). Psychology: Impediment or aid in child custody cases? *Rutgers Law Review, 29*, 117–1153.

Weithorn, L. A. (Ed.). (1987). *Psychology and child custody determinations: Knowledge, roles, and expertise.* Lincoln: University of Nebraska Press.

OTHER RESOURCES

State Guidelines

Georgia Psychological Association. (1990). *Recommendations for psychologists' involvement in child custody cases.* Atlanta, GA: Author.

Metropolitan Denver Interdisciplinary Committee on Child Custody. (1989). *Guidelines for child custody evaluations.* Denver, CO: Author.

Nebraska Psychological Association. (1986). *Guidelines for child custody evaluations.* Lincoln, NE: Author.

New Jersey State Board of Psychological Examiners. (1993). *Specialty guidelines for psychologists in custody/visitation evaluations.* Newark, NJ: Author.

North Carolina Psychological Association. (1993). *Child custody guidelines.* Unpublished manuscript.

Oklahoma Psychological Association. (1988). *Ethical guidelines for child custody evaluations.* Oklahoma City, OK: Author.

Forensic Guidelines

Committee on Ethical Guidelines for Forensic Psychologists. (1991). Specialty guidelines for forensic psychologists. *Law and Human Behavior, 6*, 655–665.

Pertinent Literature

Ackerman, M. J., & Kane, A. W. (1993). *Psychological experts in divorce, personal injury and other civil actions.* New York: Wiley.

American Psychological Association, Board of Ethnic Minority Affairs. (1991). *Guidelines for providers of psychological services to ethnic, linguistic, and culturally diverse populations.* Washington, DC: American Psychological Association.

American Psychological Association, Committee on Women in Psychology and Committee on Lesbian and Gay Concerns. (1988). *Lesbian parents and their children: A resource paper for psychologists.* Washington, DC: American Psychological Association.

Beaber, R. J. (1982, Fall). Custody quagmire: Some psycholegal dilemmas. *Journal of Psychiatry & Law,* 309–326.

Bennett, B. E., Bryant, B. K., VandenBos, G. R., & Greenwood, A. (1990). *Professional liability and risk management.* Washington, DC: American Psychological Association.

Bolocofsky, D. N. (1989). Use and abuse of mental health experts in child custody determinations. *Behavioral Sciences and the Law, 7*(2), 197–213.

Bozett, F. (1987). *Gay and lesbian parents.* New York: Praeger.

Bray, J. H. (1993). What's the best interest of the child?: Children's adjustment issues in divorce. *the Independent Practitioner, 13*, 42–45.

Bricklin, B. (1992). *Data based tests in custody evaluations.* American Journal of Family Therapy, 20, 254–265.

Cantor, D. W., & Drake, E. A. (1982). *Divorced parents and their children: A guide for mental health professionals.* New York: Springer.

Chesler, P. (1991). *Mothers on trial: The battle for children and custody.* New York: Harcourt Brace Jovanovich.

Deed, M. L. (1991). Court-ordered child custody evaluations: Helping or victimizing vulnerable families. *Psychotherapy, 28*, 76–84.

Falk, P. J. (1989). Lesbian mothers: Psychosocial assumptions in family law. *American Psychologist, 44*, 941–947.

Gardner, R. A. (1989). *Family evaluation in child custody mediation, arbitration, and litigation.* Cresskill, NJ: Creative Therapeutics.

Gardner, R. A. (1992). *The parental alienation syndrome: A guide for mental health and legal professionals.* Cresskill, NJ: Creative Therapeutics.

Gardner, R. A. (1992). *True and false accusations of child abuse.* Cresskill, NJ: Creative Therapeutics.

Goldstein, J., Freud, A., & Solnit, A. J. (1980). *Before the best interests of the child.* New York: Free Press.

Goldstein, J., Freud, A., & Solnit, A. J. (1980). *Beyond the best interests of the child.* New York: Free press.

Goldstein, J., Freud, A., Solnit, A. J., & Goldstein, S. (1986). *In the best interests of the child.* New York: Free Press.

Grisso, T. (1990). Evolving guidelines for divorce/custody evaluations. *Family and Conciliation Courts Review,* 28(1), 35–41.

Halon, R. L. (1990). The comprehensive child custody evaluation. *American Journal of Forensic Psychology,* 8(3), 19–46.

Hetherington, E. M. (1990). Coping with family transitions: Winners, losers, and survivors. *Child Development, 60*, 1–14.

Hetherington, E. M., Stanley-Hagen, M., & Anderson, E. R. (1988). Marital transitions: A child's perspective. *American Psychologist, 44*, 303–312.

Johnston, J., Kline, M., & Tschann, J. (1989). Ongoing postdivorce conflict: Effects on children of joint custody and frequent access. *Journal of Orthopsychiatry, 59*, 576–592.

Koocher, G. P., & Keith-Spiegel, P. C. (1990). *Children, ethics, and the law: Professional issues and cases.* Lincoln: University of Nebraska Press.

Kreindler, S. (1986). The role of mental health professions in custody and access disputes. In R. S. Parry, E. A. Broder, E. A. G. Schmitt, E. B. Saunders, & E. Hood (Eds.), *Custody disputes: Evaluation and intervention.* New York: Free Press.

Martindale, D. A., Martindale, J. L., & Broderick, J. E. (1991). Providing expert testimony in child custody litigation. In P. A. Keller & S. R. Heyman (Eds.), *Innovations in clinical practice: A source book* (Vol. 10, pp. 481–497). Sarasota, FL: Professional Resource Exchange.

Patterson, C. J. (in press). Children of lesbian and gay parents. *Child Development.*

Pennsylvania Psychological Association, Clinical Division Task Force on Child Custody Evaluation. (1991). *Roles for psychologists in child custody disputes.* Unpublished manuscript.

Saunders, T. R. (1991). An overview of some psycholegal issues in child physical and sexual abuse. *Psychotherapy in Private Practice,* 9(2), 61–78.

Schutz, B. M., Dixon, E. B., Lindenberger, J. C., & Ruther, N. J. (1989). *Solomon's sword: A practical guide to conducting child custody evaluations.* San Francisco: Jossey-Bass.

Stahly, G. B. (1989, August 9). *Testimony on child abuse policy to APA Board.* Paper presented at the meeting of the American Psychological Association Board of Directors, New Orleans, LA.

Thoennes, N., & Tjaden, P. G. (1991). The extent, nature, and validity of sexual abuse allegations in custody/visitation disputes. *Child Abuse & Neglect, 14*, 151–163.

Wallerstein, J. S., & Blakeslee, S. (1989). *Second chances: Men, women, and children a decade after divorce.* New York: Ticknor & Fields.

Wallerstein, J. S., & Kelly, J. B. (1980). *Surviving the breakup.* New York: Basic Books.

Weissman, H. N. (1991). Child custody evaluations: Fair and unfair professional practices. *Behavioral Sciences and the Law, 9*, 469–476.

Weithorn, L. A., & Grisso, T. (1987). Psychological evaluations in divorce custody: Problems, principles, and procedures. In L. A. Weithorn (Ed.),

Psychology and child custody determinations (pp. 157–157). Lincoln: University of Nebraska Press.

White, S. (1990). The contamination of children's interviews. *Child Youth and Family Services Quarterly, 13*(3), 6, 17–18.

Wyer, M. M., Gaylord, S. J., & Grove, E. T. The legal context of child custody evaluations. In L. A. Weithorn (Ed.), *Psychology and child custody determinations* (pp. 3–23). Lincoln: University of Nebraska Press.

Index